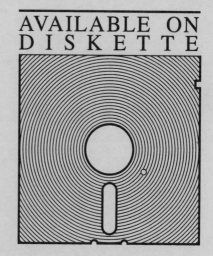

AVAILABLE ON
D I S K E T T E

BANK PROFITABILITY
Financial Statements
of Banks
[1979–1992]

The data, provided on either 5 1/4" or 3 1/2" double-sided, double-density diskettes formatted on both sides, suitable for IBM or IBM-compatible microcomputers, are supplied in a compressed format specific to OECD. The diskettes include a simple program for transferring data into DIF, SYLK, or LOTUS WKS formats. Data can therefore be readily used with such software packages as LOTUS 1-2-3, QUATTRO-PRO, EXCEL and the MS-DOS operating system.

Full technical documentation and a detailed section on "Definitions" accompanies each data package.

The price for the 1994 edition of this annual diskette has been fixed at:

FF 1 200   **US$ 215**   **£ 135**   **DM 365**

with discounts for academic circles and government agencies. Subscribers wishing to redistribute the statistics shall be required to complete a special contract.

Orders or enquiries should be sent to OECD Electronic Editions in Paris, one of OECD's Publication and Information Centres in Bonn, Tokyo or Washington, or the OECD Distributor in your country.

OECD
Electronic Editions
2, rue André-Pascal, 75775 Paris Cedex 16
Fax: (33)1-45.24.98.99

DISPONIBLE SUR DISQUETTE

RENTABILITÉ DES BANQUES
Comptes des banques
[1979–1992]

Les données sont fournies sur des disquettes double face, double densité formatées sur chaque face de format 5 pouces 1/4 ou 3 pouces 1/2 pour les micro-ordinateurs IBM ou compatibles. Les données sont enregistrées dans un format compacté particulier à l'OCDE. Un programme simple est disponible sur les disquettes permettant le transfert des données dans un format DIF, SYLK, ou LOTUS WKS. Les données peuvent ainsi être facilement utilisées avec les logiciels tels que LOTUS 1-2-3, QUATTRO-PRO, EXCEL et le système d'exploitation MS-DOS.

Chaque livraison est accompagnée d'une documentation technique complète et d'une section détaillée sur les « Définitions ».

Le prix pour l'édition 1994 de cette disquette, mise à jour annuellement, a été fixé à :

FF 1 200   US$ 215   £ 135   DM 365

Des remises sont accordées aux universités, au corps enseignant et aux organismes gouvernementaux. Les abonnés désireux d'acquérir les disquettes afin d'assurer une rediffusion des données doivent remplir un contrat spécial.

Pour vous procurer cette disquette ou pour tout renseignement, contacter les Éditions Électroniques de l'OCDE à Paris, l'un des Centres des Publications et d'Information de l'OCDE à Bonn, Tokyo ou Washington, ou le distributeur OCDE dans votre pays.

OCDE
Éditions Électroniques
2, rue André-Pascal, 75775 Paris Cedex 16, France
Fax : (33)1-45.24.98.99

BANK PROFITABILITY

◆

RENTABILITÉ DES BANQUES

FINANCIAL STATEMENTS OF BANKS
COMPTES DES BANQUES
1983-1992

ORGANISATION FOR ECONOMIC CO-OPERATION AND DEVELOPMENT
ORGANISATION DE COOPÉRATION ET DE DÉVELOPPEMENT ÉCONOMIQUES

ORGANISATION FOR ECONOMIC CO-OPERATION AND DEVELOPMENT

ORGANISATION DE COOPÉRATION ET DE DÉVELOPPEMENT ÉCONOMIQUES

Pursuant to Article 1 of the Convention signed in Paris on 14th December 1960, and which came into force on 30th September 1961, the Organisation for Economic Co-operation and Development (OECD) shall promote policies designed:

— to achieve the highest sustainable economic growth and employment and a rising standard of living in Member countries, while maintaining financial stability, and thus to contribute to the development of the world economy;

— to contribute to sound economic expansion in Member as well as non-member countries in the process of economic development; and

— to contribute to the expansion of world trade on a multilateral, non-discriminatory basis in accordance with international obligations.

The original Member countries of the OECD are Austria, Belgium, Canada, Denmark, France, Germany, Greece, Iceland, Ireland, Italy, Luxembourg, the Netherlands, Norway, Portugal, Spain, Sweden, Switzerland, Turkey, the United Kingdom and the United States. The following countries became Members subsequently through accession at the dates indicated hereafter: Japan (28th April 1964), Finland (28th January 1969), Australia (7th June 1971) and New Zealand (29th May 1973). The Commission of the European Communities takes part in the work of the OECD (Article 13 of the OECD Convention).

En vertu de l'article 1er de la Convention signée le 14 décembre 1960, à Paris, et entrée en vigueur le 30 septembre 1961, l'Organisation de Coopération et de Développement Économiques (OCDE) a pour objectif de promouvoir des politiques visant :

— à réaliser la plus forte expansion de l'économie et de l'emploi et une progression du niveau de vie dans les pays Membres, tout en maintenant la stabilité financière, et à contribuer ainsi au développement de l'économie mondiale ;

— à contribuer à une saine expansion économique dans les pays Membres, ainsi que les pays non membres, en voie de développement économique ;

— à contribuer à l'expansion du commerce mondial sur une base multilatérale et non discriminatoire conformément aux obligations internationales.

Les pays Membres originaires de l'OCDE sont : l'Allemagne, l'Autriche, la Belgique, le Canada, le Danemark, l'Espagne, les États-Unis, la France, la Grèce, l'Irlande, l'Islande, l'Italie, le Luxembourg, la Norvège, les Pays-Bas, le Portugal, le Royaume-Uni, la Suède, la Suisse et la Turquie. Les pays suivants sont ultérieurement devenus Membres par adhésion aux dates indiquées ci-après : le Japon (28 avril 1964), la Finlande (28 janvier 1969), l'Australie (7 juin 1971) et la Nouvelle-Zélande (29 mai 1973). La Commission des Communautés européennes participe aux travaux de l'OCDE (article 13 de la Convention de l'OCDE).

FOREWORD

The present publication includes data on financial statements of banks for the period 1983-1992. It thus updates the data on financial statements of banks published in *Bank Profitability, Statistical Supplement, Financial Statements of Banks 1982-91*, OECD, Paris, 1993. The coverage of banks in these statistics is not the same in each country, though the objective is to cover all institutions which conduct ordinary banking business, namely institutions which primarily take deposits from the public at large and provide finance for a wide range of purposes. Some supplementary information on the number of reporting banks, their branches and staff is also included.

The institutional coverage of the tables has been largely dictated by the availability of data on income and expenditure accounts of banks. As a result of the reporting methods which are being used in OECD countries, the tables are not integrated in the system of national accounts and are, therefore, not compatible with the *Financial Accounts of OECD Countries*. International comparisons in the field of income and expenditure accounts of banks are particularly difficult due to considerable differences in OECD countries as regards structural and regulatory features of national banking systems, accounting rules and practices, and reporting methods.

The statistical part is updated and published annually while the methodological country notes are issued less frequently. The next version of the methological notes is scheduled for publication in the course of 1994.

The preparation of this publication could not have been accomplished without the assistance of the members of the OECD Group of Financial Statisticians and the national administrations which they represent. It is published, on the Group's recommendation, under the responsibility of the Secretary-General.

3

AVANT-PROPOS

Le présent ouvrage contient les données relatives aux comptes de résultats et aux bilans des banques pour la période 1983-92. Ainsi, sont mises à jour et étendues les statistiques publiées dans *Rentabilité des Banques, Supplément Statistique, Comptes des Banques 1982-91*, OCDE, Paris, 1993. Les banques sur lesquelles portent ces statistiques ne sont pas les mêmes selon les pays, mais l'objectif est d'englober toutes les institutions qui effectuent des opérations courantes de banque, c'est-à-dire qui reçoivent des dépôts du public et offrent des concours destinés à financer un large éventail de besoins. Figurent en outre des renseignements complémentaires sur le nombre de banques qui communiquent leurs données, celui de leurs succursales et de leurs salariés.

La délimitation du cercle des institutions recensées dans les tableaux a été, en grande partie, dictée par les données existantes sur les comptes de résultats des banques. Du fait des modes de communication des données en vigueur dans les pays de l'OCDE, ces tableaux ne sont pas intégrés dans le Système de comptabilité nationale et ne sont donc pas compatibles avec les *Comptes financiers des pays de l'OCDE*. Les comparaisons internationales sont délicates étant donné les différences qui existent entre les pays en ce qui concerne la structure du système bancaire et la réglementation des banques, les règles et pratiques comptables et le système de communication des données.

La partie statistique est mise à jour et publiée annuellement tandis que les notes méthodologiques par pays sont émises moins souvent. La prochaine version des notes méthodologiques est prévue pour courant 1994.

Ces statistiques n'auraient pu être établies sans l'aide des membres du Groupe de statisticiens financiers de l'OCDE ni de celle des administrations nationales qu'ils représentent. Elles sont publiées, sur la recommandation du Groupe, sous la responsabilité du Secrétaire Général.

CONTENTS

1. Series on "Large commercial banks" are not available in this issue.
2. Series on "Savings and loan associations" are not available in this issue.

CONVENTIONAL SIGNS

N.A.	*Not available*
-	*Nil or negligible*
..	*Not applicable or breakdown not available*
:	*Decimal point*

TABLE DES MATIERES

1. Les séries relatives aux "Grandes banques commerciales" ne sont pas disponibles dans cette livraison.
2. Les séries relatives aux "Associations d'épargne et de prêts" ne sont pas disponibles dans cette livraison.

SIGNES CONVENTIONNELS

N.A. *Non disponible*
- *Nul ou négligeable*
.. *Non approprié ou*
ventilation non disponible
· *Point decimal (sépare*
les unités des décimale)

INTRODUCTION

National data on **income and expenditure accounts of banks** are grouped and, where necessary, re-classified to fit as far as possible into the following standard framework of presentation:

Income statement

1.   Interest income

2.   Interest expenses

3.   Net interest income (item 1 minus item 2)

4.   Non-interest income (net)

5.   Gross income (item 3 plus item 4)

6.   Operating expenses

7.   Net income (item 5 minus item 6)

8.   Provisions (net)

9.   Profit before tax (item 7 minus item 8)

10.   Income tax

11.   Profit after tax (item 9 minus item 10)

12.   Distributed profit

13.   Retained profit (item 11 minus item 12)

Memorandum items

14.   Staff costs (included in item 6)

15.   Net provisions on loans (included in item 8)

16.   Net provisions on securities (included in item 8)

Interest income (item 1) generally includes income on interest-bearing assets, fee income related to lending operations, and dividend income on shares and participations. In some cases it may also include income on bonds calculated as the difference between the book value and the redemption value of bonds.

Interest expenses (item 2) generally includes interest paid on liabilities, fee expenses related to borrowing operations and may include in some cases the difference between the issue price on debt instruments and their par value.

Non-interest income (net) (item 4) is generally the net result of a number of different income and expense items (other than those included in items 1 and 2) such as the following: commissions received and paid in connection with payments services, securities transactions and related services (new issues, trading, portfolio management, safe-custody) and foreign exchange transactions in the banks' own name and on behalf of clients. Other income and expenses resulting from special transactions which do not represent ordinary and regular banking business may also be included. Realised losses and gains on foreign-exchange operations and securities transactions are generally included as well.

Operating expenses (item 6) usually include all expenses relating to the ordinary and regular banking business other than those included in items 2 and 4, particularly salaries and other employee benefits, including transfers to pension reserves (staff costs), and expenses for property and equipment and related depreciation expenses. Taxes other than income or corporate taxes are also included.

Provisions (net) (item 8) generally include, in part or in full, charges for value adjustments in respect of loans, credits and securities, book gains from such adjustments, losses on loans and transfers to and from reserves for possible losses on such assets. Realised gains or losses from foreign exchange transactions and securities transactions are, however, generally included under *Non-interest income (net)* (item 4).

Any deviation from this standard presentation and classification of income and expenditure account items is generally indicated in the methodological country notes.

National data on **balance sheets of banks** are grouped and, where necessary, re-classified in order to fit as far as possible into the following standard framework of presentations:

Balance sheet

Assets

17.   Cash and balance with Central bank

18.   Interbank deposits

19.   Loans

20.   Securities

21.   Other assets

Liabilities

22.   Capital and reserves

23.   Borrowing from Central bank

24.   Interbank deposits

25.   Non-bank deposits

26.   Bonds

27.   Other liabilities

Balance sheet total

28.   End-year total (sum of items 17 to 21 or 22 to 27)

29.   Average total

Memorandum items

30.   Short-term securities (included in item 20)

31.   Bonds (included in item 20)

32.   Shares and participations (included in item 20)

33.   Claims on non-residents (included in items 18 to 21)

34.   Liabilities to non-residents (included in items 24 to 27)

Short-term securities (item 30) are, following the definition used in the European System of Integrated Accounts (paragraph 539), securities with an original maturity of usually up to 12 months, but with a maximum maturity of two years.

Bonds (item 31), are, following the definition of the European System of Integrated Accounts (paragraph 542), fixed or variable-interest rate securities with an original maturity of several years.

In countries in which there is re-discounting of commercial bills with the central bank, the volume of re-discounted bills is usually included on each side of the balance sheet, under *Loans* (item 19) on the assets side and under *Borrowing from central bank* (item 23) on the liabilities side.

The following **supplementary information** is provided:

35.   Number of institutions (covered by the data)

36.   Number of branches (covered by the data)

37.   Number of staff ('000) (of the institutions covered by the data)

In order to facilitate the interpretation and analysis of the data included in the present publication and to enable the user of the data to judge how cautiously the figures should be used for comparative purposes, national administrations have prepared methodological country notes which give detailed information on the following:

- Institutional coverage, and the relative importance of the institutions covered as compared with the whole financial system;

- Geographical coverage and degree of consolidation indicating whether domestic or foreign financial or non-financial subsidiaries of the reporting banks are covered by the data and whether branches and/or subsidiaries of foreign banks are included;

- Summary description of activities of banks indicating in particular whether the banks carry out important service activities producing fee income such as a wide range of securities-related activities and foreign exchange trading;

- Income statement reconciliation table giving detailed information on the way in which the income statement data shown in the present publication are derived from generally more detailed national data;

- Balance sheet reconciliation table giving detailed information on the way in which the balance sheet data shown in the present publication are derived from more detailed national balance sheet data;

- Explanations on some items of the income statement and balance sheet in cases in which national data cannot entirely be fitted into the standard framework. The income statement item *Provisions (net)* (item 8) receives special attention in the commentary;

- Sources of data on income statements and balance sheets of banks with indication of method of compilation.

INTRODUCTION

Les données communiquées par les pays concernant **les comptes de résultats des banques** sont groupées après, le cas échéant, reclassement pour cadrer, autant que possible, avec le modèle de présentation ci-après :

Compte de resultats

1.   Produits financiers,

2.   Frais financiers

3.   Produits financiers nets (poste 1 moins poste 2)

4.   Produits non financiers (nets)

5.   Résultat brut (poste 3 plus poste 4)

6.   Frais d'exploitation

7.   Résultat net (poste 5 moins poste 6)

8.   Provisions (nettes)

9.   Bénéfices avant impôt (poste 7 moins poste 8)

10.   Impôt sur le revenu/les sociétés

11.   Bénéfices après impôt (poste 9 moins poste 10)

12.   Bénéfices distribués

13.   Bénéfices mis en réserve (poste 11 moins poste 12)

Pour mémoire

14.   Frais de personnel (comptabilisés au poste 6)

15.   Provisions nettes sur prêts (comptabilisées au poste 8)

16.   Provisions nettes sur titres (comptabilisées au poste 8)

Le poste *Produits financiers,* (poste 1) comprend, en principe, les revenus procurés par les actifs porteurs d'intérêts, les commissions afférentes aux opérations de prêt, ainsi que les dividendes d'actions et titres de participation. Dans certains cas, il peut comprendre aussi les revenus d'obligations considérés comme étant égaux à la différence entre la valeur comptable et la valeur de remboursement des titres.

Le poste *Frais financiers* (poste 2) comprend, en principe, les intérêts versés sur les emprunts et les commissions versées sur les opérations d'emprunt. Il peut comprendre aussi la différence entre la valeur d'émission des instruments de dette et leur valeur nominale.

Le poste *Produits non financiers (nets)* (poste 4) est normalement le résultat net d'un certain nombre de produits et frais différents (autres que ceux repris aux postes 1 et 2) comme les commissions perçues et versées à l'occasion de diverses opérations -- paiements, opérations sur titres (placement d'émissions, contrepartie, gestion de portefeuille, garde de titres), opérations de change -- effectuées par les banques tant pour leur propre compte que pour celui de leurs clients. Figurent aussi à ce poste, les produits et les charges résultant d'opérations exceptionnelles et non des activités courantes des banques. Les gains et pertes de change et les plus-values et moins-values sur la réalisation de titres de placement y figurent également.

Le poste *Frais d'exploitation* (poste 6) comprend, normalement, toutes les charges afférentes aux activités courantes des banques (à l'exclusion de celles reprises aux postes 2 et 4), en particulier les salaires et autres avantages perçus par les salariés, y compris les dotations au fonds de pension (frais de personnel) et les charges afférentes aux terrains et immeubles et aux matériels, mobilier et installations ainsi que les amortissements. Sont aussi comptabilisés à ce poste les impôts autres que l'impôt sur le revenu ou les sociétés.

Le poste *Provisions (nettes)* (poste 8) comprend, en principe, en partie ou en totalité, les charges pour ajustement de la valeur comptable des prêts, crédits et titres de placement, les plus-values comptables découlant de cet ajustement, les pertes sur prêts, les dotations aux provisions pour pertes sur ces éléments d'actif et les reprises de provisions. En revanche, les gains ou pertes de change et les plus-values ou moins-values sur la réalisation de titres de placement figurent normalement au poste *Produits non financiers (nets)* (poste 4).

Toute différence de présentation avec le présent modèle des éléments du compte de résultats est en principe indiquée dans les notes méthodologiques par pays.

Les données communiquées par les pays concernant **les bilans des banques** sont groupées après, le cas échéant, reclassement pour cadrer, autant que possible, avec le modèle de présentation ci-après :

Bilan

Actif

17.   Caisse et soldes auprès de la Banque centrale

18.   Dépôts interbancaires

19.   Prêts

20. Valeurs mobilières

21. Autres actifs

Passif

22. Capital et réserves

23. Emprunts auprès de la Banque centrale

24. Dépôts interbancaires

25. Dépôts non bancaires

26. Obligations

27. Autres engagements

Total du bilan

28. Total en fin d'exercice (somme des postes 17 à 21 ou 22 à 27)

29. Total moyen

Pour mémoire

30. Titres à court terme (comptabilisés au poste 20)

31. Obligations (comptabilisées au poste 20)

32. Actions et participations (comptabilisées au poste 20)

33. Créances sur des non résidents (comptabilisées aux postes 18 à 21)

34. Engagements envers des non résidents (comptabilisés aux postes 24 à 27)

Le poste *Titres à court terme* (poste 30) comprend, selon la définition du Système européen de comptes économiques intégrés (paragraphe 539), les titres dont l'échéance initiale est normalement de 12 mois, deux ans maximum.

Le poste *Obligations* (poste 31) comprend, selon la définition du Système européen de comptes économiques intégrés (paragraphe 542), les titres à revenu fixe ou variable initialement à plusieurs années d'échéance.

Dans les pays où existe la possibilité de réescompter des effets de commerce auprès de la Banque centrale, le montant des effets réescomptés figure habituellement à la fois à l'actif du bilan poste *Prêts* (poste 19) et au passif poste *Emprunts auprès de la Banque centrale* (poste 23).

On trouvera également les **renseignements complémentaires** suivants:

35.   Nombre d'institutions (prises en compte)

36.   Nombre de succursales (prises en compte)

37.   Nombre de salariés (en milliers) (des institutions prises en compte)

Pour faciliter l'interprétation et l'analyse des données reprises dans la présente publication et pour inciter l'utilisateur à être prudent dans l'utilisation des statistiques à des fins de comparaisons internationales, les administrations nationales ont rédigé des notes par pays qui apportent des précisions sur les points suivants :

- Les institutions sur lesquelles portent les statistiques et leur importance par rapport à l'ensemble du système financier.

- Le champ géographique et le degré de consolidation des opérations de ces institutions. Il sera précisé si sont comprises dans les données les filiales financières ou non financières, domestiques ou étrangères, des banques déclarantes ainsi que les succursales/filiales des banques étrangères.

- Une description succincte des activités des banques . Il sera indiqué, en particulier, si les banques se livrent à des activités de service génératrices de commissions, telles que des activités se rapportant aux valeurs mobilières et au commerce de devises.

- Un tableau de concordance des comptes de résultats qui donne des renseignements précis sur la façon dont les informations relatives aux comptes de résultats publiées dans cette publication ont été obtenues à partir de sources nationales, en général plus détaillées.

- Un tableau de concordance des bilans qui donne des renseignements précis sur la façon dont les bilans reproduits dans cette publication ont été construits à partir des bilans, plus détaillés, publiés dans le pays.

- Des explications sur certains postes des comptes de résultats et des bilans des banques, lorsqu'il n'est pas possible de faire parfaitement cadrer les données nationales avec la présentation type retenue. Le poste du compte de résultats *Provisions (nettes)* (poste 8), notamment, donne lieu à des commentaires.

- Les sources des données concernant les comptes de résultats et les bilans des banques ainsi que le mode de collecte.

FINANCIAL STATEMENTS OF BANKS 1983-92

COMPTES DES BANQUES 1983-92

AUSTRALIA
All banks

Million Australian dollars

AUSTRALIE
Ensemble des banques

Millions de dollars australiens

#			1986	1987	1988	1989	1990	1991	1992
INCOME STATEMENT		**COMPTE DE RESULTATS**							
1.	Interest income	Produits financiers	21114	25061	27384	37341	48101	42744	33635
2.	Interest expenses	Frais financiers	15770	18869	19173	27691	37442	31712	23321
3.	Net interest income	Produits financiers nets	5344	6192	8211	9650	10659	11032	10314
4.	Non-interest income (net)	Produits non financiers (nets)	3420	4658	5327	5948	7129	10075	8143
5.	Gross income	Résultat brut	8764	10850	13538	15598	17788	21107	18457
6.	Operating expenses	Frais d'exploitation	6430	7238	8770	10144	11748	12672	13634
7.	Net income	Résultat net	2334	3612	4768	5454	6040	8435	4823
8.	Provisions (net)	Provisions (nettes)	461	803	1052	1709	3402	5117	4900
9.	Profit before tax	Bénéfices avant impôt	1873	2809	3716	3745	2638	3318	-77
10.	Income tax	Impôt	658	1198	1703	1446	1079	1500	336
11.	Profit after tax	Bénéfices après impôt	1215	1611	2013	2299	1559	1818	-413
12.	Distributed profit	Bénéfices distribués	571	579	1220	2102	1742	1390	1627
13.	Retained profit	Bénéfices mis en réserve	644	1032	793	197	-183	428	-2040
Memoranda		*Pour mémoire*							
14.	Staff costs	Frais de personnel	..	..	..	..	..	..	..
15.	Provisions on loans	Provisions sur prêts	..	..	..	..	..	..	..
16.	Provisions on securities	Provisions sur titres	..	..	..	..	..	..	..
BALANCE SHEET		**BILAN**							
Assets		**Actif**							
17.	Cash & balance with Central bank	Caisse & solde auprès de la Banque centrale	4639	4633	4714	4376	4197	3919	4215
18.	Interbank deposits	Dépôts interbancaires	18751	18121	19191	31833	34483	32884	34826
19.	Loans (1)	Prêts (1)	116315	137164	161963	206300	239051	249425	256787
20.	Securities (1)	Valeurs mobilières (1)	33487	37877	46875	49597	30852	35460	40441
21.	Other assets (1)	Autres actifs (1)	37892	49876	68955	82233	109737	111918	117808
Liabilities		**Passif**							
22.	Capital & reserves	Capital et réserves	12766	15796	22953	28363	39300	43289	45221
23.	Borrowing from Central bank	Emprunts auprès de la Banque centrale	..	..	..	..	..	..	..
24.	Interbank deposits	Dépôts interbancaires	24152	25528	26175	38352	36263	36914	42222
25.	Non-bank deposits (1)	Dépôts non bancaires (1)	..	..	..	..	228711	232934	245362
26.	Bonds	Obligations	..	..	..	..	..	..	..
27.	Other liabilities (1)	Autres engagements (1)	174166	206348	252568	307624	114046	120471	121272
Balance sheet total		**Total du bilan**							
28.	End-year total	En fin d'exercice	211085	247673	301697	374339	418322	433608	454077
29.	Average total	Moyen	184463	229379	274685	338018	396331	425965	443843
Memoranda		*Pour mémoire*							
30.	Short-term securities	Titres à court terme	2874	6405	7712	8958	5919	10780	10212
31.	Bonds	Obligations	18288	18802	19443	14369	17160	14159	16024
32.	Shares and participations (1)	Actions et participations (1)	8047	8929	13508	14219	..	..	..
33.	Claims on non-residents	Créances sur des non résidents	..	..	..	..	..	..	..
34.	Liabilities to non-residents	Engagements envers des non résidents	..	..	..	..	..	..	..
SUPPLEMENTARY INFORMATION		**RENSEIGNEMENTS COMPLEMENTAIRES**							
35.	Number of institutions	Nombre d'institutions	31	32	32	32	32	29	28
36.	Number of branches	Nombre de succursales	15462	14981	14381	15009	14617	14203	13491
37.	Number of employees (x 1000)	Nombre de salariés (x 1000)	NA	NA	NA	NA	NA	NA	NA

AUSTRALIA

All banks

Per cent	1986	1987	1988	1989	1990	1991	1992	*Pourcentage*
INCOME STATEMENT ANALYSIS								**ANALYSE DU COMPTE DE RESULTATS**
% of average balance sheet total								**% du total moyen du bilan**
38. Interest income	11.45	10.93	9.97	11.05	12.14	10.03	7.58	38. Produits financiers
39. Interest expenses	8.55	8.23	6.98	8.19	9.45	7.44	5.25	39. Frais financiers
40. Net interest income	2.90	2.70	2.99	2.85	2.69	2.59	2.32	40. Produits financiers nets
41. Non-interest income (net)	1.85	2.03	1.94	1.76	1.80	2.37	1.83	41. Produits non financiers (nets)
42. Gross income	4.75	4.73	4.93	4.61	4.49	4.96	4.16	42. Résultat brut
43. Operating expenses	3.49	3.16	3.19	3.00	2.96	2.97	3.07	43. Frais d'exploitation
44. Net income	1.27	1.57	1.74	1.61	1.52	1.98	1.09	44. Résultat net
45. Provisions (net)	0.25	0.35	0.38	0.51	0.86	1.20	1.10	45. Provisions (nettes)
46. Profit before tax	1.02	1.22	1.35	1.11	0.67	0.78	-0.02	46. Bénéfices avant impôt
47. Income tax	0.36	0.52	0.62	0.43	0.27	0.35	0.08	47. Impôt
48. Profit after tax	0.66	0.70	0.73	0.68	0.39	0.43	-0.09	48. Bénéfices après impôt
49. Distributed profit	0.31	0.25	0.44	0.62	0.44	0.33	0.37	49. Bénéfices distribués
50. Retained profit	0.35	0.45	0.29	0.06	-0.05	0.10	-0.46	50. Bénéfices mis en réserve
51. Staff costs	..	..	..	..	..	..	..	51. Frais de personnel
52. Provisions on loans	..	..	..	..	..	..	..	52. Provisions sur prêts
53. Provisions on securities	..	..	..	..	..	..	..	53. Provisions sur titres
% of gross income								**% du total du résultat brut**
54. Net interest income	60.98	57.07	60.65	61.87	59.92	52.27	55.88	54. Produits financiers nets
55. Non-interest income (net)	39.02	42.93	39.35	38.13	40.08	47.73	44.12	55. Produits non financiers (nets)
56. Operating expenses	73.37	66.71	64.78	65.03	66.04	60.04	73.87	56. Frais d'exploitation
57. Net income	26.63	33.29	35.22	34.97	33.96	39.96	26.13	57. Résultat net
58. Provisions (net)	5.26	7.40	7.77	10.96	19.13	24.24	26.55	58. Provisions (nettes)
59. Profit before tax	21.37	25.89	27.45	24.01	14.83	15.72	-0.42	59. Bénéfices avant impôt
60. Income tax	7.51	11.04	12.58	9.27	6.07	7.11	1.82	60. Impôt
61. Profit after tax	13.86	14.85	14.87	14.74	8.76	8.61	-2.24	61. Bénéfices après impôt
62. Staff costs	..	..	..	..	..	..	..	62. Frais de personnel
% of net income								**% du total du résultat net**
63. Provisions (net)	19.75	22.23	22.06	31.33	56.32	60.66	101.60	63. Provisions (nettes)
64. Profit before tax	80.25	77.77	77.94	68.67	43.68	39.34	-1.60	64. Bénéfices avant impôt
65. Income tax	28.19	33.17	35.72	26.51	17.86	17.78	6.97	65. Impôt
66. Profit after tax	52.06	44.60	42.22	42.15	25.81	21.55	-8.56	66. Bénéfices après impôt

AUSTRALIA

All banks

AUSTRALIE

Ensemble des banques

Per cent / *Pourcentage*

BALANCE SHEET ANALYSIS / **ANALYSE DU BILAN**

% of year-end balance sheet total / **% du total du bilan en fin d'exercice**

	1986	1987	1988	1989	1990	1991	1992	
Assets								**Actif**
67. Cash & balance with Central bank	2.20	1.87	1.56	1.17	1.00	0.90	0.93	67. Caisse & solde auprès de la Banque centrale
68. Interbank deposits	8.88	7.32	6.36	8.50	8.24	7.58	7.67	68. Dépôts interbancaires
69. Loans (1)	55.10	55.38	53.68	55.11	57.15	57.52	56.55	69. Prêts (1)
70. Securities (1)	15.86	15.29	15.54	13.25	7.38	8.18	8.91	70. Valeurs mobilières (1)
71. Other assets (1)	17.95	20.14	22.86	21.97	26.23	25.81	25.94	71. Autres actifs (1)
Liabilities								**Passif**
72. Capital & reserves	6.05	6.38	7.61	7.58	9.39	9.98	9.96	72. Capital et réserves
73. Borrowing from Central bank	..							73. Emprunts auprès de la Banque centrale
74. Interbank deposits	11.44	10.31	8.68	10.25	8.67	8.51	9.30	74. Dépôts interbancaires
75. Non-bank deposits (1)								75. Dépôts non bancaires (1)
76. Bonds								76. Obligations
77. Other liabilities (1)	82.51	83.31	83.72	82.18	27.26	27.78	26.71	77. Autres engagements (1)
Memoranda								*Pour mémoire*
78. Short-term securities	*1.36*	*2.59*	*2.56*	*2.39*	*1.41*	*2.49*	*2.25*	*78. Titres à court terme*
79. Bonds	*8.66*	*7.59*	*6.44*	*3.84*	*4.10*	*3.27*	*3.53*	*79. Obligations*
80. Shares and participations (1)	*3.81*	*3.61*	*4.48*	*3.80*	*..*	*..*	*..*	*80. Actions et participations (1)*
81. Claims on non-residents	*..*	*..*	*..*	*..*	*..*	*..*	*..*	*81. Créances sur des non résidents*
82. Liabilities to non-residents	*..*	*..*	*..*	*..*	*..*	*..*	*..*	*82. Engagements envers des non résidents*

1. Change in methodology.

1. Changement méthodologique.

Change in methodology:

- Introduction of revised statistical collection in 1990 resulted in reclassification of shares and participations from "Securities" (item 20 or item 70) to "Loans" (item 19 or item 69) and "Other assets" (item 21 or item 71).

- As from 1990, "Shares and participations" (item 32 or item 80) are not separately available following the introduction of revised statistical collection.

- Until 1990, "Non-bank deposits" (item 25 or item 75) were included under "Other liabilities" (item 27 or item 77). This item includes a small proportion of deposits from other banks.

Changement méthodologique :

- La reclassification des actions et participations du poste 20 (ou poste 70) "Titres" au poste 19 (ou poste 69) "Prêts" et 21 (ou poste 71) "Autres actifs" est consécutive à l'introduction en 1990 d'une révision de la collecte statistique.

- A partir de 1990, les "Actions et participations" (poste 32 ou poste 80) ne sont plus disponibles séparément suite à l'introduction d'une révision de la collecte statistique.

- Jusqu'en 1990, les "Dépôts non bancaires" (poste 25 ou poste 75) étaient inclus sous "Autres engagements" (poste 27 ou poste 77). Ce poste inclut une petite partie des dépôts des autres banques.

AUSTRIA

All banks

AUTRICHE

Ensemble des banques

Million schillings / *Millions de schillings*

	1987	1988	1989	1990	1991	1992	
INCOME STATEMENT							**COMPTE DE RESULTATS**
1. Interest income	215539	229896	275916	327360	347980	355738	1. Produits financiers
2. Interest expenses	156960	166908	210562	256357	271594	273939	2. Frais financiers
3. Net interest income	58579	62988	65354	71003	76386	81799	3. Produits financiers nets
4. Non-interest income (net)	14353	17415	25226	31767	36158	41005	4. Produits non financiers (nets)
5. Gross income	72932	80403	90580	102770	112544	122804	5. Résultat brut
6. Operating expenses	51111	55047	59340	66661	73061	78573	6. Frais d'exploitation
7. Net income	21821	25356	31240	36109	39483	44231	7. Résultat net
8. Provisions (net)	::	::	14813	20032	22077	29108	8. Provisions (nettes)
9. Profit before tax	21821	25356	16427	16077	17406	15123	9. Bénéfices avant impôt
10. Income tax	2934	3103	3157	3032	2911	2600	10. Impôt
11. Profit after tax	18887	22253	13270	13045	14495	12523	11. Bénéfices après impôt
12. Distributed profit	::	::	::	::	::	::	12. Bénéfices distribués
13. Retained profit	::	::	::	::	::	::	13. Bénéfices mis en réserve
Memoranda							***Pour mémoire***
14. Staff costs	30098	32181	34696	39547	43379	46817	14. Frais de personnel
15. Provisions on loans	::	::	6566	8050	11875	17857	15. Provisions sur prêts
16. Provisions on securities	::	::	5789	7348	3206	3749	16. Provisions sur titres
BALANCE SHEET							**BILAN**
Assets							**Actif**
17. Cash & balance with Central bank	63737	67199	76883	73166	68441	83827	17. Caisse & solde auprès de la Banque centrale
18. Interbank deposits	1220499	1231639	1223461	1235092	1242553	1303640	18. Dépôts interbancaires
19. Loans	1561331	1710902	1884902	2048063	2213849	2379219	19. Prêts
20. Securities	388599	424417	445993	468099	492964	476684	20. Valeurs mobilières
21. Other assets	184965	183171	199619	216056	258405	297082	21. Autres actifs
Liabilities							**Passif**
22. Capital & reserves	119054	141636	163595	186199	202114	220564	22. Capital et réserves
23. Borrowing from Central bank	2298	2792	1144	1533	1103	557	23. Emprunts auprès de la Banque centrale
24. Interbank deposits	1254249	1287885	1286495	1280553	1315567	1359228	24. Dépôts interbancaires
25. Non-bank deposits	1373945	1452911	1569986	1725712	1876343	2029440	25. Dépôts non bancaires
26. Bonds	517067	593320	659477	692662	705669	737231	26. Obligations
27. Other liabilities	152517	138785	150162	153816	175396	193432	27. Autres engagements
Balance sheet total							**Total du bilan**
28. End-year total	3419130	3617329	3830858	4040476	4276192	4540452	28. En fin d'exercice
29. Average total	3334251	3543249	3769759	4012331	4228420	4414568	29. Moyen
Memoranda							***Pour mémoire***
30. Short-term securities	10145	8439	5951	6807	6088	5468	30. Titres à court terme
31. Bonds	305492	334051	348443	352728	366784	361695	31. Obligations
32. Shares and participations	51819	62326	76772	93973	112789	127830	32. Actions et participations
33. Claims on non-residents	751664	816929	842040	843875	846806	915883	33. Créances sur des non résidents
34. Liabilities to non-residents	790712	877311	926274	932278	958893	1045004	34. Engagements envers des non résidents
SUPPLEMENTARY INFORMATION							**RENSEIGNEMENTS COMPLEMENTAIRES**
35. Number of institutions	1252	1250	1240	1210	1165	1104	35. Nombre d'institutions
36. Number of branches	4203	4295	4373	4497	4594	4667	36. Nombre de succursales
37. Number of employees (x 1000)	67.6	70.2	71.5	74.6	76.0	72.1	37. Nombre de salariés (x 1000)

AUSTRIA

All banks

AUTRICHE

Ensemble des banques

Per cent — *Pourcentage*

INCOME STATEMENT ANALYSIS — ANALYSE DU COMPTE DE RESULTATS

	1987	1988	1989	1990	1991	1992		
% of average balance sheet total								**% du total moyen du bilan**
38. Interest income	6.46	6.49	7.32	8.16	8.23	8.06	38.	Produits financiers
39. Interest expenses	4.71	4.71	5.59	6.39	6.42	6.21	39.	Frais financiers
40. Net interest income	1.76	1.78	1.73	1.77	1.81	1.85	40.	Produits financiers nets
41. Non-interest income (net)	0.43	0.49	0.67	0.79	0.86	0.93	41.	Produits non financiers (nets)
42. Gross income	2.19	2.27	2.40	2.56	2.66	2.78	42.	Résultat brut
43. Operating expenses	1.53	1.55	1.57	1.66	1.73	1.78	43.	Frais d'exploitation
44. Net income	0.65	0.72	0.83	0.90	0.93	1.00	44.	Résultat net
45. Provisions (net)	..	..	0.39	0.50	0.52	0.66	45.	Provisions (nettes)
46. Profit before tax	0.65	0.72	0.44	0.40	0.41	0.34	46.	Bénéfices avant impôt
47. Income tax	0.09	0.09	0.08	0.08	0.07	0.06	47.	Impôt
48. Profit after tax	0.57	0.63	0.35	0.33	0.34	0.28	48.	Bénéfices après impôt
49. Distributed profit	..	..	..	..	..	..	49.	Bénéfices distribués
50. Retained profit	..	..	..	..	..	..	50.	Bénéfices mis en réserve
51. Staff costs	0.90	0.91	0.92	0.99	1.03	1.06	51.	Frais de personnel
52. Provisions on loans	..	..	0.17	0.20	0.28	0.40	52.	Provisions sur prêts
53. Provisions on securities	..	..	0.15	0.18	0.08	0.08	53.	Provisions sur titres
% of gross income								**% du total du résultat brut**
54. Net interest income	80.32	78.34	72.15	69.09	67.87	66.61	54.	Produits financiers nets
55. Non-interest income (net)	19.68	21.66	27.85	30.91	32.13	33.39	55.	Produits non financiers (nets)
56. Operating expenses	70.08	68.46	65.51	64.86	64.92	63.98	56.	Frais d'exploitation
57. Net income	29.92	31.54	34.49	35.14	35.08	36.02	57.	Résultat net
58. Provisions (net)	..	..	16.35	19.49	19.62	23.70	58.	Provisions (nettes)
59. Profit before tax	29.92	31.54	18.14	15.64	15.47	12.31	59.	Bénéfices avant impôt
60. Income tax	4.02	3.86	3.49	2.95	2.59	2.12	60.	Impôt
61. Profit after tax	25.90	27.68	14.65	12.69	12.88	10.20	61.	Bénéfices après impôt
62. Staff costs	41.27	40.02	38.30	38.48	38.54	38.12	62.	Frais de personnel
% of net income								**% du total du résultat net**
63. Provisions (net)	..	..	47.42	55.48	55.92	65.81	63.	Provisions (nettes)
64. Profit before tax	100.00	100.00	52.58	44.52	44.08	34.19	64.	Bénéfices avant impôt
65. Income tax	13.45	12.24	10.11	8.40	7.37	5.88	65.	Impôt
66. Profit after tax	86.55	87.76	42.48	36.13	36.71	28.31	66.	Bénéfices après impôt

AUSTRIA

All banks

AUTRICHE

Ensemble des banques

Per cent

Pourcentage

BALANCE SHEET ANALYSIS

ANALYSE DU BILAN

% of year-end balance sheet total

% du total du bilan en fin d'exercice

	1987	1988	1989	1990	1991	1992		
Assets							**Actif**	
67. Cash & balance with Central bank	1.86	1.86	2.01	1.81	1.60	1.85	67.	Caisse & solde auprès de la Banque centrale
68. Interbank deposits	35.70	34.05	31.94	30.57	29.06	28.71	68.	Dépôts interbancaires
69. Loans	45.66	47.30	49.20	50.69	51.77	52.40	69.	Prêts
70. Securities	11.37	11.73	11.64	11.59	11.53	10.50	70.	Valeurs mobilières
71. Other assets	5.41	5.06	5.21	5.35	6.04	6.54	71.	Autres actifs
Liabilities							**Passif**	
72. Capital & reserves	3.48	3.92	4.27	4.61	4.73	4.86	72.	Capital et réserves
73. Borrowing from Central bank	0.07	0.08	0.03	0.04	0.03	0.01	73.	Emprunts auprès de la Banque centrale
74. Interbank deposits	36.68	35.60	33.58	31.69	30.76	29.94	74.	Dépôts interbancaires
75. Non-bank deposits	40.18	40.17	40.98	42.71	43.88	44.70	75.	Dépôts non bancaires
76. Bonds	15.12	16.40	17.21	17.14	16.50	16.24	76.	Obligations
77. Other liabilities	4.46	3.84	3.92	3.81	4.10	4.26	77.	Autres engagements
Memoranda							*Pour mémoire*	
78. Short-term securities	*0.30*	*0.23*	*0.16*	*0.17*	*0.14*	*0.12*	*78.*	*Titres à court terme*
79. Bonds	*8.93*	*9.23*	*9.10*	*8.73*	*8.58*	*7.97*	*79.*	*Obligations*
80. Shares and participations	*1.52*	*1.72*	*2.00*	*2.33*	*2.64*	*2.82*	*80.*	*Actions et participations*
81. Claims on non-residents	*21.98*	*22.58*	*21.98*	*20.89*	*19.80*	*20.17*	*81.*	*Créances sur des non résidents*
82. Liabilities to non-residents	*23.13*	*24.25*	*24.18*	*23.07*	*22.42*	*23.02*	*82.*	*Engagements envers des non résidents*

Notes

• Average balance sheet totals (item 29) are based on twelve end-month data.

Notes

• La moyenne du total des actifs/passifs (poste 29) est basée sur douze données de fin de mois.

25

BELGIUM
Commercial banks

Million Belgian francs

BELGIQUE
Banques commerciales

Millions de francs belges

		1983	1984	1985	1986	1987	1988	1989	1990	1991	1992	
INCOME STATEMENT												**COMPTE DE RESULTATS**
1.	Interest income	669100	806059	828268	737264	746312	881211	1181729	1340128	1348800	1337628	Produits financiers
2.	Interest expenses	563717	682959	691999	592534	603087	734640	1024583	1175443	1174587	1151098	Frais financiers
3.	Net interest income	105383	123100	136269	144730	143225	146571	157146	164685	174213	186530	Produits financiers nets
4.	Non-interest income (net)	34159	32245	42207	50336	52677	62690	59356	49298	57555	66355	Produits non financiers (nets)
5.	Gross income	139542	155345	178476	195106	195902	209261	216502	213983	231768	252885	Résultat brut
6.	Operating expenses	97114	107112	118868	127114	133471	129875	142420	148349	152371	163237	Frais d'exploitation
7.	Net income	42428	48233	59608	67992	62431	79386	74082	65634	79397	89648	Résultat net
8.	Provisions (net)	19985	22202	26691	27674	27283	42820	51126	24684	39710	52796	Provisions (nettes)
9.	Profit before tax	22443	26031	32917	40318	35148	36566	22956	40950	39687	36852	Bénéfices avant impôt
10.	Income tax	9817	10497	13178	16452	14019	10574	10757	7999	10132	11606	Impôt
11.	Profit after tax	12626	15534	19739	23866	21129	25992	12199	32951	29555	25246	Bénéfices après impôt
12.	Distributed profit	..	..	..	..	..	..	..	..	..	..	Bénéfices distribués
13.	Retained profit	..	..	..	..	..	..	..	..	..	..	Bénéfices mis en réserve
Memoranda												***Pour mémoire***
14.	Staff costs	*70216*	*76799*	*81949*	*87027*	*89840*	*92900*	*99174*	*104217*	*106648*	*112307*	Frais de personnel
15.	Provisions on loans	*..*	*..*	*..*	*..*	*..*	*..*	*..*	*..*	*..*	*..*	Provisions sur prêts
16.	Provisions on securities	*..*	*..*	*..*	*..*	*..*	*..*	*..*	*..*	*..*	*..*	Provisions sur titres
BALANCE SHEET												**BILAN**
Assets												**Actif**
17.	Cash & balance with Central bank	14193	18457	16192	15868	16176	16746	21245	21497	20942	20960	Caisse & solde auprès de la Banque centrale
18.	Interbank deposits	3159291	3741946	4034081	4082213	4451386	4955770	5143367	5420716	5351044	5511766	Dépôts interbancaires
19.	Loans	2198088	2455976	2365024	2360343	2457869	2830155	3382345	3504562	3681628	3876079	Prêts
20.	Securities	1524243	1743217	2104831	2452736	2584660	2679435	2765878	2947941	2855554	3137200	Valeurs mobilières
21.	Other assets	255945	349158	336801	335413	343897	472092	538690	596691	584472	570093	Autres actifs
Liabilities												**Passif**
22.	Capital & reserves	179699	209130	222335	265151	289072	334754	401677	424618	483618	534599	Capital et réserves
23.	Borrowing from Central bank (1)	..	..	..	..	..	..	..	..	..	..	Emprunts auprès de la Banque centrale (1)
24.	Interbank deposits	4472755	5332728	5626035	5738639	6024254	6658012	6866565	7104733	6636136	6800036	Dépôts interbancaires
25.	Non-bank deposits	1845512	2015844	2164325	2399149	2647782	2983769	3410030	3628596	3922770	4204454	Dépôts non bancaires
26.	Bonds	352256	390843	443984	450272	461609	470744	533357	690846	809709	897749	Obligations
27.	Other liabilities	301538	360209	400250	393362	431271	506919	639894	642609	641405	679260	Autres engagements
Balance sheet total												**Total du bilan**
28.	End-year total	7151760	8308754	8856929	9246573	9853988	10954198	11851524	12491405	12493639	13116097	En fin d'exercice
29.	Average total	6556728	7717112	8931514	8939174	9622585	10652680	11942592	12228867	12983213	13216358	Moyen
Memoranda												***Pour mémoire***
30.	Short-term securities	*562871*	*569664*	*644492*	*843583*	*901385*	*838423*	*917605*	*980824*	*718797*	*723367*	Titres à court terme
31.	Bonds	*916353*	*1123848*	*1424718*	*1569827*	*1618476*	*1752486*	*1742043*	*1871557*	*2028855*	*2308049*	Obligations
32.	Shares and participations	*45019*	*49705*	*35621*	*39327*	*64799*	*88525*	*106230*	*95560*	*107902*	*105784*	Actions et participations
33.	Claims on non-residents	*3728352*	*4479931*	*4758378*	*4856012*	*5036791*	*5740857*	*6015304*	*6069778*	*6173962*	*6406855*	Créances sur des non résidents
34.	Liabilities to non-residents	*4432503*	*5400433*	*5645082*	*5802900*	*6023515*	*6894915*	*7277340*	*7356089*	*7113229*	*7367272*	Engagements envers des non résidents
SUPPLEMENTARY INFORMATION												**RENSEIGNEMENTS COMPLEMENTAIRES**
35.	Number of institutions	84	84	85	86	86	85	85	87	91	93	Nombre d'institutions
36.	Number of branches	3680	3654	3656	3646	3631	3617	3618	3592	3547	3515	Nombre de succursales
37.	Number of employees (x 1000)	47.4	48.4	48.4	49.2	50.0	50.2	51.6	50.7	49.6	48.6	Nombre de salariés (x 1000)

BELGIUM

Commercial banks

Per cent

INCOME STATEMENT ANALYSIS

	1983	1984	1985	1986	1987	1988	1989	1990	1991	1992		
% of average balance sheet total												**% du total moyen du bilan**
38. Interest income	10.20	10.45	9.27	8.25	7.76	8.27	9.90	10.96	10.39	10.12	38.	Produits financiers
39. Interest expenses	8.60	8.85	7.75	6.63	6.27	6.90	8.58	9.61	9.05	8.71	39.	Frais financiers
40. Net interest income	1.61	1.60	1.53	1.62	1.49	1.38	1.32	1.35	1.34	1.41	40.	Produits financiers nets
41. Non-interest income (net)	0.52	0.42	0.47	0.56	0.55	0.59	0.50	0.40	0.44	0.50	41.	Produits non financiers (nets)
42. Gross income	2.13	2.01	2.00	2.18	2.04	1.96	1.81	1.75	1.79	1.91	42.	Résultat brut
43. Operating expenses	1.48	1.39	1.33	1.42	1.39	1.22	1.19	1.21	1.17	1.24	43.	Frais d'exploitation
44. Net income	0.65	0.63	0.67	0.76	0.65	0.75	0.62	0.54	0.61	0.68	44.	Résultat net
45. Provisions (net)	0.30	0.29	0.30	0.31	0.28	0.40	0.43	0.20	0.31	0.40	45.	Provisions (nettes)
46. Profit before tax	0.34	0.34	0.37	0.45	0.37	0.34	0.19	0.33	0.31	0.28	46.	Bénéfices avant impôt
47. Income tax	0.15	0.14	0.15	0.18	0.15	0.10	0.09	0.07	0.08	0.09	47.	Impôt
48. Profit after tax	0.19	0.20	0.22	0.27	0.22	0.24	0.10	0.27	0.23	0.19	48.	Bénéfices après impôt
49. Distributed profit	..	..	..	..	..	..	..	..	..	..	49.	Bénéfices distribués
50. Retained profit	..	..	..	..	..	..	..	..	..	..	50.	Bénéfices mis en réserve
51. Staff costs	1.07	1.00	0.92	0.97	0.93	0.87	0.83	0.85	0.82	0.85	51.	Frais de personnel
52. Provisions on loans	..	..	..	..	..	..	..	..	..	..	52.	Provisions sur prêts
53. Provisions on securities	..	..	..	..	..	..	..	..	..	..	53.	Provisions sur titres
% of gross income												**% du total du résultat brut**
54. Net interest income	75.52	79.24	76.35	74.18	73.11	70.04	72.58	76.96	75.17	73.76	54.	Produits financiers nets
55. Non-interest income (net)	24.48	20.76	23.65	25.82	26.89	29.96	27.42	23.04	24.83	26.24	55.	Produits non financiers (nets)
56. Operating expenses	69.59	68.95	66.60	65.15	68.13	62.06	65.78	69.33	65.74	64.55	56.	Frais d'exploitation
57. Net income	30.41	31.05	33.40	34.85	31.87	37.94	34.22	30.67	34.26	35.45	57.	Résultat net
58. Provisions (net)	14.32	14.29	14.95	14.18	13.93	20.46	23.61	11.54	17.13	20.88	58.	Provisions (nettes)
59. Profit before tax	16.08	16.76	18.44	20.66	17.94	17.47	10.60	19.14	17.12	14.57	59.	Bénéfices avant impôt
60. Income tax	7.04	6.76	7.38	8.43	7.16	5.05	4.97	3.74	4.37	4.59	60.	Impôt
61. Profit after tax	9.05	10.00	11.06	12.23	10.79	12.42	5.63	15.40	12.75	9.98	61.	Bénéfices après impôt
62. Staff costs	50.32	49.44	45.92	44.60	45.86	44.39	45.81	48.70	45.97	44.41	62.	Frais de personnel
% of net income												**% du total du résultat net**
63. Provisions (net)	47.10	46.03	44.78	40.70	43.70	53.94	69.01	37.61	50.01	58.89	63.	Provisions (nettes)
64. Profit before tax	52.90	53.97	55.22	59.30	56.30	46.06	30.99	62.39	49.99	41.11	64.	Bénéfices avant impôt
65. Income tax	23.14	21.76	22.11	24.20	22.46	13.32	14.52	12.19	12.76	12.95	65.	Impôt
66. Profit after tax	29.76	32.21	33.11	35.10	33.84	32.74	16.47	50.20	37.22	28.16	66.	Bénéfices après impôt

BELGIQUE

Banques commerciales

Pourcentage

ANALYSE DU COMPTE DE RESULTATS

BELGIUM

Commercial banks

BELGIQUE

Banques commerciales

Per cent / *Pourcentage*

BALANCE SHEET ANALYSIS / **ANALYSE DU BILAN**

% of year-end balance sheet total / % du total du bilan en fin d'exercice

		1983	1984	1985	1986	1987	1988	1989	1990	1991	1992		
Assets												**Actif**	
67.	Cash & balance with Central bank	0.20	0.22	0.18	0.17	0.16	0.15	0.18	0.17	0.17	0.16	67.	Caisse & solde auprès de la Banque centrale
68.	Interbank deposits	44.18	45.04	45.55	44.15	45.17	45.24	43.40	43.40	42.83	42.02	68.	Dépôts interbancaires
69.	Loans	30.73	29.56	26.70	25.53	24.94	25.84	28.54	28.06	29.47	29.55	69.	Prêts
70.	Securities	21.31	20.98	23.76	26.53	26.23	24.46	23.34	23.60	22.86	23.92	70.	Valeurs mobilières
71.	Other assets	3.58	4.20	3.80	3.63	3.49	4.31	4.55	4.78	4.68	4.35	71.	Autres actifs
Liabilities												**Passif**	
72.	Capital & reserves	2.51	2.52	2.51	2.87	2.93	3.06	3.39	3.40	3.87	4.08	72.	Capital et réserves
73.	Borrowing from Central bank (1)	..	..	..	..	..	..	..	..	..	..	73.	Emprunts auprès de la Banque centrale (1)
74.	Interbank deposits	62.54	64.18	63.52	62.06	61.14	60.78	57.94	56.88	53.12	51.84	74.	Dépôts interbancaires
75.	Non-bank deposits	25.81	24.26	24.44	25.95	26.87	27.24	28.77	29.05	31.40	32.06	75.	Dépôts non bancaires
76.	Bonds	4.93	4.70	5.01	4.87	4.68	4.30	4.50	5.53	6.48	6.84	76.	Obligations
77.	Other liabilities	4.22	4.34	4.52	4.25	4.38	4.63	5.40	5.14	5.13	5.18	77.	Autres engagements
Memoranda												*Pour mémoire*	
78.	*Short-term securities*	7.87	6.86	7.28	9.12	9.15	7.65	7.74	7.85	5.75	5.52	78.	*Titres à court terme*
79.	*Bonds*	12.81	13.53	16.09	16.98	16.42	16.00	14.70	14.98	16.24	17.60	79.	*Obligations*
80.	*Shares and participations*	0.63	0.60	0.40	0.43	0.66	0.81	0.90	0.77	0.86	0.81	80.	*Actions et participations*
81.	*Claims on non-residents*	52.13	53.92	53.72	52.52	51.11	52.41	50.76	48.59	49.42	48.85	81.	*Créances sur des non résidents*
82.	*Liabilities to non-residents*	61.98	65.00	63.74	62.76	61.13	62.94	61.40	58.89	56.93	56.17	82.	*Engagements envers des non résidents*

1. Included under "Interbank deposits" (item 24 or item 74).

1. Inclus sous "Dépôts interbancaires" (poste 24 ou poste 74).

Notes

- Average balance sheet totals (item 29) are based on twelve end-month data.

Notes

- La moyenne du total des actifs/passifs (poste 29) est basée sur douze données de fin de mois.

BELGIUM

Savings banks

BELGIQUE

Caisses d'épargne

Million Belgian francs / *Millions de francs belges*

No.	(English)	1983	1984	1985	1986	1987	1988	1989	1990	1991	1992	(Français)
	INCOME STATEMENT											**COMPTE DE RESULTATS**
1.	Interest income	83843	102559	113277	121355	125968	133363	146022	169453	190572	218572	Produits financiers
2.	Interest expenses	62578	75754	83382	84970	86716	91504	104267	129473	147603	171692	Frais financiers
3.	Net interest income	21265	26805	29895	36385	39252	41859	41755	39980	42969	46880	Produits financiers nets
4.	Non-interest income (net)	1130	434	973	2037	4408	5295	5025	5613	6296	7187	Produits non financiers (nets)
5.	Gross income	22395	27239	30868	38422	43660	47154	46780	45593	49265	54067	Résultat brut
6.	Operating expenses	16272	19532	22576	28172	31431	34072	35431	38480	39945	41913	Frais d'exploitation
7.	Net income	6123	7707	8292	10250	12229	13082	11349	7113	9320	12154	Résultat net
8.	Provisions (net)	3115	3338	3692	3622	4991	5892	4800	2065	3319	5350	Provisions (nettes)
9.	Profit before tax	3008	4369	4600	6628	7238	7190	6549	5048	6001	6804	Bénéfices avant impôt
10.	Income tax	1150	1755	1638	2709	2489	1796	1161	1157	1562	1423	Impôt
11.	Profit after tax	1858	2614	2962	3919	4749	5394	5388	3891	4439	5381	Bénéfices après impôt
12.	Distributed profit	..	..	..	..	..	..	..	..	..	..	Bénéfices distribués
13.	Retained profit	..	..	..	..	..	..	..	..	..	..	Bénéfices mis en réserve
	Memoranda											*Pour mémoire*
14.	*Staff costs*	*8270*	*9881*	*11188*	*12352*	*13925*	*14966*	*15617*	*17723*	*18833*	*19611*	*Frais de personnel*
15.	*Provisions on loans (1)*	*620*	*603*	*700*	*527*	*1033*	*1398*	*1720*	*656*	*1086*	*1496*	*Provisions sur prêts (1)*
16.	*Provisions on securities*											*Provisions sur titres*
	BALANCE SHEET											**BILAN**
	Assets											**Actif**
17.	Cash & balance with Central bank	2512	3019	3063	3049	3330	3560	4038	4103	4384	5345	Caisse & solde auprès de la Banque centrale
18.	Interbank deposits	38625	48209	44251	68512	105515	147927	145792	235831	282915	406477	Dépôts interbancaires
19.	Loans	361105	371076	395434	447263	495642	563040	613483	717609	793969	871153	Prêts
20.	Securities	442835	518349	608364	683574	744773	849684	891046	934398	999841	1064880	Valeurs mobilières
21.	Other assets	54754	64266	74165	78135	87532	90307	105564	118727	125592	108128	Autres actifs
	Liabilities											**Passif**
22.	Capital & reserves	34774	41554	50894	61190	73769	93754	104312	107794	114062	118977	Capital et réserves
23.	Borrowing from Central bank	123	-					500	3000	4703	4710	Emprunts auprès de la Banque centrale
24.	Interbank deposits	4191	4396	110181	133636	161371	254573	333522	418620	419914	462636	Dépôts interbancaires
25.	Non-bank deposits	594413	678992	655064	762471	888076	1022818	1070494	1212979	1361841	1548442	Dépôts non bancaires
26.	Bonds	216829	228833	250354	251190	232040	210703	162488	167968	181141	192269	Obligations
27.	Other liabilities	49501	51144	58784	72046	81537	72670	88606	100308	125039	128950	Autres engagements
	Balance sheet total											**Total du bilan**
28.	End-year total	899831	1004919	1125277	1280533	1436792	1654518	1759922	2010868	2206700	2455985	En fin d'exercice
29.	Average total	808293	948693	1065807	1201908	1351237	1548762	1712194	1870927	2105510	2314354	Moyen
	Memoranda											*Pour mémoire*
30.	*Short-term securities*	*48282*	*71246*	*66620*	*71608*	*75504*	*73426*	*96203*	*92783*	*131500*	*149569*	*Titres à court terme*
31.	*Bonds*	*381924*	*435011*	*528849*	*597747*	*654131*	*760088*	*778413*	*822355*	*847594*	*893477*	*Obligations*
32.	*Shares and participations*	*12629*	*12092*	*12895*	*14219*	*15138*	*16169*	*16430*	*19260*	*20747*	*21834*	*Actions et participations*
33.	*Claims on non-residents*	*39164*	*56627*	*84465*	*118630*	*143276*	*221209*	*301080*	*384462*	*433860*	*469740*	*Créances sur des non résidents*
34.	*Liabilities to non-residents*	*24645*	*33663*	*51387*	*81185*	*106354*	*172459*	*268177*	*352223*	*399697*	*439616*	*Engagements envers des non résidents*
	SUPPLEMENTARY INFORMATION											**RENSEIGNEMENTS COMPLEMENTAIRES**
35.	Number of institutions	31	28	29	31	32	31	29	28	28	28	Nombre d'institutions
36.	Number of branches	20659	19849	21281	20810	19804	18614	15593	14797	13531	12890	Nombre de succursales
37.	Number of employees (x 1000)	7.0	8.7	9.2	9.8	10.7	11.4	11.3	11.6	11.8	11.7	Nombre de salariés (x 1000)

BELGIUM

Savings banks

BELGIQUE

Caisses d'épargne

Per cent — *Pourcentage*

INCOME STATEMENT ANALYSIS — ANALYSE DU COMPTE DE RESULTATS

		1983	1984	1985	1986	1987	1988	1989	1990	1991	1992		
% of average balance sheet total													**% du total moyen du bilan**
38.	Interest income	10.37	10.81	10.63	10.10	9.32	8.61	8.53	9.06	9.05	9.44	38.	Produits financiers
39.	Interest expenses	7.74	7.99	7.82	7.07	6.42	5.91	6.09	6.92	7.01	7.42	39.	Frais financiers
40.	Net interest income	2.63	2.83	2.80	3.03	2.90	2.70	2.44	2.14	2.04	2.03	40.	Produits financiers nets
41.	Non-interest income (net)	0.14	0.05	0.09	0.17	0.33	0.34	0.29	0.30	0.30	0.31	41.	Produits non financiers (nets)
42.	Gross income	2.77	2.87	2.90	3.20	3.23	3.04	2.73	2.44	2.34	2.34	42.	Résultat brut
43.	Operating expenses	2.01	2.06	2.12	2.34	2.33	2.20	2.07	2.06	1.90	1.81	43.	Frais d'exploitation
44.	Net income	0.76	0.81	0.78	0.85	0.91	0.84	0.66	0.38	0.44	0.53	44.	Résultat net
45.	Provisions (net)	0.39	0.35	0.35	0.30	0.37	0.38	0.28	0.11	0.16	0.23	45.	Provisions (nettes)
46.	Profit before tax	0.37	0.46	0.43	0.55	0.54	0.46	0.38	0.27	0.29	0.29	46.	Bénéfices avant impôt
47.	Income tax	0.14	0.18	0.15	0.23	0.18	0.12	0.07	0.06	0.07	0.06	47.	Impôt
48.	Profit after tax	0.23	0.28	0.28	0.33	0.35	0.35	0.31	0.21	0.21	0.23	48.	Bénéfices après impôt
49.	Distributed profit	..	..	..	..	..	..	..	..	..	..	49.	Bénéfices distribués
50.	Retained profit	..	..	..	..	..	..	..	..	..	..	50.	Bénéfices mis en réserve
51.	Staff costs	1.02	1.04	1.05	1.03	1.03	0.97	0.91	0.95	0.89	0.85	51.	Frais de personnel
52.	Provisions on loans (1)	..	..	..	..	..	..	..	..	..	..	52.	Provisions sur prêts (1)
53.	Provisions on securities	0.08	0.06	0.07	0.04	0.08	0.09	0.10	0.04	0.05	0.06	53.	Provisions sur titres
% of gross income													**% du total du résultat brut**
54.	Net interest income	94.95	98.41	96.85	94.70	89.90	88.77	89.26	87.69	87.22	86.71	54.	Produits financiers nets
55.	Non-interest income (net)	5.05	1.59	3.15	5.30	10.10	11.23	10.74	12.31	12.78	13.29	55.	Produits non financiers (nets)
56.	Operating expenses	72.66	71.71	73.14	73.32	71.99	72.26	75.74	84.40	81.08	77.52	56.	Frais d'exploitation
57.	Net income	27.34	28.29	26.86	26.68	28.01	27.74	24.26	15.60	18.92	22.48	57.	Résultat net
58.	Provisions (net)	13.91	12.25	11.96	9.43	11.43	12.50	10.26	4.53	6.74	9.90	58.	Provisions (nettes)
59.	Profit before tax	13.43	16.04	14.90	17.25	16.58	15.25	14.00	11.07	12.18	12.58	59.	Bénéfices avant impôt
60.	Income tax	5.14	6.44	5.31	7.05	5.70	3.81	2.48	2.54	3.17	2.63	60.	Impôt
61.	Profit after tax	8.30	9.60	9.60	10.20	10.88	11.44	11.52	8.53	9.01	9.95	61.	Bénéfices après impôt
62.	Staff costs	36.93	36.28	36.24	32.15	31.89	31.74	33.38	38.87	38.23	36.27	62.	Frais de personnel
% of net income													**% du total du résultat net**
63.	Provisions (net)	50.87	43.31	44.52	35.34	40.81	45.04	42.29	29.03	35.61	44.02	63.	Provisions (nettes)
64.	Profit before tax	49.13	56.69	55.48	64.66	59.19	54.96	57.71	70.97	64.39	55.98	64.	Bénéfices avant impôt
65.	Income tax	18.78	22.77	19.75	26.43	20.35	13.73	10.23	16.27	16.76	11.71	65.	Impôt
66.	Profit after tax	30.34	33.92	35.72	38.23	38.83	41.23	47.48	54.70	47.63	44.27	66.	Bénéfices après impôt

BELGIUM

Savings banks

Per cent

BALANCE SHEET ANALYSIS

% of year-end balance sheet total

BELGIQUE

Caisses d'épargne

Pourcentage

ANALYSE DU BILAN

% du total du bilan en fin d'exercice

	1983	1984	1985	1986	1987	1988	1989	1990	1991	1992	
Assets											**Actif**
67. Cash & balance with Central bank	0.28	0.30	0.27	0.24	0.23	0.22	0.23	0.20	0.20	0.22	67. Caisse & solde auprès de la Banque centrale
68. Interbank deposits	4.29	4.80	3.93	5.35	7.34	8.94	8.28	11.73	12.82	16.55	68. Dépôts interbancaires
69. Loans	40.13	36.93	35.14	34.93	34.50	34.03	34.86	35.69	35.98	35.47	69. Prêts
70. Securities	49.21	51.58	54.06	53.38	51.84	51.36	50.63	46.47	45.31	43.36	70. Valeurs mobilières
71. Other assets	6.08	6.40	6.59	6.10	6.09	5.46	6.00	5.90	5.69	4.40	71. Autres actifs
Liabilities											**Passif**
72. Capital & reserves	3.86	4.14	4.52	4.78	5.13	5.67	5.93	5.36	5.17	4.84	72. Capital et réserves
73. Borrowing from Central bank	0.01	-	-	-	-	-	0.03	0.15	0.21	0.19	73. Emprunts auprès de la Banque centrale
74. Interbank deposits	0.47	0.44	9.79	10.44	11.23	15.39	18.95	20.82	19.03	18.84	74. Dépôts interbancaires
75. Non-bank deposits	66.06	67.57	58.21	59.54	61.81	61.82	60.83	60.33	61.71	63.05	75. Dépôts non bancaires
76. Bonds	24.10	22.77	22.25	19.62	16.15	12.74	9.23	8.35	8.21	7.83	76. Obligations
77. Other liabilities	5.50	5.09	5.22	5.63	5.67	4.39	5.03	4.99	5.67	5.25	77. Autres engagements
Memoranda											*Pour mémoire*
78. Short-term securities	*5.37*	*7.09*	*5.92*	*5.59*	*5.26*	*4.44*	*5.47*	*4.61*	*5.96*	*6.09*	*78. Titres à court terme*
79. Bonds	*42.44*	*43.29*	*47.00*	*46.68*	*45.53*	*45.94*	*44.23*	*40.90*	*38.41*	*36.38*	*79. Obligations*
80. Shares and participations	*1.40*	*1.20*	*1.15*	*1.11*	*1.05*	*0.98*	*0.93*	*0.96*	*0.94*	*0.89*	*80. Actions et participations*
81. Claims on non-residents	*4.35*	*5.63*	*7.51*	*9.26*	*9.97*	*13.37*	*17.11*	*19.12*	*19.66*	*19.13*	*81. Créances sur des non résidents*
82. Liabilities to non-residents	*2.74*	*3.35*	*4.57*	*6.34*	*7.40*	*10.42*	*15.24*	*17.52*	*17.84*	*17.90*	*82. Engagements envers des non résidents*

1. Included under "Provisions on securities" (item 16 or item 53).

Notes

- Private independent persons acting as savings bank agents are included in the number of branches.
- Average balance sheet totals (item 29) are based on twelve end-month data.

1. Inclus sous "Provisions sur titres" (poste 16 ou poste 53).

Notes

- Les agents indépendants sont compris dans le total des succursales.
- La moyenne du total des actifs/passifs (poste 29) est basée sur douze données de fin de mois.

CANADA

Commercial banks (consolidated world-wide)

CANADA

Banques commerciales (consolidées sur une base mondiale)

Million Canadian dollars / Millions de dollars canadiens

	1983	1984	1985	1986	1987	1988	1989	1990	1991	1992
INCOME STATEMENT / COMPTE DE RESULTATS										
1. Interest income / Produits financiers	36528	38368	38809	37719	35560	40482	49671	54109	51530	44115
2. Interest expenses / Frais financiers	27671	29446	28719	26758	24210	27110	35516	40006	35688	27324
3. Net interest income / Produits financiers nets	8857	8922	10090	10961	11350	13372	14155	14103	15842	16791
4. Non-interest income (net) / Produits non financiers (nets)	2364	2617	3135	3601	4491	5044	5831	6321	6821	7533
5. Gross income / Résultat brut	11221	11539	13225	14562	15841	18416	19986	20424	22663	24324
6. Operating expenses / Frais d'exploitation	6764	7120	7915	8576	9108	10362	11798	12996	14063	15367
7. Net income / Résultat net	4457	4419	5310	5986	6733	8054	8188	7428	8600	8957
8. Provisions (net) / Provisions (nettes)	1710	2003	2340	2996	2771	2520	5108	1692	2704	6035
9. Profit before tax / Bénéfices avant impôt	2747	2416	2970	2990	3962	5534	3080	5736	5896	2922
10. Income tax / Impôt	813	630	861	854	1440	2230	1106	2127	2086	969
11. Profit after tax / Bénéfices après impôt	1934	1786	2109	2136	2522	3304	1974	3609	3810	1953
12. Distributed profit / Bénéfices distribués	..	..	..	..	..	..	..	..	..	..
13. Retained profit / Bénéfices mis en réserve	..	..	..	..	..	..	..	..	..	..
Memoranda / Pour mémoire										
14. Staff costs / Frais de personnel	4123	4323	4761	4942	5186	5980	6785	7433	7970	8502
15. Provisions on loans / Provisions sur prêts	1710	2003	2340	2996	2771	2520	5108	1692	2704	6035
16. Provisions on securities / Provisions sur titres	..	..	..	..	..	..	..	..	..	..
BALANCE SHEET / BILAN										
Assets / Actif										
17. Cash & balance with Central bank / Caisse & solde auprès de la Banque centrale	6260	6080	5928	6419	6913	6834	6446	5653	6113	5897
18. Interbank deposits / Dépôts interbancaires	40668	46865	47183	50221	42233	34129	33346	32947	33609	36007
19. Loans / Prêts	241208	265778	289770	289762	307519	320722	351748	375601	393693	421772
20. Securities / Valeurs mobilières	33011	35151	40212	43867	38711	43971	46347	49147	68855	89920
21. Other assets / Autres actifs	9638	11459	11857	12772	15329	17093	18914	20289	19457	22444
Liabilities / Passif										
22. Capital & reserves / Capital et réserves	13618	16389	18383	20966	20648	22830	24926	27326	31066	31899
23. Borrowing from Central bank / Emprunts auprès de la Banque centrale	25	50	2368	71	376	342	261	38	53	6
24. Interbank deposits / Dépôts interbancaires	79283	85719	89920	80609	73953	56068	54211	60214	60955	81352
25. Non-bank deposits / Dépôts non bancaires	224261	247453	265050	280380	292328	311483	339626	354773	381258	405925
26. Bonds / Obligations	4146	4692	5921	6986	5579	7862	8270	9212	10817	12376
27. Other liabilities / Autres engagements	9452	11030	13308	14029	17821	24164	29507	32074	37578	44482
Balance sheet total / Total du bilan										
28. End-year total / En fin d'exercice	330785	365333	394950	403041	410705	422749	456801	483637	521727	576040
29. Average total / Moyen	333279	348059	380142	398996	406873	416727	439775	470219	502682	548883
Memoranda / Pour mémoire										
30. Short-term securities / Titres à court terme	..	..	..	..	..	..	..	..	..	..
31. Bonds / Obligations	..	..	..	..	..	..	..	..	..	..
32. Shares and participations / Actions et participations	..	..	..	..	..	..	..	..	..	..
33. Claims on non-residents / Créances sur des non résidents	..	..	..	..	..	..	..	..	..	..
34. Liabilities to non-residents / Engagements envers des non résidents	..	..	..	..	..	..	..	..	..	..
SUPPLEMENTARY INFORMATION / RENSEIGNEMENTS COMPLEMENTAIRES										
35. Number of institutions / Nombre d'institutions	NA	NA	NA	NA	11	10	10	10	10	10
36. Number of branches / Nombre de succursales	NA	NA	NA	NA	NA	NA	NA	NA	NA	NA
37. Number of employees (x 1000) / Nombre de salariés (x 1000)	NA	NA	NA	NA	NA	NA	NA	NA	NA	NA

CANADA

Commercial banks (consolidated world-wide)

Per cent

INCOME STATEMENT ANALYSIS

	1983	1984	1985	1986	1987	1988	1989	1990	1991	1992
% of average balance sheet total										
38. Interest income	10.96	11.02	10.21	9.45	8.74	9.71	11.29	11.51	10.25	8.04
39. Interest expenses	8.30	8.46	7.55	6.71	5.95	6.51	8.08	8.51	7.10	4.98
40. Net interest income	2.66	2.56	2.65	2.75	2.79	3.21	3.22	3.00	3.15	3.06
41. Non-interest income (net)	0.71	0.75	0.82	0.90	1.10	1.21	1.33	1.34	1.36	1.37
42. Gross income	3.37	3.32	3.48	3.65	3.89	4.42	4.54	4.34	4.51	4.43
43. Operating expenses	2.03	2.05	2.08	2.15	2.24	2.49	2.68	2.76	2.80	2.80
44. Net income	1.34	1.27	1.40	1.50	1.65	1.93	1.86	1.58	1.71	1.63
45. Provisions (net)	0.51	0.58	0.62	0.75	0.68	0.60	1.16	0.36	0.54	1.10
46. Profit before tax	0.82	0.69	0.78	0.75	0.97	1.33	0.70	1.22	1.17	0.53
47. Income tax	0.24	0.18	0.23	0.21	0.35	0.54	0.25	0.45	0.41	0.18
48. Profit after tax	0.58	0.51	0.55	0.54	0.62	0.79	0.45	0.77	0.76	0.36
49. Distributed profit	..	..	..	..	..	..	..	..	..	..
50. Retained profit	..	..	..	..	..	..	..	..	..	..
51. Staff costs	1.24	1.24	1.25	1.24	1.27	1.43	1.54	1.58	1.59	1.55
52. Provisions on loans	0.51	0.58	0.62	0.75	0.68	0.60	1.16	0.36	0.54	1.10
53. Provisions on securities	..	..	..	..	..	..	..	..	..	..
% of gross income										
54. Net interest income	78.93	77.32	76.29	75.27	71.65	72.61	70.82	69.05	69.90	69.03
55. Non-interest income (net)	21.07	22.68	23.71	24.73	28.35	27.39	29.18	30.95	30.10	30.97
56. Operating expenses	60.28	61.70	59.85	58.89	57.50	56.27	59.03	63.63	62.05	63.18
57. Net income	39.72	38.30	40.15	41.11	42.50	43.73	40.97	36.37	37.95	36.82
58. Provisions (net)	15.24	17.36	17.69	20.57	17.49	13.68	25.56	8.28	11.93	24.81
59. Profit before tax	24.48	20.94	22.46	20.53	25.01	30.05	15.41	28.08	26.02	12.01
60. Income tax	7.25	5.46	6.51	5.86	9.09	12.11	5.53	10.41	9.20	3.98
61. Profit after tax	17.24	15.48	15.95	14.67	15.92	17.94	9.88	17.67	16.81	8.03
62. Staff costs	36.74	37.46	36.00	33.94	32.74	32.47	33.95	36.39	35.17	34.95
% of net income										
63. Provisions (net)	38.37	45.33	44.07	50.05	41.16	31.29	62.38	22.78	31.44	67.38
64. Profit before tax	61.63	54.67	55.93	49.95	58.84	68.71	37.62	77.22	68.56	32.62
65. Income tax	18.24	14.26	16.21	14.27	21.39	27.69	13.51	28.63	24.26	10.82
66. Profit after tax	43.39	40.42	39.72	35.68	37.46	41.02	24.11	48.59	44.30	21.80

CANADA

Banques commerciales (consolidées sur une base mondiale)

Pourcentage

ANALYSE DU COMPTE DE RESULTATS

% du total moyen du bilan
38. Produits financiers
39. Frais financiers
40. Produits financiers nets
41. Produits non financiers (nets)
42. Résultat brut
43. Frais d'exploitation
44. Résultat net
45. Provisions (nettes)
46. Bénéfices avant impôt
47. Impôt
48. Bénéfices après impôt
49. Bénéfices distribués
50. Bénéfices mis en réserve
51. Frais de personnel
52. Provisions sur prêts
53. Provisions sur titres

% du total du résultat brut
54. Produits financiers nets
55. Produits non financiers (nets)
56. Frais d'exploitation
57. Résultat net
58. Provisions (nettes)
59. Bénéfices avant impôt
60. Impôt
61. Bénéfices après impôt
62. Frais de personnel

% du total du résultat net
63. Provisions (nettes)
64. Bénéfices avant impôt
65. Impôt
66. Bénéfices après impôt

CANADA

Commercial banks (consolidated world-wide)

CANADA

Banques commerciales (consolidées sur une base mondiale)

Per cent — *Pourcentage*

BALANCE SHEET ANALYSIS — ANALYSE DU BILAN

% of year-end balance sheet total — % du total du bilan en fin d'exercice

	1983	1984	1985	1986	1987	1988	1989	1990	1991	1992		
Assets												**Actif**
67. Cash & balance with Central bank	1.89	1.66	1.50	1.59	1.68	1.62	1.41	1.17	1.17	1.02	67.	Caisse & solde auprès de la Banque centrale
68. Interbank deposits	12.29	12.83	11.95	12.46	10.28	8.07	7.30	6.81	6.44	6.25	68.	Dépôts interbancaires
69. Loans	72.92	72.75	73.37	71.89	74.88	75.87	77.00	77.66	75.46	73.22	69.	Prêts
70. Securities	9.98	9.62	10.18	10.88	9.43	10.40	10.15	10.16	13.20	15.61	70.	Valeurs mobilières
71. Other assets	2.91	3.14	3.00	3.17	3.73	4.04	4.14	4.20	3.73	3.90	71.	Autres actifs
Liabilities												**Passif**
72. Capital & reserves	4.12	4.49	4.65	5.20	5.03	5.40	5.46	5.65	5.95	5.54	72.	Capital et réserves
73. Borrowing from Central bank	0.01	0.01	0.60	0.02	0.09	0.08	0.06	0.01	0.01	0.00	73.	Emprunts auprès de la Banque centrale
74. Interbank deposits	23.97	23.46	22.77	20.00	18.01	13.26	11.87	12.45	11.68	14.12	74.	Dépôts interbancaires
75. Non-bank deposits	67.80	67.73	67.11	69.57	71.18	73.68	74.35	73.36	73.08	70.47	75.	Dépôts non bancaires
76. Bonds	1.25	1.28	1.50	1.73	1.36	1.86	1.81	1.90	2.07	2.15	76.	Obligations
77. Other liabilities	2.86	3.02	3.37	3.48	4.34	5.72	6.46	6.63	7.20	7.72	77.	Autres engagements
Memoranda												*Pour mémoire*
78. Short-term securities	..	..	..	..	..	..	..	..	..	..	78.	Titres à court terme
79. Bonds	..	..	..	..	..	..	..	..	..	..	79.	Obligations
80. Shares and participations	..	..	..	..	..	..	..	..	..	..	80.	Actions et participations
81. Claims on non-residents	..	..	..	..	..	..	..	..	..	..	81.	Créances sur des non résidents
82. Liabilities to non-residents	..	..	..	..	..	..	..	..	..	..	82.	Engagements envers des non résidents

Notes

* Data relate to Canadian bank groups reporting on a consolidated world-wide basis.
* The reporting period is the fiscal year ending 31st October.

Notes

* Les données se rapportent au groupe de banques canadiennes qui consolident leurs comptes à l'échelle mondiale.
* La période couverte est l'exercice financier qui se termine le 31 octobre.

CANADA

Foreign commercial banks

Million Canadian dollars

CANADA

Banques commerciales étrangères

Millions de dollars canadiens

	1983	1984	1985	1986	1987	1988	1989	1990	1991	1992		
INCOME STATEMENT												**COMPTE DE RESULTATS**
1. Interest income	2050	2421	2416	2366	2845	3391	4003	4945	4669	3792	1.	Produits financiers
2. Interest expenses	1685	2038	1985	1911	2247	2671	3250	4030	3664	2908	2.	Frais financiers
3. Net interest income	365	383	431	455	598	720	753	915	1005	884	3.	Produits financiers nets
4. Non-interest income (net)	80	117	163	223	278	331	378	511	775	787	4.	Produits non financiers (nets)
5. Gross income	445	500	594	678	876	1051	1131	1426	1780	1671	5.	Résultat brut
6. Operating expenses	259	304	346	402	590	657	626	865	1143	1168	6.	Frais d'exploitation
7. Net income	186	196	248	276	286	394	505	561	637	503	7.	Résultat net
8. Provisions (net)	73	40	50	146	216	95	106	288	524	1102	8.	Provisions (nettes)
9. Profit before tax	113	156	198	130	70	299	399	273	113	-599	9.	Bénéfices avant impôt
10. Income tax	58	72	92	60	78	140	164	112	53	-212	10.	Impôt
11. Profit after tax	55	84	106	70	-8	159	235	161	60	-387	11.	Bénéfices après impôt
12. Distributed profit	..	..	..	..	..	..	..	..	..	..	12.	Bénéfices distribués
13. Retained profit	..	..	..	..	..	..	..	..	..	..	13.	Bénéfices mis en réserve
Memoranda												*Pour mémoire*
14. Staff costs	*121*	*145*	*163*	*185*	*289*	*320*	*308*	*376*	*426*	*434*	*14.*	*Frais de personnel*
15. Provisions on loans	*73*	*40*	*50*	*146*	*216*	*95*	*106*	*288*	*524*	*1102*	*15.*	*Provisions sur prêts*
16. Provisions on securities	*..*	*..*	*..*	*..*	*..*	*..*	*..*	*..*	*..*	*..*	*16.*	*Provisions sur titres*
BALANCE SHEET												**BILAN**
Assets												**Actif**
17. Cash & balance with Central bank	8	14	21	117	185	234	267	123	146	103	17.	Caisse & solde auprès de la Banque centrale
18. Interbank deposits	4863	4903	5074	6053	7050	6134	7221	6177	7427	8260	18.	Dépôts interbancaires
19. Loans	13616	15224	17085	24098	25327	28207	31037	33987	34140	36285	19.	Prêts
20. Securities	1329	1363	2168	2850	4442	4920	4664	5932	7071	9221	20.	Valeurs mobilières
21. Other assets	424	610	724	914	1008	1029	1167	1507	1303	1736	21.	Autres actifs
Liabilities												**Passif**
22. Capital & reserves	1448	1643	1857	2586	2816	3107	3416	3973	3952	3697	22.	Capital et réserves
23. Borrowing from Central bank	-	-	-	6	60	-	-	-	-	-	23.	Emprunts auprès de la Banque centrale
24. Interbank deposits	5782	5845	7491	8966	10940	12185	13080	15281	15530	17049	24.	Dépôts interbancaires
25. Non-bank deposits	12371	13917	14713	20730	22219	22752	24545	23863	24857	27680	25.	Dépôts non bancaires
26. Bonds	38	43	44	91	99	192	292	557	873	1147	26.	Obligations
27. Other liabilities	602	666	967	1653	1878	2288	3023	4052	4875	6032	27.	Autres engagements
Balance sheet total												**Total du bilan**
28. End-year total	20240	22114	25072	34032	38012	40524	44356	47726	50087	55605	28.	En fin d'exercice
29. Average total	18900	21177	23593	29552	36022	39268	42440	46041	48906	52846	29.	Moyen
Memoranda												*Pour mémoire*
30. Short-term securities	*..*	*..*	*..*	*..*	*..*	*..*	*..*	*..*	*..*	*..*	*30.*	*Titres à court terme*
31. Bonds	*..*	*..*	*..*	*..*	*..*	*..*	*..*	*..*	*..*	*..*	*31.*	*Obligations*
32. Shares and participations	*..*	*..*	*..*	*..*	*..*	*..*	*..*	*..*	*..*	*..*	*32.*	*Actions et participations*
33. Claims on non-residents	*..*	*..*	*..*	*..*	*..*	*..*	*..*	*..*	*..*	*..*	*33.*	*Créances sur des non résidents*
34. Liabilities to non-residents	*..*	*..*	*..*	*..*	*..*	*..*	*..*	*..*	*..*	*..*	*34.*	*Engagements envers des non résidents*
SUPPLEMENTARY INFORMATION												**RENSEIGNEMENTS COMPLEMENTAIRES**
35. Number of institutions	NA	NA	NA	NA	58	57	57	56	56	56	35.	Nombre d'institutions
36. Number of branches	NA	NA	NA	NA	NA	NA	NA	NA	NA	NA	36.	Nombre de succursales
37. Number of employees (x 1000)	NA	NA	NA	NA	NA	NA	NA	NA	NA	NA	37.	Nombre de salariés (x 1000)

CANADA
Foreign commercial banks

Per cent

INCOME STATEMENT ANALYSIS

	1983	1984	1985	1986	1987	1988	1989	1990	1991	1992
% of average balance sheet total										
38. Interest income	10.85	11.43	10.24	8.01	7.90	8.64	9.43	10.74	9.55	7.18
39. Interest expenses	8.92	9.62	8.41	6.47	6.24	6.80	7.66	8.75	7.49	5.50
40. Net interest income	1.93	1.81	1.83	1.54	1.66	1.83	1.77	1.99	2.05	1.67
41. Non-interest income (net)	0.42	0.55	0.69	0.75	0.77	0.84	0.89	1.11	1.58	1.49
42. Gross income	2.35	2.36	2.52	2.29	2.43	2.68	2.66	3.10	3.64	3.16
43. Operating expenses	1.37	1.44	1.47	1.36	1.64	1.67	1.48	1.88	2.34	2.21
44. Net income	0.98	0.93	1.05	0.93	0.79	1.00	1.19	1.22	1.30	0.95
45. Provisions (net)	0.39	0.19	0.21	0.49	0.60	0.24	0.25	0.63	1.07	2.09
46. Profit before tax	0.60	0.74	0.84	0.44	0.19	0.76	0.94	0.59	0.23	-1.13
47. Income tax	0.31	0.34	0.39	0.20	0.22	0.36	0.39	0.24	0.11	-0.40
48. Profit after tax	0.29	0.40	0.45	0.24	-0.02	0.40	0.55	0.35	0.12	-0.73
49. Distributed profit	:	:	:	:	:	:	:	:	:	:
50. Retained profit	:	:	:	:	:	:	:	:	:	:
51. Staff costs	0.64	0.68	0.69	0.63	0.80	0.81	0.73	0.82	0.87	0.82
52. Provisions on loans	0.39	0.19	0.21	0.49	0.60	0.24	0.25	0.63	1.07	2.09
53. Provisions on securities	:	:	:	:	:	:	:	:	:	:
% of gross income										
54. Net interest income	82.02	76.60	72.56	67.11	68.26	68.51	66.58	64.17	56.46	52.90
55. Non-interest income (net)	17.98	23.40	27.44	32.89	31.74	31.49	33.42	35.83	43.54	47.10
56. Operating expenses	58.20	60.80	58.25	59.29	67.35	62.51	55.35	60.66	64.21	69.90
57. Net income	41.80	39.20	41.75	40.71	32.65	37.49	44.65	39.34	35.79	30.10
58. Provisions (net)	16.40	8.00	8.42	21.53	24.66	9.04	9.37	20.20	29.44	65.95
59. Profit before tax	25.39	31.20	33.33	19.17	7.99	28.45	35.28	19.14	6.35	-35.85
60. Income tax	13.03	14.40	15.49	8.85	8.90	13.32	14.50	7.85	2.98	-12.69
61. Profit after tax	12.36	16.80	17.85	10.32	-0.91	15.13	20.78	11.29	3.37	-23.16
62. Staff costs	27.19	29.00	27.44	27.29	32.99	30.45	27.23	26.37	23.93	25.97
% of net income										
63. Provisions (net)	39.25	20.41	20.16	52.90	75.52	24.11	20.99	51.34	82.26	:
64. Profit before tax	60.75	79.59	79.84	47.10	24.48	75.89	79.01	48.66	17.74	:
65. Income tax	31.18	36.73	37.10	21.74	27.27	35.53	32.48	19.96	8.32	:
66. Profit after tax	29.57	42.86	42.74	25.36	-2.80	40.36	46.53	28.70	9.42	:

CANADA
Banques commerciales étrangères

Pourcentage

ANALYSE DU COMPTE DE RESULTATS

% du total moyen du bilan
38. Produits financiers
39. Frais financiers
40. Produits financiers nets
41. Produits non financiers (nets)
42. Résultat brut
43. Frais d'exploitation
44. Résultat net
45. Provisions (nettes)
46. Bénéfices avant impôt
47. Impôt
48. Bénéfices après impôt
49. Bénéfices distribués
50. Bénéfices mis en réserve
51. Frais de personnel
52. Provisions sur prêts
53. Provisions sur titres

% du total du résultat brut
54. Produits financiers nets
55. Produits non financiers (nets)
56. Frais d'exploitation
57. Résultat net
58. Provisions (nettes)
59. Bénéfices avant impôt
60. Impôt
61. Bénéfices après impôt
62. Frais de personnel

% du total du résultat net
63. Provisions (nettes)
64. Bénéfices avant impôt
65. Impôt
66. Bénéfices après impôt

CANADA

Foreign commercial banks

Per cent

BALANCE SHEET ANALYSIS

% of year-end balance sheet total

	1983	1984	1985	1986	1987	1988	1989	1990	1991	1992
Assets										
67. Cash & balance with Central bank	0.04	0.06	0.08	0.34	0.49	0.58	0.60	0.26	0.29	0.19
68. Interbank deposits	24.03	22.17	20.24	17.79	18.55	15.14	16.28	12.94	14.83	14.85
69. Loans	67.27	68.84	68.14	70.81	66.63	69.61	69.97	71.21	68.16	65.25
70. Securities	6.57	6.16	8.65	8.37	11.69	12.14	10.51	12.43	14.12	16.58
71. Other assets	2.09	2.76	2.89	2.69	2.65	2.54	2.63	3.16	2.60	3.12
Liabilities										
72. Capital & reserves	7.15	7.43	7.41	7.60	7.41	7.67	7.70	8.32	7.89	6.65
73. Borrowing from Central bank	-	-	-	0.02	0.16	-	-	-	-	-
74. Interbank deposits	28.57	26.43	29.88	26.35	28.78	30.07	29.49	32.02	31.01	30.66
75. Non-bank deposits	61.12	62.93	58.68	60.91	58.45	56.14	55.34	50.00	49.63	49.78
76. Bonds	0.19	0.19	0.18	0.27	0.26	0.47	0.66	1.17	1.74	2.06
77. Other liabilities	2.97	3.01	3.86	4.86	4.94	5.65	6.82	8.49	9.73	10.85
Memoranda										
78. Short-term securities	..	..	..	..	..	..	..	..	..	..
79. Bonds	..	..	..	..	..	..	..	..	..	..
80. Shares and participations	..	..	..	..	..	..	..	..	..	..
81. Claims on non-residents	..	..	..	..	..	..	..	..	..	..
82. Liabilities to non-residents	..	..	..	..	..	..	..	..	..	..

Notes

- The reporting period is the fiscal year ending 31st October.

CANADA

Banques commerciales étrangères

Pourcentage

ANALYSE DU BILAN

% du total du bilan en fin d'exercice

Actif
67. Caisse & solde auprès de la Banque centrale
68. Dépôts interbancaires
69. Prêts
70. Valeurs mobilières
71. Autres actifs

Passif
72. Capital et réserves
73. Emprunts auprès de la Banque centrale
74. Dépôts interbancaires
75. Dépôts non bancaires
76. Obligations
77. Autres engagements

Pour mémoire
78. Titres à court terme
79. Obligations
80. Actions et participations
81. Créances sur des non résidents
82. Engagements envers des non résidents

Notes

- La période couverte est l'exercice financier qui se termine le 31 octobre.

37

DENMARK

Commercial banks and savings banks

DANEMARK

Banques commerciales et caisses d'épargne

Million Danish kroner / *Millions de couronnes danoises*

	1983	1984	1985	1986	1987	1988	1989	1990	1991 (1)	1992	
INCOME STATEMENT											**COMPTE DE RESULTATS**
1. Interest income	41563	49736	57628	60547	66452	68776	87280	103599	100453	98915	1. Produits financiers
2. Interest expenses	28177	34551	39156	40002	43458	44703	61504	75254	66050	64453	2. Frais financiers
3. Net interest income	13386	15185	18472	20545	22994	24073	25776	28345	34403	34462	3. Produits financiers nets
4. Non-interest income (net)	24559	2780	25248	-3668	4205	13784	7170	4016	5728	-3984	4. Produits non financiers (nets)
5. Gross income	37945	17965	43720	16877	27199	37857	32946	32361	40131	30478	5. Résultat brut
6. Operating expenses	12424	13586	15106	16686	18686	20135	21383	22200	25112	24800	6. Frais d'exploitation
7. Net income	25521	4379	28614	191	8513	17722	11563	10161	15019	5678	7. Résultat net
8. Provisions (net)	5535	3904	5928	3084	5662	9416	8777	13111	15113	17331	8. Provisions (nettes)
9. Profit before tax	19986	475	22686	-2893	2851	8306	2786	-2950	-94	-11653	9. Bénéfices avant impôt
10. Income tax	7697	414	10657	-251	1067	2572	522	-238	331	189	10. Impôt
11. Profit after tax	12289	61	12029	-2642	1784	5734	2264	-2712	-425	-11842	11. Bénéfices après impôt
12. Distributed profit	882	882	1150	1242	1245	1274	1666	1320	1861	959	12. Bénéfices distribués
13. Retained profit	11407	-821	10879	-3884	539	4460	598	-4032	-2286	-12801	13. Bénéfices mis en réserve
Memoranda											***Pour mémoire***
14. Staff costs	*8142*	*8772*	*9593*	*10446*	*11776*	*12682*	*13340*	*13814*	*15165*	*15141*	14. Frais de personnel
15. Provisions on loans	*4409*	*3065*	*3985*	*2019*	*4303*	*8043*	*7388*	*11408*	*13592*	*15826*	15. Provisions sur prêts
16. Provisions on securities	*..*	*..*	*..*	*..*	*..*	*..*	*..*	*..*	*..*	*..*	16. Provisions sur titres
BALANCE SHEET											**BILAN**
Assets											**Actif**
17. Cash & balance with Central bank	8876	11800	38627	21640	11618	16180	17005	14341	19979	20858	17. Caisse & solde auprès de la Banque centrale
18. Interbank deposits	76050	104302	123235	107838	141350	169575	171700	170112	189185	160419	18. Dépôts interbancaires
19. Loans	173395	208851	269248	341748	390488	410545	456793	495821	508427	479976	19. Prêts
20. Securities	144564	162240	210632	207587	171418	200753	230152	212776	244309	227649	20. Valeurs mobilières
21. Other assets	80141	99446	123818	142785	155521	175828	184476	228538	47885	48069	21. Autres actifs
Liabilities											**Passif**
22. Capital & reserves	47963	49991	66424	70790	74779	87933	92470	88199	67564	55379	22. Capital et réserves
23. Borrowing from Central bank	6129	10327	23177	45170	18178	3513	19844	4880	19339	34573	23. Emprunts auprès de la Banque centrale
24. Interbank deposits	89159	129091	177718	162959	201379	233807	271829	292874	313462	242967	24. Dépôts interbancaires
25. Non-bank deposits	259300	305316	369105	406369	424496	471360	496049	526552	503260	499060	25. Dépôts non bancaires
26. Bonds	-	-	-	-	-	-	-	-	42821	32761	26. Obligations
27. Other liabilities	80475	91914	129136	136310	151563	176268	179934	209083	63339	72231	27. Autres engagements
Balance sheet total											**Total du bilan**
28. End-year total	483026	586639	765560	821598	870395	972881	1060126	1121588	1009785	936971	28. En fin d'exercice
29. Average total	393261	504813	608853	781707	805018	867164	1010504	1084007	1016200	967878	29. Moyen
Memoranda											***Pour mémoire***
30. Short-term securities	*17909*	*15315*	*12394*	*11712*	*21118*	*34208*	*21240*	*23713*	*48935*	*73969*	30. Titres à court terme
31. Bonds	*110257*	*129605*	*173747*	*165718*	*121559*	*132322*	*165343*	*147593*	*159252*	*120665*	31. Obligations
32. Shares and participations	*12574*	*13740*	*19525*	*22633*	*21721*	*27553*	*36782*	*34341*	*36122*	*33015*	32. Actions et participations
33. Claims on non-residents	*81314*	*117785*	*166477*	*167628*	*209273*	*276874*	*324297*	*365812*	*..*	*..*	33. Créances sur des non résidents
34. Liabilities to non-residents	*109534*	*150931*	*208806*	*212624*	*251325*	*329555*	*386679*	*420607*	*..*	*..*	34. Engagements envers des non résidents
SUPPLEMENTARY INFORMATION											**RENSEIGNEMENTS COMPLEMENTAIRES**
35. Number of institutions	224	219	217	216	214	206	199	189	119	113	35. Nombre d'institutions
36. Number of branches	3502	3480	3331	3302	3264	3159	3059	2884	2652	2467	36. Nombre de succursales
37. Number of employees (x 1000)	49	50	52	55	57	56	56	55	56	52	37. Nombre de salariés (x 1000)

DENMARK

Commercial banks and savings banks

Per cent

INCOME STATEMENT ANALYSIS

DANEMARK

Banques commerciales et caisses d'épargne

Pourcentage

ANALYSE DU COMPTE DE RESULTATS

	1983	1984	1985	1986	1987	1988	1989	1990	1991 (1)	1992		
% of average balance sheet total												**% du total moyen du bilan**
38. Interest income	10.57	9.85	9.45	7.75	8.25	7.93	8.64	9.56	9.89	10.22	38.	Produits financiers
39. Interest expenses	7.16	6.84	6.42	5.12	5.40	5.16	6.09	6.94	6.50	6.66	39.	Frais financiers
40. Net interest income	3.40	3.01	3.03	2.63	2.86	2.78	2.55	2.61	3.39	3.56	40.	Produits financiers nets
41. Non-interest income (net)	6.24	0.55	4.14	-0.47	0.52	1.59	0.71	0.37	0.56	-0.41	41.	Produits non financiers (nets)
42. Gross income	9.65	3.56	7.17	2.16	3.38	4.37	3.26	2.99	3.95	3.15	42.	Résultat brut
43. Operating expenses	3.16	2.69	2.48	2.13	2.32	2.32	2.12	2.05	2.47	2.56	43.	Frais d'exploitation
44. Net income	6.49	0.87	4.69	0.02	1.06	2.04	1.14	0.94	1.48	0.59	44.	Résultat net
45. Provisions (net)	1.41	0.77	0.97	0.39	0.70	1.09	0.87	1.21	1.49	1.79	45.	Provisions (nettes)
46. Profit before tax	5.08	0.09	3.72	-0.37	0.35	0.96	0.28	-0.27	-0.01	-1.20	46.	Bénéfices avant impôt
47. Income tax	1.96	0.08	1.75	-0.03	0.13	0.30	0.05	-0.02	0.03	0.02	47.	Impôt
48. Profit after tax	3.12	0.01	1.97	-0.34	0.22	0.66	0.22	-0.25	-0.04	-1.22	48.	Bénéfices après impôt
49. Distributed profit	0.22	0.17	0.19	0.16	0.15	0.15	0.16	0.12	0.18	0.10	49.	Bénéfices distribués
50. Retained profit	2.90	-0.16	1.78	-0.50	0.07	0.51	0.06	-0.37	-0.22	-1.32	50.	Bénéfices mis en réserve
51. Staff costs	2.07	1.74	1.57	1.34	1.46	1.46	1.32	1.27	1.49	1.56	51.	Frais de personnel
52. Provisions on loans	1.12	0.61	0.65	0.26	0.53	0.93	0.73	1.05	1.34	1.64	52.	Provisions sur prêts
53. Provisions on securities	..	..	..	..	..	..	..	..	..	..	53.	Provisions sur titres
% of gross income												**% du total du résultat brut**
54. Net interest income	35.28	84.53	42.25	121.73	84.54	63.59	78.24	87.59	85.73	113.07	54.	Produits financiers nets
55. Non-interest income (net)	64.72	15.47	57.75	-21.73	15.46	36.41	21.76	12.41	14.27	-13.07	55.	Produits non financiers (nets)
56. Operating expenses	32.74	75.62	34.55	98.87	68.70	53.19	64.90	68.60	62.58	81.37	56.	Frais d'exploitation
57. Net income	67.26	24.38	65.45	1.13	31.30	46.81	35.10	31.40	37.42	18.63	57.	Résultat net
58. Provisions (net)	14.59	21.73	13.56	18.27	20.82	24.87	26.64	40.51	37.66	56.86	58.	Provisions (nettes)
59. Profit before tax	52.67	2.64	51.89	-17.14	10.48	21.94	8.46	-9.12	-0.23	-38.23	59.	Bénéfices avant impôt
60. Income tax	20.28	2.30	24.38	-1.49	3.92	6.79	1.58	-0.74	0.82	0.62	60.	Impôt
61. Profit after tax	32.39	0.34	27.51	-15.65	6.56	15.15	6.87	-8.38	-1.06	-38.85	61.	Bénéfices après impôt
62. Staff costs	21.46	48.83	21.94	61.89	43.30	33.50	40.49	42.69	37.79	49.68	62.	Frais de personnel
% of net income												**% du total du résultat net**
63. Provisions (net)	21.69	89.15	20.72	..	66.51	53.13	75.91	129.03	100.63	..	63.	Provisions (nettes)
64. Profit before tax	78.31	10.85	79.28	..	33.49	46.87	24.09	-29.03	-0.63	..	64.	Bénéfices avant impôt
65. Income tax	30.16	9.45	37.24	..	12.53	14.51	4.51	-2.34	2.20	..	65.	Impôt
66. Profit after tax	48.15	1.39	42.04	..	20.96	32.36	19.58	-26.69	-2.83	..	66.	Bénéfices après impôt

DENMARK

Commercial banks and savings banks

Per cent

BALANCE SHEET ANALYSIS

% of year-end balance sheet total

	1983	1984	1985	1986	1987	1988	1989	1990	1991 (1)	1992
Assets										
67. Cash & balance with Central bank	1.84	2.01	5.05	2.63	1.33	1.66	1.60	1.28	1.98	2.23
68. Interbank deposits	15.74	17.78	16.10	13.13	16.24	17.43	16.20	15.17	18.74	17.12
69. Loans	35.90	35.60	35.17	41.60	44.86	42.20	43.09	44.21	50.35	51.23
70. Securities	29.93	27.66	27.51	25.27	19.69	20.63	21.71	18.97	24.19	24.30
71. Other assets	16.59	16.95	16.17	17.38	17.87	18.07	17.40	20.38	4.74	5.13
Liabilities										
72. Capital & reserves	9.93	8.52	8.68	8.62	8.59	9.04	8.72	7.86	6.69	5.91
73. Borrowing from Central bank	1.27	1.76	3.03	5.50	2.09	0.36	1.87	0.44	1.92	3.69
74. Interbank deposits	18.46	22.01	23.21	19.83	23.14	24.03	25.64	26.11	31.04	25.93
75. Non-bank deposits	53.68	52.04	48.21	49.46	48.77	48.45	46.79	46.95	49.84	53.26
76. Bonds	-	-	-	-	-	-	-	-	4.24	3.50
77. Other liabilities	16.66	15.67	16.87	16.59	17.41	18.12	16.97	18.64	6.27	7.71
Memoranda										
78. Short-term securities	*3.71*	*2.61*	*1.62*	*1.43*	*2.43*	*3.52*	*2.00*	*2.11*	*4.85*	*7.89*
79. Bonds	*22.83*	*22.09*	*22.70*	*20.17*	*13.97*	*13.60*	*15.60*	*13.16*	*15.77*	*12.88*
80. Shares and participations	*2.60*	*2.34*	*2.55*	*2.75*	*2.50*	*2.83*	*3.47*	*3.06*	*3.58*	*3.52*
81. Claims on non-residents	*16.83*	*20.08*	*21.75*	*20.40*	*24.04*	*28.46*	*30.59*	*32.62*	*..*	*..*
82. Liabilities to non-residents	*22.68*	*25.73*	*27.27*	*25.88*	*28.87*	*33.87*	*36.47*	*37.52*	*..*	*..*

1. Break in series.

Notes

- "Non-interest income (net)" (item 4) includes value adjustments on foreign currency assets and liabilities and on securities.

- Average balance sheet totals (item 29) are based on twelve end-month data.

DANEMARK

Banques commerciales et caisses d'épargne

Pourcentage

ANALYSE DU BILAN

% du total du bilan en fin d'exercice

Actif
67. Caisse & solde auprès de la Banque centrale
68. Dépôts interbancaires
69. Prêts
70. Valeurs mobilières
71. Autres actifs

Passif
72. Capital et réserves
73. Emprunts auprès de la Banque centrale
74. Dépôts interbancaires
75. Dépôts non bancaires
76. Obligations
77. Autres engagements

Pour mémoire
78. Titres à court terme
79. Obligations
80. Actions et participations
81. Créances sur des non résidents
82. Engagements envers des non résidents

1. Rupture dans les séries.

Notes

- Les "Produits non financiers (net)" (poste 4) contiennent des ajustements en valeurs concernant les actifs/passifs en monnaies étrangères et les valeurs mobilières.

- La moyenne du total des actifs/passifs (poste 29) est basée sur douze données de fin de mois.

FINLAND

All banks

Million markkaa

FINLANDE

Ensemble des banques

Millions de markkaa

	1983	1984	1985	1986	1987	1988	1989	1990	1991	1992	
INCOME STATEMENT											**COMPTE DE RESULTATS**
1. Interest income	17385	22975	26513	26760	32567	43193	60507	74459	77567	72766	1. Produits financiers
2. Interest expenses	12324	17087	19483	19540	23530	32492	48838	60676	65331	63567	2. Frais financiers
3. Net interest income	5061	5888	7030	7220	9037	10701	11669	13783	12236	9199	3. Produits financiers nets
4. Non-interest income (net)	3505	4485	5835	6603	8018	12112	10977	11750	13228	13589	4. Produits non financiers (nets)
5. Gross income	8566	10373	12865	13823	17055	22813	22646	25533	25464	22788	5. Résultat brut
6. Operating expenses	7060	8712	10177	11314	13712	16790	19199	20807	31372	43397	6. Frais d'exploitation
7. Net income	1506	1661	2688	2509	3343	6023	3447	4726	-5908	-20609	7. Résultat net
8. Provisions (net)	914	832	1558	1116	1922	2980	1618	1890	-53	-442	8. Provisions (nettes)
9. Profit before tax	592	829	1130	1393	1421	3043	1829	2836	-5855	-20167	9. Bénéfices avant impôt
10. Income tax	225	260	359	316	332	457	602	961	475	263	10. Impôt
11. Profit after tax	367	569	771	1077	1089	2586	1227	1875	-6330	-20430	11. Bénéfices après impôt
12. Distributed profit	330	515	677	835	896	1052	1177	727	273	58	12. Bénéfices distribués
13. Retained profit	37	54	94	242	193	1534	50	1148	-6603	-20488	13. Bénéfices mis en réserve
Memoranda											*Pour mémoire*
14. Staff costs (1)	*3676*	*4581*	*5130*	*5450*	*6509*	*7357*	*8014*	*8015*	*8438*	*7947*	*14. Frais de personnel (1)*
15. Provisions on loans	*653*	*688*	*1023*	*1106*	*1546*	*2084*	*2231*	*2192*	*-10*	*-259*	*15. Provisions sur prêts*
16. Provisions on securities	*..*	*..*	*..*	*..*	*376*	*675*	*-623*	*-973*	*-43*	*-182*	*16. Provisions sur titres*
BALANCE SHEET											**BILAN**
Assets											**Actif**
17. Cash & balance with Central bank	7307	13700	14257	12367	15567	24465	32085	24491	19090	26007	17. Caisse & solde auprès de la Banque centrale
18. Interbank deposits	8185	10633	13562	19865	17692	22749	24534	24072	22011	25911	18. Dépôts interbancaires
19. Loans	143840	167219	199393	232398	277749	367326	444797	483139	490581	464070	19. Prêts
20. Securities	17580	24414	30104	45230	62843	77809	89223	95149	130734	125917	20. Valeurs mobilières
21. Other assets	40978	52863	54745	72137	78623	91617	91812	107152	107975	118736	21. Autres actifs
Liabilities											**Passif**
22. Capital & reserves	12940	16304	20059	23075	27045	39098	45677	50563	53350	41264	22. Capital et réserves
23. Borrowing from Central bank	7280	7131	7144	11477	2711	4813	3871	3918	5804	8019	23. Emprunts auprès de la Banque centrale
24. Interbank deposits	7668	9437	11527	16293	13656	16480	18075	17363	18828	22158	24. Dépôts interbancaires
25. Non-bank deposits	147922	175352	200859	222640	264361	328332	347022	378838	390247	393512	25. Dépôts non bancaires
26. Bonds	2390	5765	7164	12731	17404	29922	44580	62675	78444	75613	26. Obligations
27. Other liabilities	39690	54840	65308	95781	127297	165321	223226	220646	223718	220075	27. Autres engagements
Balance sheet total											**Total du bilan**
28. End-year total	217890	268829	312061	381997	452474	583966	682451	734003	770391	760641	28. En fin d'exercice
29. Average total	200186	243361	290447	347030	417236	518221	633209	708228	752198	765517	29. Moyen
Memoranda											*Pour mémoire*
30. Short-term securities (2)		*20569*	*25165*	*2688*	*18505*	*28582*	*30029*	*36176*	*50621*	*47230*	*30. Titres à court terme (2)*
31. Bonds	*14796*			*36457*	*36675*	*38546*	*42763*	*42423*	*55802*	*64888*	*31. Obligations*
32. Shares and participations	*2784*	*3845*	*4939*	*6085*	*7663*	*10681*	*16431*	*16550*	*24311*	*13799*	*32. Actions et participations*
33. Claims on non-residents	*27335*	*42947*	*42239*	*69528*	*76255*	*88306*	*94136*	*102036*	*103688*	*116390*	*33. Créances sur des non résidents*
34. Liabilities to non-residents	*41917*	*61653*	*71030*	*98424*	*130202*	*158315*	*176339*	*218019*	*221916*	*212036*	*34. Engagements envers des non résidents*
SUPPLEMENTARY INFORMATION											**RENSEIGNEMENTS COMPLEMENTAIRES**
35. Number of institutions	652	644	635	621	610	589	553	523	438	370	35. Nombre d'institutions
36. Number of branches	2838	2886	2934	2924	2938	2956	2977	2821	2662	2393	36. Nombre de succursales
37. Number of employees (x 1000)	40.4	41.5	42.9	44.4	45.5	47.4	48.6	46.1	42.8	38.9	37. Nombre de salariés (x 1000)

FINLAND

All banks

Per cent

INCOME STATEMENT ANALYSIS

FINLANDE

Ensemble des banques

Pourcentage

ANALYSE DU COMPTE DE RESULTATS

		1983	1984	1985	1986	1987	1988	1989	1990	1991	1992		
	% of average balance sheet total											**% du total moyen du bilan**	
38.	Interest income	8.68	9.44	9.13	7.71	7.81	8.33	9.56	10.51	10.31	9.51	Produits financiers	38.
39.	Interest expenses	6.16	7.02	6.71	5.63	5.64	6.27	7.71	8.57	8.69	8.30	Frais financiers	39.
40.	Net interest income	2.53	2.42	2.42	2.08	2.17	2.06	1.84	1.95	1.63	1.20	Produits financiers nets	40.
41.	Non-interest income (net)	1.75	1.84	2.01	1.90	1.92	2.34	1.73	1.66	1.76	1.78	Produits non financiers (nets)	41.
42.	Gross income	4.28	4.26	4.43	3.98	4.09	4.40	3.58	3.61	3.39	2.98	Résultat brut	42.
43.	Operating expenses	3.53	3.58	3.50	3.26	3.29	3.24	3.03	2.94	4.17	5.67	Frais d'exploitation	43.
44.	Net income	0.75	0.68	0.93	0.72	0.80	1.16	0.54	0.67	-0.79	-2.69	Résultat net	44.
45.	Provisions (net)	0.46	0.34	0.54	0.32	0.46	0.58	0.26	0.27	-0.01	-0.06	Provisions (nettes)	45.
46.	Profit before tax	0.30	0.34	0.39	0.40	0.34	0.59	0.29	0.40	-0.78	-2.63	Bénéfices avant impôt	46.
47.	Income tax	0.11	0.11	0.12	0.09	0.08	0.09	0.10	0.14	0.06	0.03	Impôt	47.
48.	Profit after tax	0.18	0.23	0.27	0.31	0.26	0.50	0.19	0.26	-0.84	-2.67	Bénéfices après impôt	48.
49.	Distributed profit	0.16	0.21	0.23	0.24	0.21	0.20	0.19	0.10	0.04	0.01	Bénéfices distribués	49.
50.	Retained profit	0.02	0.02	0.03	0.07	0.05	0.30	0.01	0.16	-0.88	-2.68	Bénéfices mis en réserve	50.
51.	Staff costs (1)	1.84	1.88	1.77	1.57	1.56	1.42	1.27	1.13	1.12	1.04	Frais de personnel (1)	51.
52.	Provisions on loans	0.33	0.28	0.35	0.32	0.37	0.40	0.35	0.31	0.00	-0.03	Provisions sur prêts	52.
53.	Provisions on securities	..	..	..	..	0.09	0.13	-0.10	-0.14	-0.01	-0.02	Provisions sur titres	53.
	% of gross income											**% du total du résultat brut**	
54.	Net interest income	59.08	56.76	54.64	52.23	52.99	46.91	51.53	53.98	48.05	40.37	Produits financiers nets	54.
55.	Non-interest income (net)	40.92	43.24	45.36	47.77	47.01	53.09	48.47	46.02	51.95	59.63	Produits non financiers (nets)	55.
56.	Operating expenses	82.42	83.99	79.11	81.85	80.40	73.60	84.78	81.49	123.20	190.44	Frais d'exploitation	56.
57.	Net income	17.58	16.01	20.89	18.15	19.60	26.40	15.22	18.51	-23.20	-90.44	Résultat net	57.
58.	Provisions (net)	10.67	8.02	12.11	8.07	11.27	13.06	7.14	7.40	-0.21	-1.94	Provisions (nettes)	58.
59.	Profit before tax	6.91	7.99	8.78	10.08	8.33	13.34	8.08	11.11	-22.99	-88.50	Bénéfices avant impôt	59.
60.	Income tax	2.63	2.51	2.79	2.29	1.95	2.00	2.66	3.76	1.87	1.15	Impôt	60.
61.	Profit after tax	4.28	5.49	5.99	7.79	6.39	11.34	5.42	7.34	-24.86	-89.65	Bénéfices après impôt	61.
62.	Staff costs (1)	42.91	44.16	39.88	39.43	38.16	32.25	35.39	31.39	33.14	34.87	Frais de personnel (1)	62.
	% of net income											**% du total du résultat net**	
63.	Provisions (net)	60.69	50.09	57.96	44.48	57.49	49.48	46.94	39.99	..	..	Provisions (nettes)	63.
64.	Profit before tax	39.31	49.91	42.04	55.52	42.51	50.52	53.06	60.01	..	..	Bénéfices avant impôt	64.
65.	Income tax	14.94	15.65	13.36	12.59	9.93	7.59	17.46	20.33	..	..	Impôt	65.
66.	Profit after tax	24.37	34.26	28.68	42.93	32.58	42.94	35.60	39.67	..	..	Bénéfices après impôt	66.

FINLAND

All banks

Per cent

BALANCE SHEET ANALYSIS

% of year-end balance sheet total

	1983	1984	1985	1986	1987	1988	1989	1990	1991	1992
Assets										
67. Cash & balance with Central bank	3.35	5.10	4.57	3.24	3.44	4.19	4.70	3.34	2.48	3.42
68. Interbank deposits	3.76	3.96	4.35	5.20	3.91	3.90	3.59	3.28	2.86	3.41
69. Loans	66.01	62.20	63.90	60.84	61.38	62.90	65.18	65.82	63.68	61.01
70. Securities	8.07	9.08	9.65	11.84	13.89	13.32	13.07	12.96	16.97	16.55
71. Other assets	18.81	19.66	17.54	18.88	17.38	15.69	13.45	14.60	14.02	15.61
Liabilities										
72. Capital & reserves	5.94	6.06	6.43	6.04	5.98	6.70	6.69	6.89	6.93	5.42
73. Borrowing from Central bank	3.34	2.65	2.29	3.00	0.60	0.82	0.57	0.53	0.75	1.05
74. Interbank deposits	3.52	3.51	3.69	4.27	3.02	2.82	2.65	2.37	2.44	2.91
75. Non-bank deposits	67.89	65.23	64.37	58.28	58.43	56.22	50.85	51.61	50.66	51.73
76. Bonds	1.10	2.14	2.30	3.33	3.85	5.12	6.53	8.54	10.18	9.94
77. Other liabilities	18.22	20.40	20.93	25.07	28.13	28.31	32.71	30.06	29.04	28.93
Memoranda										
78. Short-term securities (2)	..	..	..	0.70	4.09	4.89	4.40	4.93	6.57	6.21
79. Bonds	6.79	7.65	8.06	9.54	8.11	6.60	6.27	5.78	7.24	8.53
80. Shares and participations	1.28	1.43	1.58	1.59	1.69	1.83	2.41	2.25	3.16	1.81
81. Claims on non-residents	12.55	15.98	13.54	18.20	16.85	15.12	13.79	13.90	13.46	15.30
82. Liabilities to non-residents	19.24	22.93	22.76	25.77	28.78	27.11	25.84	29.70	28.81	27.88

1. Change in methodology.
2. Until 1986, included under "Bonds" (item 31 or item 79).

Notes

- All banks include Commercial banks, Post office banks, Foreign commercial banks (since 1983), Savings banks and Co-operative banks.

Change in methodology:

- Historical series for "Staff costs" (item 14 or item 51 or item 62) revised to include, in addition to salaries paid, social expenditure and other staff expenses.

- As from 1984, foreign branches of Finnish commercial banks are also included in the data.

FINLANDE

Ensemble des banques

Pourcentage

ANALYSE DU BILAN

% du total du bilan en fin d'exercice

Actif
67. Caisse & solde auprès de la Banque centrale
68. Dépôts interbancaires
69. Prêts
70. Valeurs mobilières
71. Autres actifs

Passif
72. Capital et réserves
73. Emprunts auprès de la Banque centrale
74. Dépôts interbancaires
75. Dépôts non bancaires
76. Obligations
77. Autres engagements

Pour mémoire
78. Titres à court terme (2)
79. Obligations
80. Actions et participations
81. Créances sur des non résidents
82. Engagements envers des non résidents

1. Changement méthodologique.
2. Jusqu'à 1986, inclus sous "Obligations" (poste 31 ou poste 79).

Notes

- L'Ensemble des banques comprend les Banques commerciales, la Banque postale, les Banques commerciales étrangères (depuis 1983), les Caisses d'épargne et les Banques mutualistes.

Changement méthodologique :

- Les séries historiques, "Frais de personnel" (poste 14 ou poste 51 ou poste 62), ont été révisées afin d'inclure, en plus des salaires, les dépenses sociales et autres dépenses de personnel.

- Depuis 1984, les données comprennent les chiffres relatifs aux succursales étrangères des banques commerciales finlandaises.

FINLAND

Commercial banks

Million markkaa

FINLANDE

Banques commerciales

Millions de markkas

INCOME STATEMENT / COMPTE DE RESULTATS

No.	Item	Rubrique	1983	1984	1985	1986	1987	1988	1989	1990	1991	1992
1.	Interest income	Produits financiers	8801	12156	14335	14165	18048	28941	41113	51091	52508	49389
2.	Interest expenses	Frais financiers	7047	9990	11605	11682	14349	23252	35004	43382	46022	43463
3.	Net interest income	Produits financiers nets	1754	2166	2730	2483	3699	5689	6109	7709	6486	5926
4.	Non-interest income (net)	Produits non financiers (nets)	2018	2661	3719	4053	4589	7703	7679	8060	8645	7221
5.	Gross income	Résultat brut	3772	4827	6449	6536	8288	13392	13788	15769	15131	13147
6.	Operating expenses	Frais d'exploitation	3036	3767	4638	5055	6103	9951	11300	12589	20804	22942
7.	Net income	Résultat net	736	1060	1811	1481	2185	3441	2488	3180	-5673	-9795
8.	Provisions (net)	Provisions (nettes)	290	417	939	401	1131	1407	1024	924	-54	-59
9.	Profit before tax	Bénéfices avant impôt	446	643	872	1080	1054	2034	1464	2256	-5619	-9736
10.	Income tax	Impôt	143	166	250	182	189	326	421	735	272	127
11.	Profit after tax	Bénéfices après impôt	303	477	622	898	865	1708	1043	1521	-5891	-9863
12.	Distributed profit	Bénéfices distribués	298	474	616	761	812	991	1111	665	223	30
13.	Retained profit	Bénéfices mis en réserve	5	3	6	137	53	717	-68	856	-6114	-9893
	Memoranda	*Pour mémoire*										
14.	*Staff costs (1)*	*Frais de personnel (1)*	1596	1895	2250	2318	2772	3997	4500	4501	5013	4559
15.	*Provisions on loans*	*Provisions sur prêts*	278	304	546	487	871	1354	1355	1225	-465	-46
16.	*Provisions on securities*	*Provisions sur titres*	..	..	..	..	258	52	-330	-950	411	-12

BALANCE SHEET / BILAN

No.	Item	Rubrique	1983	1984	1985	1986	1987	1988	1989	1990	1991	1992
	Assets	**Actif**										
17.	Cash & balance with Central bank	Caisse & solde auprès de la Banque centrale	2530	5414	6216	5397	7147	13457	16228	12485	10489	11440
18.	Interbank deposits	Dépôts interbancaires	688	1981	1565	2292	4255	7586	8034	6464	3232	8236
19.	Loans	Prêts	69501	83730	103700	121845	149775	235294	289508	321154	327169	308638
20.	Securities	Valeurs mobilières	12834	18030	22119	33069	37963	64450	72232	77896	111357	109499
21.	Other assets	Autres actifs	30072	38318	40456	53995	56944	74991	74888	85839	80049	84579
	Liabilities	**Passif**										
22.	Capital & reserves	Capital et réserves	7980	10517	13257	15072	17490	28065	32255	36206	39140	27247
23.	Borrowing from Central bank	Emprunts auprès de la Banque centrale	6548	5987	5769	9511	856	3283	2001	2292	4013	5436
24.	Interbank deposits	Dépôts interbancaires	7358	9043	11364	15929	12744	16142	17207	17139	18706	22060
25.	Non-bank deposits	Dépôts non bancaires	68537	83354	98347	111246	137585	204387	212448	241785	245335	250665
26.	Bonds	Obligations	1966	4817	5128	7007	8784	25529	37690	54424	63503	57863
27.	Other liabilities	Autres engagements	23236	33755	40191	57833	78625	118372	159289	151992	161599	159121
	Balance sheet total	**Total du bilan**										
28.	End-year total	En fin d'exercice	115625	147473	174056	216598	256084	395778	460890	503838	532296	522392
29.	Average total	Moyen	105293	131549	160765	195327	236341	353724	428334	482364	518067	527344
	Memoranda	*Pour mémoire*										
30.	*Short-term securities (2)*	*Titres à court terme (2)*	..	..	..	954	7227	24184	25650	31939	43075	39169
31.	*Bonds*	*Obligations*	11198	15431	18677	28261	25810	32844	36928	35860	50301	59575
32.	*Shares and participations*	*Actions et participations*	1636	2599	3442	3854	4926	7422	9654	10097	17981	10755
33.	*Claims on non-residents*	*Créances sur des non résidents*	22893	35168	35588	61473	66516	87112	92621	101667	102735	114403
34.	*Liabilities to non-residents*	*Engagements envers des non résidents*	35649	52098	58491	84898	111453	154544	172104	215469	218400	205809

SUPPLEMENTARY INFORMATION / RENSEIGNEMENTS COMPLEMENTAIRES

No.	Item	Rubrique	1983	1984	1985	1986	1987	1988	1989	1990	1991	1992
35.	Number of institutions	Nombre d'institutions	7	7	7	6	6	7	10	10	12	10
36.	Number of branches	Nombre de succursales	924	942	959	930	937	1004	1010	1037	948	860
37.	Number of employees (x 1000)	Nombre de salariés (x 1000)	16.0	16.6	17.5	18.5	18.8	26.2	26.9	26.5	24.2	22.3

Per cent — *Pourcentage*

INCOME STATEMENT ANALYSIS — ANALYSE DU COMPTE DE RESULTATS

	1983	1984	1985	1986	1987	1988	1989	1990	1991	1992		
% of average balance sheet total												**% du total moyen du bilan**
38. Interest income	8.36	9.24	8.92	7.25	7.64	8.18	9.60	10.59	10.14	9.37	38.	Produits financiers
39. Interest expenses	6.69	7.59	7.22	5.98	6.07	6.57	8.17	8.99	8.88	8.24	39.	Frais financiers
40. Net interest income	1.67	1.65	1.70	1.27	1.57	1.61	1.43	1.60	1.25	1.12	40.	Produits financiers nets
41. Non-interest income (net)	1.92	2.02	2.31	2.07	1.94	2.18	1.79	1.67	1.67	1.37	41.	Produits non financiers (nets)
42. Gross income	3.58	3.67	4.01	3.35	3.51	3.79	3.22	3.27	2.92	2.49	42.	Résultat brut
43. Operating expenses	2.88	2.86	2.88	2.59	2.58	2.81	2.64	2.61	4.02	4.35	43.	Frais d'exploitation
44. Net income	0.70	0.81	1.13	0.76	0.92	0.97	0.58	0.66	-1.10	-1.86	44.	Résultat net
45. Provisions (net)	0.28	0.32	0.58	0.21	0.48	0.40	0.24	0.19	-0.01	-0.01	45.	Provisions (nettes)
46. Profit before tax	0.42	0.49	0.54	0.55	0.45	0.58	0.34	0.47	-1.08	-1.85	46.	Bénéfices avant impôt
47. Income tax	0.14	0.13	0.16	0.09	0.08	0.09	0.10	0.15	0.05	0.02	47.	Impôt
48. Profit after tax	0.29	0.36	0.39	0.46	0.37	0.48	0.24	0.32	-1.14	-1.87	48.	Bénéfices après impôt
49. Distributed profit	0.28	0.36	0.38	0.39	0.34	0.28	0.26	0.14	0.04	0.01	49.	Bénéfices distribués
50. Retained profit	0.00	0.00	0.00	0.07	0.02	0.20	-0.02	0.18	-1.18	-1.88	50.	Bénéfices mis en réserve
51. Staff costs (1)	1.52	1.44	1.40	1.19	1.17	1.13	1.05	0.93	0.97	0.86	51.	Frais de personnel (1)
52. Provisions on loans	0.26	0.23	0.34	0.25	0.37	0.38	0.32	0.25	-0.09	-0.01	52.	Provisions sur prêts
53. Provisions on securities	..	..	..	..	0.11	0.01	-0.08	-0.20	0.08	0.00	53.	Provisions sur titres
% of gross income												**% du total du résultat brut**
54. Net interest income	46.50	44.87	42.33	37.99	44.63	42.48	44.31	48.89	42.87	45.07	54.	Produits financiers nets
55. Non-interest income (net)	53.50	55.13	57.67	62.01	55.37	57.52	55.69	51.11	57.13	54.93	55.	Produits non financiers (nets)
56. Operating expenses	80.49	78.04	71.92	77.34	73.64	74.31	81.96	79.83	137.49	174.50	56.	Frais d'exploitation
57. Net income	19.51	21.96	28.08	22.66	26.36	25.69	18.04	20.17	-37.49	-74.50	57.	Résultat net
58. Provisions (net)	7.69	8.64	14.56	6.14	13.65	10.51	7.43	5.86	-0.36	-0.45	58.	Provisions (nettes)
59. Profit before tax	11.82	13.32	13.52	16.52	12.72	15.19	10.62	14.31	-37.14	-74.05	59.	Bénéfices avant impôt
60. Income tax	3.79	3.44	3.88	2.78	2.28	2.43	3.05	4.66	1.80	0.97	60.	Impôt
61. Profit after tax	8.03	9.88	9.64	13.74	10.44	12.75	7.56	9.65	-38.93	-75.02	61.	Bénéfices après impôt
62. Staff costs (1)	42.31	39.26	34.89	35.47	33.45	29.85	32.64	28.54	33.13	34.68	62.	Frais de personnel (1)
% of net income												**% du total du résultat net**
63. Provisions (net)	39.40	39.34	51.85	27.08	51.76	40.89	41.16	29.06	..	..	63.	Provisions (nettes)
64. Profit before tax	60.60	60.66	48.15	72.92	48.24	59.11	58.84	70.94	..	..	64.	Bénéfices avant impôt
65. Income tax	19.43	15.66	13.80	12.29	8.65	9.47	16.92	23.11	..	..	65.	Impôt
66. Profit after tax	41.17	45.00	34.35	60.63	39.59	49.64	41.92	47.83	..	..	66.	Bénéfices après impôt

45

FINLAND

Commercial banks

FINLANDE

Banques commerciales

Per cent — *Pourcentage*

BALANCE SHEET ANALYSIS — **ANALYSE DU BILAN**

% of year-end balance sheet total — % du total du bilan en fin d'exercice

	1983	1984	1985	1986	1987	1988	1989	1990	1991	1992		
Assets											**Actif**	
67. Cash & balance with Central bank	2.19	3.67	3.57	2.49	2.79	3.40	3.52	2.48	1.97	2.19	67.	Caisse & solde auprès de la Banque centrale
68. Interbank deposits	0.60	1.34	0.90	1.06	1.66	1.92	1.74	1.28	0.61	1.58	68.	Dépôts interbancaires
69. Loans	60.11	56.78	59.58	56.25	58.49	59.45	62.81	63.74	61.46	59.08	69.	Prêts
70. Securities	11.10	12.23	12.71	15.27	14.82	16.28	15.67	15.46	20.92	20.96	70.	Valeurs mobilières
71. Other assets	26.01	25.98	23.24	24.93	22.24	18.95	16.25	17.04	15.04	16.19	71.	Autres actifs
Liabilities											**Passif**	
72. Capital & reserves	6.90	7.13	7.62	6.96	6.83	7.09	7.00	7.19	7.35	5.22	72.	Capital et réserves
73. Borrowing from Central bank	5.66	4.06	3.31	4.39	0.33	0.83	0.43	0.45	0.75	1.04	73.	Emprunts auprès de la Banque centrale
74. Interbank deposits	6.36	6.13	6.53	7.35	4.98	4.08	3.73	3.40	3.51	4.22	74.	Dépôts interbancaires
75. Non-bank deposits	59.28	56.52	56.50	51.36	53.73	51.64	46.10	47.99	46.09	47.98	75.	Dépôts non bancaires
76. Bonds	1.70	3.27	2.95	3.24	3.43	6.45	8.18	10.80	11.93	11.08	76.	Obligations
77. Other liabilities	20.10	22.89	23.09	26.70	30.70	29.91	34.56	30.17	30.36	30.46	77.	Autres engagements
Memoranda											*Pour mémoire*	
78. Short-term securities (2)	*9.68*	*..*	*10.73*	*0.44*	*2.82*	*6.11*	*5.57*	*6.34*	*8.09*	*7.50*	*78.*	*Titres à court terme (2)*
79. Bonds		*10.46*	*..*	*13.05*	*10.08*	*8.30*	*8.01*	*7.12*	*9.45*	*11.40*	*79.*	*Obligations*
80. Shares and participations	*1.41*	*1.76*	*1.98*	*1.78*	*1.92*	*1.88*	*2.09*	*2.00*	*3.38*	*2.06*	*80.*	*Actions et participations*
81. Claims on non-residents	*19.80*	*23.85*	*20.45*	*28.38*	*25.97*	*22.01*	*20.10*	*20.18*	*19.30*	*21.90*	*81.*	*Créances sur des non résidents*
82. Liabilities to non-residents	*30.83*	*35.33*	*33.60*	*39.20*	*43.52*	*39.05*	*37.34*	*42.77*	*41.03*	*39.40*	*82.*	*Engagements envers des non résidents*

1. Change in methodology.
2. Until 1986, included under "Bonds" (item 31 or item 79).

Change in methodology:

- Historical series for "Staff costs" (item 14 or item 51 or item 62) revised to include, in addition to salaries paid, social expenditure and other staff expenses.

- As from 1984, foreign branches of Finnish commercial banks are also included in the data.

- As from 1988, data include the Post office bank (Postipankki) classified thereafter under Commercial banks.

1. Changement méthodologique.
2. Jusqu'à 1986, inclus sous "Obligations" (poste 31 ou poste 79).

Changement méthodologique :

- Les séries historiques, "Frais de personnel" (poste 14 ou poste 51 ou poste 62), ont été révisées afin d'inclure, en plus des salaires, les dépenses sociales et autres dépenses de personnel.

- Depuis 1984, les données comprennent les chiffres relatifs aux succursales étrangères des banques commerciales finlandaises.

- Depuis 1988, la Banque postale (Postipankki) est classée dans les données concernant les Banques commerciales.

FINLAND

Post office bank

Million markkaa

FINLANDE

Banque postale

Millions de markkaa

		1983	1984	1985	1986	1987		
INCOME STATEMENT								**COMPTE DE RESULTATS**
1.	Interest income	2128	2921	3434	3715	4151	1.	Produits financiers
2.	Interest expenses	1216	1830	2256	2468	2942	2.	Frais financiers
3.	Net interest income	912	1091	1178	1247	1209	3.	Produits financiers nets
4.	Non-interest income (net)	407	498	549	630	1030	4.	Produits non financiers (nets)
5.	Gross income	1319	1589	1727	1877	2239	5.	Résultat brut
6.	Operating expenses	965	1420	1493	1554	1993	6.	Frais d'exploitation
7.	Net income	354	169	234	323	246	7.	Résultat net
8.	Provisions (net)	311	110	152	217	129	8.	Provisions (nettes)
9.	Profit before tax	43	59	82	106	117	9.	Bénéfices avant impôt
10.	Income tax	22	29	32	46	47	10.	Impôt
11.	Profit after tax	21	30	50	60	70	11.	Bénéfices après impôt
12.	Distributed profit	10	15	25	30	35	12.	Bénéfices distribués
13.	Retained profit	11	15	25	30	35	13.	Bénéfices mis en réserve
Memoranda								***Pour mémoire***
14.	*Staff costs (1)*	*438*	*797*	*758*	*706*	*977*	*14.*	*Frais de personnel (1)*
15.	*Provisions on loans*	*99*	*110*	*126*	*203*	*183*	*15.*	*Provisions sur prêts*
16.	*Provisions on securities*	*..*	*..*	*..*	*..*	*-42*	*16.*	*Provisions sur titres*
BALANCE SHEET								**BILAN**
Assets								**Actif**
17.	Cash & balance with Central bank	1557	3129	2143	1536	1992	17.	Caisse & solde auprès de la Banque centrale
18.	Interbank deposits	24	60	2072	6308	1321	18.	Dépôts interbancaires
19.	Loans	16983	19143	22319	26606	27829	19.	Prêts
20.	Securities	2117	3262	4168	6705	15077	20.	Valeurs mobilières
21.	Other assets	3414	6147	5274	7774	9366	21.	Autres actifs
Liabilities								**Passif**
22.	Capital & reserves	1367	1526	1716	1980	2154	22.	Capital et réserves
23.	Borrowing from Central bank	82	254	337	755	472	23.	Emprunts auprès de la Banque centrale
24.	Interbank deposits	217	322	148	109	106	24.	Dépôts interbancaires
25.	Non-bank deposits	19019	23263	24434	24935	27030	25.	Dépôts non bancaires
26.	Bonds	270	652	1209	4360	6714	26.	Obligations
27.	Other liabilities	3140	5724	8132	16790	19109	27.	Autres engagements
Balance sheet total								**Total du bilan**
28.	End-year total	24095	31741	35976	48929	55585	28.	En fin d'exercice
29.	Average total	22954	27918	33859	42453	52257	29.	Moyen
Memoranda								***Pour mémoire***
30.	*Short-term securities (2)*	*..*	*..*	*..*	*1504*	*7990*	*30.*	*Titres à court terme (2)*
31.	*Bonds*	*1920*	*3061*	*3865*	*4687*	*6548*	*31.*	*Obligations*
32.	*Shares and participations*	*197*	*201*	*303*	*514*	*539*	*32.*	*Actions et participations*
33.	*Claims on non-residents*	*3001*	*6667*	*5812*	*7295*	*8994*	*33.*	*Créances sur des non résidents*
34.	*Liabilities to non-residents*	*4188*	*7710*	*9281*	*12194*	*15790*	*34.*	*Engagements envers des non résidents*
SUPPLEMENTARY INFORMATION								**RENSEIGNEMENTS COMPLEMENTAIRES**
35.	Number of institutions	1	1	1	1	1	35.	Nombre d'institutions
36.	Number of branches	39	39	47	49	56	36.	Nombre de succursales
37.	Number of employees (x 1000)	5.5	5.7	5.9	6.0	6.1	37.	Nombre de salariés (x 1000)

FINLAND

Post office bank

FINLANDE

Banque postale

Per cent

Pourcentage

INCOME STATEMENT ANALYSIS

ANALYSE DU COMPTE DE RESULTATS

		1983	1984	1985	1986	1987		
% of average balance sheet total								**% du total moyen du bilan**
38.	Interest income	9.27	10.46	10.14	8.75	7.94	38.	Produits financiers
39.	Interest expenses	5.30	6.55	6.66	5.81	5.63	39.	Frais financiers
40.	Net interest income	3.97	3.91	3.48	2.94	2.31	40.	Produits financiers nets
41.	Non-interest income (net)	1.77	1.78	1.62	1.48	1.97	41.	Produits non financiers (nets)
42.	Gross income	5.75	5.69	5.10	4.42	4.28	42.	Résultat brut
43.	Operating expenses	4.20	5.09	4.41	3.66	3.81	43.	Frais d'exploitation
44.	Net income	1.54	0.61	0.69	0.76	0.47	44.	Résultat net
45.	Provisions (net)	1.35	0.39	0.45	0.51	0.25	45.	Provisions (nettes)
46.	Profit before tax	0.19	0.21	0.24	0.25	0.22	46.	Bénéfices avant impôt
47.	Income tax	0.10	0.10	0.09	0.11	0.09	47.	Impôt
48.	Profit after tax	0.09	0.11	0.15	0.14	0.13	48.	Bénéfices après impôt
49.	Distributed profit	0.04	0.05	0.07	0.07	0.07	49.	Bénéfices distribués
50.	Retained profit	0.05	0.05	0.07	0.07	0.07	50.	Bénéfices mis en réserve
51.	Staff costs (1)	1.91	2.85	2.24	1.66	1.87	51.	Frais de personnel (1)
52.	Provisions on loans	0.43	0.39	0.37	0.48	0.35	52.	Provisions sur prêts
53.	Provisions on securities	..	..	..	..	-0.08	53.	Provisions sur titres
% of gross income								**% du total du résultat brut**
54.	Net interest income	69.14	68.66	68.21	66.44	54.00	54.	Produits financiers nets
55.	Non-interest income (net)	30.86	31.34	31.79	33.56	46.00	55.	Produits non financiers (nets)
56.	Operating expenses	73.16	89.36	86.45	82.79	89.01	56.	Frais d'exploitation
57.	Net income	26.84	10.64	13.55	17.21	10.99	57.	Résultat net
58.	Provisions (net)	23.58	6.92	8.80	11.56	5.76	58.	Provisions (nettes)
59.	Profit before tax	3.26	3.71	4.75	5.65	5.23	59.	Bénéfices avant impôt
60.	Income tax	1.67	1.83	1.85	2.45	2.10	60.	Impôt
61.	Profit after tax	1.59	1.89	2.90	3.20	3.13	61.	Bénéfices après impôt
62.	Staff costs (1)	33.21	50.16	43.89	37.61	43.64	62.	Frais de personnel (1)
% of net income								**% du total du résultat net**
63.	Provisions (net)	87.85	65.09	64.96	67.18	52.44	63.	Provisions (nettes)
64.	Profit before tax	12.15	34.91	35.04	32.82	47.56	64.	Bénéfices avant impôt
65.	Income tax	6.21	17.16	13.68	14.24	19.11	65.	Impôt
66.	Profit after tax	5.93	17.75	21.37	18.58	28.46	66.	Bénéfices après impôt

48

FINLAND

Post office bank

Per cent

BALANCE SHEET ANALYSIS

% of year-end balance sheet total

FINLANDE

Banque postale

Pourcentage

ANALYSE DU BILAN

% du total du bilan en fin d'exercice

	1983	1984	1985	1986	1987		
Assets							**Actif**
67. Cash & balance with Central bank	6.46	9.86	5.96	3.14	3.58	67.	Caisse & solde auprès de la Banque centrale
68. Interbank deposits	0.10	0.19	5.76	12.89	2.38	68.	Dépôts interbancaires
69. Loans	70.48	60.31	62.04	54.38	50.07	69.	Prêts
70. Securities	8.79	10.28	11.59	13.70	27.12	70.	Valeurs mobilières
71. Other assets	14.17	19.37	14.66	15.89	16.85	71.	Autres actifs
Liabilities							**Passif**
72. Capital & reserves	5.67	4.81	4.77	4.05	3.88	72.	Capital et réserves
73. Borrowing from Central bank	0.34	0.80	0.94	1.54	0.85	73.	Emprunts auprès de la Banque centrale
74. Interbank deposits	0.90	1.01	0.41	0.22	0.19	74.	Dépôts interbancaires
75. Non-bank deposits	78.93	73.29	67.92	50.96	48.63	75.	Dépôts non bancaires
76. Bonds	1.12	2.05	3.36	8.91	12.08	76.	Obligations
77. Other liabilities	13.03	18.03	22.60	34.32	34.38	77.	Autres engagements
Memoranda							***Pour mémoire***
78. Short-term securities (2)	..	..	..	3.07	14.37	78.	Titres à court terme (2)
79. Bonds	7.97	9.64	10.74	9.58	11.78	79.	Obligations
80. Shares and participations	0.82	0.63	0.84	1.05	0.97	80.	Actions et participations
81. Claims on non-residents	12.45	21.00	16.16	14.91	16.18	81.	Créances sur des non résidents
82. Liabilities to non-residents	17.38	24.29	25.80	24.92	28.41	82.	Engagements envers des non résidents

1. Change in methodology.
2. Until 1986, included under "Bonds" (item 31 or 79).

Change in methodology:

- Historical series for "Staff costs" (item 14 or item 51 or item 62) revised to include, in addition to salaries paid, social expenditure and other staff expenses.
- As from 1988, the Post office bank (Postipankki) is included under Commercial banks.

1. Changement méthodologique.
2. Jusqu'à 1986, inclus sous "Obligations" (poste 31 ou poste 79).

Changement méthodologique :

- Les séries historiques, "Frais de personnel" (poste 14 ou poste 51 ou poste 62) ont été révisées afin d'inclure, en plus des salaires, les dépenses sociales et autres dépenses de personnel.
- Depuis 1988, la Banque postale (Postipankki) est classée dans les données concernant les Banques commerciales.

FINLAND

Foreign commercial banks

Million markkaa

FINLANDE

Banques commerciales étrangères

Millions de markkaa

			1983	1984	1985	1986	1987	1988	1989	1990	1991	1992
INCOME STATEMENT		**COMPTE DE RESULTATS**										
1.	Interest income	Produits financiers	138	262	196	182	488	744	1121	984	1526	1554
2.	Interest expenses	Frais financiers	128	242	175	163	459	715	1086	923	1507	1506
3.	Net interest income	Produits financiers nets	10	20	21	19	29	29	35	61	19	48
4.	Non-interest income (net)	Produits non financiers (nets)	14	26	30	27	37	37	40	38	36	83
5.	Gross income	Résultat brut	24	46	51	46	66	66	75	99	55	131
6.	Operating expenses	Frais d'exploitation	24	30	33	37	63	70	126	95	133	149
7.	Net income	Résultat net	-	16	18	9	3	-4	-51	4	-78	-18
8.	Provisions (net)	Provisions (nettes)	2	8	5	4	11	-3	3	-	5	41
9.	Profit before tax	Bénéfices avant impôt	-2	8	13	5	-8	-1	-54	4	-83	-59
10.	Income tax	Impôt	-	-	4	2	-	3	2	4	1	3
11.	Profit after tax	Bénéfices après impôt	-2	8	4	3	-8	-4	-56	-	-84	-62
12.	Distributed profit	Bénéfices distribués	-	-	-	6	-	-	-	-	-	-
13.	Retained profit	Bénéfices mis en réserve	-2	8	5	-3	-8	-4	-56	-	-84	-62
	Memoranda	*Pour mémoire*										
14.	*Staff costs (1)*	*Frais de personnel (1)*	15	17	18	20	34	39	37	37	47	38
15.	*Provisions on loans*	*Provisions sur prêts*	2	2	3	3	3	1	1	2	5	3
16.	*Provisions on securities*	*Provisions sur titres*	..	..	..	..	8	3	2	-2	..	38
BALANCE SHEET		**BILAN**										
Assets		**Actif**										
17.	Cash & balance with Central bank	Caisse & solde auprès de la Banque centrale	1	375	358	21	126	176	154	36	108	108
18.	Interbank deposits	Dépôts interbancaires	574	465	309	528	171	323	81	297	314	33
19.	Loans	Prêts	628	410	579	887	586	447	1458	792	1771	1899
20.	Securities	Valeurs mobilières	5	21	20	305	3292	3315	2637	2896	4528	4787
21.	Other assets	Autres actifs	1408	1314	768	423	803	950	488	356	463	871
Liabilities		**Passif**										
22.	Capital & reserves	Capital et réserves	53	69	122	122	211	243	240	186	254	120
23.	Borrowing from Central bank	Emprunts auprès de la Banque centrale	-	52	38	21	-	1	-	-	99	1
24.	Interbank deposits	Dépôts interbancaires	92	68	3	183	794	244	608	51	50	-
25.	Non-bank deposits	Dépôts non bancaires	2286	2149	1664	1380	2542	2910	1966	2267	2642	287
26.	Bonds	Obligations	-	-	-	-	-	-	-	-	-	-
27.	Other liabilities	Autres engagements	185	247	207	458	1431	1813	2004	1873	4139	7290
Balance sheet total		**Total du bilan**										
28.	End-year total	En fin d'exercice	2616	2585	2034	2164	4978	5211	4818	4377	7184	7698
29.	Average total	Moyen	1715	2601	2310	2099	3571	5095	5015	4598	5781	7441
	Memoranda	*Pour mémoire*										
30.	*Short-term securities (2)*	*Titres à court terme (2)*	..	..	..	230	3094	3152	2304	2747	4298	4300
31.	*Bonds*	*Obligations*	-	16	15	70	186	150	319	136	216	479
32.	*Shares and participations*	*Actions et participations*	5	5	5	5	12	13	14	13	14	8
33.	*Claims on non-residents*	*Créances sur des non résidents*	1372	1040	757	680	604	745	714	237	918	1940
34.	*Liabilities to non-residents*	*Engagements envers des non résidents*	2080	1845	1629	1332	2828	2860	1917	2229	2517	4875
SUPPLEMENTARY INFORMATION		**RENSEIGNEMENTS COMPLEMENTAIRES**										
35.	Number of institutions	Nombre d'institutions	3	3	3	3	4	4	4	4	5	4
36.	Number of branches	Nombre de succursales	-	-	-	-	-	-	-	-	-	-
37.	Number of employees	Nombre de salariés	84	93	103	98	169	156	154	137	144	99

FINLAND
Foreign commercial banks

FINLANDE
Banques commerciales étrangères

Per cent	1983	1984	1985	1986	1987	1988	1989	1990	1991	1992		*Pourcentage*
INCOME STATEMENT ANALYSIS												**ANALYSE DU COMPTE DE RESULTATS**
% of average balance sheet total												**% du total moyen du bilan**
38. Interest income	8.05	10.07	8.48	8.67	13.67	14.60	22.35	21.40	26.40	20.88	38.	Produits financiers
39. Interest expenses	7.46	9.30	7.58	7.77	12.85	14.03	21.66	20.07	26.07	20.24	39.	Frais financiers
40. Net interest income	0.58	0.77	0.91	0.91	0.81	0.57	0.70	1.33	0.33	0.65	40.	Produits financiers nets
41. Non-interest income (net)	0.82	1.00	1.30	1.29	1.04	0.73	0.80	0.83	0.62	1.12	41.	Produits non financiers (nets)
42. Gross income	1.40	1.77	2.21	2.19	1.85	1.30	1.50	2.15	0.95	1.76	42.	Résultat brut
43. Operating expenses	1.40	1.15	1.43	1.76	1.76	1.37	2.51	2.07	2.30	2.00	43.	Frais d'exploitation
44. Net income	-	0.62	0.78	0.43	0.08	-0.08	-1.02	0.09	-1.35	-0.24	44.	Résultat net
45. Provisions (net)	0.12	0.31	0.22	0.19	0.31	-0.06	0.06	-	0.09	0.55	45.	Provisions (nettes)
46. Profit before tax	-0.12	0.31	0.56	0.24	-0.22	-0.02	-1.08	0.09	-1.44	-0.79	46.	Bénéfices avant impôt
47. Income tax	-	-	0.17	0.10	-	0.06	0.04	0.09	0.02	0.04	47.	Impôt
48. Profit after tax	-0.12	0.31	0.39	0.14	-0.22	-0.08	-1.12	-	-1.45	-0.83	48.	Bénéfices après impôt
49. Distributed profit	-	-	0.17	0.29	-	-	-	-	-	-	49.	Bénéfices distribués
50. Retained profit	-0.12	0.31	0.22	-0.14	-0.22	-0.08	-1.12	-	-1.45	-0.83	50.	Bénéfices mis en réserve
51. Staff costs (1)	0.87	0.65	0.78	0.95	0.95	0.77	0.74	0.80	0.81	0.51	51.	Frais de personnel (1)
52. Provisions on loans	0.12	0.08	0.13	0.14	0.08	0.02	0.02	0.04	0.09	0.04	52.	Provisions sur prêts
53. Provisions on securities	..	..	..	..	0.22	0.06	0.04	-0.04	..	0.51	53.	Provisions sur titres
% of gross income												**% du total du résultat brut**
54. Net interest income	41.67	43.48	41.18	41.30	43.94	43.94	46.67	61.62	34.55	36.64	54.	Produits financiers nets
55. Non-interest income (net)	58.33	56.52	58.82	58.70	56.06	56.06	53.33	38.38	65.45	63.36	55.	Produits non financiers (nets)
56. Operating expenses	100.00	65.22	64.71	80.43	95.45	106.06	168.00	95.96	241.82	113.74	56.	Frais d'exploitation
57. Net income	-	34.78	35.29	19.57	4.55	-6.06	-68.00	4.04	-141.82	-13.74	57.	Résultat net
58. Provisions (net)	8.33	17.39	9.80	8.70	16.67	-4.55	4.00	-	9.09	31.30	58.	Provisions (nettes)
59. Profit before tax	-8.33	17.39	25.49	10.87	-12.12	-1.52	-72.00	4.04	-150.91	-45.04	59.	Bénéfices avant impôt
60. Income tax	-	-	7.84	4.35	-	4.55	2.67	4.04	1.82	2.29	60.	Impôt
61. Profit after tax	-8.33	17.39	17.65	6.52	-12.12	-6.06	-74.67	-	-152.73	-47.33	61.	Bénéfices après impôt
62. Staff costs (1)	62.50	36.96	35.29	43.48	51.52	59.09	49.33	37.37	85.45	29.01	62.	Frais de personnel (1)
% of net income												**% du total du résultat net**
63. Provisions (net)	..	50.00	27.78	44.44	..	..	..	..	..	..	63.	Provisions (nettes)
64. Profit before tax	..	50.00	72.22	55.56	..	..	..	..	..	..	64.	Bénéfices avant impôt
65. Income tax	..	-	22.22	22.22	..	..	..	..	..	..	65.	Impôt
66. Profit after tax	..	50.00	50.00	33.33	..	..	..	..	..	..	66.	Bénéfices après impôt

FINLAND

Foreign commercial banks

Per cent

BALANCE SHEET ANALYSIS

% of year-end balance sheet total

	1983	1984	1985	1986	1987	1988	1989	1990	1991	1992
Assets										
67. Cash & balance with Central bank	0.04	14.51	17.60	0.97	2.53	3.38	3.20	0.82	1.50	1.40
68. Interbank deposits	21.94	17.99	15.19	24.40	3.44	6.20	1.68	6.79	4.37	0.43
69. Loans	24.01	15.86	28.47	40.99	11.77	8.58	30.26	18.09	24.65	24.67
70. Securities	0.19	0.81	0.98	14.09	66.13	63.62	54.73	66.16	63.03	62.18
71. Other assets	53.82	50.83	37.76	19.55	16.13	18.23	10.13	8.13	6.44	11.31
Liabilities										
72. Capital & reserves	2.03	2.67	6.00	5.64	4.24	4.66	4.98	4.25	3.54	1.56
73. Borrowing from Central bank	-	2.01	1.87	0.97	-	0.02	-	-	1.38	0.01
74. Interbank deposits	3.52	2.63	0.15	8.46	15.95	4.68	12.62	1.17	0.70	-
75. Non-bank deposits	87.39	83.13	81.81	63.77	51.06	55.84	40.81	51.79	36.78	3.73
76. Bonds	-	-	-	-	-	-	-	-	-	-
77. Other liabilities	7.07	9.56	10.18	21.16	28.75	34.79	41.59	42.79	57.61	94.70
Memoranda										
78. Short-term securities (2)	..	..	..	*10.63*	*62.15*	*60.49*	*47.82*	*62.76*	*59.83*	*55.86*
79. Bonds	-	*0.62*	*0.74*	*3.23*	*3.74*	*2.88*	*6.62*	*3.11*	*3.01*	*6.22*
80. Shares and participations	*0.19*	*0.19*	*0.25*	*0.23*	*0.24*	*0.25*	*0.29*	*0.30*	*0.19*	*0.10*
81. Claims on non-residents	*52.45*	*40.23*	*37.22*	*31.42*	*12.13*	*14.30*	*14.82*	*5.41*	*12.78*	*25.20*
82. Liabilities to non-residents	*79.51*	*71.37*	*80.09*	*61.55*	*56.81*	*54.88*	*39.79*	*50.93*	*35.04*	*63.33*

1. Change in methodology.
2. Until 1986, included under "Bonds" (item 31 or item 79).

Change in methodology:

- Historical series for "Staff costs" (item 14 or item 51 or item 62) revised to include, in addition to salaries paid, social expenditure and other staff expenses.

FINLANDE

Banques commerciales étrangères

Pourcentage

ANALYSE DU BILAN

% du total du bilan en fin d'exercice

Actif
67. Caisse & solde auprès de la Banque centrale
68. Dépôts interbancaires
69. Prêts
70. Valeurs mobilières
71. Autres actifs

Passif
72. Capital et réserves
73. Emprunts auprès de la Banque centrale
74. Dépôts interbancaires
75. Dépôts non bancaires
76. Obligations
77. Autres engagements

Pour mémoire
78. Titres à court terme (2)
79. Obligations
80. Actions et participations
81. Créances sur des non résidents
82. Engagements envers des non résidents

1. Changement méthodologique.
2. Jusqu'à 1986, inclus sous "Obligations" (poste 31 ou poste 79).

Changement méthodologique :

- Les séries historiques, "Frais de personnel" (poste 14 ou poste 51 ou poste 62), ont été révisées afin d'inclure, en plus des salaires, les dépenses sociales et autres dépenses de personnel.

FINLAND
Savings banks

Million markkaa

FINLANDE
Caisses d'épargne

Millions de markkas

		1983	1984	1985	1986	1987	1988	1989	1990	1991	1992
INCOME STATEMENT	**COMPTE DE RESULTATS**										
1. Interest income	1. Produits financiers	3381	4036	4498	4575	5171	7171	9967	12042	12413	10426
2. Interest expenses	2. Frais financiers	2145	2703	2886	2739	3022	4572	7041	9119	9888	10008
3. Net interest income	3. Produits financiers nets	1236	1333	1612	1836	2149	2599	2926	2923	2525	418
4. Non-interest income (net)	4. Produits non financiers (nets)	638	772	902	1098	1412	3051	1865	2128	2401	3188
5. Gross income	5. Résultat brut	1874	2105	2514	2934	3561	5650	4791	5051	4926	3606
6. Operating expenses	6. Frais d'exploitation	1685	1933	2220	2579	3087	3777	4337	4298	5760	14489
7. Net income	7. Résultat net	189	172	294	355	474	1873	454	753	-834	-10883
8. Provisions (net)	8. Provisions (nettes)	142	121	211	248	332	1028	234	508	-319	-370
9. Profit before tax	9. Bénéfices avant impôt	47	51	83	107	142	845	220	245	-515	-10513
10. Income tax	10. Impôt	29	33	38	47	51	68	100	97	50	16
11. Profit after tax	11. Bénéfices après impôt	18	18	45	60	91	777	120	148	-565	-10529
12. Distributed profit	12. Bénéfices distribués	-	-	-	-	-	-	-	-	-	-
13. Retained profit	13. Bénéfices mis en réserve	18	18	45	60	91	777	120	148	-565	-10529
Memoranda	*Pour mémoire*										
14. Staff costs (1)	*14. Frais de personnel (1)*	*895*	*1051*	*1177*	*1336*	*1556*	*1873*	*1830*	*1830*	*1714*	*1644*
15. Provisions on loans	*15. Provisions sur prêts*	*135*	*120*	*172*	*210*	*253*	*399*	*494*	*523*	*94*	*-262*
16. Provisions on securities	*16. Provisions sur titres*	*..*	*..*	*..*	*..*	*77*	*425*	*-263*	*-23*	*-413*	*-108*
BALANCE SHEET	**BILAN**										
Assets	**Actif**										
17. Cash & balance with Central bank	17. Caisse & solde auprès de la Banque centrale	1783	2583	3025	2930	3486	5960	9169	6279	4459	9577
18. Interbank deposits	18. Dépôts interbancaires	3684	4449	5160	5519	6020	8182	8564	9134	9109	7771
19. Loans	19. Prêts	29367	32743	37006	42263	51152	69181	83957	85554	82047	73871
20. Securities	20. Valeurs mobilières	1503	1815	2083	2579	3650	5603	9777	8780	8228	4910
21. Other assets	21. Autres actifs	3772	4474	5124	6184	7077	10031	9786	12072	16181	17890
Liabilities	**Passif**										
22. Capital & reserves	22. Capital et réserves	1817	2167	2546	2980	3706	6317	8144	7891	7227	6178
23. Borrowing from Central bank	23. Emprunts auprès de la Banque centrale	376	503	599	736	855	1028	1178	1107	1150	2108
24. Interbank deposits	24. Dépôts interbancaires	1	4	2	2	2	84	250	173	72	96
25. Non-bank deposits	25. Dépôts non bancaires	31757	36266	41562	45933	52440	65717	71340	68107	70422	66714
26. Bonds	26. Obligations	73	155	612	709	835	1891	3238	2229	5516	7912
27. Other liabilities	27. Autres engagements	6085	6969	7077	9115	13547	23920	37103	42312	35637	31011
Balance sheet total	**Total du bilan**										
28. End-year total	28. En fin d'exercice	40109	46064	52398	59475	71385	98957	121253	121819	120024	114019
29. Average total	29. Moyen	37357	43087	49231	55937	65430	85171	110105	121536	120922	117022
Memoranda	*Pour mémoire*										
30. Short-term securities (2)	*30. Titres à court terme (2)*	*968*	*1203*	*1394*	*1725*	*169*	*953*	*1946*	*1329*	*1810*	*2236*
31. Bonds	*31. Obligations*	*535*	*612*	*689*	*854*	*2210*	*2861*	*2611*	*2420*	*1742*	*1291*
32. Shares and participations	*32. Actions et participations*	*-*	*-*	*2*	*6*	*1271*	*1789*	*5220*	*5031*	*4676*	*1383*
33. Claims on non-residents	*33. Créances sur des non résidents*	*-*	*-*	*2*	*-*	*92*	*394*	*742*	*54*	*28*	*39*
34. Liabilities to non-residents	*34. Engagements envers des non résidents*	*-*	*-*	*1629*	*-*	*129*	*911*	*2318*	*321*	*4*	*1334*
SUPPLEMENTARY INFORMATION	**RENSEIGNEMENTS COMPLEMENTAIRES**										
35. Number of institutions	35. Nombre d'institutions	270	263	254	241	230	211	178	150	86	39
36. Number of branches	36. Nombre de succursales	1035	1056	1076	1091	1093	1102	1130	984	967	845
37. Number of employees (x 1000)	37. Nombre de salariés (x 1000)	10.5	10.7	10.7	10.9	11.2	11.7	11.9	10.1	9.5	7.8

FINLAND

Savings banks

Per cent

INCOME STATEMENT ANALYSIS

FINLANDE

Caisses d'épargne

Pourcentage

ANALYSE DU COMPTE DE RESULTATS

		1983	1984	1985	1986	1987	1988	1989	1990	1991	1992		
% of average balance sheet total												**% du total moyen du bilan**	
38.	Interest income	9.05	9.37	9.14	8.18	7.90	8.42	9.05	9.91	10.27	8.91	Produits financiers	38.
39.	Interest expenses	5.74	6.27	5.86	4.90	4.62	5.37	6.39	7.50	8.18	8.55	Frais financiers	39.
40.	Net interest income	3.31	3.09	3.27	3.28	3.28	3.05	2.66	2.41	2.09	0.36	Produits financiers nets	40.
41.	Non-interest income (net)	1.71	1.79	1.83	1.96	2.16	3.58	1.69	1.75	1.99	2.72	Produits non financiers (nets)	41.
42.	Gross income	5.02	4.89	5.11	5.25	5.44	6.63	4.35	4.16	4.07	3.08	Résultat brut	42.
43.	Operating expenses	4.51	4.49	4.51	4.61	4.72	4.43	3.94	3.54	4.76	12.38	Frais d'exploitation	43.
44.	Net income	0.51	0.40	0.60	0.63	0.72	2.20	0.41	0.62	-0.69	-9.30	Résultat net	44.
45.	Provisions (net)	0.38	0.28	0.43	0.44	0.51	1.21	0.21	0.42	-0.26	-0.32	Provisions (nettes)	45.
46.	Profit before tax	0.13	0.12	0.17	0.19	0.22	0.99	0.20	0.20	-0.43	-8.98	Bénéfices avant impôt	46.
47.	Income tax	0.08	0.08	0.08	0.08	0.08	0.08	0.09	0.08	0.04	0.01	Impôt	47.
48.	Profit after tax	0.05	0.04	0.09	0.11	0.14	0.91	0.11	0.12	-0.47	-9.00	Bénéfices après impôt	48.
49.	Distributed profit	-	-	-	-	-	-	-	-	-	-	Bénéfices distribués	49.
50.	Retained profit	0.05	0.04	0.09	0.11	0.14	0.91	0.11	0.12	-0.47	-9.00	Bénéfices mis en réserve	50.
51.	Staff costs (1)	2.40	2.44	2.39	2.39	2.38	2.20	1.66	1.51	1.42	1.40	Frais de personnel (1)	51.
52.	Provisions on loans	0.36	0.28	0.35	0.38	0.39	0.47	0.45	0.43	0.08	-0.22	Provisions sur prêts	52.
53.	Provisions on securities	..	..	..	..	0.12	0.50	-0.24	-0.02	-0.34	-0.09	Provisions sur titres	53.
% of gross income												**% du total du résultat brut**	
54.	Net interest income	65.96	63.33	64.12	62.58	60.35	46.00	61.07	57.87	51.26	..	Produits financiers nets	54.
55.	Non-interest income (net)	34.04	36.67	35.88	37.42	39.65	54.00	38.93	42.13	48.74	..	Produits non financiers (nets)	55.
56.	Operating expenses	89.91	91.83	88.31	87.90	86.69	66.85	90.52	85.09	116.93	..	Frais d'exploitation	56.
57.	Net income	10.09	8.17	11.69	12.10	13.31	33.15	9.48	14.91	-16.93	..	Résultat net	57.
58.	Provisions (net)	7.58	5.75	8.39	8.45	9.32	18.19	4.88	10.06	-6.48	..	Provisions (nettes)	58.
59.	Profit before tax	2.51	2.42	3.30	3.65	3.99	14.96	4.59	4.85	-10.45	..	Bénéfices avant impôt	59.
60.	Income tax	1.55	1.57	1.51	1.60	1.43	1.20	2.09	1.92	1.02	..	Impôt	60.
61.	Profit after tax	0.96	0.86	1.79	2.04	2.56	13.75	2.50	2.93	-11.47	..	Bénéfices après impôt	61.
62.	Staff costs (1)	47.76	49.93	46.82	45.54	43.70	33.15	38.20	36.23	34.79	..	Frais de personnel (1)	62.
% of net income												**% du total du résultat net**	
63.	Provisions (net)	75.13	70.35	71.77	69.86	70.04	54.89	51.54	67.46	..	..	Provisions (nettes)	63.
64.	Profit before tax	24.87	29.65	28.23	30.14	29.96	45.11	48.46	32.54	..	..	Bénéfices avant impôt	64.
65.	Income tax	15.34	19.19	12.93	13.24	10.76	3.63	22.03	12.88	..	..	Impôt	65.
66.	Profit after tax	9.52	10.47	15.31	16.90	19.20	41.48	26.43	19.65	..	..	Bénéfices après impôt	66.

FINLAND

Savings banks

Per cent

BALANCE SHEET ANALYSIS

% of year-end balance sheet total

	1983	1984	1985	1986	1987	1988	1989	1990	1991	1992
Assets										
67. Cash & balance with Central bank	4.45	5.61	5.77	4.93	4.88	6.02	7.56	5.15	3.72	8.40
68. Interbank deposits	9.18	9.66	9.85	9.28	8.43	8.27	7.06	7.50	7.59	6.82
69. Loans	73.22	71.08	70.62	71.06	71.66	69.91	69.24	70.23	68.36	64.79
70. Securities	3.75	3.94	3.98	4.34	5.11	5.66	8.06	7.21	6.86	4.31
71. Other assets	9.40	9.71	9.78	10.40	9.91	10.14	8.07	9.91	13.48	15.69
Liabilities										
72. Capital & reserves	4.53	4.70	4.86	5.01	5.19	6.38	6.72	6.48	6.02	5.42
73. Borrowing from Central bank	0.94	1.09	1.14	1.24	1.20	1.04	0.97	0.91	0.96	1.85
74. Interbank deposits	0.00	0.01	0.00	0.00	0.00	0.08	0.21	0.14	0.06	0.08
75. Non-bank deposits	79.18	78.73	79.32	77.23	73.46	66.41	58.84	55.91	58.67	58.51
76. Bonds	0.18	0.34	1.17	1.19	1.17	1.91	2.67	1.83	4.60	6.94
77. Other liabilities	15.17	15.13	13.51	15.33	18.98	24.17	30.60	34.73	29.69	27.20
Memoranda										
78. Short-term securities (2)	*..*	*..*	*..*	*..*	*0.24*	*0.96*	*1.60*	*1.09*	*1.51*	*1.96*
79. Bonds	*2.41*	*2.61*	*2.66*	*2.90*	*3.10*	*2.89*	*2.15*	*1.99*	*1.45*	*1.13*
80. Shares and participations	*1.33*	*1.33*	*1.31*	*1.44*	*1.78*	*1.81*	*4.31*	*4.13*	*3.90*	*1.21*
81. Claims on non-residents	*-*	*-*	*0.00*	*0.01*	*0.13*	*0.40*	*0.61*	*0.04*	*0.02*	*0.03*
82. Liabilities to non-residents	*-*	*-*	*3.11*	*-*	*0.18*	*0.92*	*1.91*	*0.26*	*0.00*	*1.17*

1. Change in methodology.
2. Until 1987, included under "Bonds" (item 31 or item 79).

Change in methodology:

• Historical series for "Staff costs" (item 14 or item 51 or item 62) revised to include, in addition to salaries paid, social expenditure and other staff expenses.

FINLANDE

Caisses d'épargne

Pourcentage

ANALYSE DU BILAN

% du total du bilan en fin d'exercice

Actif
67. Caisse & solde auprès de la Banque centrale
68. Dépôts interbancaires
69. Prêts
70. Valeurs mobilières
71. Autres actifs

Passif
72. Capital et réserves
73. Emprunts auprès de la Banque centrale
74. Dépôts interbancaires
75. Dépôts non bancaires
76. Obligations
77. Autres engagements

Pour mémoire
78. Titres à court terme (2)
79. Obligations
80. Actions et participations
81. Créances sur des non résidents
82. Engagements envers des non résidents

1. Changement méthodologique.
2. Jusqu'à 1987, inclus sous "Obligations" (poste 31 ou poste 79).

Changement méthodologique :

• Les séries historiques, "Frais de personnel" (poste 14 ou poste 51 ou poste 62), ont été révisées afin d'inclure, en plus des salaires, les dépenses sociales et autres dépenses de personnel.

FINLAND
Co-operative banks

Million markkaa

INCOME STATEMENT	1983	1984	1985	1986	1987	1988	1989	1990	1991	1992
1. Interest income	2937	3600	4050	4123	4709	6337	8306	10342	11120	11397
2. Interest expenses	1788	2322	2561	2488	2758	3953	5707	7252	7914	8590
3. Net interest income	1149	1278	1489	1635	1951	2384	2599	3090	3206	2807
4. Non-interest income (net)	428	528	635	795	950	1321	1393	1524	2146	3097
5. Gross income	1577	1806	2124	2430	2901	3705	3992	4614	5352	5904
6. Operating expenses	1350	1562	1793	2089	2466	2992	3436	3825	4675	5817
7. Net income	227	244	331	341	435	713	556	789	677	87
8. Provisions (net)	169	176	251	246	319	548	357	458	315	-54
9. Profit before tax	58	68	80	95	116	165	199	331	362	141
10. Income tax	31	32	35	39	45	60	79	125	152	117
11. Profit after tax	27	36	45	56	71	105	120	206	210	24
12. Distributed profit	22	26	32	38	49	61	66	62	50	28
13. Retained profit	5	10	13	18	22	44	54	144	160	-4
Memoranda										
14. Staff costs (1)	*732*	*821*	*927*	*1070*	*1170*	*1448*	*1647*	*1647*	*1664*	*1706*
15. Provisions on loans	*139*	*152*	*176*	*203*	*236*	*330*	*381*	*442*	*356*	*46*
16. Provisions on securities	*..*	*..*	*..*	*..*	*75*	*195*	*-32*	*2*	*-41*	*-100*
BALANCE SHEET										
Assets										
17. Cash & balance with Central bank	1436	2199	2515	2483	2816	4872	6534	5691	4034	4882
18. Interbank deposits	3215	3678	4456	5218	5925	6658	7855	8177	9356	9871
19. Loans	27361	31193	35789	40797	48407	62404	69874	75639	79594	79662
20. Securities	1121	1286	1714	2572	2861	4441	4577	5577	6621	6721
21. Other assets	2312	2610	3123	3761	4433	5645	6650	8885	11282	15396
Liabilities										
22. Capital & reserves	1723	2025	2418	2921	3484	4473	5038	6280	6729	7719
23. Borrowing from Central bank	274	335	401	454	528	501	692	519	542	474
24. Interbank deposits	-	-	10	70	10	10	10	-	-	2
25. Non-bank deposits	26323	30320	34852	39146	44784	55318	61268	66679	71848	75846
26. Bonds	81	141	215	655	1071	2502	3652	6022	9425	9838
27. Other liabilities	7044	8145	9701	11585	14585	21216	24830	24469	22343	22653
Balance sheet total										
28. End-year total	35445	40966	47597	54831	64442	84020	95490	103969	110887	116532
29. Average total	32867	38206	44282	51214	59637	74231	89755	99730	107428	113710
Memoranda										
30. Short-term securities (2)	*..*	*..*	*..*	*..*	*25*	*293*	*129*	*161*	*1438*	*1525*
31. Bonds	*710*	*858*	*1214*	*1714*	*1921*	*2691*	*2905*	*4007*	*3543*	*3543*
32. Shares and participations	*411*	*428*	*500*	*858*	*915*	*1457*	*1543*	*1409*	*1640*	*1653*
33. Claims on non-residents	*69*	*72*	*80*	*74*	*49*	*55*	*59*	*78*	*7*	*8*
34. Liabilities to non-residents	*-*	*-*	*-*	*-*	*2*	*-*	*-*	*-*	*995*	*18*
SUPPLEMENTARY INFORMATION										
35. Number of institutions	371	370	370	370	369	367	361	359	335	317
36. Number of branches	840	849	852	854	852	850	837	800	747	688
37. Number of employees (x 1000)	8.3	8.5	8.7	9.0	9.2	9.4	9.6	9.3	9.0	8.7

FINLANDE
Banques mutualistes

Millions de markkas

COMPTE DE RESULTATS
1. Produits financiers
2. Frais financiers
3. Produits financiers nets
4. Produits non financiers (nets)
5. Résultat brut
6. Frais d'exploitation
7. Résultat net
8. Provisions (nettes)
9. Bénéfices avant impôt
10. Impôt
11. Bénéfices après impôt
12. Bénéfices distribués
13. Bénéfices mis en réserve

Pour mémoire
14. Frais de personnel (1)
15. Provisions sur prêts
16. Provisions sur titres

BILAN

Actif
17. Caisse & solde auprès de la Banque centrale
18. Dépôts interbancaires
19. Prêts
20. Valeurs mobilières
21. Autres actifs

Passif
22. Capital et réserves
23. Emprunts auprès de la Banque centrale
24. Dépôts interbancaires
25. Dépôts non bancaires
26. Obligations
27. Autres engagements

Total du bilan
28. En fin d'exercice
29. Moyen

Pour mémoire
30. Titres à court terme (2)
31. Obligations
32. Actions et participations
33. Créances sur des non résidents
34. Engagements envers des non résidents

RENSEIGNEMENTS COMPLEMENTAIRES
35. Nombre d'institutions
36. Nombre de succursales
37. Nombre de salariés (x 1000)

FINLAND

Co-operative banks

FINLANDE

Banques mutualistes

		1983	1984	1985	1986	1987	1988	1989	1990	1991	1992		
INCOME STATEMENT ANALYSIS													**ANALYSE DU COMPTE DE RESULTATS**
% of average balance sheet total													**% du total moyen du bilan**
38.	Interest income	8.94	9.42	9.15	8.05	7.90	8.54	9.25	10.37	10.35	10.02	38.	Produits financiers
39.	Interest expenses	5.44	6.08	5.78	4.86	4.62	5.33	6.36	7.27	7.37	7.55	39.	Frais financiers
40.	Net interest income	3.50	3.35	3.36	3.19	3.27	3.21	2.90	3.10	2.98	2.47	40.	Produits financiers nets
41.	Non-interest income (net)	1.30	1.38	1.43	1.55	1.59	1.78	1.55	1.53	2.00	2.72	41.	Produits non financiers (nets)
42.	Gross income	4.80	4.73	4.80	4.74	4.86	4.99	4.45	4.63	4.98	5.19	42.	Résultat brut
43.	Operating expenses	4.11	4.09	4.05	4.08	4.14	4.03	3.83	3.84	4.35	5.12	43.	Frais d'exploitation
44.	Net income	0.69	0.64	0.75	0.67	0.73	0.96	0.62	0.79	0.63	0.08	44.	Résultat net
45.	Provisions (net)	0.51	0.46	0.57	0.48	0.53	0.74	0.40	0.46	0.29	-0.05	45.	Provisions (nettes)
46.	Profit before tax	0.18	0.18	0.18	0.19	0.19	0.22	0.22	0.33	0.34	0.12	46.	Bénéfices avant impôt
47.	Income tax	0.09	0.08	0.08	0.08	0.08	0.08	0.09	0.13	0.14	0.10	47.	Impôt
48.	Profit after tax	0.08	0.09	0.10	0.11	0.12	0.14	0.13	0.21	0.20	0.02	48.	Bénéfices après impôt
49.	Distributed profit	0.07	0.07	0.07	0.07	0.08	0.08	0.07	0.06	0.05	0.02	49.	Bénéfices distribués
50.	Retained profit	0.02	0.03	0.03	0.04	0.04	0.06	0.06	0.14	0.15	0.00	50.	Bénéfices mis en réserve
51.	Staff costs (1)	2.23	2.15	2.09	2.09	1.96	1.95	1.83	1.65	1.55	1.50	51.	Frais de personnel (1)
52.	Provisions on loans	0.42	0.40	0.40	0.40	0.40	0.44	0.42	0.44	0.33	0.04	52.	Provisions sur prêts
53.	Provisions on securities	..	..	..	..	0.13	0.26	-0.04	0.00	-0.04	-0.09	53.	Provisions sur titres
% of gross income													**% du total du résultat brut**
54.	Net interest income	72.86	70.76	70.10	67.28	67.25	64.35	65.11	66.97	59.90	47.54	54.	Produits financiers nets
55.	Non-interest income (net)	27.14	29.24	29.90	32.72	32.75	35.65	34.89	33.03	40.10	52.46	55.	Produits non financiers (nets)
56.	Operating expenses	85.61	86.49	84.42	85.97	85.01	80.76	86.07	82.90	87.35	98.53	56.	Frais d'exploitation
57.	Net income	14.39	13.51	15.58	14.03	14.99	19.24	13.93	17.10	12.65	1.47	57.	Résultat net
58.	Provisions (net)	10.72	9.75	11.82	10.12	11.00	14.79	8.94	9.93	5.89	-0.91	58.	Provisions (nettes)
59.	Profit before tax	3.68	3.77	3.77	3.91	4.00	4.45	4.98	7.17	6.76	2.39	59.	Bénéfices avant impôt
60.	Income tax	1.97	1.77	1.65	1.60	1.55	1.62	1.98	2.71	2.84	1.98	60.	Impôt
61.	Profit after tax	1.71	1.99	2.12	2.30	2.45	2.83	3.01	4.46	3.92	0.41	61.	Bénéfices après impôt
62.	Staff costs (1)	46.42	45.46	43.64	44.03	40.33	39.08	41.26	35.70	31.09	28.90	62.	Frais de personnel (1)
% of net income													**% du total du résultat net**
63.	Provisions (net)	74.45	72.13	75.83	72.14	73.33	76.86	64.21	58.05	46.53	-62.07	63.	Provisions (nettes)
64.	Profit before tax	25.55	27.87	24.17	27.86	26.67	23.14	35.79	41.95	53.47	162.07	64.	Bénéfices avant impôt
65.	Income tax	13.66	13.11	10.57	11.44	10.34	8.42	14.21	15.84	22.45	134.48	65.	Impôt
66.	Profit after tax	11.89	14.75	13.60	16.42	16.32	14.73	21.58	26.11	31.02	27.59	66.	Bénéfices après impôt

FINLAND
Co-operative banks

FINLANDE
Banques mutualistes

Per cent — *Pourcentage*

BALANCE SHEET ANALYSIS — **ANALYSE DU BILAN**

% of year-end balance sheet total — **% du total du bilan en fin d'exercice**

	1983	1984	1985	1986	1987	1988	1989	1990	1991	1992	
Assets											**Actif**
67. Cash & balance with Central bank	4.05	5.37	5.28	4.53	4.37	5.80	6.84	5.47	3.64	4.19	67. Caisse & solde auprès de la Banque centrale
68. Interbank deposits	9.07	8.98	9.36	9.52	9.19	7.92	8.23	7.86	8.44	8.47	68. Dépôts interbancaires
69. Loans	77.19	76.14	75.19	74.40	75.12	74.27	73.17	72.75	71.78	68.36	69. Prêts
70. Securities	3.16	3.14	3.60	4.69	4.44	5.29	4.79	5.36	5.97	5.77	70. Valeurs mobilières
71. Other assets	6.52	6.37	6.56	6.86	6.88	6.72	6.96	8.55	10.17	13.21	71. Autres actifs
Liabilities											**Passif**
72. Capital & reserves	4.86	4.94	5.08	5.33	5.41	5.32	5.28	6.04	6.07	6.62	72. Capital et réserves
73. Borrowing from Central bank	0.77	0.82	0.84	0.83	0.82	0.60	0.72	0.50	0.49	0.41	73. Emprunts auprès de la Banque centrale
74. Interbank deposits	-	-	0.02	0.13	0.02	0.01	0.01	-	-	0.00	74. Dépôts interbancaires
75. Non-bank deposits	74.26	74.01	73.22	71.39	69.46	65.84	64.16	64.13	64.79	65.09	75. Dépôts non bancaires
76. Bonds	0.23	0.34	0.45	1.19	1.66	2.98	3.82	5.79	8.50	8.44	76. Obligations
77. Other liabilities	19.87	19.88	20.38	21.13	22.63	25.25	26.00	23.53	20.15	19.44	77. Autres engagements
Memoranda											*Pour mémoire*
78. Short-term securities (2)	*2.00*	*2.09*	*2.55*	*3.13*	*0.04*	*0.35*	*0.14*	*0.15*	*1.30*	*1.31*	*78. Titres à court terme (2)*
79. Bonds					*2.98*	*3.20*	*3.04*	*3.85*	*3.20*	*3.04*	*79. Obligations*
80. Shares and participations	*1.16*	*1.04*	*1.05*	*1.56*	*1.42*	*1.73*	*1.62*	*1.36*	*1.48*	*1.42*	*80. Actions et participations*
81. Claims on non-residents	*0.19*	*0.18*	*0.17*	*0.13*	*0.08*	*0.07*	*0.06*	*0.08*	*0.01*	*0.01*	*81. Créances sur des non résidents*
82. Liabilities to non-residents	-	-	-	-	*0.00*	-	-	-	*0.90*	*0.02*	*82. Engagements envers des non résidents*

1. Change in methodology.
2. Until 1986, included under "Bonds" (item 31 or item 79).

Change in methodology:

• Historical series for "Staff costs" (item 14 or item 51 or item 62) revised to include, in addition to salaries paid, social expenditure and other staff expenses.

1. Changement méthodologique.
2. Jusqu'à 1986, inclus sous "Obligations" (poste 31 ou poste 79).

Changement méthodologique :

• Les séries historiques, "Frais de personnel" (poste 14 ou poste 51 ou poste 62), ont été révisées afin d'inclure, en plus des salaires, les dépenses sociales et autres dépenses de personnel.

FRANCE

Commercial banks and credit co-operatives

FRANCE

Banques commerciales et mutualistes

Million French francs / *Millions de francs français*

	1983	1984	1985	1986 (2)	1987	1988	1989	1990	1991	1992
INCOME STATEMENT / COMPTE DE RESULTATS										
1. Interest income / Produits financiers	538151	628469	562425	579965	601939	695263	853155	965053	973966	960313
2. Interest expenses / Frais financiers	408770	482132	409493	408865	426755	503338	658953	765556	773421	769993
3. Net interest income / Produits financiers nets	129381	146337	152932	171100	175184	191925	194202	199497	200545	190320
4. Non-interest income (net) / Produits non financiers (nets)	26069	22230	25052	28835	31863	33452	45182	48403	69851	93580
5. Gross income / Résultat brut	155450	168567	177984	199935	207047	225377	239384	247900	270396	283900
6. Operating expenses / Frais d'exploitation	105174	116971	124648	133227	141543	150377	159652	169324	177241	185680
7. Net income / Résultat net	50276	51596	53336	66708	65504	75000	79732	78576	93155	98220
8. Provisions (net) / Provisions (nettes)	33549	34394	34412	42482	39397	43516	51630	52180	59916	78862
9. Profit before tax / Bénéfices avant impôt	16727	17202	18924	24226	26107	31484	28102	26396	33239	19358
10. Income tax / Impôt	7404	6927	8432	9324	9172	10333	9393	7647	9658	11827
11. Profit after tax / Bénéfices après impôt	9323	10275	10492	14902	16935	21151	18709	18749	23581	7531
12. Distributed profit / Bénéfices distribués	..	..	..	5645	6362	8348	9478	9587	10677	9673
13. Retained profit / Bénéfices mis en réserve	..	..	..	9257	10573	12803	9231	9162	12904	-2142
Memoranda / Pour mémoire										
14. Staff costs / Frais de personnel	69600	76134	80437	84740	88278	92415	97157	102094	105482	109034
15. Provisions on loans / Provisions sur prêts	..	..	..	22645	15968	26139	30159	32923	42595	65842
16. Provisions on securities / Provisions sur titres	..	..	..	2691	6027	-2764	2254	6644	292	9216
BALANCE SHEET / BILAN										
Assets / Actif										
17. Cash & balance with Central bank / Caisse & solde auprès de la Banque centrale	112866	130010	152714	186978	143610	158030	158977	116272	103291	57345
18. Interbank deposits / Dépôts interbancaires	2216412	2623425	2571559	3204683	3490402	3901829	4274116	4639338	4419624	4805960
19. Loans / Prêts	2269879	2526317	2417469	2491881	2785380	3274425	3746561	4193607	4413169	4564257
20. Securities / Valeurs mobilières	157104	196659	243633	500447	636019	690656	797998	893069	1330776	1607578
21. Other assets / Autres actifs	509408	619171	602699	743625	761527	921162	1116835	1340114	1153924	1407244
Liabilities / Passif										
22. Capital & reserves / Capital et réserves	125890	143247	145038	173221	199629	244488	285828	338487	389370	454432
23. Borrowing from Central bank (1) / Emprunts auprès de la Banque centrale (1)										
24. Interbank deposits / Dépôts interbancaires	2571799	2957347	2717110	3464918	3818201	4277345	4757650	4913847	4629260	4859998
25. Non-bank deposits / Dépôts non bancaires	1836298	2033452	2138051	2264839	2512900	2876815	3289459	3896984	4025008	4429581
26. Bonds / Obligations	274940	388368	402609	507441	539396	676504	733507	772666	853375	902178
27. Other liabilities / Autres engagements	456742	573168	585266	717195	746813	870950	1028133	1260415	1523772	1796196
Balance sheet total / Total du bilan										
28. End-year total / En fin d'exercice	5265669	6095582	5988074	7127614	7816939	8946102	10094577	11182400	11420785	12442384
29. Average total / Moyen	4910797	5680626	6041828	6934649	7450417	8369027	9658989	10521007	11522443	11998615
Memoranda / Pour mémoire										
30. Short-term securities / Titres à court terme	..	..	..	..	..	..	..	..	..	..
31. Bonds / Obligations	..	..	..	..	..	..	..	..	..	..
32. Shares and participations / Actions et participations	..	..	..	..	..	..	..	..	..	..
33. Claims on non-residents / Créances sur des non résidents	2160039	2575183	2277469	2230900	2366657	2878458	3179968	3645239	3632368	4101638
34. Liabilities to non-residents / Engagements envers des non résidents	2075894	2449924	2112122	2143305	2249641	2827614	3213276	3739650	3817369	4108514
SUPPLEMENTARY INFORMATION / RENSEIGNEMENTS COMPLEMENTAIRES										
35. Number of institutions / Nombre d'institutions	429	435	390	389	399	411	424	427	431	440
36. Number of branches / Nombre de succursales	21395	21323	21030	21025	21362	20943	21119	20771	20680	20492
37. Number of employees (x 1000) / Nombre de salariés (x 1000)	368.0	375.6	372.9	373.3	371.7	370.2	369.9	365.5	258.6	350.6

FRANCE

Commercial banks and credit co-operatives

Per cent

INCOME STATEMENT ANALYSIS

FRANCE

Banques commerciales et mutualistes

Pourcentage

ANALYSE DU COMPTE DE RESULTATS

			1983	1984	1985	1986 (2)	1987	1988	1989	1990	1991	1992
	% of average balance sheet total	**% du total moyen du bilan**										
38.	Interest income	Produits financiers	10.96	11.06	9.31	8.36	8.08	8.31	8.83	9.17	8.45	8.00
39.	Interest expenses	Frais financiers	8.32	8.49	6.78	5.90	5.73	6.01	6.82	7.28	6.71	6.42
40.	Net interest income	Produits financiers nets	2.63	2.58	2.53	2.47	2.35	2.29	2.01	1.90	1.74	1.59
41.	Non-interest income (net)	Produits non financiers (nets)	0.53	0.39	0.41	0.42	0.43	0.40	0.47	0.46	0.61	0.78
42.	Gross income	Résultat brut	3.17	2.97	2.95	2.88	2.78	2.69	2.48	2.36	2.35	2.37
43.	Operating expenses	Frais d'exploitation	2.14	2.06	2.06	1.92	1.90	1.80	1.65	1.61	1.54	1.55
44.	Net income	Résultat net	1.02	0.91	0.88	0.96	0.88	0.90	0.83	0.75	0.81	0.82
45.	Provisions (net)	Provisions (nettes)	0.68	0.61	0.57	0.61	0.53	0.52	0.53	0.50	0.52	0.66
46.	Profit before tax	Bénéfices avant impôt	0.34	0.30	0.31	0.35	0.35	0.38	0.29	0.25	0.29	0.16
47.	Income tax	Impôt	0.15	0.12	0.14	0.13	0.12	0.12	0.10	0.07	0.08	0.10
48.	Profit after tax	Bénéfices après impôt	0.19	0.18	0.17	0.21	0.23	0.25	0.19	0.18	0.20	0.06
49.	Distributed profit	Bénéfices distribués	..	..	..	0.08	0.09	0.10	0.10	0.09	0.09	0.08
50.	Retained profit	Bénéfices mis en réserve	..	..	..	0.13	0.14	0.15	0.10	0.09	0.11	-0.02
51.	Staff costs	Frais de personnel	1.42	1.34	1.33	1.22	1.18	1.10	1.01	0.97	0.92	0.91
52.	Provisions on loans	Provisions sur prêts	..	..	..	0.33	0.21	0.31	0.31	0.31	0.37	0.55
53.	Provisions on securities	Provisions sur titres	..	..	..	0.04	0.08	-0.03	0.02	0.06	0.00	0.08
	% of gross income	**% du total du résultat brut**										
54.	Net interest income	Produits financiers nets	83.23	86.81	85.92	85.58	84.61	85.16	81.13	80.47	74.17	67.04
55.	Non-interest income (net)	Produits non financiers (nets)	16.77	13.19	14.08	14.42	15.39	14.84	18.87	19.53	25.83	32.96
56.	Operating expenses	Frais d'exploitation	67.66	69.39	70.03	66.64	68.36	66.72	66.69	68.30	65.55	65.40
57.	Net income	Résultat net	32.34	30.61	29.97	33.36	31.64	33.28	33.31	31.70	34.45	34.60
58.	Provisions (net)	Provisions (nettes)	21.58	20.40	19.33	21.25	19.03	19.31	21.57	21.05	22.16	27.78
59.	Profit before tax	Bénéfices avant impôt	10.76	10.20	10.63	12.12	12.61	13.97	11.74	10.65	12.29	6.82
60.	Income tax	Impôt	4.76	4.11	4.74	4.66	4.43	4.58	3.92	3.08	3.57	4.17
61.	Profit after tax	Bénéfices après impôt	6.00	6.10	5.89	7.45	8.18	9.38	7.82	7.56	8.72	2.65
62.	Staff costs	Frais de personnel	44.77	45.17	45.19	42.38	42.64	41.00	40.59	41.18	39.01	38.41
	% of net income	**% du total du résultat net**										
63.	Provisions (net)	Provisions (nettes)	66.73	66.66	64.52	63.68	60.14	58.02	64.75	66.41	64.32	80.29
64.	Profit before tax	Bénéfices avant impôt	33.27	33.34	35.48	36.32	39.86	41.98	35.25	33.59	35.68	19.71
65.	Income tax	Impôt	14.73	13.43	15.81	13.98	14.00	13.78	11.78	9.73	10.37	12.04
66.	Profit after tax	Bénéfices après impôt	18.54	19.91	19.67	22.34	25.85	28.20	23.46	23.86	25.31	7.67

FRANCE

Commercial banks and credit co-operatives

Per cent

BALANCE SHEET ANALYSIS

% of year-end balance sheet total

FRANCE

Banques commerciales et mutualistes

Pourcentage

ANALYSE DU BILAN

% du total du bilan en fin d'exercice

	1983	1984	1985	1986 (2)	1987	1988	1989	1990	1991	1992		
Assets												**Actif**
67. Cash & balance with Central bank	2.14	2.13	2.55	2.62	1.84	1.77	1.57	1.04	0.90	0.46	67.	Caisse & solde auprès de la Banque centrale
68. Interbank deposits	42.09	43.04	42.94	44.96	44.65	43.61	42.34	41.49	38.70	38.63	68.	Dépôts interbancaires
69. Loans	43.11	41.45	40.37	34.96	35.63	36.60	37.12	37.50	38.64	36.68	69.	Prêts
70. Securities	2.98	3.23	4.07	7.02	8.14	7.72	7.91	7.99	11.65	12.92	70.	Valeurs mobilières
71. Other assets	9.67	10.16	10.06	10.43	9.74	10.30	11.06	11.98	10.10	11.31	71.	Autres actifs
Liabilities												**Passif**
72. Capital & reserves	2.39	2.35	2.42	2.43	2.55	2.73	2.83	3.03	3.41	3.65	72.	Capital et réserves
73. Borrowing from Central bank (1)	..	..	..	..	..	..	..	..	..	..	73.	Emprunts auprès de la Banque centrale (1)
74. Interbank deposits	48.84	48.52	45.38	48.61	48.85	47.81	47.13	43.94	40.53	39.06	74.	Dépôts interbancaires
75. Non-bank deposits	34.87	33.36	35.71	31.78	32.15	32.16	32.59	34.85	35.24	35.60	75.	Dépôts non bancaires
76. Bonds	5.22	6.37	6.72	7.12	6.90	7.56	7.27	6.91	7.47	7.25	76.	Obligations
77. Other liabilities	8.67	9.40	9.77	10.06	9.55	9.74	10.19	11.27	13.34	14.44	77.	Autres engagements
Memoranda												*Pour mémoire*
78. Short-term securities	..	..	..	..	..	..	..	..	..	..	*78.*	*Titres à court terme*
79. Bonds	..	..	..	..	..	..	..	..	..	..	*79.*	*Obligations*
80. Shares and participations	..	..	..	..	..	..	..	..	..	..	*80.*	*Actions et participations*
81. Claims on non-residents	*41.02*	*42.25*	*38.03*	*31.30*	*30.30*	*32.18*	*31.50*	*32.60*	*31.80*	*32.97*	*81.*	*Créances sur des non résidents*
82. Liabilities to non-residents	*39.42*	*40.19*	*35.27*	*30.07*	*28.78*	*31.61*	*31.83*	*33.44*	*33.42*	*33.02*	*82.*	*Engagements envers des non résidents*

1. Included under "Interbank deposits" (item 24 or item 74).
2. Change in methodology as from 1986.

Change in methodology:

• Following the accounting reform of 1991, the presentation of "Securities" items in the balance sheet and income statement was modified. Data, as from 1986, were recalculated on the basis of these modifications.

• As from 1986, average balance sheet totals (item 29) are based on the average of quarterly totals.

1. Inclus sous "Dépôts interbancaires" (poste 24 ou poste 74).
2. Changement méthodologique à partir de 1986.

Changement méthodologique :

• Une réforme comptable intervenue en 1991 a entraîné des modifications dans la présentation des opérations sur titres dans le bilan et le compte de résultat. Les données, à partir de 1986, ont été recalculées selon ces modifications.

• A partir de 1986 la moyenne du total des actifs/passifs (poste 29) est basée sur la moyenne des totaux des situations trimestrielles.

FRANCE

Large commercial banks / Grandes banques commerciales

Million French francs / Millions de francs français

INCOME STATEMENT / COMPTE DE RESULTATS	1983	1984	1985	1986 (2)	1987	1988	1989	1990	1991	1992	
1. Interest income	333528	391406	345399	351130	356026	401540	490370	555315	561510	553514	1. Produits financiers
2. Interest expenses	254343	302348	251589	252016	255096	293382	377307	440707	446446	446541	2. Frais financiers
3. Net interest income	79185	89058	93810	99114	100930	108158	113063	114608	115064	106973	3. Produits financiers nets
4. Non-interest income (net)	16237	13263	17460	20424	24225	25285	30732	32065	46273	59678	4. Produits non financiers (nets)
5. Gross income	95422	102321	111270	119538	125155	133443	143795	146673	161337	166651	5. Résultat brut
6. Operating expenses	65130	72065	77694	80104	84024	88434	93711	99388	104081	109966	6. Frais d'exploitation
7. Net income	30292	30256	33576	39434	41131	45009	50084	47285	57256	56685	7. Résultat net
8. Provisions (net)	23120	23339	25379	30046	26763	30652	34073	34073	36155	34240	8. Provisions (nettes)
9. Profit before tax	7172	6917	8197	9388	14368	14357	15243	13212	21101	22445	9. Bénéfices avant impôt
10. Income tax	3950	3807	4551	4531	5016	5280	5072	3570	5605	7833	10. Impôt
11. Profit after tax	3222	3110	3646	4857	9352	9077	10171	9642	15496	14612	11. Bénéfices après impôt
12. Distributed profit	..	..	..	2198	2590	3627	4393	4150	4785	4669	12. Bénéfices distribués
13. Retained profit	..	..	..	2659	6762	5450	5778	5492	10711	9943	13. Bénéfices mis en réserve
Memoranda											*Pour mémoire*
14. Staff costs	44120	47822	51057	52316	54068	56219	59099	62068	64434	67416	14. Frais de personnel
15. Provisions on loans	..	..	..	16132	9964	18661	20591	21226	24575	33302	15. Provisions sur prêts
16. Provisions on securities	..	..	..	2011	4238	-1975	776	4214	-784	3931	16. Provisions sur titres
BALANCE SHEET											**BILAN**
Assets											**Actif**
17. Cash & balance with Central bank	71034	84021	105693	103408	86041	101200	93336	77326	71870	37410	17. Caisse & solde auprès de la Banque centrale
18. Interbank deposits	1346855	1598632	1545198	1905147	2018331	2272590	2456510	2735222	2547642	2820529	18. Dépôts interbancaires
19. Loans	1481751	1663103	1661410	1652581	1810929	2113731	2403158	2673198	2812344	2920278	19. Prêts
20. Securities	77845	90453	105333	253128	305635	323492	384174	427499	728643	913157	20. Valeurs mobilières
21. Other assets	298971	419666	418192	487633	488265	575967	716147	908076	747557	952815	21. Autres actifs
Liabilities											**Passif**
22. Capital & reserves	61105	66205	73183	81077	89728	116334	131226	172624	192201	232638	22. Capital et réserves
23. Borrowing from Central bank (1)	..	..	..	..	..	..	..	..	..	..	23. Emprunts auprès de la Banque centrale (1)
24. Interbank deposits	1477802	1726155	1585187	2003491	2146014	2442461	2724819	2887902	2710582	2943609	24. Dépôts interbancaires
25. Non-bank deposits	1267005	1425156	1496823	1557540	1674689	1897973	2129064	2512440	2557516	2824732	25. Dépôts non bancaires
26. Bonds	169610	232187	266552	277859	293689	368874	392809	411924	462954	493403	26. Obligations
27. Other liabilities	300934	406172	414081	481931	505080	561337	675408	836430	984802	1149807	27. Autres engagements
Balance sheet total											**Total du bilan**
28. End-year total	3276456	3855875	3835826	4401897	4709201	5386980	6053326	6821321	6908056	7644189	28. En fin d'exercice
29. Average total	3066419	3566166	3845851	4324061	4527626	5033297	5751364	6316663	6969143	7210118	29. Moyen
Memoranda											*Pour mémoire*
30. Short-term securities	..	..	..	..	..	..	..	..	..	..	30. Titres à court terme
31. Bonds	..	..	..	..	..	..	..	..	..	..	31. Obligations
32. Shares and participations	..	..	..	..	..	..	..	..	..	..	32. Actions et participations
33. Claims on non-residents	1606047	1939830	1701130	1592649	1611696	1971750	2138301	2492038	2475228	2910282	33. Créances sur des non résidents
34. Liabilities to non-residents	1535807	1829965	1552763	1524045	1510481	1907909	2133156	2555351	2637372	2998860	34. Engagements envers des non résidents
SUPPLEMENTARY INFORMATION											**RENSEIGNEMENTS COMPLEMENTAIRES**
35. Number of institutions	8	8	8	8	8	8	8	8	8	8	35. Nombre d'institutions
36. Number of branches	12272	12276	12300	12412	12357	12305	12365	12233	12202	12197	36. Nombre de succursales
37. Number of employees (x 1000)	231.5	236.2	236.4	232.5	230.9	229.6	228.3	224.9	222.2	218.2	37. Nombre de salariés (x 1000)

FRANCE

Large commercial banks

Per cent

INCOME STATEMENT ANALYSIS

	1983	1984	1985	1986 (2)	1987	1988	1989	1990	1991	1992
% of average balance sheet total										
38. Interest income	10.88	10.98	8.98	8.12	7.86	7.98	8.53	8.79	8.06	7.68
39. Interest expenses	8.29	8.48	6.54	5.83	5.63	5.83	6.56	6.98	6.41	6.19
40. Net interest income	2.58	2.50	2.44	2.29	2.23	2.15	1.97	1.81	1.65	1.48
41. Non-interest income (net)	0.53	0.37	0.45	0.47	0.54	0.50	0.53	0.51	0.66	0.83
42. Gross income	3.11	2.87	2.89	2.76	2.76	2.65	2.50	2.32	2.32	2.31
43. Operating expenses	2.12	2.02	2.02	1.85	1.86	1.76	1.63	1.57	1.49	1.53
44. Net income	0.99	0.85	0.87	0.91	0.91	0.89	0.87	0.75	0.82	0.79
45. Provisions (net)	0.75	0.65	0.66	0.69	0.59	0.61	0.61	0.54	0.52	0.47
46. Profit before tax	0.23	0.19	0.21	0.22	0.32	0.29	0.27	0.21	0.30	0.31
47. Income tax	0.13	0.11	0.12	0.10	0.11	0.10	0.09	0.06	0.08	0.11
48. Profit after tax	0.11	0.09	0.09	0.11	0.21	0.18	0.18	0.15	0.22	0.20
49. Distributed profit	:	:	:	0.05	0.06	0.07	0.08	0.07	0.07	0.06
50. Retained profit	:	:	:	0.06	0.15	0.11	0.10	0.09	0.15	0.14
51. Staff costs	1.44	1.34	1.33	1.21	1.19	1.12	1.03	0.98	0.92	0.94
52. Provisions on loans	:	:	:	0.37	0.22	0.37	0.36	0.34	0.35	0.46
53. Provisions on securities	:	:	:	0.05	0.09	-0.04	0.01	0.07	-0.01	0.05
% of gross income										
54. Net interest income	82.98	87.04	84.31	82.91	80.64	81.05	78.63	78.14	71.32	64.19
55. Non-interest income (net)	17.02	12.96	15.69	17.09	19.36	18.95	21.37	21.86	28.68	35.81
56. Operating expenses	68.25	70.43	69.82	67.01	67.14	66.27	65.17	67.76	64.51	65.99
57. Net income	31.75	29.57	30.18	32.99	32.86	33.73	34.83	32.24	35.49	34.01
58. Provisions (net)	24.23	22.81	22.81	25.14	21.38	22.97	24.23	23.23	22.41	20.55
59. Profit before tax	7.52	6.76	7.37	7.85	11.48	10.76	10.60	9.01	13.08	13.47
60. Income tax	4.14	3.72	4.09	3.79	4.01	3.96	3.53	2.43	3.47	4.70
61. Profit after tax	3.38	3.04	3.28	4.06	7.47	6.80	7.07	6.57	9.60	8.77
62. Staff costs	46.24	46.74	45.89	43.77	43.20	42.13	41.10	42.32	39.94	40.45
% of net income										
63. Provisions (net)	76.32	77.14	75.59	76.19	65.07	68.10	69.57	72.06	63.15	60.40
64. Profit before tax	23.68	22.86	24.41	23.81	34.93	31.90	30.43	27.94	36.85	39.60
65. Income tax	13.04	12.58	13.55	11.49	12.20	11.73	10.13	7.55	9.79	13.82
66. Profit after tax	10.64	10.28	10.86	12.32	22.74	20.17	20.31	20.39	27.06	25.78

FRANCE

Grandes banques commerciales

Pourcentage

ANALYSE DU COMPTE DE RESULTATS

% du total moyen du bilan
38. Produits financiers
39. Frais financiers
40. Produits financiers nets
41. Produits non financiers (nets)
42. Résultat brut
43. Frais d'exploitation
44. Résultat net
45. Provisions (nettes)
46. Bénéfices avant impôt
47. Impôt
48. Bénéfices après impôt
49. Bénéfices distribués
50. Bénéfices mis en réserve

51. Frais de personnel
52. Provisions sur prêts
53. Provisions sur titres

% du total du résultat brut
54. Produits financiers nets
55. Produits non financiers (nets)
56. Frais d'exploitation
57. Résultat net
58. Provisions (nettes)
59. Bénéfices avant impôt
60. Impôt
61. Bénéfices après impôt
62. Frais de personnel

% du total du résultat net
63. Provisions (nettes)
64. Bénéfices avant impôt
65. Impôt
66. Bénéfices après impôt

63

FRANCE

Large commercial banks

Per cent

BALANCE SHEET ANALYSIS

% of year-end balance sheet total

		1983	1984	1985	1986 (2)	1987	1988	1989	1990	1991	1992
	Assets										
67.	Cash & balance with Central bank	2.17	2.18	2.76	2.35	1.83	1.88	1.54	1.13	1.04	0.49
68.	Interbank deposits	41.11	41.46	40.28	43.28	42.86	42.19	40.58	40.10	36.88	36.90
69.	Loans	45.22	43.13	43.31	37.54	38.46	39.24	39.70	39.19	40.71	38.20
70.	Securities	2.38	2.35	2.75	5.75	6.49	6.01	6.35	6.27	10.55	11.95
71.	Other assets	9.12	10.88	10.90	11.08	10.37	10.69	11.83	13.31	10.82	12.46
	Liabilities										
72.	Capital & reserves	1.86	1.72	1.91	1.84	1.91	2.16	2.17	2.53	2.78	3.04
73.	Borrowing from Central bank (1)	..	..	..	..	..	..	..	..	..	..
74.	Interbank deposits	45.10	44.77	41.33	45.51	45.57	45.34	45.01	42.34	39.24	38.51
75.	Non-bank deposits	38.67	36.96	39.02	35.38	35.56	35.23	35.17	36.83	37.02	36.95
76.	Bonds	5.18	6.02	6.95	6.31	6.24	6.85	6.49	6.04	6.70	6.45
77.	Other liabilities	9.18	10.53	10.80	10.95	10.73	10.42	11.16	12.26	14.26	15.04
	Memoranda										
78.	*Short-term securities*	..	..	..	..	..	..	..	..	..	..
79.	*Bonds*	..	..	..	..	..	..	..	..	..	..
80.	*Shares and participations*	..	..	..	..	..	..	..	..	..	..
81.	*Claims on non-residents*	49.02	50.31	44.35	36.18	34.22	36.60	35.32	36.53	35.83	38.07
82.	*Liabilities to non-residents*	46.87	47.46	40.48	34.62	32.08	35.42	35.24	37.46	38.18	39.23

1. Included under "Interbank deposits" (item 24 or item 74).
2. Change in methodology as from 1986.

Notes

- Large commercial banks are a subgroup of Commercial banks and credit co-operatives.

Change in methodology:

- Following the accounting reform of 1991, the presentation of "Securities" items in the balance sheet and income statement was modified. Data, as from 1986, were recalculated on the basis of these modifications.

- As from 1986, average balance sheet totals (item 29) are based on the average of quarterly totals.

FRANCE

Grandes banques commerciales

Pourcentage

ANALYSE DU BILAN

% du total du bilan en fin d'exercice

Actif
67. Caisse & solde auprès de la Banque centrale
68. Dépôts interbancaires
69. Prêts
70. Valeurs mobilières
71. Autres actifs

Passif
72. Capital et réserves
73. Emprunts auprès de la Banque centrale (1)
74. Dépôts interbancaires
75. Dépôts non bancaires
76. Obligations
77. Autres engagements

Pour mémoire
78. *Titres à court terme*
79. *Obligations*
80. *Actions et participations*
81. *Créances sur des non résidents*
82. *Engagements envers des non résidents*

1. Inclus sous "Dépôts interbancaires" (poste 24 ou poste 74).
2. Changement méthodologique à partir de 1986.

Notes

- Les Grandes banques commerciales sont un sous-groupe des Banques commerciales et mutualistes.

Changement méthodologique :

- Une réforme comptable intervenue en 1991 a entraîné des modifications dans la présentation des opérations sur titres dans le bilan et le compte de résultat. Les données, à partir de 1986, ont été recalculées selon ces modifications.

- A partir de 1986 la moyenne du total des actifs/passifs (poste 29) est basée sur la moyenne des totaux des situations trimestrielles.

GERMANY
All banks

ALLEMAGNE
Ensemble des banques

Million DM / *Millions de DM*

	1983	1984	1985	1986	1987	1988	1989	1990	1991	1992	
INCOME STATEMENT											**COMPTE DE RESULTATS**
1. Interest income	166935	175343	180527	181159	182155	191817	224774	272413	317946	356962	1. Produits financiers
2. Interest expenses	110129	118350	120692	116811	117875	125596	157915	201200	236652	266815	2. Frais financiers
3. Net interest income	56806	56993	59835	64348	64280	66221	66859	71213	81294	90147	3. Produits financiers nets
4. Non-interest income (net)	11366	12541	15515	16335	16131	15442	22957	26055	25789	28250	4. Produits non financiers (nets)
5. Gross income	68172	69534	75350	80683	80411	81663	89816	97268	107083	118397	5. Résultat brut
6. Operating expenses	38803	41230	45627	50530	53176	55598	57993	62987	69779	76406	6. Frais d'exploitation
7. Net income	29369	28304	29723	30153	27235	26065	31823	34281	37304	41991	7. Résultat net
8. Provisions (net)	12849	10938	11958	11488	10477	6808	15294	16807	14008	17325	8. Provisions (nettes)
9. Profit before tax	16520	17366	17765	18665	16758	19257	16529	17474	23296	24666	9. Bénéfices avant impôt
10. Income tax	11009	11060	11393	11595	10316	11965	9275	9408	13585	15266	10. Impôt
11. Profit after tax	5511	6306	6372	7070	6442	7292	7254	8066	9711	9400	11. Bénéfices après impôt
12. Distributed profit	3321	4150	4417	5063	4844	5088	5506	5828	6192	6522	12. Bénéfices distribués
13. Retained profit	2190	2156	1955	2007	1598	2204	1748	2238	3519	2878	13. Bénéfices mis en réserve
Memoranda											*Pour mémoire*
14. *Staff costs*	*25575*	*26819*	*29379*	*32328*	*34180*	*35770*	*36971*	*40178*	*44264*	*48301*	14. *Frais de personnel*
15. *Provisions on loans*	*12597*	*10707*	*11661*	*11142*	*10218*	*6736*	*15093*	*16295*	*13680*	*16900*	15. *Provisions sur prêts*
16. *Provisions on securities (1)*	..	..	..	..	..	..	..	..	..	..	16. *Provisions sur titres (1)*
BALANCE SHEET											**BILAN**
Assets											**Actif**
17. Cash & balance with Central bank	62643	67390	69835	71528	75478	76127	85858	92447	93057	101914	17. Caisse & solde auprès de la Banque centrale
18. Interbank deposits	446230	498412	541786	641874	703121	773067	855091	942832	957079	1008667	18. Dépôts interbancaires
19. Loans	1358061	1438759	1525921	1616444	1684653	1802314	1923523	2103045	2369096	2594859	19. Prêts
20. Securities	328544	356306	398718	433365	476356	511376	535369	627941	667974	753966	20. Valeurs mobilières
21. Other assets	61964	66464	73062	80010	81740	84842	90902	95027	114479	113267	21. Autres actifs
Liabilities											**Passif**
22. Capital & reserves	75815	82239	92823	105015	113259	119755	133480	146444	161709	187401	22. Capital et réserves
23. Borrowing from Central bank	70444	79332	87133	81888	71563	125163	153961	164043	186258	152691	23. Emprunts auprès de la Banque centrale
24. Interbank deposits	505793	548764	568000	640764	694531	758172	798405	914820	964155	1100162	24. Dépôts interbancaires
25. Non-bank deposits	1202849	1294839	1408483	1532971	1632736	1733511	1843035	2010213	2197726	2354476	25. Dépôts non bancaires
26. Bonds	324161	338999	358217	374807	397643	392924	434797	480036	526178	586482	26. Obligations
27. Other liabilities	78380	83158	94666	107776	111616	118201	127065	145736	165659	191461	27. Autres engagements
Balance sheet total											**Total du bilan**
28. End-year total	2257442	2427331	2609322	2843221	3021348	3247726	3490743	3861292	4201685	4572673	28. En fin d'exercice
29. Average total	2154333	2281097	2481800	2695352	2901013	3101033	3318573	3625716	3993446	4359930	29. Moyen
Memoranda											*Pour mémoire*
30. *Short-term securities*	*69538*	*68562*	*69639*	*64291*	*67080*	*58176*	*51859*	*104948*	*132600*	*134122*	30. *Titres à court terme*
31. *Bonds*	*225426*	*251071*	*287412*	*318939*	*353433*	*394145*	*412249*	*431455*	*432463*	*497933*	31. *Obligations*
32. *Shares and participations*	*33580*	*36673*	*41667*	*50135*	*55843*	*59055*	*71261*	*91538*	*102911*	*121911*	32. *Actions et participations*
33. *Claims on non-residents*	*233429*	*269861*	*298645*	*374699*	*413771*	*494438*	*572825*	*745902*	*687172*	*730577*	33. *Créances sur des non résidents*
34. *Liabilities to non-residents*	*222982*	*255675*	*249585*	*251922*	*275524*	*328618*	*337417*	*440078*	*423857*	*530575*	34. *Engagements envers des non résidents*
SUPPLEMENTARY INFORMATION											**RENSEIGNEMENTS COMPLEMENTAIRES**
35. Number of institutions	3039	3025	4439	4465	4340	4223	4089	3913	3716	3517	35. Nombre d'institutions
36. Number of branches	35611	35752	38867	39812	39744	39679	39651	39576	39228	39295	36. Nombre de succursales
37. Number of employees (x 1000)	NA	NA	NA	NA	NA	NA	NA	NA	NA	NA	37. Nombre de salariés (x 1000)

GERMANY

All banks

Per cent

INCOME STATEMENT ANALYSIS

ALLEMAGNE

Ensemble des banques

Pourcentage

ANALYSE DU COMPTE DE RESULTATS

		1983	1984	1985	1986	1987	1988	1989	1990	1991	1992		
	% of average balance sheet total												**% du total moyen du bilan**
38.	Interest income	7.75	7.69	7.27	6.72	6.28	6.19	6.77	7.51	7.96	8.19	38.	Produits financiers
39.	Interest expenses	5.11	5.19	4.86	4.33	4.06	4.05	4.76	5.55	5.93	6.12	39.	Frais financiers
40.	Net interest income	2.64	2.50	2.41	2.39	2.22	2.14	2.01	1.96	2.04	2.07	40.	Produits financiers nets
41.	Non-interest income (net)	0.53	0.55	0.63	0.61	0.56	0.50	0.69	0.72	0.65	0.65	41.	Produits non financiers (nets)
42.	Gross income	3.16	3.05	3.04	2.99	2.77	2.63	2.71	2.68	2.68	2.72	42.	Résultat brut
43.	Operating expenses	1.80	1.81	1.84	1.87	1.83	1.79	1.75	1.74	1.75	1.75	43.	Frais d'exploitation
44.	Net income	1.36	1.24	1.20	1.12	0.94	0.84	0.96	0.95	0.93	0.96	44.	Résultat net
45.	Provisions (net)	0.60	0.48	0.48	0.43	0.36	0.22	0.46	0.46	0.35	0.40	45.	Provisions (nettes)
46.	Profit before tax	0.77	0.76	0.72	0.69	0.58	0.62	0.50	0.48	0.58	0.57	46.	Bénéfices avant impôt
47.	Income tax	0.51	0.48	0.46	0.43	0.36	0.39	0.28	0.26	0.34	0.35	47.	Impôt
48.	Profit after tax	0.26	0.28	0.26	0.26	0.22	0.24	0.22	0.22	0.24	0.22	48.	Bénéfices après impôt
49.	Distributed profit	0.15	0.18	0.18	0.19	0.17	0.16	0.17	0.16	0.16	0.15	49.	Bénéfices distribués
50.	Retained profit	0.10	0.09	0.08	0.07	0.06	0.07	0.05	0.06	0.09	0.07	50.	Bénéfices mis en réserve
51.	Staff costs	1.19	1.18	1.18	1.20	1.18	1.15	1.11	1.11	1.11	1.11	51.	Frais de personnel
52.	Provisions on loans	0.58	0.47	0.47	0.41	0.35	0.22	0.45	0.45	0.34	0.39	52.	Provisions sur prêts
53.	Provisions on securities (1)	:	:	:	:	:	:	:	:	:	:	53.	Provisions sur titres (1)
	% of gross income												**% du total du résultat brut**
54.	Net interest income	83.33	81.96	79.41	79.75	79.94	81.09	74.44	73.21	75.92	76.14	54.	Produits financiers nets
55.	Non-interest income (net)	16.67	18.04	20.59	20.25	20.06	18.91	25.56	26.79	24.08	23.86	55.	Produits non financiers (nets)
56.	Operating expenses	56.92	59.29	60.55	62.63	66.13	68.08	64.57	64.76	65.16	64.53	56.	Frais d'exploitation
57.	Net income	43.08	40.71	39.45	37.37	33.87	31.92	35.43	35.24	34.84	35.47	57.	Résultat net
58.	Provisions (net)	18.85	15.73	15.87	14.24	13.03	8.34	17.03	17.28	13.08	14.63	58.	Provisions (nettes)
59.	Profit before tax	24.23	24.97	23.58	23.13	20.84	23.58	18.40	17.96	21.76	20.83	59.	Bénéfices avant impôt
60.	Income tax	16.15	15.91	15.12	14.37	12.83	14.65	10.33	9.67	12.69	12.89	60.	Impôt
61.	Profit after tax	8.08	9.07	8.46	8.76	8.01	8.93	8.08	8.29	9.07	7.94	61.	Bénéfices après impôt
62.	Staff costs	37.52	38.57	38.99	40.07	42.51	43.80	41.16	41.31	41.34	40.80	62.	Frais de personnel
	% of net income												**% du total du résultat net**
63.	Provisions (net)	43.75	38.64	40.23	38.10	38.47	26.12	48.06	49.03	37.55	41.26	63.	Provisions (nettes)
64.	Profit before tax	56.25	61.36	59.77	61.90	61.53	73.88	51.94	50.97	62.45	58.74	64.	Bénéfices avant impôt
65.	Income tax	37.49	39.08	38.33	38.45	37.88	45.90	29.15	27.44	36.42	36.36	65.	Impôt
66.	Profit after tax	18.76	22.28	21.44	23.45	23.65	27.98	22.79	23.53	26.03	22.39	66.	Bénéfices après impôt

GERMANY

All banks

ALLEMAGNE

Ensemble des banques

Per cent — *Pourcentage*

BALANCE SHEET ANALYSIS — ANALYSE DU BILAN

% of year-end balance sheet total — **% du total du bilan en fin d'exercice**

	1983	1984	1985	1986	1987	1988	1989	1990	1991	1992		
Assets												**Actif**
67. Cash & balance with Central bank	2.77	2.78	2.68	2.52	2.50	2.34	2.46	2.39	2.21	2.23	67.	Caisse & solde auprès de la Banque centrale
68. Interbank deposits	19.77	20.53	20.76	22.58	23.27	23.80	24.50	24.42	22.78	22.06	68.	Dépôts interbancaires
69. Loans	60.16	59.27	58.48	56.85	55.76	55.49	55.10	54.46	56.38	56.75	69.	Prêts
70. Securities	14.55	14.68	15.28	15.24	15.77	15.75	15.34	16.26	15.90	16.49	70.	Valeurs mobilières
71. Other assets	2.74	2.74	2.80	2.81	2.71	2.61	2.60	2.46	2.72	2.48	71.	Autres actifs
Liabilities												**Passif**
72. Capital & reserves	3.36	3.39	3.56	3.69	3.75	3.69	3.82	3.79	3.85	4.10	72.	Capital et réserves
73. Borrowing from Central bank	3.12	3.27	3.34	2.88	2.37	3.85	4.41	4.25	4.43	3.34	73.	Emprunts auprès de la Banque centrale
74. Interbank deposits	22.41	22.61	21.77	22.54	22.99	23.34	22.87	23.69	22.95	24.06	74.	Dépôts interbancaires
75. Non-bank deposits	53.28	53.34	53.98	53.92	54.04	53.38	52.80	52.06	52.31	51.49	75.	Dépôts non bancaires
76. Bonds	14.36	13.97	13.73	13.18	13.16	12.10	12.46	12.43	12.52	12.83	76.	Obligations
77. Other liabilities	3.47	3.43	3.63	3.79	3.69	3.64	3.64	3.77	3.94	4.19	77.	Autres engagements
Memoranda												*Pour mémoire*
78. Short-term securities	*3.08*	*2.82*	*2.67*	*2.26*	*2.22*	*1.79*	*1.49*	*2.72*	*3.16*	*2.93*	*78.*	*Titres à court terme*
79. Bonds	*9.99*	*10.34*	*11.01*	*11.22*	*11.70*	*12.14*	*11.81*	*11.17*	*10.29*	*10.89*	*79.*	*Obligations*
80. Shares and participations	*1.49*	*1.51*	*1.60*	*1.76*	*1.85*	*1.82*	*2.04*	*2.37*	*2.45*	*2.67*	*80.*	*Actions et participations*
81. Claims on non-residents	*10.34*	*11.12*	*11.45*	*13.18*	*13.69*	*15.22*	*16.41*	*19.32*	*16.35*	*15.98*	*81.*	*Créances sur des non résidents*
82. Liabilities to non-residents	*9.88*	*10.53*	*9.57*	*8.86*	*9.12*	*10.12*	*9.67*	*11.40*	*10.09*	*11.60*	*82.*	*Engagements envers des non résidents*

1. Included under "Provisions on loans" (item 15 or item 52).

1. Inclus sous "Provisions sur prêts" (poste 15 ou poste 52).

Notes

• All banks include Commercial banks, Regional giro institutions, Savings banks, Regional institutions of co-operative banks and Co-operative banks.

• Average balance sheet totals (item 29) are based on twelve end-month data.

• Data for banks domiciled in the new Länder of the Federal Republic of Germany are not included.

Change in methodology:

• As from 1985, all credit co-operatives are included in the data.

• As from 1986, the so-called Instalment sales financing institutions are included in the data.

Notes

• L'Ensemble des banques comprend les Banques commerciales, les Organismes régionaux de compensation, les Caisses d'épargne, les Institutions régionales des banques mutualistes et les Banques mutualistes.

• La moyenne du total des actifs/passifs (poste 29) est basée sur douze données de fin de mois.

• Les données portant sur les banques domiciliées dans les nouveaux Länder de la République fédérale d'Allemagne ne sont pas incluses.

Changement méthodologique :

• Depuis 1985, l'ensemble des banques mutualistes est compris dans les données.

• Depuis 1986, les Etablissements de financement des ventes à crédit sont compris dans les données.

GERMANY

Commercial banks

ALLEMAGNE

Banques commerciales

Million DM / *Millions de DM*

		1983	1984	1985	1986	1987	1988	1989	1990	1991	1992	
INCOME STATEMENT												**COMPTE DE RESULTATS**
1.	Interest income	48735	51953	51916	54708	55057	60714	75952	93502	109785	125197	Produits financiers
2.	Interest expenses	31745	35062	34339	33552	34574	39455	54081	68910	80576	92094	Frais financiers
3.	Net interest income	16990	16891	17577	21156	20483	21259	21871	24592	29209	33103	Produits financiers nets
4.	Non-interest income (net)	5608	5915	7551	8872	8709	9283	12315	13742	12825	14735	Produits non financiers (nets)
5.	Gross income	22598	22806	25128	30028	29192	30542	34186	38334	42034	47838	Résultat brut
6.	Operating expenses	13738	14552	15799	18911	19976	21137	22245	24427	27834	30451	Frais d'exploitation
7.	Net income	8860	8254	9329	11117	9216	9405	11941	13907	14200	17387	Résultat net
8.	Provisions (net)	5104	3487	3377	4518	3872	2374	4467	6328	6317	10313	Provisions (nettes)
9.	Profit before tax	3756	4767	5952	6599	5344	7031	7474	7579	7883	7074	Bénéfices avant impôt
10.	Income tax	2320	2561	3234	3481	2737	3839	3994	3434	3883	3821	Impôt
11.	Profit after tax	1436	2206	2718	3118	2607	3192	3480	4145	4000	3253	Bénéfices après impôt
12.	Distributed profit	868	1635	1889	2329	2202	2309	2584	3041	2840	2894	Bénéfices distribués
13.	Retained profit	568	571	829	789	405	883	896	1104	1160	359	Bénéfices mis en réserve
Memoranda												*Pour mémoire*
14.	*Staff costs*	*9401*	*9790*	*10465*	*12336*	*12985*	*13729*	*14259*	*15555*	*17477*	*18961*	*Frais de personnel*
15.	*Provisions on loans*	*5004*	*3368*	*3183*	*4304*	*3697*	*2353*	*4314*	*5983*	*6157*	*10046*	*Provisions sur prêts*
16.	*Provisions on securities (1)*	..	..	..	..	..	..	..	..	..	..	*Provisions sur titres (1)*
BALANCE SHEET												**BILAN**
Assets												**Actif**
17.	Cash & balance with Central bank	24798	27297	29095	29491	30940	28116	32043	35665	37627	38792	Caisse & solde auprès de la Banque centrale
18.	Interbank deposits	157380	177389	187019	213482	230538	254751	283241	311569	314517	345687	Dépôts interbancaires
19.	Loans	383289	413529	438301	506244	537300	602864	664124	757560	865040	938289	Prêts
20.	Securities	79358	90627	100452	108981	111209	117005	132739	156499	177994	205865	Valeurs mobilières
21.	Other assets	14517	14586	15655	21459	22180	24399	26549	25353	26308	34854	Autres actifs
Liabilities												**Passif**
22.	Capital & reserves	26533	28456	32633	40298	44399	47034	55417	64922	72356	82228	Capital et réserves
23.	Borrowing from Central bank	27120	31725	34776	41126	34090	50803	60371	57210	60178	56101	Emprunts auprès de la Banque centrale
24.	Interbank deposits	189075	205990	211301	247319	266114	293506	314931	348978	362609	415905	Dépôts interbancaires
25.	Non-bank deposits	325662	356513	377964	423698	454523	501012	551267	634532	727226	784343	Dépôts non bancaires
26.	Bonds	63991	71419	77443	81095	84686	84760	101409	115170	125832	141938	Obligations
27.	Other liabilities	26961	29325	36405	46121	48355	50020	55301	65834	73285	82972	Autres engagements
Balance sheet total												**Total du bilan**
28.	End-year total	659342	723428	770522	879657	932167	1027135	1138696	1286646	1421486	1563487	En fin d'exercice
29.	Average total	626162	665005	719619	818825	889239	968536	1072589	1203377	1350934	1495870	Moyen
Memoranda												*Pour mémoire*
30.	*Short-term securities*	*23687*	*25803*	*22960*	*18210*	*17037*	*16986*	*13915*	*23196*	*38346*	*39895*	*Titres à court terme*
31.	*Bonds*	*35326*	*42681*	*52792*	*60112*	*61295*	*65546*	*75707*	*76814*	*79780*	*98773*	*Obligations*
32.	*Shares and participations*	*20345*	*22143*	*24700*	*30659*	*32877*	*34473*	*43117*	*56489*	*59968*	*67197*	*Actions et participations*
33.	*Claims on non-residents*	*147927*	*174079*	*185372*	*227950*	*246090*	*298773*	*330289*	*397119*	*405332*	*437475*	*Créances sur des non résidents*
34.	*Liabilities to non-residents*	*162699*	*191273*	*190391*	*195971*	*211822*	*252393*	*260075*	*306926*	*319405*	*373253*	*Engagements envers des non résidents*
SUPPLEMENTARY INFORMATION												**RENSEIGNEMENTS COMPLEMENTAIRES**
35.	Number of institutions	176	174	173	252	255	259	264	274	281	276	Nombre d'institutions
36.	Number of branches	5433	5430	5449	6346	6260	6242	6252	6255	6044	6394	Nombre de succursales
37.	Number of employees (x 1000)	NA	NA	NA	NA	NA	NA	NA	NA	NA	NA	Nombre de salariés (x 1000)

GERMANY

Commercial banks

ALLEMAGNE

Banques commerciales

Per cent

Pourcentage

INCOME STATEMENT ANALYSIS

ANALYSE DU COMPTE DE RESULTATS

	1983	1984	1985	1986	1987	1988	1989	1990	1991	1992		
% of average balance sheet total												**% du total moyen du bilan**
38. Interest income	7.78	7.81	7.21	6.68	6.19	6.27	7.08	7.77	8.13	8.37	38.	Produits financiers
39. Interest expenses	5.07	5.27	4.77	4.10	3.89	4.07	5.04	5.73	5.96	6.16	39.	Frais financiers
40. Net interest income	2.71	2.54	2.44	2.58	2.30	2.19	2.04	2.04	2.16	2.21	40.	Produits financiers nets
41. Non-interest income (net)	0.90	0.89	1.05	1.08	0.98	0.96	1.15	1.14	0.95	0.99	41.	Produits non financiers (nets)
42. Gross income	3.61	3.43	3.49	3.67	3.28	3.15	3.19	3.19	3.11	3.20	42.	Résultat brut
43. Operating expenses	2.19	2.19	2.20	2.31	2.25	2.18	2.07	2.03	2.06	2.04	43.	Frais d'exploitation
44. Net income	1.41	1.24	1.30	1.36	1.04	0.97	1.11	1.16	1.05	1.16	44.	Résultat net
45. Provisions (net)	0.82	0.52	0.47	0.55	0.44	0.25	0.42	0.53	0.47	0.69	45.	Provisions (nettes)
46. Profit before tax	0.60	0.72	0.83	0.81	0.60	0.73	0.70	0.63	0.58	0.47	46.	Bénéfices avant impôt
47. Income tax	0.37	0.39	0.45	0.43	0.31	0.40	0.37	0.29	0.29	0.26	47.	Impôt
48. Profit after tax	0.23	0.33	0.38	0.38	0.29	0.33	0.32	0.34	0.30	0.22	48.	Bénéfices après impôt
49. Distributed profit	0.14	0.25	0.26	0.28	0.25	0.24	0.24	0.25	0.21	0.19	49.	Bénéfices distribués
50. Retained profit	0.09	0.09	0.12	0.10	0.05	0.09	0.08	0.09	0.09	0.02	50.	Bénéfices mis en réserve
51. Staff costs	1.50	1.47	1.45	1.51	1.46	1.42	1.33	1.29	1.29	1.27	51.	Frais de personnel
52. Provisions on loans	0.80	0.51	0.44	0.53	0.42	0.24	0.40	0.50	0.46	0.67	52.	Provisions sur prêts
53. Provisions on securities (1)	..	..	..	..	..	..	..	..	..	..	53.	Provisions sur titres (1)
% of gross income												**% du total du résultat brut**
54. Net interest income	75.18	74.06	69.95	70.45	70.17	69.61	63.98	64.15	69.49	69.20	54.	Produits financiers nets
55. Non-interest income (net)	24.82	25.94	30.05	29.55	29.83	30.39	36.02	35.85	30.51	30.80	55.	Produits non financiers (nets)
56. Operating expenses	60.79	63.81	62.87	62.98	68.43	69.21	65.07	63.72	66.22	63.65	56.	Frais d'exploitation
57. Net income	39.21	36.19	37.13	37.02	31.57	30.79	34.93	36.28	33.78	36.35	57.	Résultat net
58. Provisions (net)	22.59	15.29	13.44	15.05	13.26	7.77	13.07	16.51	15.03	21.56	58.	Provisions (nettes)
59. Profit before tax	16.62	20.90	23.69	21.98	18.31	23.02	21.86	19.77	18.75	14.79	59.	Bénéfices avant impôt
60. Income tax	10.27	11.23	12.87	11.59	9.38	12.57	11.68	8.96	9.24	7.99	60.	Impôt
61. Profit after tax	6.35	9.67	10.82	10.38	8.93	10.45	10.18	10.81	9.52	6.80	61.	Bénéfices après impôt
62. Staff costs	41.60	42.93	41.65	41.08	44.48	44.95	41.71	40.58	41.58	39.64	62.	Frais de personnel
% of net income												**% du total du résultat net**
63. Provisions (net)	57.61	42.25	36.20	40.64	42.01	25.24	37.41	45.50	44.49	59.31	63.	Provisions (nettes)
64. Profit before tax	42.39	57.75	63.80	59.36	57.99	74.76	62.59	54.50	55.51	40.69	64.	Bénéfices avant impôt
65. Income tax	26.19	31.03	34.67	31.31	29.70	40.82	33.45	24.69	27.35	21.98	65.	Impôt
66. Profit after tax	16.21	26.73	29.13	28.05	28.29	33.94	29.14	29.81	28.17	18.71	66.	Bénéfices après impôt

GERMANY

Commercial banks

Per cent

BALANCE SHEET ANALYSIS

% of year-end balance sheet total

	1983	1984	1985	1986	1987	1988	1989	1990	1991	1992
Assets										
67. Cash & balance with Central bank	3.76	3.77	3.78	3.35	3.32	2.74	2.81	2.77	2.65	2.48
68. Interbank deposits	23.87	24.52	24.27	24.27	24.73	24.80	24.87	24.22	22.13	22.11
69. Loans	58.13	57.16	56.88	57.55	57.64	58.69	58.32	58.88	60.85	60.01
70. Securities	12.04	12.53	13.04	12.39	11.93	11.39	11.66	12.16	12.52	13.17
71. Other assets	2.20	2.02	2.03	2.44	2.38	2.38	2.33	1.97	1.85	2.23
Liabilities										
72. Capital & reserves	4.02	3.93	4.24	4.58	4.76	4.58	4.87	5.05	5.09	5.26
73. Borrowing from Central bank	4.11	4.39	4.51	4.68	3.66	4.95	5.30	4.45	4.23	3.59
74. Interbank deposits	28.68	28.47	27.42	28.12	28.55	28.58	27.66	27.12	25.51	26.60
75. Non-bank deposits	49.39	49.28	49.05	48.17	48.76	48.78	48.41	49.32	51.16	50.17
76. Bonds	9.71	9.87	10.05	9.22	9.08	8.25	8.91	8.95	8.85	9.08
77. Other liabilities	4.09	4.05	4.72	5.24	5.19	4.87	4.86	5.12	5.16	5.31
Memoranda										
78. Short-term securities	*3.59*	*3.57*	*2.98*	*2.07*	*1.83*	*1.65*	*1.22*	*1.80*	*2.70*	*2.55*
79. Bonds	*5.36*	*5.90*	*6.85*	*6.83*	*6.58*	*6.38*	*6.65*	*5.97*	*5.61*	*6.32*
80. Shares and participations	*3.09*	*3.06*	*3.21*	*3.49*	*3.53*	*3.36*	*3.79*	*4.39*	*4.21*	*4.30*
81. Claims on non-residents	*22.44*	*24.06*	*24.06*	*25.91*	*26.40*	*29.09*	*29.01*	*30.86*	*28.51*	*27.98*
82. Liabilities to non-residents	*24.68*	*26.44*	*24.71*	*22.28*	*22.72*	*24.57*	*22.84*	*23.85*	*22.47*	*23.87*

1. Included under "Provisions on loans" (item 15 or item 52).

Notes

• Average balance sheet totals (item 29) are based on twelve end-month data.

Change in methodology:

• As from 1986, the so called Instalment sales financing institutions are included in the data.

ALLEMAGNE

Banques commerciales

Pourcentage

ANALYSE DU BILAN

% du total du bilan en fin d'exercice

Actif
67. Caisse & solde auprès de la Banque centrale
68. Dépôts interbancaires
69. Prêts
70. Valeurs mobilières
71. Autres actifs

Passif
72. Capital et réserves
73. Emprunts auprès de la Banque centrale
74. Dépôts interbancaires
75. Dépôts non bancaires
76. Obligations
77. Autres engagements

Pour mémoire
78. Titres à court terme
79. Obligations
80. Actions et participations
81. Créances sur des non résidents
82. Engagements envers des non résidents

1. Inclus sous "Provisions sur prêts" (poste 15 ou poste 52).

Notes

• La moyenne du total des actifs/passifs (poste 29) est basée sur douze données de fin de mois.

Changement méthodologique :

• Depuis 1986, les Etablissements de financement des ventes à crédit sont compris dans les données.

GERMANY

Large commercial banks

ALLEMAGNE

Grandes banques commerciales

Million DM	1983	1984	1985	1986	1987	1988	1989	1990	1991	1992	Millions de DM
INCOME STATEMENT											**COMPTE DE RESULTATS**
1. Interest income	22863	24389	24185	24338	24256	28090	35221	43650	50489	55719	1. Produits financiers
2. Interest expenses	13853	15294	14769	13370	14257	17400	23823	30612	34827	38594	2. Frais financiers
3. Net interest income	9010	9095	9416	10968	9999	10690	11398	13038	15662	17125	3. Produits financiers nets
4. Non-interest income (net)	3279	3392	4261	4169	4313	4901	5773	6997	6315	8204	4. Produits non financiers (nets)
5. Gross income	12289	12487	13677	15137	14312	15591	17171	20035	21977	25329	5. Résultat brut
6. Operating expenses	7858	8290	9063	10056	10442	11105	11571	12657	14795	16027	6. Frais d'exploitation
7. Net income	4431	4197	4614	5081	3870	4486	5600	7378	7182	9302	7. Résultat net
8. Provisions (net)	1998	1554	1095	1443	1452	517	1053	2708	2395	4423	8. Provisions (nettes)
9. Profit before tax	2433	2643	3519	3638	2418	3969	4547	4670	4787	4879	9. Bénéfices avant impôt
10. Income tax	1470	1576	2017	1987	1201	2245	2493	1915	2320	1999	10. Impôt
11. Profit after tax	963	1067	1502	1651	1217	1724	2054	2755	2467	2880	11. Bénéfices après impôt
12. Distributed profit	606	675	862	1114	1003	1037	1304	1962	1543	1586	12. Bénéfices distribués
13. Retained profit	357	392	640	537	214	687	750	793	924	1294	13. Bénéfices mis en réserve
Memoranda											*Pour mémoire*
14. *Staff costs*	*5509*	*5702*	*6104*	*6770*	*7012*	*7457*	*7702*	*8348*	*9671*	*10378*	14. *Frais de personnel*
15. *Provisions on loans*	*1980*	*1465*	*933*	*1296*	*1329*	*504*	*1035*	*2491*	*2327*	*4217*	15. *Provisions sur prêts*
16. *Provisions on securities (1)*	*..*	*..*	*..*	*..*	*..*	*..*	*..*	*..*	*..*	*..*	16. *Provisions sur titres (1)*
BALANCE SHEET											**BILAN**
Assets											**Actif**
17. Cash & balance with Central bank	11990	14215	15575	15771	17090	14265	17006	20034	22041	21456	17. Caisse & solde auprès de la Banque centrale
18. Interbank deposits	75274	88275	93352	101248	110062	126057	135759	155820	151688	173501	18. Dépôts interbancaires
19. Loans	166805	179551	191921	212505	227226	267545	296500	345721	405306	418642	19. Prêts
20. Securities	39366	43492	50246	55225	53877	55507	63955	74472	83023	92907	20. Valeurs mobilières
21. Other assets	7939	7312	6983	7391	7735	8133	8385	8254	8240	10760	21. Autres actifs
Liabilities											**Passif**
22. Capital & reserves	12166	13240	15839	18766	20761	22133	26944	31303	34258	38059	22. Capital et réserves
23. Borrowing from Central bank	10652	12984	15539	16388	13552	17319	23045	17203	24044	18426	23. Emprunts auprès de la Banque centrale
24. Interbank deposits	83431	88724	91277	99229	105502	123272	127905	151037	148965	175391	24. Dépôts interbancaires
25. Non-bank deposits	169307	189729	200721	217879	233581	264367	291839	343846	402067	423614	25. Dépôts non bancaires
26. Bonds	10392	11434	13948	16008	17005	17585	23021	26870	26312	28232	26. Obligations
27. Other liabilities	15426	16734	20753	23870	25589	26831	28851	34042	34652	33544	27. Autres engagements
Balance sheet total											**Total du bilan**
28. End-year total	301374	332845	358077	392140	415990	471507	521605	604301	670298	717266	28. En fin d'exercice
29. Average total	288832	306864	335269	365894	399553	446084	494426	563239	641255	694382	29. Moyen
Memoranda											*Pour mémoire*
30. *Short-term securities*	*12566*	*13119*	*12216*	*9151*	*7653*	*8334*	*8291*	*10071*	*14800*	*15548*	30. *Titres à court terme*
31. *Bonds*	*14039*	*16323*	*22016*	*24818*	*23050*	*24103*	*26290*	*25355*	*28915*	*33627*	31. *Obligations*
32. *Shares and participations*	*12761*	*14050*	*16014*	*21256*	*23174*	*23070*	*29374*	*39046*	*39308*	*43732*	32. *Actions et participations*
33. *Claims on non-residents*	*90535*	*108495*	*114577*	*138091*	*147374*	*183131*	*194585*	*233940*	*235265*	*257909*	33. *Créances sur des non résidents*
34. *Liabilities to non-residents*	*100111*	*119268*	*119745*	*124004*	*131661*	*163674*	*166807*	*197384*	*202878*	*232226*	34. *Engagements envers des non résidents*
SUPPLEMENTARY INFORMATION											**RENSEIGNEMENTS COMPLEMENTAIRES**
35. Number of institutions	6	6	6	6	6	6	6	6	4	4	35. Nombre d'institutions
36. Number of branches	3113	3119	3115	3118	3120	3108	3110	3105	3043	3036	36. Nombre de succursales
37. Number of employees (x 1000)	NA	NA	NA	NA	NA	NA	NA	NA	NA	NA	37. Nombre de salariés (x 1000)

71

GERMANY

Large commercial banks

ALLEMAGNE

Grandes banques commerciales

Per cent — *Pourcentage*

INCOME STATEMENT ANALYSIS — ANALYSE DU COMPTE DE RESULTATS

	1983	1984	1985	1986	1987	1988	1989	1990	1991	1992		
% of average balance sheet total												**% du total moyen du bilan**
38. Interest income	7.92	7.95	7.21	6.65	6.07	6.30	7.12	7.75	7.87	8.02	38.	Produits financiers
39. Interest expenses	4.80	4.98	4.41	3.65	3.57	3.90	4.82	5.43	5.43	5.56	39.	Frais financiers
40. Net interest income	3.12	2.96	2.81	3.00	2.50	2.40	2.31	2.31	2.44	2.47	40.	Produits financiers nets
41. Non-interest income (net)	1.14	1.11	1.27	1.14	1.08	1.10	1.17	1.24	0.98	1.18	41.	Produits non financiers (nets)
42. Gross income	4.25	4.07	4.08	4.14	3.58	3.50	3.47	3.56	3.43	3.65	42.	Résultat brut
43. Operating expenses	2.72	2.70	2.70	2.75	2.61	2.49	2.34	2.25	2.31	2.31	43.	Frais d'exploitation
44. Net income	1.53	1.37	1.38	1.39	0.97	1.01	1.13	1.31	1.12	1.34	44.	Résultat net
45. Provisions (net)	0.69	0.51	0.33	0.39	0.36	0.12	0.21	0.48	0.37	0.64	45.	Provisions (nettes)
46. Profit before tax	0.84	0.86	1.05	0.99	0.61	0.89	0.92	0.83	0.75	0.70	46.	Bénéfices avant impôt
47. Income tax	0.51	0.51	0.60	0.54	0.30	0.50	0.50	0.34	0.36	0.29	47.	Impôt
48. Profit after tax	0.33	0.35	0.45	0.45	0.30	0.39	0.42	0.49	0.38	0.41	48.	Bénéfices après impôt
49. Distributed profit	0.21	0.22	0.26	0.30	0.25	0.23	0.26	0.35	0.24	0.23	49.	Bénéfices distribués
50. Retained profit	0.12	0.13	0.19	0.15	0.05	0.15	0.15	0.14	0.14	0.19	50.	Bénéfices mis en réserve
51. Staff costs	1.91	1.86	1.82	1.85	1.75	1.67	1.56	1.48	1.51	1.49	51.	Frais de personnel
52. Provisions on loans	0.69	0.48	0.28	0.35	0.33	0.11	0.21	0.44	0.36	0.61	52.	Provisions sur prêts
53. Provisions on securities (1)	:	:	:	:	:	:	:	:	:	:	53.	Provisions sur titres (1)
% of gross income												**% du total du résultat brut**
54. Net interest income	73.32	72.84	68.85	72.46	69.86	68.57	66.38	65.08	71.27	67.61	54.	Produits financiers nets
55. Non-interest income (net)	26.68	27.16	31.15	27.54	30.14	31.43	33.62	34.92	28.73	32.39	55.	Produits non financiers (nets)
56. Operating expenses	63.94	66.39	66.26	66.43	72.96	71.23	67.39	63.17	67.32	63.28	56.	Frais d'exploitation
57. Net income	36.06	33.61	33.74	33.57	27.04	28.77	32.61	36.83	32.68	36.72	57.	Résultat net
58. Provisions (net)	16.26	12.44	8.01	9.53	10.15	3.32	6.13	13.52	10.90	17.46	58.	Provisions (nettes)
59. Profit before tax	19.80	21.17	25.73	24.03	16.89	25.46	26.48	23.31	21.78	19.26	59.	Bénéfices avant impôt
60. Income tax	11.96	12.62	14.75	13.13	8.39	14.40	14.52	9.56	10.56	7.89	60.	Impôt
61. Profit after tax	7.84	8.54	10.98	10.91	8.50	11.06	11.96	13.75	11.23	11.37	61.	Bénéfices après impôt
62. Staff costs	44.83	45.66	44.63	44.72	48.99	47.83	44.85	41.67	44.01	40.97	62.	Frais de personnel
% of net income												**% du total du résultat net**
63. Provisions (net)	45.09	37.03	23.73	28.40	37.52	11.52	18.80	36.70	33.35	47.55	63.	Provisions (nettes)
64. Profit before tax	54.91	62.97	76.27	71.60	62.48	88.48	81.20	63.30	66.65	52.45	64.	Bénéfices avant impôt
65. Income tax	33.18	37.55	43.71	39.11	31.03	50.04	44.52	25.96	32.30	21.49	65.	Impôt
66. Profit after tax	21.73	25.42	32.55	32.49	31.45	38.43	36.68	37.34	34.35	30.96	66.	Bénéfices après impôt

GERMANY

Large commercial banks

Per cent

BALANCE SHEET ANALYSIS

% of year-end balance sheet total

	1983	1984	1985	1986	1987	1988	1989	1990	1991	1992
Assets										
67. Cash & balance with Central bank	3.98	4.27	4.35	4.02	4.11	3.03	3.26	3.32	3.29	2.99
68. Interbank deposits	24.98	26.52	26.07	25.82	26.46	26.73	26.03	25.79	22.63	24.19
69. Loans	55.35	53.94	53.60	54.19	54.62	56.74	56.84	57.21	60.47	58.37
70. Securities	13.06	13.07	14.03	14.08	12.95	11.77	12.26	12.32	12.39	12.95
71. Other assets	2.63	2.20	1.95	1.88	1.86	1.72	1.61	1.37	1.23	1.50
Liabilities										
72. Capital & reserves	4.04	3.98	4.42	4.79	4.99	4.69	5.17	5.18	5.11	5.31
73. Borrowing from Central bank	3.53	3.90	4.34	4.18	3.26	3.67	4.42	2.85	3.59	2.57
74. Interbank deposits	27.68	26.66	25.49	25.30	25.36	26.14	24.52	24.99	22.22	24.45
75. Non-bank deposits	56.18	57.00	56.06	55.56	56.15	56.07	55.95	56.90	59.98	59.06
76. Bonds	3.45	3.44	3.90	4.08	4.09	3.73	4.41	4.45	3.93	3.94
77. Other liabilities	5.12	5.03	5.80	6.09	6.15	5.69	5.53	5.63	5.17	4.68
Memoranda										
78. Short-term securities	*4.17*	*3.94*	*3.41*	*2.33*	*1.84*	*1.77*	*1.59*	*1.67*	*2.21*	*2.17*
79. Bonds	*4.66*	*4.90*	*6.15*	*6.33*	*5.54*	*5.11*	*5.04*	*4.20*	*4.31*	*4.69*
80. Shares and participations	*4.23*	*4.22*	*4.47*	*5.42*	*5.57*	*4.89*	*5.63*	*6.46*	*5.86*	*6.10*
81. Claims on non-residents	*30.04*	*32.60*	*32.00*	*35.21*	*35.43*	*38.84*	*37.31*	*38.71*	*35.10*	*35.96*
82. Liabilities to non-residents	*33.22*	*35.83*	*33.44*	*31.62*	*31.65*	*34.71*	*31.98*	*32.66*	*30.27*	*32.38*

1. Included under "Provisions on loans" (item 15 or item 52).

Notes

• Large commercial banks are a sub-group of Commercial banks.

• Average balance sheet totals (item 29) are based on twelve end-month data.

ALLEMAGNE

Grandes banques commerciales

Pourcentage

ANALYSE DU BILAN

% du total du bilan en fin d'exercice

Actif
67. Caisse & solde auprès de la Banque centrale
68. Dépôts interbancaires
69. Prêts
70. Valeurs mobilières
71. Autres actifs

Passif
72. Capital et réserves
73. Emprunts auprès de la Banque centrale
74. Dépôts interbancaires
75. Dépôts non bancaires
76. Obligations
77. Autres engagements

Pour mémoire
78. Titres à court terme
79. Obligations
80. Actions et participations
81. Créances sur des non résidents
82. Engagements envers des non résidents

1. Inclus sous "Provisions sur prêts" (poste 15 ou poste 52).

Notes

• Les Grandes banques commerciales sont un sous-groupe des Banques commerciales.

• La moyenne du total des actifs/passifs (poste 29) est basée sur douze données de fin de mois.

GERMANY

Regional giro institutions

ALLEMAGNE

Organismes régionaux de compensation

Million DM / Millions de DM

	1983	1984	1985	1986	1987	1988	1989	1990	1991	1992	
INCOME STATEMENT											**COMPTE DE RESULTATS**
1. Interest income	36771	38271	38132	37898	38471	40388	46856	56817	67101	76780	1. Produits financiers
2. Interest expenses	32306	33652	33348	33068	33756	35646	42153	52078	61750	70142	2. Frais financiers
3. Net interest income	4465	4619	4784	4830	4715	4742	4703	4739	5351	6638	3. Produits financiers nets
4. Non-interest income (net)	1259	1118	1797	1389	1287	1188	1473	1349	1857	2006	4. Produits non financiers (nets)
5. Gross income	5724	5737	6581	6219	6002	5930	6176	6088	7208	8644	5. Résultat brut
6. Operating expenses	2265	2427	2576	2776	2919	3117	3308	3604	3873	5063	6. Frais d'exploitation
7. Net income	3459	3310	4005	3443	3083	2813	2868	2484	3335	3581	7. Résultat net
8. Provisions (net)	2389	2217	2788	2104	1839	1200	1122	1579	1899	1771	8. Provisions (nettes)
9. Profit before tax	1070	1093	1217	1339	1244	1613	1746	905	1436	1810	9. Bénéfices avant impôt
10. Income tax	693	738	796	880	747	1089	1016	433	766	889	10. Impôt
11. Profit after tax	377	355	421	459	497	524	730	472	670	921	11. Bénéfices après impôt
12. Distributed profit	237	219	283	321	350	359	374	336	327	434	12. Bénéfices distribués
13. Retained profit	140	136	138	138	147	165	356	136	343	487	13. Bénéfices mis en réserve
Memoranda											*Pour mémoire*
14. Staff costs	*1499*	*1616*	*1738*	*1842*	*1942*	*2069*	*2171*	*2393*	*2468*	*3220*	14. Frais de personnel
15. Provisions on loans	*2250*	*2156*	*2740*	*2005*	*1787*	*1174*	*1090*	*1551*	*1825*	*1697*	15. Provisions sur prêts
16. Provisions on securities (1)	*..*	*..*	*..*	*..*	*..*	*..*	*..*	*..*	*..*	*..*	16. Provisions sur titres (1)
BALANCE SHEET											**BILAN**
Assets											*Actif*
17. Cash & balance with Central bank	4871	4350	4543	4590	3708	4030	5325	7106	4334	5357	17. Caisse & solde auprès de la Banque centrale
18. Interbank deposits	125732	141016	154205	187446	218430	254734	286439	317729	329932	368961	18. Dépôts interbancaires
19. Loans	315685	321595	328885	333939	342577	349487	354110	382774	444196	523715	19. Prêts
20. Securities	50735	55469	59383	59305	60068	62549	69504	116932	124858	158334	20. Valeurs mobilières
21. Other assets	8289	9247	9215	9595	11052	12591	13529	14559	16378	20179	21. Autres actifs
Liabilities											*Passif*
22. Capital & reserves	11283	11741	12160	13341	13930	14624	16331	17442	20265	29846	22. Capital et réserves
23. Borrowing from Central bank	8970	9688	13920	7879	6816	21939	25183	32448	43979	31831	23. Emprunts auprès de la Banque centrale
24. Interbank deposits	136285	142568	141307	158442	171508	198227	213735	280076	305577	371072	24. Dépôts interbancaires
25. Non-bank deposits	92567	103655	112754	130238	149124	165298	178316	191566	211546	260784	25. Dépôts non bancaires
26. Bonds	242915	250456	260911	268873	279056	266228	277285	295797	312236	344492	26. Obligations
27. Other liabilities	13292	13569	15179	16102	15401	17075	18057	21771	26095	38521	27. Autres engagements
Balance sheet total											*Total du bilan*
28. End-year total	505312	531677	556231	594875	635835	683391	728907	839100	919698	1076546	28. En fin d'exercice
29. Average total	488702	503875	533905	573933	617561	655600	699495	774961	872439	1021846	29. Moyen
Memoranda											*Pour mémoire*
30. Short-term securities	*14611*	*14667*	*15398*	*12062*	*10605*	*7331*	*7514*	*40637*	*44877*	*42029*	30. Titres à court terme
31. Bonds	*30996*	*35445*	*37879*	*40633*	*42226*	*47644*	*52600*	*63689*	*65843*	*97520*	31. Obligations
32. Shares and participations	*5128*	*5357*	*6106*	*6610*	*7237*	*7574*	*9390*	*12606*	*14138*	*18785*	32. Actions et participations
33. Claims on non-residents	*74741*	*83481*	*94562*	*118012*	*130839*	*155053*	*184436*	*272157*	*222613*	*247934*	33. Créances sur des non résidents
34. Liabilities to non-residents	*51477*	*53272*	*46261*	*43867*	*50691*	*61614*	*61469*	*104877*	*87723*	*134346*	34. Engagements envers des non résidents
SUPPLEMENTARY INFORMATION											**RENSEIGNEMENTS COMPLEMENTAIRES**
35. Number of institutions	12	12	12	12	12	12	11	11	11	12	35. Nombre d'institutions
36. Number of branches	257	245	239	235	231	226	219	309	290	329	36. Nombre de succursales
37. Number of employees (x 1000)	NA	NA	NA	NA	NA	NA	NA	NA	NA	NA	37. Nombre de salariés (x 1000)

ALLEMAGNE

Regional giro institutions

Organismes régionaux de compensation

Per cent

Pourcentage

INCOME STATEMENT ANALYSIS

ANALYSE DU COMPTE DE RESULTATS

		1983	1984	1985	1986	1987	1988	1989	1990	1991	1992			
	% of average balance sheet total											**% du total moyen du bilan**		
38.	Interest income	7.52	7.60	7.14	6.60	6.23	6.16	6.70	7.33	7.69	7.51	Produits financiers	38.
39.	Interest expenses	6.61	6.68	6.25	5.76	5.47	5.44	6.03	6.72	7.08	6.86	Frais financiers	39.
40.	Net interest income	0.91	0.92	0.90	0.84	0.76	0.72	0.67	0.61	0.61	0.65	Produits financiers nets	40.
41.	Non-interest income (net)	0.26	0.22	0.34	0.24	0.21	0.18	0.21	0.17	0.21	0.20	Produits non financiers (nets)	41.
42.	Gross income	1.17	1.14	1.23	1.08	0.97	0.90	0.88	0.79	0.83	0.85	Résultat brut	42.
43.	Operating expenses	0.46	0.48	0.48	0.48	0.47	0.48	0.47	0.47	0.44	0.50	Frais d'exploitation	43.
44.	Net income	0.71	0.66	0.75	0.60	0.50	0.43	0.41	0.32	0.38	0.35	Résultat net	44.
45.	Provisions (net)	0.49	0.44	0.52	0.37	0.30	0.18	0.16	0.20	0.22	0.17	Provisions (nettes)	45.
46.	Profit before tax	0.22	0.22	0.23	0.23	0.20	0.25	0.25	0.12	0.16	0.18	Bénéfices avant impôt	46.
47.	Income tax	0.14	0.15	0.15	0.15	0.12	0.17	0.15	0.06	0.09	0.09	Impôt	47.
48.	Profit after tax	0.08	0.07	0.08	0.08	0.08	0.08	0.10	0.06	0.08	0.09	Bénéfices après impôt	48.
49.	Distributed profit	0.05	0.04	0.05	0.06	0.06	0.05	0.05	0.04	0.04	0.04	Bénéfices distribués	49.
50.	Retained profit	0.03	0.03	0.03	0.02	0.02	0.03	0.05	0.02	0.04	0.05	Bénéfices mis en réserve	50.
51.	Staff costs	0.31	0.32	0.33	0.32	0.31	0.32	0.31	0.31	0.28	0.32	Frais de personnel	51.
52.	Provisions on loans	0.46	0.43	0.51	0.35	0.29	0.18	0.16	0.20	0.21	0.17	Provisions sur prêts	52.
53.	Provisions on securities (1)	..	..	..	..	..	..	..	..	..	..	Provisions sur titres (1)	53.
	% of gross income											**% du total du résultat brut**		
54.	Net interest income	78.00	80.51	72.69	77.67	78.56	79.97	76.15	77.84	74.24	76.79	Produits financiers nets	54.
55.	Non-interest income (net)	22.00	19.49	27.31	22.33	21.44	20.03	23.85	22.16	25.76	23.21	Produits non financiers (nets)	55.
56.	Operating expenses	39.57	42.30	39.14	44.64	48.63	52.56	53.56	59.20	53.73	58.57	Frais d'exploitation	56.
57.	Net income	60.43	57.70	60.86	55.36	51.37	47.44	46.44	40.80	46.27	41.43	Résultat net	57.
58.	Provisions (net)	41.74	38.64	42.36	33.83	30.64	20.24	18.17	25.94	26.35	20.49	Provisions (nettes)	58.
59.	Profit before tax	18.69	19.05	18.49	21.53	20.73	27.20	28.27	14.87	19.92	20.94	Bénéfices avant impôt	59.
60.	Income tax	12.11	12.86	12.10	14.15	12.45	18.36	16.45	7.11	10.63	10.28	Impôt	60.
61.	Profit after tax	6.59	6.19	6.40	7.38	8.28	8.84	11.82	7.75	9.30	10.65	Bénéfices après impôt	61.
62.	Staff costs	26.19	28.17	26.41	29.62	32.36	34.89	35.15	39.31	34.24	37.25	Frais de personnel	62.
	% of net income											**% du total du résultat net**		
63.	Provisions (net)	69.07	66.98	69.61	61.11	59.65	42.66	39.12	63.57	56.94	49.46	Provisions (nettes)	63.
64.	Profit before tax	30.93	33.02	30.39	38.89	40.35	57.34	60.88	36.43	43.06	50.54	Bénéfices avant impôt	64.
65.	Income tax	20.03	22.30	19.88	25.56	24.23	38.71	35.43	17.43	22.97	24.83	Impôt	65.
66.	Profit after tax	10.90	10.73	10.51	13.33	16.12	18.63	25.45	19.00	20.09	25.72	Bénéfices après impôt	66.

GERMANY

Regional giro institutions

ALLEMAGNE

Organismes régionaux de compensation

Per cent	1983	1984	1985	1986	1987	1988	1989	1990	1991	1992	Pourcentage
BALANCE SHEET ANALYSIS											**ANALYSE DU BILAN**
% of year-end balance sheet total											**% du total du bilan en fin d'exercice**
Assets											**Actif**
67. Cash & balance with Central bank	0.96	0.82	0.82	0.77	0.58	0.59	0.73	0.85	0.47	0.50	67. Caisse & solde auprès de la Banque centrale
68. Interbank deposits	24.88	26.52	27.72	31.51	34.35	37.28	39.30	37.87	35.87	34.27	68. Dépôts interbancaires
69. Loans	62.47	60.49	59.13	56.14	53.88	51.14	48.58	45.62	48.30	48.65	69. Prêts
70. Securities	10.04	10.43	10.68	9.97	9.45	9.15	9.54	13.94	13.58	14.71	70. Valeurs mobilières
71. Other assets	1.64	1.74	1.66	1.61	1.74	1.84	1.86	1.74	1.78	1.87	71. Autres actifs
Liabilities											**Passif**
72. Capital & reserves	2.23	2.21	2.19	2.24	2.19	2.14	2.24	2.08	2.20	2.77	72. Capital et réserves
73. Borrowing from Central bank	1.78	1.82	2.50	1.32	1.07	3.21	3.45	3.87	4.78	2.96	73. Emprunts auprès de la Banque centrale
74. Interbank deposits	26.97	26.81	25.40	26.63	26.97	29.01	29.32	33.38	33.23	34.47	74. Dépôts interbancaires
75. Non-bank deposits	18.32	19.50	20.27	21.89	23.45	24.19	24.46	22.83	23.00	24.22	75. Dépôts non bancaires
76. Bonds	48.07	47.11	46.91	45.20	43.89	38.96	38.04	35.25	33.95	32.00	76. Obligations
77. Other liabilities	2.63	2.55	2.73	2.71	2.42	2.50	2.48	2.59	2.84	3.58	77. Autres engagements
Memoranda											***Pour mémoire***
78. Short-term securities	*2.89*	*2.76*	*2.77*	*2.03*	*1.67*	*1.07*	*1.03*	*4.84*	*4.88*	*3.90*	*78. Titres à court terme*
79. Bonds	*6.13*	*6.67*	*6.81*	*6.83*	*6.64*	*6.97*	*7.22*	*7.59*	*7.16*	*9.06*	*79. Obligations*
80. Shares and participations	*1.01*	*1.01*	*1.10*	*1.11*	*1.14*	*1.11*	*1.29*	*1.50*	*1.54*	*1.74*	*80. Actions et participations*
81. Claims on non-residents	*14.79*	*15.70*	*17.00*	*19.84*	*20.58*	*22.69*	*25.30*	*32.43*	*24.21*	*23.03*	*81. Créances sur des non résidents*
82. Liabilities to non-residents	*10.19*	*10.02*	*8.32*	*7.37*	*7.97*	*9.02*	*8.43*	*12.50*	*9.54*	*12.48*	*82. Engagements envers des non résidents*

1. Included under "Provisions on loans" (item 15 or item 52).

Notes

• Average balance sheet totals (item 29) are based on twelve end-month data.

1. Inclus sous "Provisions sur prêts" (poste 15 ou poste 52).

Notes

• La moyenne du total des actifs/passifs (poste 29) est basée sur douze données de fin de mois.

GERMANY

Savings banks

Million DM

ALLEMAGNE

Caisses d'épargne

Millions de DM

		1983	1984	1985	1986	1987	1988	1989	1990	1991	1992	
INCOME STATEMENT												**COMPTE DE RESULTATS**
1.	Interest income	47262	49295	50911	50338	50450	51762	57466	67561	78362	85138	1. Produits financiers
2.	Interest expenses	25289	27019	28055	26984	26864	27319	33152	42593	50204	55437	2. Frais financiers
3.	Net interest income	21993	22276	22856	23354	23586	24443	24314	24968	28158	29701	3. Produits financiers nets
4.	Non-interest income (net)	2292	2425	2390	2588	2728	1837	4097	5387	5633	6164	4. Produits non financiers (nets)
5.	Gross income	24285	24701	25246	25942	26314	26280	28411	30355	33791	35865	5. Résultat brut
6.	Operating expenses	13392	14054	14946	15881	16876	17680	18409	19731	21782	22991	6. Frais d'exploitation
7.	Net income	10893	10647	10300	10061	9438	8600	10002	10624	12009	12874	7. Résultat net
8.	Provisions (net)	3475	3057	3202	3160	3216	2425	5859	5681	3573	3467	8. Provisions (nettes)
9.	Profit before tax	7418	7590	7098	6901	6222	6175	4143	4943	8436	9407	9. Bénéfices avant impôt
10.	Income tax	5196	5256	4900	4762	4224	4095	2466	3133	5612	6475	10. Impôt
11.	Profit after tax	2222	2334	2198	2139	1998	2080	1677	1810	2824	2932	11. Bénéfices après impôt
12.	Distributed profit	1316	1397	1379	1377	1317	1345	1159	1240	1614	1726	12. Bénéfices distribués
13.	Retained profit	906	937	819	762	681	735	518	570	1210	1206	13. Bénéfices mis en réserve
Memoranda												**Pour mémoire**
14.	Staff costs	8830	9152	9677	10283	11045	11542	11864	12776	14231	15040	14. Frais de personnel
15.	Provisions on loans	3470	3038	3181	3142	3205	2420	5850	5671	3550	3446	15. Provisions sur prêts
16.	Provisions on securities (1)	..	..	..	..	..	..	..	..	..	..	16. Provisions sur titres (1)
BALANCE SHEET												**BILAN**
Assets												**Actif**
17.	Cash & balance with Central bank	20751	21641	21726	22576	25753	27440	29921	30259	29855	33908	17. Caisse & solde auprès de la Banque centrale
18.	Interbank deposits	46771	55310	59931	73203	70015	76311	95999	107769	112200	92305	18. Dépôts interbancaires
19.	Loans	419180	446785	466780	482066	501094	528417	561165	595639	652187	685475	19. Prêts
20.	Securities	122534	128945	141064	160719	186938	203826	200023	213906	220649	230666	20. Valeurs mobilières
21.	Other assets	23952	26056	27331	27950	28136	28016	28700	31408	36680	32972	21. Autres actifs
Liabilities												**Passif**
22.	Capital & reserves	22209	24332	26540	28541	30564	32526	34655	36411	38900	40977	22. Capital et réserves
23.	Borrowing from Central bank	17601	19828	19853	17492	15744	27825	38355	42747	48466	38075	23. Emprunts auprès de la Banque centrale
24.	Interbank deposits	56650	63892	68608	77549	86147	91503	94993	100577	110026	118366	24. Dépôts interbancaires
25.	Non-bank deposits	508843	540313	569248	606075	636267	660439	684637	721904	760428	775360	25. Dépôts non bancaires
26.	Bonds	2330	3051	4000	6783	11589	18246	28102	40537	52476	58781	26. Obligations
27.	Other liabilities	25555	27321	28583	30074	31625	33471	35066	36805	41275	43767	27. Autres engagements
Balance sheet total												**Total du bilan**
28.	End-year total	633188	678737	716832	766514	811936	864010	915808	978981	1051571	1075326	28. En fin d'exercice
29.	Average total	606704	645764	689295	733290	783133	831211	875042	934259	999930	1029488	29. Moyen
Memoranda												**Pour mémoire**
30.	Short-term securities	14947	12649	13683	17580	20792	18534	16671	20248	23108	22241	30. Titres à court terme
31.	Bonds	104015	112319	122644	137562	159219	177850	174336	181083	180251	185685	31. Obligations
32.	Shares and participations	3572	3977	4737	5577	6927	7442	9016	12575	17290	22740	32. Actions et participations
33.	Claims on non-residents	2747	3413	4253	7521	8416	11326	21563	27051	24154	17581	33. Créances sur des non résidents
34.	Liabilities to non-residents	3712	4722	5097	5116	5863	6864	7637	12385	7891	11002	34. Engagements envers des non résidents
SUPPLEMENTARY INFORMATION												**RENSEIGNEMENTS COMPLEMENTAIRES**
35.	Number of institutions	592	591	590	589	586	585	583	575	558	542	35. Nombre d'institutions
36.	Number of branches	17076	17131	17204	17248	17307	17355	17359	17212	17033	16923	36. Nombre de succursales
37.	Number of employees (x 1000)	NA	NA	NA	NA	NA	NA	NA	NA	NA	NA	37. Nombre de salariés (x 1000)

GERMANY

Savings banks

ALLEMAGNE

Caisses d'épargne

Per cent / *Pourcentage*

INCOME STATEMENT ANALYSIS / **ANALYSE DU COMPTE DE RESULTATS**

	1983	1984	1985	1986	1987	1988	1989	1990	1991	1992		
% of average balance sheet total												**% du total moyen du bilan**
38. Interest income	7.79	7.63	7.39	6.86	6.44	6.23	6.57	7.23	7.84	8.27	38.	Produits financiers
39. Interest expenses	4.16	4.18	4.07	3.68	3.43	3.29	3.79	4.56	5.02	5.38	39.	Frais financiers
40. Net interest income	3.62	3.45	3.32	3.18	3.01	2.94	2.78	2.67	2.82	2.89	40.	Produits financiers nets
41. Non-interest income (net)	0.38	0.38	0.35	0.35	0.35	0.22	0.47	0.58	0.56	0.60	41.	Produits non financiers (nets)
42. Gross income	4.00	3.83	3.66	3.54	3.36	3.16	3.25	3.25	3.38	3.48	42.	Résultat brut
43. Operating expenses	2.21	2.18	2.17	2.17	2.15	2.13	2.10	2.11	2.18	2.23	43.	Frais d'exploitation
44. Net income	1.80	1.65	1.49	1.37	1.21	1.03	1.14	1.14	1.20	1.25	44.	Résultat net
45. Provisions (net)	0.57	0.47	0.46	0.43	0.41	0.29	0.67	0.61	0.36	0.34	45.	Provisions (nettes)
46. Profit before tax	1.22	1.18	1.03	0.94	0.79	0.74	0.47	0.53	0.84	0.91	46.	Bénéfices avant impôt
47. Income tax	0.86	0.81	0.71	0.65	0.54	0.49	0.28	0.34	0.56	0.63	47.	Impôt
48. Profit after tax	0.37	0.36	0.32	0.29	0.26	0.25	0.19	0.19	0.28	0.28	48.	Bénéfices après impôt
49. Distributed profit	0.22	0.22	0.20	0.19	0.17	0.16	0.13	0.13	0.16	0.17	49.	Bénéfices distribués
50. Retained profit	0.15	0.15	0.12	0.10	0.09	0.09	0.06	0.06	0.12	0.12	50.	Bénéfices mis en réserve
51. Staff costs	1.46	1.42	1.40	1.40	1.41	1.39	1.36	1.37	1.42	1.46	51.	Frais de personnel
52. Provisions on loans	0.57	0.47	0.46	0.43	0.41	0.29	0.67	0.61	0.36	0.33	52.	Provisions sur prêts
53. Provisions on securities (1)	..	..	..	..	..	..	..	..	..	..	53.	Provisions sur titres (1)
% of gross income												**% du total du résultat brut**
54. Net interest income	90.56	90.18	90.53	90.02	89.63	93.01	85.58	82.25	83.33	82.81	54.	Produits financiers nets
55. Non-interest income (net)	9.44	9.82	9.47	9.98	10.37	6.99	14.42	17.75	16.67	17.19	55.	Produits non financiers (nets)
56. Operating expenses	55.15	56.90	59.20	61.22	64.13	67.28	64.80	65.00	64.46	64.10	56.	Frais d'exploitation
57. Net income	44.85	43.10	40.80	38.78	35.87	32.72	35.20	35.00	35.54	35.90	57.	Résultat net
58. Provisions (net)	14.31	12.38	12.68	12.18	12.22	9.23	20.62	18.72	10.57	9.67	58.	Provisions (nettes)
59. Profit before tax	30.55	30.73	28.12	26.60	23.65	23.50	14.58	16.28	24.97	26.23	59.	Bénéfices avant impôt
60. Income tax	21.40	21.28	19.41	18.36	16.05	15.58	8.68	10.32	16.61	18.05	60.	Impôt
61. Profit after tax	9.15	9.45	8.71	8.25	7.59	7.91	5.90	5.96	8.36	8.18	61.	Bénéfices après impôt
62. Staff costs	36.36	37.05	38.33	39.64	41.97	43.92	41.76	42.09	42.11	41.94	62.	Frais de personnel
% of net income												**% du total du résultat net**
63. Provisions (net)	31.90	28.71	31.09	31.41	34.08	28.20	58.58	53.47	29.75	26.93	63.	Provisions (nettes)
64. Profit before tax	68.10	71.29	68.91	68.59	65.92	71.80	41.42	46.53	70.25	73.07	64.	Bénéfices avant impôt
65. Income tax	47.70	49.37	47.57	47.33	44.76	47.62	24.66	29.49	46.73	50.30	65.	Impôt
66. Profit after tax	20.40	21.92	21.34	21.26	21.17	24.19	16.77	17.04	23.52	22.77	66.	Bénéfices après impôt

GERMANY

Savings banks

Per cent

BALANCE SHEET ANALYSIS

% of year-end balance sheet total

ALLEMAGNE

Caisses d'épargne

Pourcentage

ANALYSE DU BILAN

% du total du bilan en fin d'exercice

	1983	1984	1985	1986	1987	1988	1989	1990	1991	1992	
Assets											**Actif**
67. Cash & balance with Central bank	3.28	3.19	3.03	2.95	3.17	3.18	3.27	3.09	2.84	3.15	67. Caisse & solde auprès de la Banque centrale
68. Interbank deposits	7.39	8.15	8.36	9.55	8.62	8.83	10.48	11.01	10.67	8.58	68. Dépôts interbancaires
69. Loans	66.20	65.83	65.12	62.89	61.72	61.16	61.28	60.84	62.02	63.75	69. Prêts
70. Securities	19.35	19.00	19.68	20.97	23.02	23.59	21.84	21.85	20.98	21.45	70. Valeurs mobilières
71. Other assets	3.78	3.84	3.81	3.65	3.47	3.24	3.13	3.21	3.49	3.07	71. Autres actifs
Liabilities											**Passif**
72. Capital & reserves	3.51	3.58	3.70	3.72	3.76	3.76	3.78	3.72	3.70	3.81	72. Capital et réserves
73. Borrowing from Central bank	2.78	2.92	2.77	2.28	1.94	3.22	4.19	4.37	4.61	3.54	73. Emprunts auprès de la Banque centrale
74. Interbank deposits	8.95	9.41	9.57	10.12	10.61	10.59	10.37	10.27	10.46	11.01	74. Dépôts interbancaires
75. Non-bank deposits	80.36	79.61	79.41	79.07	78.36	76.44	74.76	73.74	72.31	72.10	75. Dépôts non bancaires
76. Bonds	0.37	0.45	0.56	0.88	1.43	2.11	3.07	4.14	4.99	5.47	76. Obligations
77. Other liabilities	4.04	4.03	3.99	3.92	3.90	3.87	3.83	3.76	3.93	4.07	77. Autres engagements
Memoranda											*Pour mémoire*
78. Short-term securities	2.36	1.86	1.91	2.29	2.56	2.15	1.82	2.07	2.20	2.07	78. Titres à court terme
79. Bonds	16.43	16.55	17.11	17.95	19.61	20.58	19.04	18.50	17.14	17.27	79. Obligations
80. Shares and participations	0.56	0.59	0.66	0.73	0.85	0.86	0.98	1.28	1.64	2.11	80. Actions et participations
81. Claims on non-residents	0.43	0.50	0.59	0.98	1.04	1.31	2.35	2.76	2.30	1.63	81. Créances sur des non résidents
82. Liabilities to non-residents	0.59	0.70	0.71	0.67	0.72	0.79	0.83	1.27	0.75	1.02	82. Engagements envers des non résidents

1. Included under "Provisions on loans" (item 15 or item 52).

1. Inclus sous "Provisions sur prêts" (poste 15 ou poste 52).

Notes

• Average balance sheet totals (item 29) are based on twelve end-month data.

Notes

• La moyenne du total des actifs/passifs (poste 29) est basée sur douze données de fin de mois.

GERMANY

Regional institutions of co-operative banks

Institutions régionales des banques mutualistes

Million DM / Millions de DM	1983	1984	1985	1986	1987	1988	1989	1990	1991	1992	
INCOME STATEMENT											**COMPTE DE RESULTATS**
1. Interest income	9228	9644	9675	9036	9216	9630	11113	14172	15773	16099	1. Produits financiers
2. Interest expenses	7375	7940	8098	7329	7413	7898	9891	12999	14684	14635	2. Frais financiers
3. Net interest income	1853	1704	1577	1707	1803	1732	1222	1173	1089	1464	3. Produits financiers nets
4. Non-interest income (net)	311	341	1160	578	433	358	938	1307	1271	585	4. Produits non financiers (nets)
5. Gross income	2164	2045	2737	2285	2236	2090	2160	2480	2360	2049	5. Résultat brut
6. Operating expenses	773	796	906	1032	1053	1029	1055	1175	1222	1344	6. Frais d'exploitation
7. Net income	1391	1249	1831	1253	1183	1061	1105	1305	1138	705	7. Résultat net
8. Provisions (net)	417	245	1206	290	245	47	623	844	728	244	8. Provisions (nettes)
9. Profit before tax	974	1004	625	963	938	1014	482	461	410	461	9. Bénéfices avant impôt
10. Income tax	532	537	506	529	542	585	93	177	228	261	10. Impôt
11. Profit after tax	442	467	119	434	396	429	389	284	182	200	11. Bénéfices après impôt
12. Distributed profit	185	226	148	276	200	219	559	219	119	78	12. Bénéfices distribués
13. Retained profit	257	241	-29	158	196	210	-170	65	63	122	13. Bénéfices mis en réserve
Memoranda											**Pour mémoire**
14. Staff costs	447	471	524	536	572	554	577	647	660	723	14. Frais de personnel
15. Provisions on loans	414	241	1198	283	234	34	623	725	670	189	15. Provisions sur prêts
16. Provisions on securities (1)	..	..	..	..	..	..	..	..	..	..	16. Provisions sur titres (1)
BALANCE SHEET											**BILAN**
Assets											**Actif**
17. Cash & balance with Central bank	2335	3456	3029	3319	2351	2389	2739	2247	2925	2102	17. Caisse & solde auprès de la Banque centrale
18. Interbank deposits	70397	74892	78937	90268	103468	106397	102158	107746	102957	106576	18. Dépôts interbancaires
19. Loans	24903	27530	29305	28722	31166	35220	36028	38412	51773	58011	19. Prêts
20. Securities	26789	28967	32501	31844	33460	35375	38995	40883	38670	39914	20. Valeurs mobilières
21. Other assets	2513	2206	2904	2707	2596	2167	4217	4258	14284	3980	21. Autres actifs
Liabilities											**Passif**
22. Capital & reserves	3796	4561	5394	5556	6013	6218	6725	6446	7180	7890	22. Capital et réserves
23. Borrowing from Central bank	6962	6689	7069	4842	4802	10001	11529	11993	15690	10254	23. Emprunts auprès de la Banque centrale
24. Interbank deposits	87862	98453	106247	116949	129249	131965	130758	139772	145210	148468	24. Dépôts interbancaires
25. Non-bank deposits	12472	13002	12603	12734	12874	12595	12563	14712	17599	19028	25. Dépôts non bancaires
26. Bonds	13447	11694	12477	13676	16677	16654	18525	15454	18346	19042	26. Obligations
27. Other liabilities	2398	2652	2886	3103	3426	4115	4037	5169	6584	5901	27. Autres engagements
Balance sheet total											**Total du bilan**
28. End-year total	126937	137051	146676	156860	173041	181548	184137	193546	210609	210583	28. En fin d'exercice
29. Average total	118133	128336	136874	144403	159944	171195	173658	178846	194435	188434	29. Moyen
Memoranda											**Pour mémoire**
30. Short-term securities	8193	8003	9033	7351	7352	3575	2446	7982	10499	11801	30. Titres à court terme
31. Bonds	15541	17402	19406	19908	20656	25849	30436	27049	21166	20777	31. Obligations
32. Shares and participations	3055	3562	4062	4585	5452	5951	6113	5852	7005	7336	32. Actions et participations
33. Claims on non-residents	7105	7775	12952	19246	25807	25893	31136	42780	34701	27719	33. Créances sur des non résidents
34. Liabilities to non-residents	2106	2923	3979	3128	3150	3530	3745	10054	7674	7998	34. Engagements envers des non résidents
SUPPLEMENTARY INFORMATION											**RENSEIGNEMENTS COMPLEMENTAIRES**
35. Number of institutions	9	9	9	8	7	6	6	4	4	4	35. Nombre d'institutions
36. Number of branches	45	46	46	48	36	32	32	31	29	31	36. Nombre de succursales
37. Number of employees (x 1000)	NA	NA	NA	NA	NA	NA	NA	NA	NA	NA	37. Nombre de salariés (x 1000)

GERMANY

Regional institutions of co-operative banks

ALLEMAGNE

Institutions régionales des banques mutualistes

Per cent — *Pourcentage*

	1983	1984	1985	1986	1987	1988	1989	1990	1991	1992		
INCOME STATEMENT ANALYSIS												**ANALYSE DU COMPTE DE RESULTATS**
% of average balance sheet total												**% du total moyen du bilan**
38. Interest income	7.81	7.51	7.07	6.26	5.76	5.63	6.40	7.92	8.11	8.54	38.	Produits financiers
39. Interest expenses	6.24	6.19	5.92	5.08	4.63	4.61	5.70	7.27	7.55	7.77	39.	Frais financiers
40. Net interest income	1.57	1.33	1.15	1.18	1.13	1.01	0.70	0.66	0.56	0.78	40.	Produits financiers nets
41. Non-interest income (net)	0.26	0.27	0.85	0.40	0.27	0.21	0.54	0.73	0.65	0.31	41.	Produits non financiers (nets)
42. Gross income	1.83	1.59	2.00	1.58	1.40	1.22	1.24	1.39	1.21	1.09	42.	Résultat brut
43. Operating expenses	0.65	0.62	0.66	0.71	0.66	0.60	0.61	0.66	0.63	0.71	43.	Frais d'exploitation
44. Net income	1.18	0.97	1.34	0.87	0.74	0.62	0.64	0.73	0.59	0.37	44.	Résultat net
45. Provisions (net)	0.35	0.19	0.88	0.20	0.15	0.03	0.36	0.47	0.37	0.13	45.	Provisions (nettes)
46. Profit before tax	0.82	0.78	0.46	0.67	0.59	0.59	0.28	0.26	0.21	0.24	46.	Bénéfices avant impôt
47. Income tax	0.45	0.42	0.37	0.37	0.34	0.34	0.05	0.10	0.12	0.14	47.	Impôt
48. Profit after tax	0.37	0.36	0.09	0.30	0.25	0.25	0.22	0.16	0.09	0.11	48.	Bénéfices après impôt
49. Distributed profit	0.16	0.18	0.11	0.19	0.13	0.13	0.32	0.12	0.06	0.04	49.	Bénéfices distribués
50. Retained profit	0.22	0.19	-0.02	0.11	0.12	0.12	-0.10	0.04	0.03	0.06	50.	Bénéfices mis en réserve
51. Staff costs	0.38	0.37	0.38	0.37	0.36	0.32	0.33	0.36	0.34	0.38	51.	Frais de personnel
52. Provisions on loans	0.35	0.19	0.88	0.20	0.15	0.02	0.36	0.41	0.34	0.10	52.	Provisions sur prêts
53. Provisions on securities (1)	..	..	..	..	..	..	..	..	..	..	53.	Provisions sur titres (1)
% of gross income												**% du total du résultat brut**
54. Net interest income	85.63	83.33	57.62	74.70	80.64	82.87	56.57	47.30	46.14	71.45	54.	Produits financiers nets
55. Non-interest income (net)	14.37	16.67	42.38	25.30	19.36	17.13	43.43	52.70	53.86	28.55	55.	Produits non financiers (nets)
56. Operating expenses	35.72	38.92	33.10	45.16	47.09	49.23	48.84	47.38	51.78	65.59	56.	Frais d'exploitation
57. Net income	64.28	61.08	66.90	54.84	52.91	50.77	51.16	52.62	48.22	34.41	57.	Résultat net
58. Provisions (net)	19.27	11.98	44.06	12.69	10.96	2.25	28.84	34.03	30.85	11.91	58.	Provisions (nettes)
59. Profit before tax	45.01	49.10	22.84	42.14	41.95	48.52	22.31	18.59	17.37	22.50	59.	Bénéfices avant impôt
60. Income tax	24.58	26.26	18.49	23.15	24.24	27.99	4.31	7.14	9.66	12.74	60.	Impôt
61. Profit after tax	20.43	22.84	4.35	18.99	17.71	20.53	18.01	11.45	7.71	9.76	61.	Bénéfices après impôt
62. Staff costs	20.66	23.03	19.15	23.46	25.58	26.51	26.71	26.09	27.97	35.29	62.	Frais de personnel
% of net income												**% du total du résultat net**
63. Provisions (net)	29.98	19.62	65.87	23.14	20.71	4.43	56.38	64.67	63.97	34.61	63.	Provisions (nettes)
64. Profit before tax	70.02	80.38	34.13	76.86	79.29	95.57	43.62	35.33	36.03	65.39	64.	Bénéfices avant impôt
65. Income tax	38.25	42.99	27.64	42.22	45.82	55.14	8.42	13.56	20.04	37.02	65.	Impôt
66. Profit after tax	31.78	37.39	6.50	34.64	33.47	40.43	35.20	21.76	15.99	28.37	66.	Bénéfices après impôt

GERMANY

Regional institutions of co-operative banks

ALLEMAGNE

Institutions régionales des banques mutualistes

		1983	1984	1985	1986	1987	1988	1989	1990	1991	1992		
Per cent													*Pourcentage*
BALANCE SHEET ANALYSIS													**ANALYSE DU BILAN**
% of year-end balance sheet total													**% du total du bilan en fin d'exercice**
Assets													**Actif**
67.	Cash & balance with Central bank	1.84	2.52	2.07	2.12	1.36	1.32	1.49	1.16	1.39	1.00	67.	Caisse & solde auprès de la Banque centrale
68.	Interbank deposits	55.46	54.65	53.82	57.55	59.79	58.61	55.48	55.67	48.89	50.61	68.	Dépôts interbancaires
69.	Loans	19.62	20.09	19.98	18.31	18.01	19.40	19.57	19.85	24.58	27.55	69.	Prêts
70.	Securities	21.10	21.14	22.16	20.30	19.34	19.49	21.18	21.12	18.36	18.95	70.	Valeurs mobilières
71.	Other assets	1.98	1.61	1.98	1.73	1.50	1.19	2.29	2.20	6.78	1.89	71.	Autres actifs
Liabilities													**Passif**
72.	Capital & reserves	2.99	3.33	3.68	3.54	3.47	3.42	3.65	3.33	3.41	3.75	72.	Capital et réserves
73.	Borrowing from Central bank	5.48	4.88	4.82	3.09	2.78	5.51	6.26	6.20	7.45	4.87	73.	Emprunts auprès de la Banque centrale
74.	Interbank deposits	69.22	71.84	72.44	74.56	74.69	72.69	71.01	72.22	68.95	70.50	74.	Dépôts interbancaires
75.	Non-bank deposits	9.83	9.49	8.59	8.12	7.44	6.94	6.82	7.60	8.36	9.04	75.	Dépôts non bancaires
76.	Bonds	10.59	8.53	8.51	8.72	9.64	9.17	10.06	7.98	8.71	9.04	76.	Obligations
77.	Other liabilities	1.89	1.94	1.97	1.98	1.98	2.27	2.19	2.67	3.13	2.80	77.	Autres engagements
Memoranda													**Pour mémoire**
78.	*Short-term securities*	*6.45*	*5.84*	*6.16*	*4.69*	*4.25*	*1.97*	*1.33*	*4.12*	*4.99*	*5.60*	78.	*Titres à court terme*
79.	*Bonds*	*12.24*	*12.70*	*13.23*	*12.69*	*11.94*	*14.24*	*16.53*	*13.98*	*10.05*	*9.87*	79.	*Obligations*
80.	*Shares and participations*	*2.41*	*2.60*	*2.77*	*2.92*	*3.15*	*3.28*	*3.32*	*3.02*	*3.33*	*3.48*	80.	*Actions et participations*
81.	*Claims on non-residents*	*5.60*	*5.67*	*8.83*	*12.27*	*14.91*	*14.26*	*16.91*	*22.10*	*16.48*	*13.16*	81.	*Créances sur des non résidents*
82.	*Liabilities to non-residents*	*1.66*	*2.13*	*2.71*	*1.99*	*1.82*	*1.94*	*2.03*	*5.19*	*3.64*	*3.80*	82.	*Engagements envers des non résidents*

1. Included under "Provisions on loans" (item 15 or item 52).

1. Inclus sous "Provisions sur prêts" (poste 15 ou poste 52).

Notes

- Average balance sheet totals (item 29) are based on twelve end-month data.

Notes

- La moyenne du total des actifs/passifs (poste 29) est basée sur douze données de fin de mois.

82

GERMANY
Co-operative banks

ALLEMAGNE
Banques mutualistes

Million DM / *Millions de DM*

	1983	1984	1985	1986	1987	1988	1989	1990	1991	1992	
INCOME STATEMENT											**COMPTE DE RESULTATS**
1. Interest income	24939	26180	29893	29179	28961	29323	33387	40361	46925	53748	1. Produits financiers
2. Interest expenses	13434	14677	16852	15878	15268	15278	18638	24620	29438	34507	2. Frais financiers
3. Net interest income	11505	11503	13041	13301	13693	14045	14749	15741	17487	19241	3. Produits financiers nets
4. Non-interest income (net)	1896	2742	2617	2908	2974	2776	4134	4270	4203	4760	4. Produits non financiers (nets)
5. Gross income	13401	14245	15658	16209	16667	16821	18883	20011	21690	24001	5. Résultat brut
6. Operating expenses	8643	9401	11400	11930	12352	12635	12976	14050	15068	16557	6. Frais d'exploitation
7. Net income	4758	4844	4258	4279	4315	4186	5907	5961	6622	7444	7. Résultat net
8. Provisions (net)	1464	1932	1385	1416	1305	762	3223	2375	1491	1530	8. Provisions (nettes)
9. Profit before tax	3294	2912	2873	2863	3010	3424	2684	3586	5131	5914	9. Bénéfices avant impôt
10. Income tax	2268	1968	1957	1943	2066	2357	1706	2231	3096	3820	10. Impôt
11. Profit after tax	1026	944	916	920	944	1067	978	1355	2035	2094	11. Bénéfices après impôt
12. Distributed profit	715	673	718	760	775	856	830	992	1292	1390	12. Bénéfices distribués
13. Retained profit	311	271	198	160	169	211	148	363	743	704	13. Bénéfices mis en réserve
Memoranda											*Pour mémoire*
14. *Staff costs*	*5398*	*5790*	*6975*	*7331*	*7636*	*7876*	*8100*	*8807*	*9428*	*10357*	14. *Frais de personnel*
15. *Provisions on loans*	*1459*	*1904*	*1359*	*1408*	*1295*	*755*	*3216*	*2365*	*1478*	*1522*	15. *Provisions sur prêts*
16. *Provisions on securities (1)*	*..*	*..*	*..*	*..*	*..*	*..*	*..*	*..*	*..*	*..*	16. *Provisions sur titres (1)*
BALANCE SHEET											**BILAN**
Assets											**Actif**
17. Cash & balance with Central bank	9888	10646	11442	11552	12726	14152	15830	17170	18317	21756	17. Caisse & solde auprès de la Banque centrale
18. Interbank deposits	45950	49805	61694	77475	80670	80874	87254	98019	101699	99288	18. Dépôts interbancaires
19. Loans	215004	229320	262650	265473	272516	286326	308096	328660	360749	395299	19. Prêts
20. Securities	49128	52298	65318	72516	84681	92621	94108	99721	105973	119457	20. Valeurs mobilières
21. Other assets	12693	14369	17957	18299	17776	17669	17907	19449	20833	21221	21. Autres actifs
Liabilities											**Passif**
22. Capital & reserves	11994	13149	16096	17279	18353	19353	20352	21223	23008	26460	22. Capital et réserves
23. Borrowing from Central bank	9791	11402	11515	10549	10111	14595	18523	19645	17945	16430	23. Emprunts auprès de la Banque centrale
24. Interbank deposits	35921	37861	40537	40505	41513	42971	43988	45417	45706	49800	24. Dépôts interbancaires
25. Non-bank deposits	263305	281356	335914	360226	379948	394167	416252	447499	485201	521466	25. Dépôts non bancaires
26. Bonds	1478	2379	3386	4380	5635	7036	9476	13078	17288	22229	26. Obligations
27. Other liabilities	10174	10291	11613	12376	12809	13520	14604	16157	18423	20636	27. Autres engagements
Balance sheet total											**Total du bilan**
28. End-year total	332663	356438	419061	445315	468369	491642	523195	563019	607571	657021	28. En fin d'exercice
29. Average total	314632	338117	402107	424901	451136	474491	497789	534273	575708	624292	29. Moyen
Memoranda											*Pour mémoire*
30. *Short-term securities*	*8100*	*7440*	*8565*	*9088*	*11294*	*11750*	*11313*	*12885*	*15821*	*18236*	30. *Titres à court terme*
31. *Bonds*	*39548*	*43224*	*54691*	*60724*	*70037*	*77256*	*79170*	*82820*	*85535*	*95354*	31. *Obligations*
32. *Shares and participations*	*1480*	*1634*	*2062*	*2704*	*3350*	*3615*	*3625*	*4016*	*4617*	*5867*	32. *Actions et participations*
33. *Claims on non-residents*	*909*	*1113*	*1506*	*1970*	*2619*	*3393*	*5401*	*6795*	*8269*	*7585*	33. *Créances sur des non résidents*
34. *Liabilities to non-residents*	*2988*	*3485*	*3857*	*3840*	*3998*	*4217*	*4491*	*5636*	*4973*	*6989*	34. *Engagements envers des non résidents*
SUPPLEMENTARY INFORMATION											**RENSEIGNEMENTS COMPLEMENTAIRES**
35. Number of institutions	2250	2239	3655	3604	3480	3361	3225	3049	2862	2683	35. Nombre d'institutions
36. Number of branches	12800	12900	15929	15935	15910	15824	15789	15769	15815	15618	36. Nombre de succursales
37. Number of employees (x 1000)	NA	NA	NA	NA	NA	NA	NA	NA	NA	NA	37. Nombre de salariés (x 1000)

GERMANY

Co-operative banks

ALLEMAGNE

Banques mutualistes

Per cent / *Pourcentage*

INCOME STATEMENT ANALYSIS / ANALYSE DU COMPTE DE RESULTATS

	1983	1984	1985	1986	1987	1988	1989	1990	1991	1992		
% of average balance sheet total												**% du total moyen du bilan**
38. Interest income	7.93	7.74	7.43	6.87	6.42	6.18	6.71	7.55	8.15	8.61	38.	Produits financiers
39. Interest expenses	4.27	4.34	4.19	3.74	3.38	3.22	3.74	4.61	5.11	5.53	39.	Frais financiers
40. Net interest income	3.66	3.40	3.24	3.13	3.04	2.96	2.96	2.95	3.04	3.08	40.	Produits financiers nets
41. Non-interest income (net)	0.60	0.81	0.65	0.68	0.66	0.59	0.83	0.80	0.73	0.76	41.	Produits non financiers (nets)
42. Gross income	4.26	4.21	3.89	3.81	3.69	3.55	3.79	3.75	3.77	3.84	42.	Résultat brut
43. Operating expenses	2.75	2.78	2.84	2.81	2.74	2.66	2.61	2.63	2.62	2.65	43.	Frais d'exploitation
44. Net income	1.51	1.43	1.06	1.01	0.96	0.88	1.19	1.12	1.15	1.19	44.	Résultat net
45. Provisions (net)	0.47	0.57	0.34	0.33	0.29	0.16	0.65	0.44	0.26	0.25	45.	Provisions (nettes)
46. Profit before tax	1.05	0.86	0.71	0.67	0.67	0.72	0.54	0.67	0.89	0.95	46.	Bénéfices avant impôt
47. Income tax	0.72	0.58	0.49	0.46	0.46	0.50	0.34	0.42	0.54	0.61	47.	Impôt
48. Profit after tax	0.33	0.28	0.23	0.22	0.21	0.22	0.20	0.25	0.35	0.34	48.	Bénéfices après impôt
49. Distributed profit	0.23	0.20	0.18	0.18	0.17	0.18	0.17	0.19	0.22	0.22	49.	Bénéfices distribués
50. Retained profit	0.10	0.08	0.05	0.04	0.04	0.04	0.03	0.07	0.13	0.11	50.	Bénéfices mis en réserve
51. Staff costs	1.72	1.71	1.73	1.73	1.69	1.66	1.63	1.65	1.64	1.66	51.	Frais de personnel
52. Provisions on loans	0.46	0.56	0.34	0.33	0.29	0.16	0.65	0.44	0.26	0.24	52.	Provisions sur prêts
53. Provisions on securities (1)	:	:	:	:	:	:	:	:	:	:	53.	Provisions sur titres (1)
% of gross income												**% du total du résultat brut**
54. Net interest income	85.85	80.75	83.29	82.06	82.16	83.50	78.11	78.66	80.62	80.17	54.	Produits financiers nets
55. Non-interest income (net)	14.15	19.25	16.71	17.94	17.84	16.50	21.89	21.34	19.38	19.83	55.	Produits non financiers (nets)
56. Operating expenses	64.50	66.00	72.81	73.60	74.11	75.11	68.72	70.21	69.47	68.98	56.	Frais d'exploitation
57. Net income	35.50	34.00	27.19	26.40	25.89	24.89	31.28	29.79	30.53	31.02	57.	Résultat net
58. Provisions (net)	10.92	13.56	8.85	8.74	7.83	4.53	17.07	11.87	6.87	6.37	58.	Provisions (nettes)
59. Profit before tax	24.58	20.44	18.35	17.66	18.06	20.36	14.21	17.92	23.66	24.64	59.	Bénéfices avant impôt
60. Income tax	16.92	13.82	12.50	11.99	12.40	14.01	9.03	11.15	14.27	15.92	60.	Impôt
61. Profit after tax	7.66	6.63	5.85	5.68	5.66	6.34	5.18	6.77	9.38	8.72	61.	Bénéfices après impôt
62. Staff costs	40.28	40.65	44.55	45.23	45.82	46.82	42.90	44.01	43.47	43.15	62.	Frais de personnel
% of net income												**% du total du résultat net**
63. Provisions (net)	30.77	39.88	32.53	33.09	30.24	18.20	54.56	39.84	22.52	20.55	63.	Provisions (nettes)
64. Profit before tax	69.23	60.12	67.47	66.91	69.76	81.80	45.44	60.16	77.48	79.45	64.	Bénéfices avant impôt
65. Income tax	47.67	40.63	45.96	45.41	47.88	56.31	28.88	37.43	46.75	51.32	65.	Impôt
66. Profit after tax	21.56	19.49	21.51	21.50	21.88	25.49	16.56	22.73	30.73	28.13	66.	Bénéfices après impôt

Co-operative banks   Banques mutualistes

Per cent   *Pourcentage*

BALANCE SHEET ANALYSIS   **ANALYSE DU BILAN**

	1983	1984	1985	1986	1987	1988	1989	1990	1991	1992	
% of year-end balance sheet total											**% du total du bilan en fin d'exercice**
Assets											**Actif**
67. Cash & balance with Central bank	2.97	2.99	2.73	2.59	2.72	2.88	3.03	3.05	3.01	3.31	67. Caisse & solde auprès de la Banque centrale
68. Interbank deposits	13.81	13.97	14.72	17.40	17.22	16.45	16.68	17.41	16.74	15.11	68. Dépôts interbancaires
69. Loans	64.63	64.34	62.68	59.61	58.18	58.24	58.89	58.37	59.38	60.17	69. Prêts
70. Securities	14.77	14.67	15.59	16.28	18.08	18.84	17.99	17.71	17.44	18.18	70. Valeurs mobilières
71. Other assets	3.82	4.03	4.29	4.11	3.80	3.59	3.42	3.45	3.43	3.23	71. Autres actifs
Liabilities											**Passif**
72. Capital & reserves	3.61	3.69	3.84	3.88	3.92	3.94	3.89	3.77	3.79	4.03	72. Capital et réserves
73. Borrowing from Central bank	2.94	3.20	2.75	2.37	2.16	2.97	3.54	3.49	2.95	2.50	73. Emprunts auprès de la Banque centrale
74. Interbank deposits	10.80	10.62	9.67	9.10	8.86	8.74	8.41	8.07	7.52	7.58	74. Dépôts interbancaires
75. Non-bank deposits	79.15	78.94	80.16	80.89	81.12	80.17	79.56	79.48	79.86	79.37	75. Dépôts non bancaires
76. Bonds	0.44	0.67	0.81	0.98	1.20	1.43	1.81	2.32	2.85	3.38	76. Obligations
77. Other liabilities	3.06	2.89	2.77	2.78	2.73	2.75	2.79	2.87	3.03	3.14	77. Autres engagements
Memoranda											*Pour mémoire*
78. Short-term securities	*2.43*	*2.09*	*2.04*	*2.04*	*2.41*	*2.39*	*2.16*	*2.29*	*2.60*	*2.78*	*78. Titres à court terme*
79. Bonds	*11.89*	*12.13*	*13.05*	*13.64*	*14.95*	*15.71*	*15.13*	*14.71*	*14.08*	*14.51*	*79. Obligations*
80. Shares and participations	*0.44*	*0.46*	*0.49*	*0.61*	*0.72*	*0.74*	*0.69*	*0.71*	*0.76*	*0.89*	*80. Actions et participations*
81. Claims on non-residents	*0.27*	*0.31*	*0.36*	*0.44*	*0.56*	*0.69*	*1.03*	*1.21*	*1.36*	*1.15*	*81. Créances sur des non résidents*
82. Liabilities to non-residents	*0.90*	*0.98*	*0.92*	*0.86*	*0.85*	*0.86*	*0.86*	*1.04*	*0.82*	*1.06*	*82. Engagements envers des non résidents*

1. Included under "Provisions on loans" (item 15 or item 52).

1. Inclus sous "Provisions sur prêts" (poste 15 ou poste 52).

Notes

• Average balance sheet totals (item 29) are based on twelve end-month data.

Change in methodology:

• As from 1985, all credit co-operatives are included in the data.

Notes

• La moyenne du total des actifs/passifs (poste 29) est basée sur douze données de fin de mois.

Changement méthodologique :

• Depuis 1985, l'ensemble des banques mutualistes est compris dans les données.

GREECE

Commercial banks

Million drachmas

GREECE

Banques commerciales

Millions de drachmes

	English	French	1989	1990	1991	1992
INCOME STATEMENT		**COMPTE DE RESULTATS**				
1.	Interest income	Produits financiers	809952	1035190	1261913	1443939
2.	Interest expenses	Frais financiers	725805	906422	1057989	1254566
3.	Net interest income	Produits financiers nets	84147	128768	203924	189373
4.	Non-interest income (net)	Produits non financiers (nets)	124662	162719	233960	233826
5.	Gross income	Résultat brut	208809	291487	437884	423199
6.	Operating expenses	Frais d'exploitation	156098	186857	224721	258344
7.	Net income	Résultat net	52711	104630	213163	164855
8.	Provisions (net)	Provisions (nettes)	22034	35758	63983	35902
9.	Profit before tax	Bénéfices avant impôt	30677	68872	149180	128953
10.	Income tax	Impôt	3847	14296	24108	42032
11.	Profit after tax	Bénéfices après impôt	26830	54576	125072	86921
12.	Distributed profit	Bénéfices distribués	15572	32859	59333	42248
13.	Retained profit	Bénéfices mis en réserve	11258	21717	65739	44673
Memoranda		***Pour mémoire***				
14.	Staff costs	Frais de personnel	119660	143565	170332	184808
15.	Provisions on loans	Provisions sur prêts	18589	32052	60506	32985
16.	Provisions on securities	Provisions sur titres	..	..	..	..
BALANCE SHEET		**BILAN**				
Assets		**Actif**				
17.	Cash & balance with Central bank	Caisse & solde auprès de la Banque centrale	955274	1055865	1244087	1503293
18.	Interbank deposits	Dépôts interbancaires	400934	459030	572950	797191
19.	Loans	Prêts	2291176	2418951	2605460	2937304
20.	Securities	Valeurs mobilières	2694370	3290618	3870488	4449403
21.	Other assets	Autres actifs	386183	463230	920229	1276138
Liabilities		**Passif**				
22.	Capital & reserves	Capital et réserves	230484	340331	479424	564540
23.	Borrowing from Central bank	Emprunts auprès de la Banque centrale	29734	37482	30198	25045
24.	Interbank deposits	Dépôts interbancaires	71987	77288	153731	202400
25.	Non-bank deposits	Dépôts non bancaires	6035693	6884194	7996031	9452494
26.	Bonds	Obligations	-	-	119125	119125
27.	Other liabilities	Autres engagements	360039	348399	434705	599725
Balance sheet total		**Total du bilan**				
28.	End-year total	En fin d'exercice	6727937	7687694	9213214	10963329
29.	Average total	Moyen	6173791	7207815	8450454	10088272
Memoranda		***Pour mémoire***				
30.	Short-term securities	Titres à court terme	2287331	2609630	1332128	771354
31.	Bonds	Obligations	156967	382999	2166431	3196832
32.	Shares and participations	Actions et participations	250072	297989	371929	481217
33.	Claims on non-residents	Créances sur des non résidents	..	..	..	..
34.	Liabilities to non-residents	Engagements envers des non résidents	..	..	..	..
SUPPLEMENTARY INFORMATION		**RENSEIGNEMENTS COMPLEMENTAIRES**				
35.	Number of institutions	Nombre d'institutions	15	18	20	21
36.	Number of branches	Nombre de succursales	1065	1082	1121	1162
37.	Number of employees (x 1000)	Nombre de salariés (x 1000)	37.2	36.5	37.3	37.4

GREECE

Commercial banks

Per cent

	1989	1990	1991	1992	
INCOME STATEMENT ANALYSIS					**ANALYSE DU COMPTE DE RESULTATS**
% of average balance sheet total					**% du total moyen du bilan**
38. Interest income	13.12	14.36	14.93	14.31	38. Produits financiers
39. Interest expenses	11.76	12.58	12.52	12.44	39. Frais financiers
40. Net interest income	1.36	1.79	2.41	1.88	40. Produits financiers nets
41. Non-interest income (net)	2.02	2.26	2.77	2.32	41. Produits non financiers (nets)
42. Gross income	3.38	4.04	5.18	4.19	42. Résultat brut
43. Operating expenses	2.53	2.59	2.66	2.56	43. Frais d'exploitation
44. Net income	0.85	1.45	2.52	1.63	44. Résultat net
45. Provisions (net)	0.36	0.50	0.76	0.36	45. Provisions (nettes)
46. Profit before tax	0.50	0.96	1.77	1.28	46. Bénéfices avant impôt
47. Income tax	0.06	0.20	0.29	0.42	47. Impôt
48. Profit after tax	0.43	0.76	1.48	0.86	48. Bénéfices après impôt
49. Distributed profit	0.25	0.46	0.70	0.42	49. Bénéfices distribués
50. Retained profit	0.18	0.30	0.78	0.44	50. Bénéfices mis en réserve
51. Staff costs	1.94	1.99	2.02	1.83	51. Frais de personnel
52. Provisions on loans	0.30	0.44	0.72	0.33	52. Provisions sur prêts
53. Provisions on securities	..	..	..	..	53. Provisions sur titres
% of gross income					**% du total du résultat brut**
54. Net interest income	40.30	44.18	46.57	44.75	54. Produits financiers nets
55. Non-interest income (net)	59.70	55.82	53.43	55.25	55. Produits non financiers (nets)
56. Operating expenses	74.76	64.10	51.32	61.05	56. Frais d'exploitation
57. Net income	25.24	35.90	48.68	38.95	57. Résultat net
58. Provisions (net)	10.55	12.27	14.61	8.48	58. Provisions (nettes)
59. Profit before tax	14.69	23.63	34.07	30.47	59. Bénéfices avant impôt
60. Income tax	1.84	4.90	5.51	9.93	60. Impôt
61. Profit after tax	12.85	18.72	28.56	20.54	61. Bénéfices après impôt
62. Staff costs	57.31	49.25	38.90	43.67	62. Frais de personnel
% of net income					**% du total du résultat net**
63. Provisions (net)	41.80	34.18	30.02	21.78	63. Provisions (nettes)
64. Profit before tax	58.20	65.82	69.98	78.22	64. Bénéfices avant impôt
65. Income tax	7.30	13.66	11.31	25.50	65. Impôt
66. Profit after tax	50.90	52.16	58.67	52.73	66. Bénéfices après impôt

87

GREECE

Commercial banks

GRECE

Banques commerciales

Per cent

BALANCE SHEET ANALYSIS

Pourcentage

ANALYSE DU BILAN

% of year-end balance sheet total

% du total du bilan en fin d'exercice

	1989	1990	1991	1992		
Assets						**Actif**
67. Cash & balance with Central bank	14.20	13.73	13.50	13.71	67.	Caisse & solde auprès de la Banque centrale
68. Interbank deposits	5.96	5.97	6.22	7.27	68.	Dépôts interbancaires
69. Loans	34.05	31.47	28.28	26.79	69.	Prêts
70. Securities	40.05	42.80	42.01	40.58	70.	Valeurs mobilières
71. Other assets	5.74	6.03	9.99	11.64	71.	Autres actifs
Liabilities						**Passif**
72. Capital & reserves	3.43	4.43	5.20	5.15	72.	Capital et réserves
73. Borrowing from Central bank	0.44	0.49	0.33	0.23	73.	Emprunts auprès de la Banque centrale
74. Interbank deposits	1.07	1.01	1.67	1.85	74.	Dépôts interbancaires
75. Non-bank deposits	89.71	89.55	86.79	86.22	75.	Dépôts non bancaires
76. Bonds	-	-	1.29	1.09	76.	Obligations
77. Other liabilities	5.35	4.53	4.72	5.47	77.	Autres engagements
Memoranda						*Pour mémoire*
78. Short-term securities	34.00	33.95	14.46	7.04	78.	Titres à court terme
79. Bonds	2.33	4.98	23.51	29.16	79.	Obligations
80. Shares and participations	3.72	3.88	4.04	4.39	80.	Actions et participations
81. Claims on non-residents	..	..	..	..	81.	Créances sur des non résidents
82. Liabilities to non-residents	..	..	..	..	82.	Engagements envers des non résidents

88

GREECE

Large commercial banks

Million drachmas

	1983	1984	1985	1986	1987	1988	1989	1990	1991	1992
INCOME STATEMENT										
1. Interest income	211197	283474	362938	421524	470044	575166	708956	890880	1068795	1214742
2. Interest expenses	179691	248519	327762	380934	444522	538274	644999	798348	912049	1085177
3. Net interest income	31506	34955	35176	40590	25522	36892	63957	92532	156746	129565
4. Non-interest income (net)	20640	32912	46042	56926	80966	96544	103671	135770	196760	185477
5. Gross income	52146	67867	81218	97516	106488	133436	167628	228302	353506	315042
6. Operating expenses	39914	51568	63849	73121	83179	108286	128358	151969	178455	198993
7. Net income	12232	16299	17369	24395	23309	25150	39270	76333	175051	116049
8. Provisions (net)	5679	7590	8598	10344	9491	10760	19350	31240	59044	24506
9. Profit before tax	6553	8709	8771	14051	13818	14390	19920	45093	116007	91543
10. Income tax	971	932	990	1243	2288	2244	2714	9498	17547	26789
11. Profit after tax	5582	7777	7781	12808	11530	12146	17206	35595	98460	64754
12. Distributed profit	4502	5170	3765	6810	8572	9763	8768	19583	41679	29745
13. Retained profit	1080	2607	4016	5998	2958	2383	8438	16012	56781	35009
Memoranda										
14. *Staff costs*	*32376*	*41811*	*51695*	*58343*	*63957*	*83952*	*100241*	*118929*	*138279*	*147857*
15. *Provisions on loans*	..	..	..	..	*9491*	*9920*	*16178*	*29200*	*56171*	*24112*
16. *Provisions on securities*	..	..	..	..	..	..	..	..	..	..
BALANCE SHEET										
Assets										
17. Cash & balance with Central bank	268971	468459	509022	512909	737241	851581	787858	937939	1080606	1257843
18. Interbank deposits	110457	144891	202194	155764	159245	281820	296536	320288	388178	582607
19. Loans	747668	902002	1074734	1295144	1410280	1647158	1948042	1996282	2120142	2293430
20. Securities	525453	674909	969482	1210724	1509263	1949543	2527840	2968372	3453143	3823378
21. Other assets	101748	94285	173612	294366	216138	155636	283183	350354	724762	1132346
Liabilities										
22. Capital & reserves	64529	67156	71217	77377	81929	149671	167870	247835	351624	408236
23. Borrowing from Central bank	90727	137221	194405	186261	136750	41278	5523	12086	5896	1385
24. Interbank deposits	31122	29979	44946	34488	37923	47554	59282	65595	129009	156326
25. Non-bank deposits	1459427	1932202	2507426	2998305	3675497	4453687	5395410	6035308	6848311	8017463
26. Bonds	-	-	-	-	-	-	-	-	119125	119125
27. Other liabilities	108492	117988	111050	172476	100068	193548	215374	212411	312866	387069
Balance sheet total										
28. End-year total	1754297	2284546	2929044	3468907	4032167	4885738	5843459	6573235	7766831	9089604
29. Average total	1586812	2019422	2606795	3198976	3750537	4458953	5364599	6208347	7170033	8428218
Memoranda										
30. *Short-term securities*	*463493*	*608586*	*893488*	*1073423*	*1235980*	*1607086*	*2133756*	*2317709*	*969054*	*506022*
31. *Bonds*	*24753*	*22438*	*21494*	*31206*	*73101*	*115355*	*149571*	*366025*	*2135623*	*2916980*
32. *Shares and participations*	*37207*	*43885*	*54500*	*106095*	*200182*	*227102*	*244513*	*284638*	*348466*	*400376*
33. *Claims on non-residents*	..	..	..	..	..	..	..	..	..	..
34. *Liabilities to non-residents*	..	..	..	..	..	..	..	..	..	..
SUPPLEMENTARY INFORMATION										
35. Number of institutions	4	4	4	4	4	4	4	4	4	4
36. Number of branches	748	759	782	795	794	797	799	802	812	824
37. Number of employees (x 1000)	24.0	25.1	27.4	28.4	29.0	29.4	29.7	28.7	28.7	28.3

GRECE

Grandes banques commerciales

Millions de drachmes

COMPTE DE RESULTATS
1. Produits financiers
2. Frais financiers
3. Produits financiers nets
4. Produits non financiers (nets)
5. Résultat brut
6. Frais d'exploitation
7. Résultat net
8. Provisions (nettes)
9. Bénéfices avant impôt
10. Impôt
11. Bénéfices après impôt
12. Bénéfices distribués
13. Bénéfices mis en réserve

Pour mémoire
14. *Frais de personnel*
15. *Provisions sur prêts*
16. *Provisions sur titres*

BILAN

Actif
17. Caisse & solde auprès de la Banque centrale
18. Dépôts interbancaires
19. Prêts
20. Valeurs mobilières
21. Autres actifs

Passif
22. Capital et réserves
23. Emprunts auprès de la Banque centrale
24. Dépôts interbancaires
25. Dépôts non bancaires
26. Obligations
27. Autres engagements

Total du bilan
28. En fin d'exercice
29. Moyen

Pour mémoire
30. *Titres à court terme*
31. *Obligations*
32. *Actions et participations*
33. *Créances sur des non résidents*
34. *Engagements envers des non résidents*

RENSEIGNEMENTS COMPLEMENTAIRES
35. Nombre d'institutions
36. Nombre de succursales
37. Nombre de salariés (x 1000)

GREECE

Large commercial banks

Per cent

GREECE

Grandes banques commerciales

Pourcentage

		1983	1984	1985	1986	1987	1988	1989	1990	1991	1992			
INCOME STATEMENT ANALYSIS												**ANALYSE DU COMPTE DE RESULTATS**		
% of average balance sheet total												**% du total moyen du bilan**		
38.	Interest income	13.31	14.04	13.92	13.18	12.53	12.90	13.22	14.35	14.91	14.41	38.	Produits financiers
39.	Interest expenses	11.32	12.31	12.57	11.91	11.85	12.07	12.02	12.86	12.72	12.88	39.	Frais financiers
40.	Net interest income	1.99	1.73	1.35	1.27	0.68	0.83	1.19	1.49	2.19	1.54	40.	Produits financiers nets
41.	Non-interest income (net)	1.30	1.63	1.77	1.78	2.16	2.17	1.93	2.19	2.74	2.20	41.	Produits non financiers (nets)
42.	Gross income	3.29	3.36	3.12	3.05	2.84	2.99	3.12	3.68	4.93	3.74	42.	Résultat brut
43.	Operating expenses	2.52	2.55	2.45	2.29	2.22	2.43	2.39	2.45	2.49	2.36	43.	Frais d'exploitation
44.	Net income	0.77	0.81	0.67	0.76	0.62	0.56	0.73	1.23	2.44	1.38	44.	Résultat net
45.	Provisions (net)	0.36	0.38	0.33	0.32	0.25	0.24	0.36	0.50	0.82	0.29	45.	Provisions (nettes)
46.	Profit before tax	0.41	0.43	0.34	0.44	0.37	0.32	0.37	0.73	1.62	1.09	46.	Bénéfices avant impôt
47.	Income tax	0.06	0.05	0.04	0.04	0.06	0.05	0.05	0.15	0.24	0.32	47.	Impôt
48.	Profit after tax	0.35	0.39	0.30	0.40	0.31	0.27	0.32	0.57	1.37	0.77	48.	Bénéfices après impôt
49.	Distributed profit	0.28	0.26	0.14	0.21	0.23	0.22	0.16	0.32	0.58	0.35	49.	Bénéfices distribués
50.	Retained profit	0.07	0.13	0.15	0.19	0.08	0.05	0.16	0.26	0.79	0.42	50.	Bénéfices mis en réserve
51.	Staff costs	2.04	2.07	1.98	1.82	1.71	1.88	1.87	1.92	1.93	1.75	51.	Frais de personnel
52.	Provisions on loans	..	..	..	..	0.25	0.22	0.30	0.47	0.78	0.29	52.	Provisions sur prêts
53.	Provisions on securities	..	..	..	..	..	..	..	..	..	..	53.	Provisions sur titres
% of gross income												**% du total du résultat brut**		
54.	Net interest income	60.42	51.51	43.31	41.62	23.97	27.65	38.15	40.53	44.34	41.13	54.	Produits financiers nets
55.	Non-interest income (net)	39.58	48.49	56.69	58.38	76.03	72.35	61.85	59.47	55.66	58.87	55.	Produits non financiers (nets)
56.	Operating expenses	76.54	75.98	78.61	74.98	78.11	81.15	76.57	66.56	50.48	63.16	56.	Frais d'exploitation
57.	Net income	23.46	24.02	21.39	25.02	21.89	18.85	23.43	33.44	49.52	36.84	57.	Résultat net
58.	Provisions (net)	10.89	11.18	10.59	10.61	8.91	8.06	11.54	13.68	16.70	7.78	58.	Provisions (nettes)
59.	Profit before tax	12.57	12.83	10.80	14.41	12.98	10.78	11.88	19.75	32.82	29.06	59.	Bénéfices avant impôt
60.	Income tax	1.86	1.37	1.22	1.27	2.15	1.68	1.62	4.16	4.96	8.50	60.	Impôt
61.	Profit after tax	10.70	11.46	9.58	13.13	10.83	9.10	10.26	15.59	27.85	20.55	61.	Bénéfices après impôt
62.	Staff costs	62.09	61.61	63.65	59.83	60.06	62.92	59.80	52.09	39.12	46.93	62.	Frais de personnel
% of net income												**% du total du résultat net**		
63.	Provisions (net)	46.43	46.57	49.50	42.40	40.72	42.78	49.27	40.93	33.73	21.12	63.	Provisions (nettes)
64.	Profit before tax	53.57	53.43	50.50	57.60	59.28	57.22	50.73	59.07	66.27	78.88	64.	Bénéfices avant impôt
65.	Income tax	7.94	5.72	5.70	5.10	9.82	8.92	6.91	12.44	10.02	23.08	65.	Impôt
66.	Profit after tax	45.63	47.71	44.80	52.50	49.47	48.29	43.81	46.63	56.25	55.80	66.	Bénéfices après impôt

GREECE

Large commercial banks

Per cent

BALANCE SHEET ANALYSIS

% of year-end balance sheet total

	1983	1984	1985	1986	1987	1988	1989	1990	1991	1992
Assets										
67. Cash & balance with Central bank	15.33	20.51	17.38	14.79	18.28	17.43	13.48	14.27	13.91	13.84
68. Interbank deposits	6.30	6.34	6.90	4.49	3.95	5.77	5.07	4.87	5.00	6.41
69. Loans	42.62	39.48	36.69	37.34	34.98	33.71	33.34	30.37	27.30	25.23
70. Securities	29.95	29.54	33.10	34.90	37.43	39.90	43.26	45.16	44.46	42.06
71. Other assets	5.80	4.13	5.93	8.49	5.36	3.19	4.85	5.33	9.33	12.46
Liabilities										
72. Capital & reserves	3.68	2.94	2.43	2.23	2.03	3.06	2.87	3.77	4.53	4.49
73. Borrowing from Central bank	5.17	6.01	6.64	5.37	3.39	0.84	0.09	0.18	0.08	0.02
74. Interbank deposits	1.77	1.31	1.53	0.99	0.94	0.97	1.01	1.00	1.66	1.72
75. Non-bank deposits	83.19	84.58	85.61	86.43	91.15	91.16	92.33	91.82	88.17	88.20
76. Bonds	-	-	-	-	-	-	-	-	1.53	1.31
77. Other liabilities	6.18	5.16	3.79	4.97	2.48	3.96	3.69	3.23	4.03	4.26
Memoranda										
78. Short-term securities	*26.42*	*26.64*	*30.50*	*30.94*	*30.65*	*32.89*	*36.52*	*35.26*	*12.48*	*5.57*
79. Bonds	*1.41*	*0.98*	*0.73*	*0.90*	*1.81*	*2.36*	*2.56*	*5.57*	*27.50*	*32.09*
80. Shares and participations	*2.12*	*1.92*	*1.86*	*3.06*	*4.96*	*4.65*	*4.18*	*4.33*	*4.49*	*4.40*
81. Claims on non-residents	*..*	*..*	*..*	*..*	*..*	*..*	*..*	*..*	*..*	*..*
82. Liabilities to non-residents	*..*	*..*	*..*	*..*	*..*	*..*	*..*	*..*	*..*	*..*

Notes

- Large commercial banks are a sub-group of Commercial banks.

GREECE

Grandes banques commerciales

Pourcentage

ANALYSE DU BILAN

% du total du bilan en fin d'exercice

Actif
67. Caisse & solde auprès de la Banque centrale
68. Dépôts interbancaires
69. Prêts
70. Valeurs mobilières
71. Autres actifs

Passif
72. Capital et réserves
73. Emprunts auprès de la Banque centrale
74. Dépôts interbancaires
75. Dépôts non bancaires
76. Obligations
77. Autres engagements

Pour mémoire
78. Titres à court terme
79. Obligations
80. Actions et participations
81. Créances sur des non résidents
82. Engagements envers des non résidents

Notes

- Les Grandes banques commerciales sont un sous-groupe des Banques commerciales.

91

ITALY

Commercial banks

ITALIE

Banques commerciales

Billion lire / *Milliards de lires*

		1983	1984	1985	1986	1987	1988	1989	1990	1991 (2)	1992		
INCOME STATEMENT													**COMPTE DE RESULTATS**
1.	Interest income	53673	60229	63683	60145	57900	61725	71824	79772	86582	105077	1.	Produits financiers
2.	Interest expenses	39189	44053	45581	38994	35815	36942	43915	48321	51753	63406	2.	Frais financiers
3.	Net interest income	14484	16176	18102	21151	22085	24783	27909	31451	34829	41671	3.	Produits financiers nets
4.	Non-interest income (net)	5403	6666	8328	9900	8580	9439	9673	11321	12335	10396	4.	Produits non financiers (nets)
5.	Gross income	19887	22842	26430	31051	30665	34222	37582	42772	47164	52067	5.	Résultat brut
6.	Operating expenses	13710	15775	17751	19476	21497	23074	24061	26861	30149	33110	6.	Frais d'exploitation
7.	Net income	6177	7067	8679	11575	9168	11148	13521	15911	17015	18957	7.	Résultat net
8.	Provisions (net)	2808	3007	3310	3783	3409	4247	4320	4999	4977	7479	8.	Provisions (nettes)
9.	Profit before tax	3369	4060	5369	7792	5759	6901	9201	10912	12038	11478	9.	Bénéfices avant impôt
10.	Income tax	1863	1978	2593	3541	2301	2983	3301	3767	4297	4488	10.	Impôt
11.	Profit after tax	1506	2082	2776	4251	3458	3918	5900	7145	7741	6990	11.	Bénéfices après impôt
12.	Distributed profit	641	902	1123	1506	1631	1696	1812	2108	2298	2301	12.	Bénéfices distribués
13.	Retained profit	865	1180	1653	2745	1827	2222	4088	5037	5443	4689	13.	Bénéfices mis en réserve
Memoranda													*Pour mémoire*
14.	Staff costs	10038	11324	12768	13938	15370	16564	17183	18927	21221	23133	14.	Frais de personnel
15.	Provisions on loans	2421	2640	2361	2796	2564	3329	4183	5084	4934	5916	15.	Provisions sur prêts
16.	Provisions on securities	109	115	81	314	1270	951	1361	840	1104	2695	16.	Provisions sur titres
BALANCE SHEET													**BILAN**
Assets													*Actif*
17.	Cash & balance with Central bank(1)	3068	50569	59669	65884	71816	79120	85882	95995	98501	99570	17.	Caisse & solde auprès de la Banque centrale(1)
18.	Interbank deposits (1)	72338	75236	78905	84646	77780	75209	91212	67991	73381	122811	18.	Dépôts interbancaires (1)
19.	Loans	133051	167469	188828	204929	220573	262148	316595	370511	427159	480756	19.	Prêts
20.	Securities	117281	128309	135948	146684	148538	137469	129640	120146	131245	138377	20.	Valeurs mobilières
21.	Other assets	203433	208502	226043	238252	233980	265489	360382	333516	375250	417718	21.	Autres actifs
Liabilities													*Passif*
22.	Capital & reserves	22447	33298	38858	46275	53052	56194	62474	68246	83896	102131	22.	Capital et réserves
23.	Borrowing from Central bank	5556	1993	6917	3205	3754	3601	3615	4360	6767	5316	23.	Emprunts auprès de la Banque centrale
24.	Interbank deposits	66097	76194	77858	85216	79046	72112	90839	63218	66005	109859	24.	Dépôts interbancaires
25.	Non-bank deposits	265530	292428	322701	352366	376067	404475	444005	486337	539855	557081	25.	Dépôts non bancaires
26.	Bonds	-	-	-	-	-	-	-	-	-	-	26.	Obligations
27.	Other liabilities	169541	226172	243058	253334	240767	283054	382779	365999	409013	484845	27.	Autres engagements
Balance sheet total													*Total du bilan*
28.	End-year total	529171	630085	689392	740396	752687	819435	983711	988159	1105536	1259233	28.	En fin d'exercice
29.	Average total	461612	520940	601149	649765	701002	758922	844587	922348	983101	1119449	29.	Moyen
Memoranda													*Pour mémoire*
30.	Short-term securities	32678	30481	18361	22388	18961	16856	15663	18086	19043	13722	30.	Titres à court terme
31.	Bonds	89425	97828	117587	124296	129577	120613	113777	102060	112202	124655	31.	Obligations
32.	Shares and participations	4805	6419	6930	8822	9664	10914	14386	15540	23492	24907	32.	Actions et participations
33.	Claims on non-residents	50306	69758	76245	73434	67902	72820	92031	92377	92311	107578	33.	Créances sur des non résidents
34.	Liabilities to non-residents	65530	93910	93115	90391	92651	108960	135678	137107	160538	220485	34.	Engagements envers des non résidents
SUPPLEMENTARY INFORMATION													**RENSEIGNEMENTS COMPLEMENTAIRES**
35.	Number of institutions	205	235	235	232	226	219	198	197	188	177	35.	Nombre d'institutions
36.	Number of branches	9025	10304	10388	10427	10540	10556	10564	11328	12353	13332	36.	Nombre de succursales
37.	Number of employees (x 1000)	226.3	234.5	235.3	238.2	240.9	241.3	240.7	240.9	245.4	245.8	37.	Nombre de salariés (x 1000)

ITALY

Commercial banks

Per cent

INCOME STATEMENT ANALYSIS

		1983	1984	1985	1986	1987	1988	1989	1990	1991 (2)	1992		
% of average balance sheet total													**% du total moyen du bilan**
38.	Interest income	11.63	11.56	10.59	9.26	8.26	8.13	8.50	8.65	8.81	9.39	38.	Produits financiers
39.	Interest expenses	8.49	8.46	7.58	6.00	5.11	4.87	5.20	5.24	5.26	5.66	39.	Frais financiers
40.	Net interest income	3.14	3.11	3.01	3.26	3.15	3.27	3.30	3.41	3.54	3.72	40.	Produits financiers nets
41.	Non-interest income (net)	1.17	1.28	1.39	1.52	1.22	1.24	1.15	1.23	1.25	0.93	41.	Produits non financiers (nets)
42.	Gross income	4.31	4.38	4.40	4.78	4.37	4.51	4.45	4.64	4.80	4.65	42.	Résultat brut
43.	Operating expenses	2.97	3.03	2.95	3.00	3.07	3.04	2.85	2.91	3.07	2.96	43.	Frais d'exploitation
44.	Net income	1.34	1.36	1.44	1.78	1.31	1.47	1.60	1.73	1.73	1.69	44.	Résultat net
45.	Provisions (net)	0.61	0.58	0.55	0.58	0.49	0.56	0.51	0.54	0.51	0.67	45.	Provisions (nettes)
46.	Profit before tax	0.73	0.78	0.89	1.20	0.82	0.91	1.09	1.18	1.22	1.03	46.	Bénéfices avant impôt
47.	Income tax	0.40	0.38	0.43	0.54	0.33	0.39	0.39	0.41	0.44	0.40	47.	Impôt
48.	Profit after tax	0.33	0.40	0.46	0.65	0.49	0.52	0.70	0.77	0.79	0.62	48.	Bénéfices après impôt
49.	Distributed profit	0.14	0.17	0.19	0.23	0.23	0.22	0.21	0.23	0.23	0.21	49.	Bénéfices distribués
50.	Retained profit	0.19	0.23	0.27	0.42	0.26	0.29	0.48	0.55	0.55	0.42	50.	Bénéfices mis en réserve
51.	Staff costs	2.17	2.17	2.12	2.15	2.19	2.18	2.03	2.05	2.16	2.07	51.	Frais de personnel
52.	Provisions on loans	0.52	0.51	0.39	0.43	0.37	0.44	0.50	0.55	0.50	0.53	52.	Provisions sur prêts
53.	Provisions on securities	0.02	0.02	0.01	0.05	0.18	0.13	0.16	0.09	0.11	0.24	53.	Provisions sur titres
% of gross income													**% du total du résultat brut**
54.	Net interest income	72.83	70.82	68.49	68.12	72.02	72.42	74.26	73.53	73.85	80.03	54.	Produits financiers nets
55.	Non-interest income (net)	27.17	29.18	31.51	31.88	27.98	27.58	25.74	26.47	26.15	19.97	55.	Produits non financiers (nets)
56.	Operating expenses	68.94	69.06	67.16	62.72	70.10	67.42	64.02	62.80	63.92	63.59	56.	Frais d'exploitation
57.	Net income	31.06	30.94	32.84	37.28	29.90	32.58	35.98	37.20	36.08	36.41	57.	Résultat net
58.	Provisions (net)	14.12	13.16	12.52	12.18	11.12	12.41	11.49	11.69	10.55	14.36	58.	Provisions (nettes)
59.	Profit before tax	16.94	17.77	20.31	25.09	18.78	20.17	24.48	25.51	25.52	22.04	59.	Bénéfices avant impôt
60.	Income tax	9.37	8.66	9.81	11.40	7.50	8.72	8.78	8.81	9.11	8.62	60.	Impôt
61.	Profit after tax	7.57	9.11	10.50	13.69	11.28	11.45	15.70	16.70	16.41	13.43	61.	Bénéfices après impôt
62.	Staff costs	50.48	49.58	48.31	44.89	50.12	48.40	45.72	44.25	44.99	44.43	62.	Frais de personnel
% of net income													**% du total du résultat net**
63.	Provisions (net)	45.46	42.55	38.14	32.68	37.18	38.10	31.95	31.42	29.25	39.45	63.	Provisions (nettes)
64.	Profit before tax	54.54	57.45	61.86	67.32	62.82	61.90	68.05	68.58	70.75	60.55	64.	Bénéfices avant impôt
65.	Income tax	30.16	27.99	29.88	30.59	25.10	26.76	24.41	23.68	25.25	23.67	65.	Impôt
66.	Profit after tax	24.38	29.46	31.99	36.73	37.72	35.15	43.64	44.91	45.50	36.87	66.	Bénéfices après impôt

ITALY

Commercial banks

ITALIE

Banques commerciales

Per cent — *Pourcentage*

BALANCE SHEET ANALYSIS — ANALYSE DU BILAN

% of year-end balance sheet total — % du total du bilan en fin d'exercice

	1983	1984	1985	1986	1987	1988	1989	1990	1991 (2)	1992	
Assets											**Actif**
67. Cash & balance with Central bank(1)	0.58	8.03	8.66	8.90	9.54	9.66	8.73	9.71	8.91	7.91	67. Caisse & solde auprès de la Banque centrale(1)
68. Interbank deposits (1)	13.67	11.94	11.45	11.43	10.33	9.18	9.27	6.88	6.64	9.75	68. Dépôts interbancaires (1)
69. Loans	25.14	26.58	27.39	27.68	29.30	31.99	32.18	37.50	38.64	38.18	69. Prêts
70. Securities	22.16	20.36	19.72	19.81	19.73	16.78	13.18	12.16	11.87	10.99	70. Valeurs mobilières
71. Other assets	38.44	33.09	32.79	32.18	31.09	32.40	36.63	33.75	33.94	33.17	71. Autres actifs
Liabilities											**Passif**
72. Capital & reserves	4.24	5.28	5.64	6.25	7.05	6.86	6.35	6.91	7.59	8.11	72. Capital et réserves
73. Borrowing from Central bank	1.05	0.32	1.00	0.43	0.50	0.44	0.37	0.44	0.61	0.42	73. Emprunts auprès de la Banque centrale
74. Interbank deposits	12.49	12.09	11.29	11.51	10.50	8.80	9.23	6.40	5.97	8.72	74. Dépôts interbancaires
75. Non-bank deposits	50.18	46.41	46.81	47.59	49.96	49.36	45.14	49.22	48.83	44.24	75. Dépôts non bancaires
76. Bonds	-	-	-	-	-	-	-	-	-	-	76. Obligations
77. Other liabilities	32.04	35.90	35.26	34.22	31.99	34.54	38.91	37.04	37.00	38.50	77. Autres engagements
Memoranda											*Pour mémoire*
78. Short-term securities	6.18	4.84	2.66	3.02	2.52	2.06	1.61	1.83	1.72	1.09	78. Titres à court terme
79. Bonds	16.90	15.53	17.06	16.79	17.22	14.72	11.57	10.33	10.15	9.90	79. Obligations
80. Shares and participations	0.91	1.02	1.01	1.19	1.28	1.33	1.46	1.57	2.12	1.98	80. Actions et participations
81. Claims on non-residents	9.51	11.07	11.06	9.92	9.02	8.89	9.36	9.35	8.35	8.54	81. Créances sur des non résidents
82. Liabilities to non-residents	12.38	14.90	13.51	12.21	12.31	13.30	13.79	13.87	14.52	17.51	82. Engagements envers des non résidents

1. Change in methodology.
2. In 1991, break in series due to mergers and acquisitions.

Notes

• Average balance sheet totals (item 29) are based on twelve end-month data.

Change in methodology:

• As from 1984, data relate to a larger number of banks.
• As from 1984, "Cash and balance with Central bank" (item 17 or item 67) also includes required reserves and "Interbank deposits" (item 18 or item 68) includes both domestic and foreign currency deposits.

1. Changement méthodologique.
2. En 1991, rupture de comparabilité dans les séries due aux fusions et acquisitions.

Notes

• La moyenne du total des actifs/passifs (poste 29) est basée sur douze données de fin de mois.

Changement méthodologique :

• Depuis 1984, les données se rapportent à un plus grand nombre de banques.
• A partir de 1984 le poste "Caisse et solde auprès de la Banque centrale" (poste 17 ou poste 67) comprend également les réserves obligatoires ; le poste "Dépôts interbancaires" (poste 18 ou poste 68) comprend à la fois les dépôts en monnaie nationale et ceux en devises.

ITALY

Large commercial banks

Billion lire

ITALIE

Grandes banques commerciales

Milliards de lires

			1983	1984	1985	1986	1987	1988	1989	1990	1991	1992 (2)
INCOME STATEMENT		**COMPTE DE RESULTATS**										
1.	Interest income	Produits financiers	24150	24110	25687	23792	23308	24883	29897	33116	35245	46692
2.	Interest expenses	Frais financiers	18178	18080	19055	15811	15040	15495	19325	21192	22435	29169
3.	Net interest income	Produits financiers nets	5972	6030	6632	7981	8268	9388	10572	11924	12810	17523
4.	Non-interest income (net)	Produits non financiers (nets)	2824	3184	4288	5032	4034	4909	4529	5142	5247	4949
5.	Gross income	Résultat brut	8796	9214	10920	13013	12302	14297	15101	17066	18057	22472
6.	Operating expenses	Frais d'exploitation	6832	7149	7803	8628	9480	10028	10226	11241	12381	14817
7.	Net income	Résultat net	1964	2065	3117	4385	2822	4269	4875	5825	5676	7655
8.	Provisions (net)	Provisions (nettes)	1035	1046	1485	1547	1261	1986	1958	2230	1757	3470
9.	Profit before tax	Bénéfices avant impôt	929	1019	1632	2838	1561	2283	2917	3595	3919	4185
10.	Income tax	Impôt	658	553	862	1143	416	781	778	814	1205	1282
11.	Profit after tax	Bénéfices après impôt	271	466	770	1695	1145	1502	2139	2781	2714	2903
12.	Distributed profit	Bénéfices distribués	109	173	188	344	395	412	392	467	524	760
13.	Retained profit	Bénéfices mis en réserve	162	293	582	1351	750	1090	1747	2314	2190	2143
	Memoranda	*Pour mémoire*										
14.	*Staff costs*	*Frais de personnel*	*5257*	*5384*	*5874*	*6460*	*7118*	*7570*	*7677*	*8203*	*9139*	*10908*
15.	*Provisions on loans*	*Provisions sur prêts*	*1129*	*1032*	*669*	*965*	*1076*	*1591*	*1844*	*2234*	*1847*	*2507*
16.	*Provisions on securities*	*Provisions sur titres*	*20*	*46*	*73*	*147*	*436*	*367*	*684*	*289*	*466*	*1574*
BALANCE SHEET		**BILAN**										
Assets		**Actif**										
17.	Cash & balance with Central bank(1)	Caisse & solde auprès de la Banque centrale(1)	1186	20292	24131	26633	28769	31095	33268	37173	36727	41178
18.	Interbank deposits (1)	Dépôts interbancaires (1)	29442	24640	32260	31252	25940	29203	38681	21313	25593	55697
19.	Loans	Prêts	59501	68012	75346	80859	86691	102915	128029	151912	170741	218956
20.	Securities	Valeurs mobilières	54535	54695	53817	59762	65913	55187	54737	47247	47865	54369
21.	Other assets	Autres actifs	121932	127559	132873	140814	128294	143357	208354	175814	189080	223188
Liabilities		**Passif**										
22.	Capital & reserves	Capital et réserves	8423	11377	13498	16739	20577	21538	25250	27148	32888	49097
23.	Borrowing from Central bank	Emprunts auprès de la Banque centrale	1886	849	5561	1877	2313	2348	1759	3028	5059	2992
24.	Interbank deposits	Dépôts interbancaires	33812	36772	35651	42584	40786	32922	52333	25949	27467	50830
25.	Non-bank deposits	Dépôts non bancaires	114052	112770	124480	137106	143589	153261	168383	184965	201227	238960
26.	Bonds	Obligations	-	-	-	-	-	-	-	-	-	-
27.	Other liabilities	Autres engagements	108423	133429	139237	141013	128341	151687	215345	192369	203366	251509
	Balance sheet total	**Total du bilan**										
28.	End-year total	En fin d'exercice	266596	295197	318427	339320	335607	361757	463069	433460	470007	593388
29.	Average total	Moyen	236973	234015	272465	289641	310944	338444	381329	410425	414279	491043
	Memoranda	*Pour mémoire*										
30.	*Short-term securities*	*Titres à court terme*	*19207*	*18036*	*9608*	*12297*	*8511*	*5321*	*4823*	*6808*	*9781*	*5053*
31.	*Bonds*	*Obligations*	*38153*	*36659*	*44208*	*47466*	*57402*	*49866*	*49915*	*40439*	*38084*	*49316*
32.	*Shares and participations*	*Actions et participations*	*2826*	*3643*	*3448*	*4702*	*5117*	*5568*	*7788*	*7953*	*14205*	*15693*
33.	*Claims on non-residents*	*Créances sur des non résidents*	*36759*	*47071*	*49743*	*48751*	*44345*	*49213*	*65915*	*64005*	*61343*	*67418*
34.	*Liabilities to non-residents*	*Engagements envers des non résidents*	*48430*	*58689*	*58254*	*54817*	*55731*	*67771*	*88417*	*86087*	*95575*	*126280*
SUPPLEMENTARY INFORMATION		**RENSEIGNEMENTS COMPLEMENTAIRES**										
35.	Number of institutions	Nombre d'institutions	8	7	7	7	7	7	7	7	7	7
36.	Number of branches	Nombre de succursales	3293	3187	3204	3230	3272	3276	3303	3665	4010	4947
37.	Number of employees (x 1000)	Nombre de salariés (x 1000)	114.9	107.8	107.4	109.3	109.9	108.7	104.0	105.0	105.4	115.1

ITALY

Large commercial banks

Per cent

INCOME STATEMENT ANALYSIS

ITALIE

Grandes banques commerciales

Pourcentage

ANALYSE DU COMPTE DE RESULTATS

		1983	1984	1985	1986	1987	1988	1989	1990	1991	1992 (2)		
% of average balance sheet total													**% du total moyen du bilan**
38.	Interest income	10.19	10.30	9.43	8.21	7.50	7.35	7.84	8.07	8.51	9.51	38.	Produits financiers
39.	Interest expenses	7.67	7.73	6.99	5.46	4.84	4.58	5.07	5.16	5.42	5.94	39.	Frais financiers
40.	Net interest income	2.52	2.58	2.43	2.76	2.66	2.77	2.77	2.91	3.09	3.57	40.	Produits financiers nets
41.	Non-interest income (net)	1.19	1.36	1.57	1.74	1.30	1.45	1.19	1.25	1.27	1.01	41.	Produits non financiers (nets)
42.	Gross income	3.71	3.94	4.01	4.49	3.96	4.22	3.96	4.16	4.36	4.58	42.	Résultat brut
43.	Operating expenses	2.88	3.05	2.86	2.98	3.05	2.96	2.68	2.74	2.99	3.02	43.	Frais d'exploitation
44.	Net income	0.83	0.88	1.14	1.51	0.91	1.26	1.28	1.42	1.37	1.56	44.	Résultat net
45.	Provisions (net)	0.44	0.45	0.55	0.53	0.41	0.59	0.51	0.54	0.42	0.71	45.	Provisions (nettes)
46.	Profit before tax	0.39	0.44	0.60	0.98	0.50	0.67	0.76	0.88	0.95	0.85	46.	Bénéfices avant impôt
47.	Income tax	0.28	0.24	0.32	0.39	0.13	0.23	0.20	0.20	0.29	0.26	47.	Impôt
48.	Profit after tax	0.11	0.20	0.28	0.59	0.37	0.44	0.56	0.68	0.66	0.59	48.	Bénéfices après impôt
49.	Distributed profit	0.05	0.07	0.07	0.12	0.13	0.12	0.10	0.11	0.13	0.15	49.	Bénéfices distribués
50.	Retained profit	0.07	0.13	0.21	0.47	0.24	0.32	0.46	0.56	0.53	0.44	50.	Bénéfices mis en réserve
51.	Staff costs	2.22	2.30	2.16	2.23	2.29	2.24	2.01	2.00	2.21	2.22	51.	Frais de personnel
52.	Provisions on loans	0.48	0.44	0.25	0.33	0.35	0.47	0.48	0.54	0.45	0.51	52.	Provisions sur prêts
53.	Provisions on securities	0.01	0.02	0.03	0.05	0.14	0.11	0.18	0.07	0.11	0.32	53.	Provisions sur titres
% of gross income													**% du total du résultat brut**
54.	Net interest income	67.89	65.44	60.73	61.33	67.21	65.66	70.01	69.87	70.94	77.98	54.	Produits financiers nets
55.	Non-interest income (net)	32.11	34.56	39.27	38.67	32.79	34.34	29.99	30.13	29.06	22.02	55.	Produits non financiers (nets)
56.	Operating expenses	77.67	77.59	71.46	66.30	77.06	70.14	67.72	65.87	68.57	65.94	56.	Frais d'exploitation
57.	Net income	22.33	22.41	28.54	33.70	22.94	29.86	32.28	34.13	31.43	34.06	57.	Résultat net
58.	Provisions (net)	11.77	11.35	13.60	11.89	10.25	13.89	12.97	13.07	9.73	15.44	58.	Provisions (nettes)
59.	Profit before tax	10.56	11.06	14.95	21.81	12.69	15.97	19.32	21.07	21.70	18.62	59.	Bénéfices avant impôt
60.	Income tax	7.48	6.00	7.89	8.78	3.38	5.46	5.15	4.77	6.67	5.70	60.	Impôt
61.	Profit after tax	3.08	5.06	7.05	13.03	9.31	10.51	14.16	16.30	15.03	12.92	61.	Bénéfices après impôt
62.	Staff costs	59.77	58.43	53.79	49.64	57.86	52.95	50.84	48.07	50.61	48.54	62.	Frais de personnel
% of net income													**% du total du résultat net**
63.	Provisions (net)	52.70	50.65	47.64	35.28	44.68	46.52	40.16	38.28	30.95	45.33	63.	Provisions (nettes)
64.	Profit before tax	47.30	49.35	52.36	64.72	55.32	53.48	59.84	61.72	69.05	54.67	64.	Bénéfices avant impôt
65.	Income tax	33.50	26.78	27.65	26.07	14.74	18.29	15.96	13.97	21.23	16.75	65.	Impôt
66.	Profit after tax	13.80	22.57	24.70	38.65	40.57	35.18	43.88	47.74	47.82	37.92	66.	Bénéfices après impôt

ITALY

Large commercial banks

ITALIE

Grandes banques commerciales

Per cent

Pourcentage

BALANCE SHEET ANALYSIS

ANALYSE DU BILAN

% of year-end balance sheet total

% du total du bilan en fin d'exercice

	1983	1984	1985	1986	1987	1988	1989	1990	1991	1992 (2)		
Assets												**Actif**
67. Cash & balance with Central bank(1)	0.44	6.87	7.58	7.85	8.57	8.60	7.18	8.58	7.81	6.94	67.	Caisse & solde auprès de la Banque centrale(1)
68. Interbank deposits (1)	11.04	8.35	10.13	9.21	7.73	8.07	8.35	4.92	5.45	9.39	68.	Dépôts interbancaires (1)
69. Loans	22.32	23.04	23.66	23.83	25.83	28.45	27.65	35.05	36.33	36.90	69.	Prêts
70. Securities	20.46	18.53	16.90	17.61	19.64	15.26	11.82	10.90	10.18	9.16	70.	Valeurs mobilières
71. Other assets	45.74	43.21	41.73	41.50	38.23	39.63	44.99	40.56	40.23	37.61	71.	Autres actifs
Liabilities												**Passif**
72. Capital & reserves	3.16	3.85	4.24	4.93	6.13	5.95	5.45	6.26	7.00	8.27	72.	Capital et réserves
73. Borrowing from Central bank	0.71	0.29	1.75	0.55	0.69	0.65	0.38	0.70	1.08	0.50	73.	Emprunts auprès de la Banque centrale
74. Interbank deposits	12.68	12.46	11.20	12.55	12.15	9.10	11.30	5.99	5.84	8.57	74.	Dépôts interbancaires
75. Non-bank deposits	42.78	38.20	39.09	40.41	42.78	42.37	36.36	42.67	42.81	40.27	75.	Dépôts non bancaires
76. Bonds	-	-	-	-	-	-	-	-	-	-	76.	Obligations
77. Other liabilities	40.67	45.20	43.73	41.56	38.24	41.93	46.50	44.38	43.27	42.39	77.	Autres engagements
Memoranda												*Pour mémoire*
78. Short-term securities	*7.20*	*6.11*	*3.02*	*3.62*	*2.54*	*1.47*	*1.04*	*1.57*	*2.08*	*0.85*	*78.*	*Titres à court terme*
79. Bonds	*14.31*	*12.42*	*13.88*	*13.99*	*17.10*	*13.78*	*10.78*	*9.33*	*8.10*	*8.31*	*79.*	*Obligations*
80. Shares and participations	*1.06*	*1.23*	*1.08*	*1.39*	*1.52*	*1.54*	*1.68*	*1.83*	*3.02*	*2.64*	*80.*	*Actions et participations*
81. Claims on non-residents	*13.79*	*15.95*	*15.62*	*14.37*	*13.21*	*13.60*	*14.23*	*14.77*	*13.05*	*11.36*	*81.*	*Créances sur des non résidents*
82. Liabilities to non-residents	*18.17*	*19.88*	*18.29*	*16.15*	*16.61*	*18.73*	*19.09*	*19.86*	*20.33*	*21.28*	*82.*	*Engagements envers des non résidents*

1. Change in methodology.
2. In 1992, break in series due to mergers and acquisitions.

Notes

- Large commercial banks are a sub-group of Commercial banks.

- Average balance sheet totals (item 29) are based on twelve end-month data.

Change in methodology:

- As from 1984, "Cash and balance with Central bank" (item 17 or item 67) also includes required reserves and "Interbank deposits" (item 18 or item 68) includes both domestic and foreign currency deposits.

1. Changement méthodologique.
2. En 1992, rupture de comparabilité dans les séries dûe aux fusions et acquisitions.

Notes

- Les Grandes banques commerciales sont un sous-groupe des Banques commerciales.

- La moyenne du total des actifs/passifs (poste 29) est basée sur douze données de fin de mois.

Changement méthodologique :

- A partir de 1984 le poste "Caisse et solde auprès de la Banque centrale" (poste 17 ou poste 67) comprend également les réserves obligatoires ; le poste "Dépôts interbancaires" (poste 18 ou poste 68) comprend à la fois les dépôts en monnaie nationale et ceux en devises.

ITALY

Savings banks

Billion lire

ITALIE

Caisses d'épargne

Milliards de lires

	1983	1984	1985	1986	1987	1988	1989	1990	1991 (2)	1992	
INCOME STATEMENT											**COMPTE DE RESULTATS**
1. Interest income	18680	20839	22214	21801	20000	22173	25694	28610	29254	35321	1. Produits financiers
2. Interest expenses	13215	14453	15082	13318	11342	12364	14551	16126	16476	20196	2. Frais financiers
3. Net interest income	5465	6386	7132	8483	8658	9809	11143	12484	12778	15125	3. Produits financiers nets
4. Non-interest income (net)	1885	2242	2219	2833	3043	3060	3562	4043	4554	4551	4. Produits non financiers (nets)
5. Gross income	7350	8628	9351	11316	11701	12869	14705	16527	17332	19676	5. Résultat brut
6. Operating expenses	4934	5410	5890	6575	7186	7680	8045	9199	10151	11602	6. Frais d'exploitation
7. Net income	2416	3218	3461	4741	4515	5189	6660	7328	7181	8074	7. Résultat net
8. Provisions (net)	1469	1865	1692	1930	2203	2479	2048	2145	1700	2738	8. Provisions (nettes)
9. Profit before tax	947	1353	1769	2811	2312	2710	4612	5183	5481	5336	9. Bénéfices avant impôt
10. Income tax	702	946	1109	1644	1430	1685	1956	2123	2008	1970	10. Impôt
11. Profit after tax	245	407	660	1167	882	1025	2656	3060	3473	3366	11. Bénéfices après impôt
12. Distributed profit	-	-	3	4	5	12	38	52	174	726	12. Bénéfices distribués
13. Retained profit	245	407	657	1163	877	1013	2618	3008	3299	2640	13. Bénéfices mis en réserve
Memoranda											*Pour mémoire*
14. Staff costs	3630	3882	4180	4678	5160	5436	5721	6479	7229	8075	14. Frais de personnel
15. Provisions on loans	1193	1296	1298	1174	1420	1493	1838	1843	1830	2203	15. Provisions sur prêts
16. Provisions on securities	185	99	54	53	507	464	355	323	125	1133	16. Provisions sur titres
BALANCE SHEET											**BILAN**
Assets											**Actif**
17. Cash & balance with Central bank(1)	998	16919	20511	22823	24423	27910	30643	36528	37148	35702	17. Caisse & solde auprès de la Banque centrale(1)
18. Interbank deposits (1)	17137	21144	19796	23044	23251	21810	24767	24378	24621	33228	18. Dépôts interbancaires (1)
19. Loans	41535	51260	59171	65289	69548	82932	101312	117735	133947	147987	19. Prêts
20. Securities	48528	51356	57643	59659	60653	62197	62109	61272	55387	62738	20. Valeurs mobilières
21. Other assets	50906	41540	50972	58367	65862	80170	106053	105763	116751	127448	21. Autres actifs
Liabilities											**Passif**
22. Capital & reserves	6178	9416	11493	13666	16715	19151	22554	25125	35042	43160	22. Capital et réserves
23. Borrowing from Central bank	388	466	403	407	1517	1679	2162	2370	1430	3049	23. Emprunts auprès de la Banque centrale
24. Interbank deposits	7626	7968	9889	10374	13427	14260	15708	17488	15493	26211	24. Dépôts interbancaires
25. Non-bank deposits	106452	116877	128411	140308	145804	162219	175583	194949	201689	211105	25. Dépôts non bancaires
26. Bonds											26. Obligations
27. Other liabilities	38460	47492	57897	64426	66275	77711	108876	105745	114200	123576	27. Autres engagements
Balance sheet total											**Total du bilan**
28. End-year total	159104	182219	208094	229181	243737	275019	324883	345677	367854	407102	28. En fin d'exercice
29. Average total	142674	165252	190549	209841	228879	260424	289849	320819	322016	375866	29. Moyen
Memoranda											*Pour mémoire*
30. Short-term securities	11141	9544	5605	6502	4842	5004	4442	7366	7670	5341	30. Titres à court terme
31. Bonds	39057	41812	52038	53157	55811	57194	57667	53906	47716	57397	31. Obligations
32. Shares and participations	1678	1943	2217	2565	2903	3365	4767	5421	8072	10741	32. Actions et participations
33. Claims on non-residents	1946	2624	3550	4071	5275	6941	8179	9850	12782	12624	33. Créances sur des non résidents
34. Liabilities to non-residents	4583	5915	6729	8326	10412	13090	16137	18964	24163	29253	34. Engagements envers des non résidents
SUPPLEMENTARY INFORMATION											**RENSEIGNEMENTS COMPLEMENTAIRES**
35. Number of institutions	85	83	83	83	79	79	78	78	76	76	35. Nombre d'institutions
36. Number of branches	4074	4466	4481	4483	4391	4508	4535	4765	4958	5269	36. Nombre de succursales
37. Number of employees (x 1000)	69.2	70.3	71.0	72.2	70.9	75.1	77.5	80.0	80.5	81.4	37. Nombre de salariés (x 1000)

Savings banks

Caisses d'épargne

Per cent

Pourcentage

INCOME STATEMENT ANALYSIS

ANALYSE DU COMPTE DE RESULTATS

	1983	1984	1985	1986	1987	1988	1989	1990	1991 (2)	1992		
% of average balance sheet total												**% du total moyen du bilan**
38. Interest income	13.09	12.61	11.66	10.39	8.74	8.51	8.86	8.92	9.08	9.40	38.	Produits financiers
39. Interest expenses	9.26	8.75	7.92	6.35	4.96	4.75	5.02	5.03	5.12	5.37	39.	Frais financiers
40. Net interest income	3.83	3.86	3.74	4.04	3.78	3.77	3.84	3.89	3.97	4.02	40.	Produits financiers nets
41. Non-interest income (net)	1.32	1.36	1.16	1.35	1.33	1.18	1.23	1.26	1.41	1.21	41.	Produits non financiers (nets)
42. Gross income	5.15	5.22	4.91	5.39	5.11	4.94	5.07	5.15	5.38	5.23	42.	Résultat brut
43. Operating expenses	3.46	3.27	3.09	3.13	3.14	2.95	2.78	2.87	3.15	3.09	43.	Frais d'exploitation
44. Net income	1.69	1.95	1.82	2.26	1.97	1.99	2.30	2.28	2.23	2.15	44.	Résultat net
45. Provisions (net)	1.03	1.13	0.89	0.92	0.96	0.95	0.71	0.67	0.53	0.73	45.	Provisions (nettes)
46. Profit before tax	0.66	0.82	0.93	1.34	1.01	1.04	1.59	1.62	1.70	1.42	46.	Bénéfices avant impôt
47. Income tax	0.49	0.57	0.58	0.78	0.62	0.65	0.67	0.66	0.62	0.52	47.	Impôt
48. Profit after tax	0.17	0.25	0.35	0.56	0.39	0.39	0.92	0.95	1.08	0.90	48.	Bénéfices après impôt
49. Distributed profit	-	-	0.00	0.00	0.00	0.00	0.01	0.02	0.05	0.19	49.	Bénéfices distribués
50. Retained profit	0.17	0.25	0.34	0.55	0.38	0.39	0.90	0.94	1.02	0.70	50.	Bénéfices mis en réserve
51. Staff costs	2.54	2.35	2.19	2.23	2.25	2.09	1.97	2.02	2.24	2.15	51.	Frais de personnel
52. Provisions on loans	0.84	0.78	0.68	0.56	0.62	0.57	0.63	0.57	0.57	0.59	52.	Provisions sur prêts
53. Provisions on securities	0.13	0.06	0.03	0.03	0.22	0.18	0.12	0.10	0.04	0.30	53.	Provisions sur titres
% of gross income												**% du total du résultat brut**
54. Net interest income	74.35	74.01	76.27	74.96	73.99	76.22	75.78	75.54	73.72	76.87	54.	Produits financiers nets
55. Non-interest income (net)	25.65	25.99	23.73	25.04	26.01	23.78	24.22	24.46	26.28	23.13	55.	Produits non financiers (nets)
56. Operating expenses	67.13	62.70	62.99	58.10	61.41	59.68	54.71	55.66	58.57	58.97	56.	Frais d'exploitation
57. Net income	32.87	37.30	37.01	41.90	38.59	40.32	45.29	44.34	41.43	41.03	57.	Résultat net
58. Provisions (net)	19.99	21.62	18.09	17.06	18.83	19.26	13.93	12.98	9.81	13.92	58.	Provisions (nettes)
59. Profit before tax	12.88	15.68	18.92	24.84	19.76	21.06	31.36	31.36	31.62	27.12	59.	Bénéfices avant impôt
60. Income tax	9.55	10.96	11.86	14.53	12.22	13.09	13.30	12.85	11.59	10.01	60.	Impôt
61. Profit after tax	3.33	4.72	7.06	10.31	7.54	7.96	18.06	18.52	20.04	17.11	61.	Bénéfices après impôt
62. Staff costs	49.39	44.99	44.70	41.34	44.10	42.24	38.91	39.20	41.71	41.04	62.	Frais de personnel
% of net income												**% du total du résultat net**
63. Provisions (net)	60.80	57.96	48.89	40.71	48.79	47.77	30.75	29.27	23.67	33.91	63.	Provisions (nettes)
64. Profit before tax	39.20	42.04	51.11	59.29	51.21	52.23	69.25	70.73	76.33	66.09	64.	Bénéfices avant impôt
65. Income tax	29.06	29.40	32.04	34.68	31.67	32.47	29.37	28.97	27.96	24.40	65.	Impôt
66. Profit after tax	10.14	12.65	19.07	24.62	19.53	19.75	39.88	41.76	48.36	41.69	66.	Bénéfices après impôt

ITALY

Savings banks

Per cent

BALANCE SHEET ANALYSIS

% of year-end balance sheet total

	1983	1984	1985	1986	1987	1988	1989	1990	1991 (2)	1992
Assets										
67. Cash & balance with Central bank(1)	0.63	9.28	9.86	9.96	10.02	10.15	9.43	10.57	10.10	8.77
68. Interbank deposits (1)	10.77	11.60	9.51	10.05	9.54	7.93	7.62	7.05	6.69	8.16
69. Loans	26.11	28.13	28.43	28.49	28.53	30.16	31.18	34.06	36.41	36.35
70. Securities	30.50	28.18	27.70	26.03	24.88	22.62	19.12	17.73	15.06	15.41
71. Other assets	32.00	22.80	24.49	25.47	27.02	29.15	32.64	30.60	31.74	31.31
Liabilities										
72. Capital & reserves	3.88	5.17	5.52	5.96	6.86	6.96	6.94	7.27	9.53	10.60
73. Borrowing from Central bank	0.24	0.26	0.19	0.18	0.62	0.61	0.67	0.69	0.39	0.75
74. Interbank deposits	4.79	4.37	4.75	4.53	5.51	5.19	4.83	5.06	4.21	6.44
75. Non-bank deposits	66.91	64.14	61.71	61.22	59.82	58.98	54.04	56.40	54.83	51.86
76. Bonds	-	-	-	-	-	-	-	-	-	-
77. Other liabilities	24.17	26.06	27.82	28.11	27.19	28.26	33.51	30.59	31.04	30.36
Memoranda										
78. Short-term securities	*7.00*	*5.24*	*2.69*	*2.84*	*1.99*	*1.82*	*1.37*	*2.13*	*2.09*	*1.31*
79. Bonds	*24.55*	*22.95*	*25.01*	*23.19*	*22.90*	*20.80*	*17.75*	*15.59*	*12.97*	*14.10*
80. Shares and participations	*1.05*	*1.07*	*1.07*	*1.12*	*1.19*	*1.22*	*1.47*	*1.57*	*2.19*	*2.64*
81. Claims on non-residents	*1.22*	*1.44*	*1.71*	*1.78*	*2.16*	*2.52*	*2.52*	*2.85*	*3.47*	*3.10*
82. Liabilities to non-residents	*2.88*	*3.25*	*3.23*	*3.63*	*4.27*	*4.76*	*4.97*	*5.49*	*6.57*	*7.19*

1. Change in methodology.
2. In 1991, break in series due to mergers and acquisitions.

Notes

- Average balance sheet totals (item 29) are based on twelve end-month data.

Change in methodology:

- As from 1984, "Cash and balance with Central bank" (item 17 or item 67) also includes required reserves and "Interbank deposits" (item 18 or item 68) includes both domestic and foreign currency deposits.

ITALIE

Caisses d'épargne

Pourcentage

ANALYSE DU BILAN

% du total du bilan en fin d'exercice

Actif
67. Caisse & solde auprès de la Banque centrale(1)
68. Dépôts interbancaires (1)
69. Prêts
70. Valeurs mobilières
71. Autres actifs

Passif
72. Capital et réserves
73. Emprunts auprès de la Banque centrale
74. Dépôts interbancaires
75. Dépôts non bancaires
76. Obligations
77. Autres engagements

Pour mémoire
78. Titres à court terme
79. Obligations
80. Actions et participations
81. Créances sur des non résidents
82. Engagements envers des non résidents

1. Changement méthodologique.
2. En 1991, rupture de comparabilité dans les séries dûe aux fusions et acquisitions.

Notes

- La moyenne du total des actifs/passifs (poste 29) est basée sur douze données de fin de mois.

Changement méthodologique :

- A partir de 1984 le poste "Caisse et solde auprès de la Banque centrale" (poste 17 ou poste 67) comprend également les réserves obligatoires ; le poste "Dépôts interbancaires" (poste 18 ou poste 68) comprend à la fois les dépôts en monnaie nationale et ceux en devises.

JAPAN / JAPON

Commercial banks / Banques commerciales

100 million Japanese yen / *100 millions de yen japonais*

No.	Item	1983	1984	1985	1986	1987	1988	1989	1990	1991	1992	Poste
	INCOME STATEMENT											**COMPTE DE RESULTATS**
1.	Interest income	191308	226645	212785	205504	225242	281848	388258	481476	462453	360912	Produits financiers
2.	Interest expenses	144755	179559	166626	152514	168596	211888	318008	413323	379443	269818	Frais financiers
3.	Net interest income	46553	47086	46159	52990	56646	69960	70250	68153	83010	91094	Produits financiers nets
4.	Non-interest income (net)	8010	10113	12311	12988	18998	24369	21992	21663	10197	3489	Produits non financiers (nets)
5.	Gross income	54563	57199	58470	65978	75644	94329	92242	89816	93207	94583	Résultat brut
6.	Operating expenses	36804	38943	40353	42516	45629	52811	56619	60639	64193	66294	Frais d'exploitation
7.	Net income	17759	18256	18117	23462	30015	41518	35623	29177	29014	28289	Résultat net
8.	Provisions (net)	1184	1295	723	1596	1631	3147	3101	2125	5335	9612	Provisions (nettes)
9.	Profit before tax	16575	16961	17394	21866	28384	38371	32522	27052	23679	18677	Bénéfices avant impôt
10.	Income tax	9100	9363	9209	11770	15625	20235	15521	12743	12628	11084	Impôt
11.	Profit after tax	7475	7598	8185	10096	12759	18136	17001	14309	11051	7593	Bénéfices après impôt
12.	Distributed profit	1916	2018	2089	2274	2337	1493	1638	1694	1697	1706	Bénéfices distribués
13.	Retained profit	5559	5580	6096	7822	10422	16643	15363	12615	9354	5887	Bénéfices mis en réserve
	Memoranda											*Pour mémoire*
14.	Staff costs	21583	22421	23032	23600	23774	29558	30796	32255	33713	34624	Frais de personnel
15.	Provisions on loans	1064	1182	494	1085	1320	2851	2937	2009	5480	9329	Provisions sur prêts
16.	Provisions on securities	120	113	229	511	311	296	164	116	-145	283	Provisions sur titres
	BALANCE SHEET											**BILAN**
	Assets											**Actif**
17.	Cash & balance with Central bank(1)	541687	635772	594525	724358	820228	994636	1232259	1010134	845110	710380	Caisse & solde auprès de la Banque centrale(1)
18.	Interbank deposits	..	..	..	..	..	..	..	..	..	..	Dépôts interbancaires
19.	Loans	1764333	2022864	2175910	2456586	2783332	3537651	4098926	4330050	4484647	4538361	Prêts
20.	Securities	401326	447676	474340	581051	648140	835621	1014487	1022177	978035	960568	Valeurs mobilières
21.	Other assets	524120	580352	657274	674373	758522	1037496	1287869	1170455	1138940	786390	Autres actifs
	Liabilities											**Passif**
22.	Capital & reserves	75675	82498	91335	101614	124197	175958	226715	239712	249044	253907	Capital et réserves
23.	Borrowing from Central bank	22922	13588	26192	40878	47166	46336	33141	35555	30535	39738	Emprunts auprès de la Banque centrale
24.	Interbank deposits (2)	..	..	..	..	..	..	..	..	..	..	Dépôts interbancaires (2)
25.	Non-bank deposits	2511214	2865314	2959597	3361047	3797408	4906164	5808225	5736884	5554169	5357468	Dépôts non bancaires
26.	Bonds	21460	22900	30934	33266	44854	57657	58214	55069	56237	56566	Obligations
27.	Other liabilities	600195	702364	793991	899563	996597	1219289	1507246	1465655	1556746	1288020	Autres engagements
	Balance sheet total											**Total du bilan**
28.	End-year total	3231466	3686664	3902049	4436368	5010222	6405404	7633541	7532875	7446732	6995699	En fin d'exercice
29.	Average total	3095353	3459065	3794356	4169208	4723295	5971836	7019472	7583208	7489804	7221216	Moyen
	Memoranda											*Pour mémoire*
30.	Short-term securities	..	..	..	..	..	..	..	..	..	..	Titres à court terme
31.	Bonds	..	..	..	..	..	..	..	..	..	..	Obligations
32.	Shares and participations	67159	76365	84597	94218	122050	173678	219140	247808	258658	258058	Actions et participations
33.	Claims on non-residents	..	..	..	..	..	..	..	..	..	..	Créances sur des non résidents
34.	Liabilities to non-residents	..	..	..	..	..	..	..	..	..	..	Engagements envers des non résidents
	SUPPLEMENTARY INFORMATION											**RENSEIGNEMENTS COMPLEMENTAIRES**
35.	Number of institutions	76	77	77	77	77	145	145	144	143	141	Nombre d'institutions
36.	Number of branches	8550	8899	9037	9251	9355	13727	14045	14325	14632	14782	Nombre de succursales
37.	Number of employees (x 1000)	337	333	325	320	314	397	397	399	406	412	Nombre de salariés (x 1000)

JAPAN

Commercial banks

JAPON

Banques commerciales

	1983	1984	1985	1986	1987	1988	1989	1990	1991	1992
Per cent / *Pourcentage*										
INCOME STATEMENT ANALYSIS / **ANALYSE DU COMPTE DE RESULTATS**										
% of average balance sheet total / **% du total moyen du bilan**										
38. Interest income / Produits financiers	6.18	6.55	5.61	4.93	4.77	4.72	5.53	6.35	6.17	5.00
39. Interest expenses / Frais financiers	4.68	5.19	4.39	3.66	3.57	3.55	4.53	5.45	5.07	3.74
40. Net interest income / Produits financiers nets	1.50	1.36	1.22	1.27	1.20	1.17	1.00	0.90	1.11	1.26
41. Non-interest income (net) / Produits non financiers (nets)	0.26	0.29	0.32	0.31	0.40	0.41	0.31	0.29	0.14	0.05
42. Gross income / Résultat brut	1.76	1.65	1.54	1.58	1.60	1.58	1.31	1.18	1.24	1.31
43. Operating expenses / Frais d'exploitation	1.19	1.13	1.06	1.02	0.97	0.88	0.81	0.80	0.86	0.92
44. Net income / Résultat net	0.57	0.53	0.48	0.56	0.64	0.70	0.51	0.38	0.39	0.39
45. Provisions (net) / Provisions (nettes)	0.04	0.04	0.02	0.04	0.03	0.05	0.04	0.03	0.07	0.13
46. Profit before tax / Bénéfices avant impôt	0.54	0.49	0.46	0.52	0.60	0.64	0.46	0.36	0.32	0.26
47. Income tax / Impôt	0.29	0.27	0.24	0.28	0.33	0.34	0.22	0.17	0.17	0.15
48. Profit after tax / Bénéfices après impôt	0.24	0.22	0.22	0.24	0.27	0.30	0.24	0.19	0.15	0.11
49. Distributed profit / Bénéfices distribués	0.06	0.06	0.06	0.05	0.05	0.03	0.02	0.02	0.02	0.02
50. Retained profit / Bénéfices mis en réserve	0.18	0.16	0.16	0.19	0.22	0.28	0.22	0.17	0.12	0.08
51. Staff costs / Frais de personnel	0.70	0.65	0.61	0.57	0.50	0.49	0.44	0.43	0.45	0.48
52. Provisions on loans / Provisions sur prêts	0.03	0.03	0.01	0.03	0.03	0.05	0.04	0.03	0.07	0.13
53. Provisions on securities / Provisions sur titres	0.00	0.00	0.01	0.01	0.01	0.00	0.00	0.00	0.00	0.00
% of gross income / **% du total du résultat brut**										
54. Net interest income / Produits financiers nets	85.32	82.32	78.94	80.31	74.88	74.17	76.16	75.88	89.06	96.31
55. Non-interest income (net) / Produits non financiers (nets)	14.68	17.68	21.06	19.69	25.12	25.83	23.84	24.12	10.94	3.69
56. Operating expenses / Frais d'exploitation	67.45	68.08	69.01	64.44	60.32	55.99	61.38	67.51	68.87	70.09
57. Net income / Résultat net	32.55	31.92	30.99	35.56	39.68	44.01	38.62	32.49	31.13	29.91
58. Provisions (net) / Provisions (nettes)	2.17	2.26	1.24	2.42	2.16	3.34	3.36	2.37	5.72	10.16
59. Profit before tax / Bénéfices avant impôt	30.38	29.65	29.75	33.14	37.52	40.68	35.26	30.12	25.40	19.75
60. Income tax / Impôt	16.68	16.37	15.75	17.84	20.66	21.45	16.83	14.19	13.55	11.72
61. Profit after tax / Bénéfices après impôt	13.70	13.28	14.00	15.30	16.87	19.23	18.43	15.93	11.86	8.03
62. Staff costs / Frais de personnel	39.56	39.20	39.39	35.77	31.43	31.34	33.39	35.91	36.17	36.61
% of net income / **% du total du résultat net**										
63. Provisions (net) / Provisions (nettes)	6.67	7.09	3.99	6.80	5.43	7.58	8.71	7.28	18.39	33.98
64. Profit before tax / Bénéfices avant impôt	93.33	92.91	96.01	93.20	94.57	92.42	91.29	92.72	81.61	66.02
65. Income tax / Impôt	51.24	51.29	50.83	50.17	52.06	48.74	43.57	43.67	43.52	39.18
66. Profit after tax / Bénéfices après impôt	42.09	41.62	45.18	43.03	42.51	43.68	47.72	49.04	38.09	26.84

Commercial banks

Per cent

BALANCE SHEET ANALYSIS

% of year-end balance sheet total

	1983	1984	1985	1986	1987	1988	1989	1990	1991	1992
Assets										
67. Cash & balance with Central bank (1)	..	..	..	..	..	..	..	..	..	..
68. Interbank deposits	16.76	17.25	15.24	16.33	16.37	15.53	16.14	13.41	11.35	10.15
69. Loans	54.60	54.87	55.76	55.37	55.55	55.23	53.70	57.48	60.22	64.87
70. Securities	12.42	12.14	12.16	13.10	12.94	13.05	13.29	13.57	13.13	13.73
71. Other assets	16.22	15.74	16.84	15.20	15.14	16.20	16.87	15.54	15.29	11.24
Liabilities										
72. Capital & reserves	2.34	2.24	2.34	2.29	2.48	2.75	2.97	3.18	3.34	3.63
73. Borrowing from Central bank	0.71	0.37	0.67	0.92	0.94	0.72	0.43	0.47	0.41	0.57
74. Interbank deposits (2)	..	..	..	..	..	..	..	..	..	..
75. Non-bank deposits	77.71	77.72	75.85	75.76	75.79	76.59	76.09	76.16	74.59	76.58
76. Bonds	0.66	0.62	0.79	0.75	0.90	0.90	0.76	0.73	0.76	0.81
77. Other liabilities	18.57	19.05	20.35	20.28	19.89	19.04	19.75	19.46	20.91	18.41
Memoranda										
78. Short-term securities	..	..	..	..	..	..	..	..	..	..
79. Bonds	..	..	..	..	..	..	..	..	..	..
80. Shares and participations	2.08	2.07	2.17	2.12	2.44	2.71	2.87	3.29	3.47	3.69
81. Claims on non-residents	..	..	..	..	..	..	..	..	..	..
82. Liabilities to non-residents	..	..	..	..	..	..	..	..	..	..

Notes

1. Included under "Interbank deposits" (item 18 or item 68).
2. Included under "Non-bank deposits" (item 25 or item 75).

Notes

- Data relate to fiscal years ending 31st March.

Change in methodology

- As from 1988, data also include Sogo banks (banks for medium- and small-size industries).

JAPON

Banques commerciales

Pourcentage

ANALYSE DU BILAN

% du total du bilan en fin d'exercice

Actif
67. Caisse & solde auprès de la Banque centrale(1)
68. Dépôts interbancaires
69. Prêts
70. Valeurs mobilières
71. Autres actifs

Passif
72. Capital et réserves
73. Emprunts auprès de la Banque centrale
74. Dépôts interbancaires (2)
75. Dépôts non bancaires
76. Obligations
77. Autres engagements

Pour mémoire
78. Titres à court terme
79. Obligations
80. Actions et participations
81. Créances sur des non résidents
82. Engagements envers des non résidents

Notes

- Les données portent sur l'exercice financier, qui se termine le 31 mars.

Changement méthodologique

- Depuis 1988, sont aussi reprises dans les données des Sogo Banks (les banques pour les petites et moyennes entreprises).

1. Inclus sous "Dépôts interbancaires" (poste 18 ou poste 68).
2. Inclus sous "Dépôts non bancaires" (poste 25 ou poste 75).

JAPAN

Large commercial banks

JAPON

Grandes banques commerciales

100 million Japanese yen / *100 millions de yen japonais*

#	Item	1983	1984	1985	1986	1987	1988	1989	1990	1991	1992
	INCOME STATEMENT / COMPTE DE RESULTATS										
1.	Interest income / Produits financiers	136601	167142	150656	144688	163562	204088	270559	323647	298368	226675
2.	Interest expenses / Frais financiers	110370	140820	125425	114577	130371	167313	238474	293346	257605	180932
3.	Net interest income / Produits financiers nets	26231	26322	25231	30111	33191	36775	32085	30301	40763	45743
4.	Non-interest income (net) / Produits non financiers (nets)	6132	7759	9140	9787	15787	24566	19003	17000	9026	2807
5.	Gross income / Résultat brut	32363	34081	34371	39898	48978	61341	51088	47301	49789	48550
6.	Operating expenses / Frais d'exploitation	20941	21973	22554	24074	26620	28559	27233	29367	31018	31779
7.	Net income / Résultat net	11422	12108	11817	15824	22358	32782	23855	17934	18771	16771
8.	Provisions (net) / Provisions (nettes)	766	903	368	928	1091	6361	2354	1503	4330	7368
9.	Profit before tax / Bénéfices avant impôt	10656	11205	11449	14896	21267	26421	21501	16431	14441	9403
10.	Income tax / Impôt	5716	6176	5868	7836	12066	13940	10470	7577	7965	5727
11.	Profit after tax / Bénéfices après impôt	4940	5029	5581	7060	9201	12481	11031	8854	6476	3676
12.	Distributed profit / Bénéfices distribués	1308	1371	1417	1581	1624	1838	1069	1115	1113	1113
13.	Retained profit / Bénéfices mis en réserve	3632	3658	4164	5479	7577	10643	9962	7739	5363	2563
	Memoranda / Pour mémoire										
14.	*Staff costs / Frais de personnel*	11630	11898	12070	12511	12498	12772	13378	14079	14658	14970
15.	*Provisions on loans / Provisions sur prêts*	753	853	214	576	925	2080	2224	1425	4354	7114
16.	*Provisions on securities / Provisions sur titres*	13	50	154	352	166	4281	130	78	-24	254
	BALANCE SHEET / BILAN										
	Assets / Actif										
17.	Cash & balance with Central bank(1) / Caisse & solde auprès de la Banque centrale(1)	483725	573427	527488	648761	723304	883583	1046119	858603	694322	556503
18.	Interbank deposits / Dépôts interbancaires	..	..	..	..	..	..	..	..	..	..
19.	Loans / Prêts	1162708	1340795	1453591	1672764	1909408	2159315	2520336	2660295	2736541	2743890
20.	Securities / Valeurs mobilières	224028	255537	289760	344058	391775	449216	560295	538856	513847	513673
21.	Other assets / Autres actifs	411396	457343	485490	518040	583935	720189	956143	858749	804944	546982
	Liabilities / Passif										
22.	Capital & reserves / Capital et réserves	43394	47196	53621	60837	78740	104939	137039	144097	148493	149928
23.	Borrowing from Central bank / Emprunts auprès de la Banque centrale	21253	11771	24265	38492	44685	43204	27135	28024	26353	34859
24.	Interbank deposits (2) / Dépôts interbancaires (2)	..	..	..	..	..	..	..	..	..	..
25.	Non-bank deposits / Dépôts non bancaires	1698496	1951891	1991385	2303880	2622945	3045140	3644553	3535869	3292328	3087810
26.	Bonds / Obligations	21460	22900	30934	32908	41384	52623	53948	51568	53546	54181
27.	Other liabilities / Autres engagements	497254	593344	656124	747506	820668	966397	1220218	1156945	1228934	1034270
	Balance sheet total / Total du bilan										
28.	End-year total / En fin d'exercice	2281857	2627102	2756329	3183623	3608422	4212303	5082893	4916503	4749654	4361048
29.	Average total / Moyen	2186357	2454479	2691715	2969976	3396022	3910362	4647598	4999698	4833079	4555351
	Memoranda / Pour mémoire										
30.	*Short-term securities / Titres à court terme*	..	..	..	..	..	..	..	..	..	..
31.	*Bonds / Obligations*	..	..	..	..	..	..	..	..	..	..
32.	*Shares and participations / Actions et participations*	53796	61152	67468	74847	97885	132497	169114	192011	201849	200637
33.	*Claims on non-residents / Créances sur des non résidents*	..	..	..	..	..	..	..	..	..	..
34.	*Liabilities to non-residents / Engagements envers des non résidents*	..	..	..	..	..	..	..	..	..	..
	SUPPLEMENTARY INFORMATION / RENSEIGNEMENTS COMPLEMENTAIRES										
35.	Number of institutions / Nombre d'institutions	13	13	13	13	13	13	13	12	11	11
36.	Number of branches / Nombre de succursales	2859	2883	2904	3032	3050	3099	3182	3249	3280	3293
37.	Number of employees (x 1000) / Nombre de salariés (x 1000)	172	166	160	157	154	152	152	152	154	157

JAPAN

Large commercial banks

JAPON

Grandes banques commerciales

Per cent / *Pourcentage*

INCOME STATEMENT ANALYSIS / **ANALYSE DU COMPTE DE RESULTATS**

		1983	1984	1985	1986	1987	1988	1989	1990	1991	1992	
% of average balance sheet total												**% du total moyen du bilan**
38.	Interest income	6.25	6.81	5.60	4.87	4.82	5.22	5.82	6.47	6.17	4.98	Produits financiers 38.
39.	Interest expenses	5.05	5.74	4.66	3.86	3.84	4.28	5.13	5.87	5.33	3.97	Frais financiers 39.
40.	Net interest income	1.20	1.07	0.94	1.01	0.98	0.94	0.69	0.61	0.84	1.00	Produits financiers nets 40.
41.	Non-interest income (net)	0.28	0.32	0.34	0.33	0.46	0.63	0.41	0.34	0.19	0.06	Produits non financiers (nets) 41.
42.	Gross income	1.48	1.39	1.28	1.34	1.44	1.57	1.10	0.95	1.03	1.07	Résultat brut 42.
43.	Operating expenses	0.96	0.90	0.84	0.81	0.78	0.73	0.59	0.59	0.64	0.70	Frais d'exploitation 43.
44.	Net income	0.52	0.49	0.44	0.53	0.66	0.84	0.51	0.36	0.39	0.37	Résultat net 44.
45.	Provisions (net)	0.04	0.04	0.01	0.03	0.03	0.16	0.05	0.03	0.09	0.16	Provisions (nettes) 45.
46.	Profit before tax	0.49	0.46	0.43	0.50	0.63	0.68	0.46	0.33	0.30	0.21	Bénéfices avant impôt 46.
47.	Income tax	0.26	0.25	0.22	0.26	0.36	0.36	0.23	0.15	0.16	0.13	Impôt 47.
48.	Profit after tax	0.23	0.20	0.21	0.24	0.27	0.32	0.24	0.18	0.13	0.08	Bénéfices après impôt 48.
49.	Distributed profit	0.06	0.06	0.05	0.05	0.05	0.05	0.02	0.02	0.02	0.02	Bénéfices distribués 49.
50.	Retained profit	0.17	0.15	0.15	0.18	0.22	0.27	0.21	0.15	0.11	0.06	Bénéfices mis en réserve 50.
51.	Staff costs	0.53	0.48	0.45	0.42	0.37	0.33	0.29	0.28	0.30	0.33	Frais de personnel 51.
52.	Provisions on loans	0.03	0.03	0.01	0.02	0.03	0.05	0.05	0.03	0.09	0.16	Provisions sur prêts 52.
53.	Provisions on securities	0.00	0.00	0.01	0.01	0.00	0.11	0.00	0.00	0.00	0.01	Provisions sur titres 53.
% of gross income												**% du total du résultat brut**
54.	Net interest income	81.05	77.23	73.41	75.47	67.77	59.95	62.80	64.06	81.87	94.22	Produits financiers nets 54.
55.	Non-interest income (net)	18.95	22.77	26.59	24.53	32.23	40.05	37.20	35.94	18.13	5.78	Produits non financiers (nets) 55.
56.	Operating expenses	64.71	64.47	65.62	60.34	54.35	46.56	53.31	62.09	62.30	65.46	Frais d'exploitation 56.
57.	Net income	35.29	35.53	34.38	39.66	45.65	53.44	46.69	37.91	37.70	34.54	Résultat net 57.
58.	Provisions (net)	2.37	2.65	1.07	2.33	2.23	10.37	4.61	3.18	8.70	15.18	Provisions (nettes) 58.
59.	Profit before tax	32.93	32.88	33.31	37.34	43.42	43.07	42.09	34.74	29.00	19.37	Bénéfices avant impôt 59.
60.	Income tax	17.66	18.12	17.07	19.64	24.64	22.73	20.49	16.02	16.00	11.80	Impôt 60.
61.	Profit after tax	15.26	14.76	16.24	17.70	18.79	20.35	21.59	18.72	13.01	7.57	Bénéfices après impôt 61.
62.	Staff costs	35.94	34.91	35.12	31.36	25.52	20.82	26.19	29.76	29.44	30.83	Frais de personnel 62.
% of net income												**% du total du résultat net**
63.	Provisions (net)	6.71	7.46	3.11	5.86	4.88	19.40	9.87	8.38	23.07	43.93	Provisions (nettes) 63.
64.	Profit before tax	93.29	92.54	96.89	94.14	95.12	80.60	90.13	91.62	76.93	56.07	Bénéfices avant impôt 64.
65.	Income tax	50.04	51.01	49.66	49.52	53.97	42.52	43.89	42.25	42.43	34.15	Impôt 65.
66.	Profit after tax	43.25	41.53	47.23	44.62	41.15	38.07	46.24	49.37	34.50	21.92	Bénéfices après impôt 66.

JAPAN

Large commercial banks

Per cent

BALANCE SHEET ANALYSIS

% of year-end balance sheet total

	1983	1984	1985	1986	1987	1988	1989	1990	1991	1992
Assets										
67. Cash & balance with Central bank (1)	..	..	..	..	..	..	..	..	..	..
68. Interbank deposits	21.20	21.83	19.14	20.38	20.04	20.98	20.58	17.46	14.62	12.76
69. Loans	50.95	51.04	52.74	52.54	52.92	51.26	49.58	54.11	57.62	62.92
70. Securities	9.82	9.73	10.51	10.81	10.86	10.66	11.02	10.96	10.82	11.78
71. Other assets	18.03	17.41	17.61	16.27	16.18	17.10	18.81	17.47	16.95	12.54
Liabilities										
72. Capital & reserves	1.90	1.80	1.95	1.91	2.18	2.49	2.70	2.93	3.13	3.44
73. Borrowing from Central bank	0.93	0.45	0.88	1.21	1.24	1.03	0.53	0.57	0.55	0.80
74. Interbank deposits (2)	..	..	..	..	..	..	..	..	..	..
75. Non-bank deposits (2)	74.43	74.30	72.25	72.37	72.69	72.29	71.70	71.92	69.32	70.80
76. Bonds	0.94	0.87	1.12	1.03	1.15	1.25	1.06	1.05	1.13	1.24
77. Other liabilities	21.79	22.59	23.80	23.48	22.74	22.94	24.01	23.53	25.87	23.72
Memoranda										
78. Short-term securities	..	..	..	..	..	..	..	..	..	..
79. Bonds	..	..	..	..	..	..	..	..	..	..
80. Shares and participations	2.36	2.33	2.45	2.35	2.71	3.15	3.33	3.91	4.25	4.60
81. Claims on non-residents	..	..	..	..	..	..	..	..	..	..
82. Liabilities to non-residents	..	..	..	..	..	..	..	..	..	..

1. Included under "Interbank deposits" (item 18 or item 68).
2. Included under "Non-bank deposits" (item 25 or item 75).

Notes

- Data are based on the annual publication of the Federation of Bankers Association of Japan "Analysis of Financial Statements of All Banks". The term Large commercial banks corresponds to the term City banks used in Japanese publications.

- Data relate to fiscal years ending 31st March.

JAPON

Grandes banques commerciales

Pourcentage

ANALYSE DU BILAN

% du total du bilan en fin d'exercice

Actif
67. Caisse & solde auprès de la Banque centrale(1)
68. Dépôts interbancaires
69. Prêts
70. Valeurs mobilières
71. Autres actifs

Passif
72. Capital et réserves
73. Emprunts auprès de la Banque centrale
74. Dépôts interbancaires (2)
75. Dépôts non bancaires
76. Obligations
77. Autres engagements

Pour mémoire
78. Titres à court terme
79. Obligations
80. Actions et participations
81. Créances sur des non résidents
82. Engagements envers des non résidents

1. Inclus sous "Dépôts interbancaires" (poste 18 ou poste 68).
2. Inclus sous "Dépôts non bancaires" (poste 25 ou poste 75).

Notes

- Les données sont extraites d'une publication annuelle de la Fédération des associations de banquiers du Japon "Analysis of Financial Statements of All Banks". Le terme, Grandes banques commerciales correspond au terme City banks utilisé dans les publications japonaises.

- Les données portent sur l'exercice financier, qui se termine le 31 mars.

LUXEMBOURG

Commercial banks

Million Luxembourg francs

LUXEMBOURG

Banques commerciales

Millions de francs luxembourgeois

	English	French	1983	1984	1985	1986	1987	1988	1989	1990	1991	1992
	INCOME STATEMENT	**COMPTE DE RESULTATS**										
1.	Interest income	Produits financiers	578423	661542	659869	593525	605706	702452	1001719	1185123	1251957	1375962
2.	Interest expenses	Frais financiers	501612	579470	571174	506503	519999	612743	910018	1090911	1143722	1259077
3.	Net interest income	Produits financiers nets	76811	82072	88695	87022	85707	89709	91701	94212	108235	116885
4.	Non-interest income (net)	Produits non financiers (nets)	16281	12525	21712	23657	21418	28762	36062	50738	39044	48172
5.	Gross income	Résultat brut	93092	94597	110407	110679	107125	118471	127763	144950	147279	165057
6.	Operating expenses	Frais d'exploitation	24388	27049	30777	34110	37767	45361	52259	54089	59720	65000
7.	Net income	Résultat net	68704	67548	79630	76569	69358	73110	75504	90861	87559	100057
8.	Provisions (net)	Provisions (nettes)	52606	47203	54515	50973	42488	35000	41357	63860	54302	55180
9.	Profit before tax	Bénéfices avant impôt	16098	20345	25115	25596	26870	38110	34147	27001	33257	44877
10.	Income tax	Impôt	8192	9816	11817	11426	11246	14579	10912	7919	9539	16498
11.	Profit after tax	Bénéfices après impôt	7906	10529	13298	14170	15624	23531	23235	19082	23718	28379
12.	Distributed profit	Bénéfices distribués	2177	5306	5437	5753	7861	8716	NA	NA	NA	NA
13.	Retained profit	Bénéfices mis en réserve	5729	5223	7861	8417	7763	14815	NA	NA	NA	NA
	Memoranda	*Pour mémoire*										
14.	*Staff costs*	*Frais de personnel*	13766	15049	16751	18717	20810	24038	27326	28291	31205	33820
15.	*Provisions on loans*	*Provisions sur prêts*	..	..	..	..	..	..	..	..	..	..
16.	*Provisions on securities*	*Provisions sur titres*	..	..	..	..	..	..	..	..	..	..
	BALANCE SHEET	**BILAN**										
	Assets	**Actif**										
17.	Cash & balance with Central bank	Caisse & solde auprès de la Banque centrale	7706	12407	15896	17822	14954	22731	22550	21999	23912	25247
18.	Interbank deposits	Dépôts interbancaires	3325734	3743593	4153414	4493575	5091042	5895411	6827903	7542436	7595436	8514637
19.	Loans	Prêts	2454326	2680945	2444418	2291377	2239670	2488137	2705253	2991164	3111790	3560101
20.	Securities	Valeurs mobilières	341257	408332	519801	626933	644846	747022	825196	947786	1030649	1366487
21.	Other assets	Autres actifs	462615	485407	494278	577407	695968	784481	955869	976829	989324	957609
	Liabilities	**Passif**										
22.	Capital & reserves	Capital et réserves	210619	241075	264572	278847	292956	326944	362536	400727	437490	509944
23.	Borrowing from Central bank	Emprunts auprès de la Banque centrale	-	-	-	-	-	-	-	-	-	-
24.	Interbank deposits	Dépôts interbancaires	4655969	5064551	5087914	5021751	5213590	5456033	5664861	5862019	5781106	6308312
25.	Non-bank deposits	Dépôts non bancaires	1334310	1580956	1756196	2165763	2567373	3338309	4362287	5018640	5233632	6122701
26.	Bonds	Obligations	96987	125722	110723	108212	133500	291661	361339	557124	643922	683190
27.	Other liabilities	Autres engagements	293753	318380	408402	432541	479061	524835	585748	641704	654961	799934
	Balance sheet total	**Total du bilan**										
28.	End-year total	En fin d'exercice	6591638	7330684	7627807	8007114	8686480	9937782	11336771	12480214	12751111	14424081
29.	Average total	Moyen	6244024	6830970	7509547	7669959	8275464	9467853	11126632	12212272	13003686	13841317
	Memoranda	*Pour mémoire*										
30.	*Short-term securities*	*Titres à court terme*	151163	208068	292268	310070	308259	333652	324005	380893	480731	700081
31.	*Bonds*	*Obligations*	28440	27827	31087	33769	35795	49897	86293	121414	86639	89378
32.	*Shares and participations*	*Actions et participations*										
33.	*Claims on non-residents*	*Créances sur des non résidents*	5752587	6409467	6598617	6941873	7525666	8663424	10020284	11050104	11263515	12563961
34.	*Liabilities to non-residents*	*Engagements envers des non résidents*	5280549	6233881	6373914	6645544	7066412	8015812	9226691	10258514	10468546	11559901
	SUPPLEMENTARY INFORMATION	**RENSEIGNEMENTS COMPLEMENTAIRES**										
35.	Number of institutions	Nombre d'institutions	114	115	118	122	127	143	166	177	187	213
36.	Number of branches	Nombre de succursales	241	237	243	250	258	258	295	297	308	303
37.	Number of employees (x 1000)	Nombre de salariés (x 1000)	9.0	9.4	10.2	11.4	12.7	13.7	15.2	16.3	17.1	17.6

LUXEMBOURG

Commercial banks

Per cent

INCOME STATEMENT ANALYSIS

LUXEMBOURG

Banques commerciales

Pourcentage

ANALYSE DU COMPTE DE RESULTATS

	1983	1984	1985	1986	1987	1988	1989	1990	1991	1992	
% of average balance sheet total											**% du total moyen du bilan**
38. Interest income	9.26	9.68	8.79	7.74	7.32	7.42	9.00	9.70	9.63	9.94	38. Produits financiers
39. Interest expenses	8.03	8.48	7.61	6.60	6.28	6.47	8.18	8.93	8.80	9.10	39. Frais financiers
40. Net interest income	1.23	1.20	1.18	1.13	1.04	0.95	0.82	0.77	0.83	0.84	40. Produits financiers nets
41. Non-interest income (net)	0.26	0.18	0.29	0.31	0.26	0.30	0.32	0.42	0.30	0.35	41. Produits non financiers (nets)
42. Gross income	1.49	1.38	1.47	1.44	1.29	1.25	1.15	1.19	1.13	1.19	42. Résultat brut
43. Operating expenses	0.39	0.40	0.41	0.44	0.46	0.48	0.47	0.44	0.46	0.47	43. Frais d'exploitation
44. Net income	1.10	0.99	1.06	1.00	0.84	0.77	0.68	0.74	0.67	0.72	44. Résultat net
45. Provisions (net)	0.84	0.69	0.73	0.66	0.51	0.37	0.37	0.52	0.42	0.40	45. Provisions (nettes)
46. Profit before tax	0.26	0.30	0.33	0.33	0.32	0.40	0.31	0.22	0.26	0.32	46. Bénéfices avant impôt
47. Income tax	0.13	0.14	0.16	0.15	0.14	0.15	0.10	0.06	0.07	0.12	47. Impôt
48. Profit after tax	0.13	0.15	0.18	0.18	0.19	0.25	0.21	0.16	0.18	0.21	48. Bénéfices après impôt
49. Distributed profit	0.03	0.08	0.07	0.08	0.09	0.09	NA	NA	NA	NA	49. Bénéfices distribués
50. Retained profit	0.09	0.08	0.10	0.11	0.09	0.16	NA	NA	NA	NA	50. Bénéfices mis en réserve
51. Staff costs	0.22	0.22	0.22	0.24	0.25	0.25	0.25	0.23	0.24	0.24	51. Frais de personnel
52. Provisions on loans	..	..	..	..	..	..	..	..	..	..	52. Provisions sur prêts
53. Provisions on securities	..	..	..	..	..	..	..	..	..	..	53. Provisions sur titres
% of gross income											**% du total du résultat brut**
54. Net interest income	82.51	86.76	80.33	78.63	80.01	75.72	71.77	65.00	73.49	70.81	54. Produits financiers nets
55. Non-interest income (net)	17.49	13.24	19.67	21.37	19.99	24.28	28.23	35.00	26.51	29.19	55. Produits non financiers (nets)
56. Operating expenses	26.20	28.59	27.88	30.82	35.26	38.29	40.90	37.32	40.55	39.38	56. Frais d'exploitation
57. Net income	73.80	71.41	72.12	69.18	64.74	61.71	59.10	62.68	59.45	60.62	57. Résultat net
58. Provisions (net)	56.51	49.90	49.38	46.05	39.66	29.54	32.37	44.06	36.87	33.43	58. Provisions (nettes)
59. Profit before tax	17.29	21.51	22.75	23.13	25.08	32.17	26.73	18.63	22.58	27.19	59. Bénéfices avant impôt
60. Income tax	8.80	10.38	10.70	10.32	10.50	12.31	8.54	5.46	6.48	10.00	60. Impôt
61. Profit after tax	8.49	11.13	12.04	12.80	14.58	19.86	18.19	13.16	16.10	17.19	61. Bénéfices après impôt
62. Staff costs	14.79	15.91	15.17	16.91	19.43	20.29	21.39	19.52	21.19	20.49	62. Frais de personnel
% of net income											**% du total du résultat net**
63. Provisions (net)	76.57	69.88	68.46	66.57	61.26	47.87	54.77	70.28	62.02	55.15	63. Provisions (nettes)
64. Profit before tax	23.43	30.12	31.54	33.43	38.74	52.13	45.23	29.72	37.98	44.85	64. Bénéfices avant impôt
65. Income tax	11.92	14.53	14.84	14.92	16.21	19.94	14.45	8.72	10.89	16.49	65. Impôt
66. Profit after tax	11.51	15.59	16.70	18.51	22.53	32.19	30.77	21.00	27.09	28.36	66. Bénéfices après impôt

LUXEMBOURG

Commercial banks

LUXEMBOURG

Banques commerciales

Per cent — *Pourcentage*

BALANCE SHEET ANALYSIS — **ANALYSE DU BILAN**

% of year-end balance sheet total — % du total du bilan en fin d'exercice

	1983	1984	1985	1986	1987	1988	1989	1990	1991	1992	
Assets											**Actif**
67. Cash & balance with Central bank	0.12	0.17	0.21	0.22	0.17	0.23	0.20	0.18	0.19	0.18	67. Caisse & solde auprès de la Banque centrale
68. Interbank deposits	50.45	51.07	54.45	56.12	58.61	59.32	60.23	60.44	59.57	59.03	68. Dépôts interbancaires
69. Loans	37.23	36.57	32.05	28.62	25.78	25.04	23.86	23.97	24.40	24.68	69. Prêts
70. Securities	5.18	5.57	6.81	7.83	7.42	7.52	7.28	7.59	8.08	9.47	70. Valeurs mobilières
71. Other assets	7.02	6.62	6.48	7.21	8.01	7.89	8.43	7.83	7.76	6.64	71. Autres actifs
Liabilities											**Passif**
72. Capital & reserves	3.20	3.29	3.47	3.48	3.37	3.29	3.20	3.21	3.43	3.54	72. Capital et réserves
73. Borrowing from Central bank	-	-	-	-	-	-	-	-	-	-	73. Emprunts auprès de la Banque centrale
74. Interbank deposits	70.63	69.09	66.70	62.72	60.02	54.90	49.97	46.97	45.34	43.73	74. Dépôts interbancaires
75. Non-bank deposits	20.24	21.57	23.02	27.05	29.56	33.59	38.48	40.21	41.04	42.45	75. Dépôts non bancaires
76. Bonds	1.47	1.72	1.45	1.35	1.54	2.93	3.19	4.46	5.05	4.74	76. Obligations
77. Other liabilities	4.46	4.34	5.35	5.40	5.52	5.28	5.17	5.14	5.14	5.55	77. Autres engagements
Memoranda											*Pour mémoire*
78. Short-term securities	*..*	*..*	*..*	*..*	*..*	*..*	*..*	*..*	*..*	*..*	*78. Titres à court terme*
79. Bonds	*2.29*	*2.84*	*3.83*	*3.87*	*3.55*	*3.36*	*2.86*	*3.05*	*3.77*	*4.85*	*79. Obligations*
80. Shares and participations	*0.43*	*0.38*	*0.41*	*0.42*	*0.41*	*0.50*	*0.76*	*0.97*	*0.68*	*0.62*	*80. Actions et participations*
81. Claims on non-residents	*87.27*	*87.43*	*86.51*	*86.70*	*86.64*	*87.18*	*88.39*	*88.54*	*88.33*	*87.10*	*81. Créances sur des non résidents*
82. Liabilities to non-residents	*80.11*	*85.04*	*83.56*	*83.00*	*81.37*	*80.66*	*81.39*	*82.20*	*82.10*	*80.14*	*82. Engagements envers des non résidents*

Notes

- Average balance sheet totals (item 29) are based on thirteen end-month data.

Notes

- La moyenne du total des actifs/passifs (poste 29) est basée sur treize données de fin de mois.

NETHERLANDS
All banks

PAYS-BAS
Ensemble des banques

Million guilders / *Millions de florins*

INCOME STATEMENT / COMPTE DE RESULTATS

	1983	1984	1985	1986	1987	1988	1989 (2)	1990 (2)	1991	1992
1. Interest income — Produits financiers	..	..	..	..	..	..	..	..	..	..
2. Interest expenses — Frais financiers	..	..	..	..	..	..	..	..	..	..
3. Net interest income — Produits financiers nets	10826	10707	11182	13478	14036	15038	16987	18309	20331	22215
4. Non-interest income (net) — Produits non financiers (nets)	3328	3505	3858	4237	4918	5632	7062	7336	8360	8912
5. Gross income — Résultat brut	14154	14212	15040	17715	18954	20670	24049	25645	28691	31127
6. Operating expenses — Frais d'exploitation	8703	8876	9436	11682	13053	13986	15862	17612	19510	21074
7. Net income — Résultat net	5451	5336	5604	6033	5901	6684	8187	8033	9181	10053
8. Provisions (net) — Provisions (nettes)	2787	2907	1843	1892	1161	2741	2931	3006	3293	3609
9. Profit before tax — Bénéfices avant impôt	2664	2429	3761	4141	4740	3943	5256	5027	5888	6444
10. Income tax — Impôt	..	..	..	..	1374	1102	1254	1273	1683	1933
11. Profit after tax — Bénéfices après impôt	..	..	..	..	3366	2841	4002	3754	4205	4511
12. Distributed profit — Bénéfices distribués	..	..	..	..	..	..	..	..	..	..
13. Retained profit — Bénéfices mis en réserve	..	..	..	..	..	..	..	..	..	..
Memoranda — Pour mémoire										
14. Staff costs — Frais de personnel	5729	5854	6150	7085	7925	8371	9162	10183	11242	12245
15. Provisions on loans — Provisions sur prêts	..	..	..	..	..	..	..	..	..	..
16. Provisions on securities — Provisions sur titres	..	..	..	..	..	..	..	..	..	..

BALANCE SHEET / BILAN

	1983	1984	1985	1986	1987	1988	1989 (2)	1990 (2)	1991	1992
Assets — Actif										
17. Cash & bal. with Central bank — Caisse & solde auprès de la Banque centrale	4235	4599	4679	6077	8377	7622	22879	26110	22511	29446
18. Interbank deposits — Dépôts interbancaires	134042	154422	153339	151908	161571	186233	223004	261984	259165	265622
19. Loans — Prêts	260636	270342	280217	332268	338626	374264	501308	685356	731174	789757
20. Securities — Valeurs mobilières	36570	41734	47132	69246	66150	73059	77642	118789	122342	139692
21. Other assets — Autres actifs	26343	28052	31122	37466	42822	48856	62595	30251	32468	31019
Liabilities — Passif										
22. Capital & reserves — Capital et réserves	15706	17345	19296	23717	26532	29058	38756	45047	47634	50459
23. Borrowing from Central bank — Emprunts auprès de la Banque centrale	6675	5527	5610	10701	7351	6093	4891	9328	3045	6647
24. Interbank deposits — Dépôts interbancaires	147681	154553	150742	154974	164676	179108	197499	265314	285345	296965
25. Non-bank deposits — Dépôts non bancaires	213133	237901	253320	307565	311773	342967	422644	510650	535246	580987
26. Bonds — Obligations	37456	39662	42909	49600	54773	67145	138017	167192	167845	168702
27. Other liabilities — Autres engagements	41175	44161	44612	50408	52441	65663	85621	124959	128545	151776
Balance sheet total — Total du bilan										
28. End-year total — En fin d'exercice	461826	499149	516489	596965	617546	690034	887428	1122490	1167660	1255536
29. Average total — Moyen	450660	480488	507819	556727	607256	653790	817041	1004959	1145075	1211598
Memoranda — Pour mémoire										
30. Short-term securities (1) — Titres à court terme (1)	35141	40564	45863	66459	63459	69532	74111	27525	23333	24900
31. Bonds — Obligations	1429	1170	1269	2787	2691	3527	3531	86122	93604	110535
32. Shares and participations — Actions et participations	..	..	..	..	..	..	..	6281	6708	6898
33. Claims on non-residents — Créances sur des non résidents	178651	202017	199717	199689	203974	238791	280183	314206	321725	343747
34. Liabilities to non-residents — Engagements envers des non résidents	171987	187904	181741	182778	192450	220035	232405	259304	267940	298789

SUPPLEMENTARY INFORMATION / RENSEIGNEMENTS COMPLEMENTAIRES

	1983	1984	1985	1986	1987	1988	1989 (2)	1990 (2)	1991	1992
35. Number of institutions — Nombre d'institutions	92	86	84	83	85	86	170	180	173	177
36. Number of branches — Nombre de succursales	5406	5475	4786	7388	7352	7233	8006	7992	7827	7518
37. Number of employees (x 1000) — Nombre de salariés (x 1000)	90.7	91.1	92.4	104.1	106.0	106.4	117.4	122.9	119.9	119.9

NETHERLANDS

All banks

Per cent

INCOME STATEMENT ANALYSIS

PAYS-BAS

Ensemble des banques

Pourcentage

ANALYSE DU COMPTE DE RESULTATS

		1983	1984	1985	1986	1987	1988	1989 (2)	1990 (2)	1991	1992		
% of average balance sheet total													**% du total moyen du bilan**
38.	Interest income	..	..	..	..	..	..	..	..	0.00	0.00	38.	Produits financiers
39.	Interest expenses	..	..	..	..	..	..	..	..	..	..	39.	Frais financiers
40.	Net interest income	2.40	2.23	2.20	2.42	2.31	2.30	2.08	1.82	1.78	1.83	40.	Produits financiers nets
41.	Non-interest income (net)	0.74	0.73	0.76	0.76	0.81	0.86	0.86	0.73	0.73	0.74	41.	Produits non financiers (nets)
42.	Gross income	3.14	2.96	2.96	3.18	3.12	3.16	2.94	2.55	2.51	2.57	42.	Résultat brut
43.	Operating expenses	1.93	1.85	1.86	2.10	2.15	2.14	1.94	1.75	1.70	1.74	43.	Frais d'exploitation
44.	Net income	1.21	1.11	1.10	1.08	0.97	1.02	1.00	0.80	0.80	0.83	44.	Résultat net
45.	Provisions (net)	0.62	0.61	0.36	0.34	0.19	0.42	0.36	0.30	0.29	0.30	45.	Provisions (nettes)
46.	Profit before tax	0.59	0.51	0.74	0.74	0.78	0.60	0.64	0.50	0.51	0.53	46.	Bénéfices avant impôt
47.	Income tax	..	..	..	..	0.23	0.17	0.15	0.13	0.15	0.16	47.	Impôt
48.	Profit after tax	..	..	..	..	0.55	0.43	0.49	0.37	0.37	0.37	48.	Bénéfices après impôt
49.	Distributed profit	..	..	..	..	..	..	..	..	..	..	49.	Bénéfices distribués
50.	Retained profit	..	..	..	..	..	..	..	..	..	..	50.	Bénéfices mis en réserve
51.	Staff costs	1.27	1.22	1.21	1.27	1.31	1.28	1.12	1.01	0.98	1.01	51.	Frais de personnel
52.	Provisions on loans	..	..	..	..	..	..	..	..	..	..	52.	Provisions sur prêts
53.	Provisions on securities	..	..	..	..	..	..	..	..	..	..	53.	Provisions sur titres
% of gross income													**% du total du résultat brut**
54.	Net interest income	76.49	75.34	74.35	76.08	74.05	72.75	70.63	71.39	70.86	71.37	54.	Produits financiers nets
55.	Non-interest income (net)	23.51	24.66	25.65	23.92	25.95	27.25	29.37	28.61	29.14	28.63	55.	Produits non financiers (nets)
56.	Operating expenses	61.49	62.45	62.74	65.94	68.87	67.66	65.96	68.68	68.00	67.70	56.	Frais d'exploitation
57.	Net income	38.51	37.55	37.26	34.06	31.13	32.34	34.04	31.32	32.00	32.30	57.	Résultat net
58.	Provisions (net)	19.69	20.45	12.25	10.68	6.13	13.26	12.19	11.72	11.48	11.59	58.	Provisions (nettes)
59.	Profit before tax	18.82	17.09	25.01	23.38	25.01	19.08	21.86	19.60	20.52	20.70	59.	Bénéfices avant impôt
60.	Income tax	..	..	..	..	7.25	5.33	5.21	4.96	5.87	6.21	60.	Impôt
61.	Profit after tax	..	..	..	..	17.76	13.74	16.64	14.64	14.66	14.49	61.	Bénéfices après impôt
62.	Staff costs	40.48	41.19	40.89	39.99	41.81	40.50	38.10	39.71	39.18	39.34	62.	Frais de personnel
% of net income													**% du total du résultat net**
63.	Provisions (net)	51.13	54.48	32.89	31.36	19.67	41.01	35.80	37.42	35.87	35.90	63.	Provisions (nettes)
64.	Profit before tax	48.87	45.52	67.11	68.64	80.33	58.99	64.20	62.58	64.13	64.10	64.	Bénéfices avant impôt
65.	Income tax	..	..	..	..	23.28	16.49	15.32	15.85	18.33	19.23	65.	Impôt
66.	Profit after tax	..	..	..	..	57.04	42.50	48.88	46.73	45.80	44.87	66.	Bénéfices après impôt

NETHERLANDS

All banks

PAYS-BAS

Ensemble des banques

Per cent — *Pourcentage*

BALANCE SHEET ANALYSIS — ANALYSE DU BILAN

% of year-end balance sheet total — % du total du bilan en fin d'exercice

		1983	1984	1985	1986	1987	1988	1989 (2)	1990 (2)	1991	1992	
Assets												**Actif**
67.	Cash & bal. with Central bank	0.92	0.92	0.91	1.02	1.36	1.10	2.58	2.33	1.93	2.35	67. Caisse & solde auprès de la Banque centrale
68.	Interbank deposits	29.02	30.94	29.69	25.45	26.16	26.99	25.13	23.34	22.20	21.16	68. Dépôts interbancaires
69.	Loans	56.44	54.16	54.25	55.66	54.83	54.24	56.49	61.06	62.62	62.90	69. Prêts
70.	Securities	7.92	8.36	9.13	11.60	10.71	10.59	8.75	10.58	10.48	11.13	70. Valeurs mobilières
71.	Other assets	5.70	5.62	6.03	6.28	6.93	7.08	7.05	2.69	2.78	2.47	71. Autres actifs
Liabilities												**Passif**
72.	Capital & reserves	3.40	3.47	3.74	3.97	4.30	4.21	4.37	4.01	4.08	4.02	72. Capital et réserves
73.	Borrowing from Central bank	1.45	1.11	1.09	1.79	1.19	0.88	0.55	0.83	0.26	0.53	73. Emprunts auprès de la Banque centrale
74.	Interbank deposits	31.98	30.96	29.19	25.96	26.67	25.96	22.26	23.64	24.44	23.65	74. Dépôts interbancaires
75.	Non-bank deposits	46.15	47.66	49.05	51.52	50.49	49.70	47.63	45.49	45.84	46.27	75. Dépôts non bancaires
76.	Bonds	8.11	7.95	8.31	8.31	8.87	9.73	15.55	14.89	14.37	13.44	76. Obligations
77.	Other liabilities	8.92	8.85	8.64	8.44	8.49	9.52	9.65	11.13	11.01	12.09	77. Autres engagements
Memoranda												***Pour mémoire***
78.	*Short-term securities (1)*	*7.61*	*8.13*	*8.88*	*11.13*	*10.28*	*10.08*	*8.35*	*2.45*	*2.00*	*1.98*	78. *Titres à court terme (1)*
79.	*Bonds*	*..*	*..*	*..*	*..*	*..*	*..*	*..*	*7.67*	*8.02*	*8.80*	79. *Obligations*
80.	*Shares and participations*	*0.31*	*0.23*	*0.25*	*0.47*	*0.44*	*0.51*	*0.40*	*0.56*	*0.57*	*0.55*	80. *Actions et participations*
81.	*Claims on non-residents*	*38.68*	*40.47*	*38.67*	*33.45*	*33.03*	*34.61*	*31.57*	*27.99*	*27.55*	*27.38*	81. *Créances sur des non résidents*
82.	*Liabilities to non-residents*	*37.24*	*37.64*	*35.19*	*30.62*	*31.16*	*31.89*	*26.19*	*23.10*	*22.95*	*23.80*	82. *Engagements envers des non résidents*

1. Up to 1990 (old series), included under "Bonds" (item 31 or item 79).
2. New series. See change in methodology.

1. Jusqu'à 1990 (ancienne série) inclus sous "Obligations" (poste 31 ou poste 79).
2. Nouvelle série. Voir changement méthodologique.

Change in methodology:

- As from 1986, the data include the Postbank.
- As from 1988, Provisions (net) (item 8) consists of "transfers to the provision for general business risks". The addition to the lending/country risk provision out of this "provision for general business risks" in 1990 (new series), 1991 and 1992 amounts to Gld 2 410 million, Gld 3 328 million and Gld 3 283 respectively.
- As from 1989, balance sheet data, in addition to universal banks and banks organised on a co-operative basis (old series), also include savings banks, mortgage banks, capital market institutions and security credit institutions. The income statement data, for the same series (1989 and 1990 old series), include universal banks, banks organised on a credit co-operative basis and savings banks. The old series for 1989 were published in Bank Profitablity, Statistical Supplement 1981-1990 (OECD, Paris, 1992).
- The new series for 1990 cover, both for income statement and balance sheet data, universal banks, banks organised on a co-operative basis, savings banks, mortgage banks, capital market institutions and security credit institutions. The old series for 1990 were published in Bank Profitability, Statistical Supplement 1982-1991 (OECD, Paris, 1993).

Changement méthodologique :

- A compter de 1986, les données incluent la Banque postale.
- Depuis 1988, les Provisions (nettes) (poste 8), concernent les "dotations aux provisions pour risques généraux". La partie correspondant à la "provision pour risques" dans cette provision générale s'est élevée en 1990 (nouvelle série), 1991 et 1992 à fl2 410 millions, fl3 328 millions et fl3 283 millions respectivement.
- A partir de 1989, les données de bilan, en plus des banques universelles et des banques organisées en mutuelles (anciennes séries), incluent également les caisses d'épargne, les banques hypothécaires, les institutions du marché financier et les institutions des titres de crédit. Les données du compte de résultat, pour les mêmes séries (1989 et 1990 ancienne série), incluent les banques universelles, les banques organisées en mutuelles et les caisses d'épargne. L'ancienne série pour 1989 a été publiée dans Rentabilité des banques, Supplément statistique 1981-1990 (OCDE, Paris, 1992).
- La nouvelle série pour 1990 concerne, aussi bien pour les données du compte de résultat que pour celles du bilan, les banques universelles, les banques organisées en mutuelles, les caisses d'épargne, les banques hypothécaires, les institutions du marché financier et les institutions des titres de crédit. L'ancienne série pour 1990 a été publiée dans Rentabilité des banques, Supplément statistique 1982-1991 (OCDE, Paris, 1992).

NORWAY

All banks

NORVEGE

Ensemble des banques

Million Norwegian kroner / *Millions de couronnes norvégiennes*

	1983	1984	1985	1986	1987	1988	1989	1990	1991	1992	
INCOME STATEMENT											**COMPTE DE RESULTATS**
1. Interest income	28272	33966	40872	55270	73541	80265	76422	75021	70070	67670	1. Produits financiers
2. Interest expenses	18413	23060	28976	40490	55847	61632	55286	54808	50888	46937	2. Frais financiers
3. Net interest income	9859	10906	11896	14780	17694	18633	21136	20213	19182	20733	3. Produits financiers nets
4. Non-interest income (net)	2399	3481	4557	5805	3740	6320	7455	5155	3604	5555	4. Produits non financiers (nets)
5. Gross income	12258	14387	16453	20585	21434	24953	28591	25368	22786	26288	5. Résultat brut
6. Operating expenses (1)	8367	9859	11720	13926	16322	17438	17250	17933	20051	15859	6. Frais d'exploitation (1)
7. Net income	3891	4528	4733	6659	5112	7515	11341	7435	2735	10429	7. Résultat net
8. Provisions (net) (1)	1732	2251	2745	4049	4444	8882	9891	11655	21632	11707	8. Provisions (nettes) (1)
9. Profit before tax	2159	2277	1988	2610	668	-1367	1450	-4220	-18897	-1278	9. Bénéfices avant impôt
10. Income tax	399	410	403	468	384	279	570	272	201	404	10. Impôt
11. Profit after tax	1760	1867	1585	2142	284	-1646	880	-4492	-19098	-1682	11. Bénéfices après impôt
12. Distributed profit	423	541	651	501	239	167	775	35	25	122	12. Bénéfices distribués
13. Retained profit	1337	1326	934	1641	45	-1813	105	-4527	-19123	-1804	13. Bénéfices mis en réserve
Memoranda											*Pour mémoire*
14. Staff costs	*4523*	*5035*	*5787*	*6868*	*7670*	*8436*	*8262*	*8557*	*8416*	*7868*	14. Frais de personnel
15. Provisions on loans	*1113*	*1332*	*1432*	*1720*	*4432*	*8769*	*10481*	*10919*	*21370*	*11692*	15. Provisions sur prêts
16. Provisions on securities	*..*	*..*	*..*	*..*	*..*	*..*	*..*	*..*	*..*	*..*	16. Provisions sur titres
BALANCE SHEET											**BILAN**
Assets											**Actif**
17. Cash & balance with Central bank	3051	2088	2529	2893	3881	3136	3083	3136	3634	4890	17. Caisse & solde auprès de la Banque centrale
18. Interbank deposits	15517	18257	21717	40840	35734	23367	17799	20753	28470	41658	18. Dépôts interbancaires
19. Loans	156582	199689	263201	350155	405581	427506	459632	474753	451560	468575	19. Prêts
20. Securities	69321	83928	86863	83299	117509	96853	91045	84430	65803	67493	20. Valeurs mobilières
21. Other assets	4643	8913	8051	13107	27968	32167	33147	31573	28612	28094	21. Autres actifs
Liabilities											**Passif**
22. Capital & reserves	13397	16162	19450	23168	23461	22831	26204	23768	16785	21509	22. Capital et réserves
23. Borrowing from Central bank	3101	1162	2982	67676	73727	76254	58562	55880	44492	39171	23. Emprunts auprès de la Banque centrale
24. Interbank deposits	30523	42731	58975	69789	97704	80146	77217	76437	68072	50669	24. Dépôts interbancaires
25. Non-bank deposits	186453	227350	262064	268106	312465	326167	354185	370880	374350	407414	25. Dépôts non bancaires
26. Bonds	3456	7121	10147	32310	34569	43738	48038	50602	43858	64814	26. Obligations
27. Other liabilities	12184	18349	28743	29245	48746	33899	40499	37077	30523	27128	27. Autres engagements
Balance sheet total											**Total du bilan**
28. End-year total	249114	312875	382361	490294	590672	583033	604707	614645	578080	610710	28. En fin d'exercice
29. Average total	247763	294024	364215	458355	541430	613904	612183	639192	621560	591255	29. Moyen
Memoranda											*Pour mémoire*
30. Short-term securities	*4692*	*22380*	*28935*	*20470*	*33266*	*10354*	*9813*	*13128*	*8549*	*5420*	30. Titres à court terme
31. Bonds	*60534*	*55780*	*49769*	*51655*	*73705*	*75859*	*69770*	*58263*	*47245*	*52360*	31. Obligations
32. Shares and participations	*4095*	*5768*	*8158*	*11174*	*10539*	*10640*	*11462*	*13037*	*10008*	*9713*	32. Actions et participations
33. Claims on non-residents	*19381*	*27593*	*27843*	*49049*	*31792*	*26135*	*31201*	*34083*	*30638*	*43157*	33. Créances sur des non résidents
34. Liabilities to non-residents	*33381*	*50646*	*70471*	*98120*	*132070*	*131271*	*134193*	*129315*	*96144*	*75435*	34. Engagements envers des non résidents
SUPPLEMENTARY INFORMATION											**RENSEIGNEMENTS COMPLEMENTAIRES**
35. Number of institutions	275	248	225	221	201	187	179	164	156	155	35. Nombre d'institutions
36. Number of branches	1940	1970	2001	1930	2166	2032	1796	1796	1661	1593	36. Nombre de succursales
37. Number of employees (x 1000)	27.9	29.0	29.9	32.7	34.6	34.4	32.0	31.2	27.8	26.7	37. Nombre de salariés (x 1000)

NORVEGE

All banks

Ensemble des banques

Per cent

Pourcentage

INCOME STATEMENT ANALYSIS / ANALYSE DU COMPTE DE RESULTATS

	1983	1984	1985	1986	1987	1988	1989	1990	1991	1992		
% of average balance sheet total												**% du total moyen du bilan**
38. Interest income	11.41	11.55	11.22	12.06	13.58	13.07	12.48	11.74	11.27	11.45	38.	Produits financiers
39. Interest expenses	7.43	7.84	7.96	8.83	10.31	10.04	9.03	8.57	8.19	7.94	39.	Frais financiers
40. Net interest income	3.98	3.71	3.27	3.22	3.27	3.04	3.45	3.16	3.09	3.51	40.	Produits financiers nets
41. Non-interest income (net)	0.97	1.18	1.25	1.27	0.69	1.03	1.22	0.81	0.58	0.94	41.	Produits non financiers (nets)
42. Gross income	4.95	4.89	4.52	4.49	3.96	4.06	4.67	3.97	3.67	4.45	42.	Résultat brut
43. Operating expenses (1)	3.38	3.35	3.22	3.04	3.01	2.84	2.82	2.81	3.23	2.68	43.	Frais d'exploitation (1)
44. Net income	1.57	1.54	1.30	1.45	0.94	1.22	1.85	1.16	0.44	1.76	44.	Résultat net
45. Provisions (net) (1)	0.70	0.77	0.75	0.88	0.82	1.45	1.62	1.82	3.48	1.98	45.	Provisions (nettes) (1)
46. Profit before tax	0.87	0.77	0.55	0.57	0.12	-0.22	0.24	-0.66	-3.04	-0.22	46.	Bénéfices avant impôt
47. Income tax	0.16	0.14	0.11	0.10	0.07	0.05	0.09	0.04	0.03	0.07	47.	Impôt
48. Profit after tax	0.71	0.63	0.44	0.47	0.05	-0.27	0.14	-0.70	-3.07	-0.28	48.	Bénéfices après impôt
49. Distributed profit	0.17	0.18	0.18	0.11	0.04	0.03	0.13	0.01	0.00	0.02	49.	Bénéfices distribués
50. Retained profit	0.54	0.45	0.26	0.36	0.01	-0.30	0.02	-0.71	-3.08	-0.31	50.	Bénéfices mis en réserve
51. Staff costs	1.83	1.71	1.59	1.50	1.42	1.37	1.35	1.34	1.35	1.33	51.	Frais de personnel
52. Provisions on loans	0.45	0.45	0.39	0.38	0.82	1.43	1.71	1.71	3.44	1.98	52.	Provisions sur prêts
53. Provisions on securities	..	..	..	..	..	..	..	..	..	..	53.	Provisions sur titres
% of gross income												**% du total du résultat brut**
54. Net interest income	80.43	75.80	72.30	71.80	82.55	74.67	73.93	79.68	84.18	78.87	54.	Produits financiers nets
55. Non-interest income (net)	19.57	24.20	27.70	28.20	17.45	25.33	26.07	20.32	15.82	21.13	55.	Produits non financiers (nets)
56. Operating expenses (1)	68.26	68.53	71.23	67.65	76.15	69.88	60.33	70.69	88.00	60.33	56.	Frais d'exploitation (1)
57. Net income	31.74	31.47	28.77	32.35	23.85	30.12	39.67	29.31	12.00	39.67	57.	Résultat net
58. Provisions (net) (1)	14.13	15.65	16.68	19.67	20.73	35.59	34.59	45.94	94.94	44.53	58.	Provisions (nettes) (1)
59. Profit before tax	17.61	15.83	12.08	12.68	3.12	-5.48	5.07	-16.64	-82.93	-4.86	59.	Bénéfices avant impôt
60. Income tax	3.26	2.85	2.45	2.27	1.79	1.12	1.99	1.07	0.88	1.54	60.	Impôt
61. Profit after tax	14.36	12.98	9.63	10.41	1.32	-6.60	3.08	-17.71	-83.81	-6.40	61.	Bénéfices après impôt
62. Staff costs	36.90	35.00	35.17	33.36	35.78	33.81	28.90	33.73	36.93	29.93	62.	Frais de personnel
% of net income												**% du total du résultat net**
63. Provisions (net)	44.51	49.71	58.00	60.80	86.93	118.19	87.21	156.76	..	112.25	63.	Provisions (nettes)
64. Profit before tax	55.49	50.29	42.00	39.20	13.07	-18.19	12.79	-56.76	..	-12.25	64.	Bénéfices avant impôt
65. Income tax	10.25	9.05	8.51	7.03	7.51	3.71	5.03	3.66	..	3.87	65.	Impôt
66. Profit after tax	45.23	41.23	33.49	32.17	5.56	-21.90	7.76	-60.42	..	-16.13	66.	Bénéfices après impôt

NORWAY

All banks

Per cent

BALANCE SHEET ANALYSIS

% of year-end balance sheet total

	1983	1984	1985	1986	1987	1988	1989	1990	1991	1992
Assets										
67. Cash & balance with Central bank	1.22	0.67	0.66	0.59	0.66	0.54	0.51	0.51	0.63	0.80
68. Interbank deposits	6.23	5.84	5.68	8.33	6.05	4.01	2.94	3.38	4.92	6.82
69. Loans	62.86	63.82	68.84	71.42	68.66	73.32	76.01	77.24	78.11	76.73
70. Securities	27.83	26.82	22.72	16.99	19.89	16.61	15.06	13.74	11.38	11.05
71. Other assets	1.86	2.85	2.11	2.67	4.73	5.52	5.48	5.14	4.95	4.60
Liabilities										
72. Capital & reserves	5.38	5.17	5.09	4.73	3.97	3.92	4.33	3.87	2.90	3.52
73. Borrowing from Central bank	1.24	0.37	0.78	13.80	12.48	13.08	9.68	9.09	7.70	6.41
74. Interbank deposits	12.25	13.66	15.42	14.23	16.54	13.75	12.77	12.44	11.78	8.30
75. Non-bank deposits	74.85	72.66	68.54	54.68	52.90	55.94	58.57	60.34	64.76	66.71
76. Bonds	1.39	2.28	2.65	6.59	5.85	7.50	7.94	8.23	7.59	10.61
77. Other liabilities	4.89	5.86	7.52	5.96	8.25	5.81	6.70	6.03	5.28	4.44
Memoranda										
78. Short-term securities	*1.88*	*7.15*	*7.57*	*4.18*	*5.63*	*1.78*	*1.62*	*2.14*	*1.48*	*0.89*
79. Bonds	*24.30*	*17.83*	*13.02*	*10.54*	*12.48*	*13.01*	*11.54*	*9.48*	*8.17*	*8.57*
80. Shares and participations	*1.64*	*1.84*	*2.13*	*2.28*	*1.78*	*1.82*	*1.90*	*2.12*	*1.73*	*1.59*
81. Claims on non-residents	*7.78*	*8.82*	*7.28*	*10.00*	*5.38*	*4.48*	*5.16*	*5.55*	*5.33*	*7.07*
82. Liabilities to non-residents	*13.40*	*16.19*	*18.43*	*20.01*	*22.36*	*22.52*	*22.19*	*21.04*	*16.63*	*12.35*

1. Change in methodology.

Notes

- Average balance sheet totals (item 29) are based on thirteen end-month data.

- All banks include Commercial banks and Savings banks.

Change in methodology:

- Due to methodological changes, in 1991, value adjustments (NKr 1.1 billion in 1990) are included under "Operating expenses" (item 6 or item 43 or item 56) and not under "Provisions (net)" (item 8 or item 45 or item 58).

NORVEGE

Ensemble des banques

Pourcentage

ANALYSE DU BILAN

% du total du bilan en fin d'exercice

Actif
67. Caisse & solde auprès de la Banque centrale
68. Dépôts interbancaires
69. Prêts
70. Valeurs mobilières
71. Autres actifs

Passif
72. Capital et réserves
73. Emprunts auprès de la Banque centrale
74. Dépôts interbancaires
75. Dépôts non bancaires
76. Obligations
77. Autres engagements

Pour mémoire
78. Titres à court terme
79. Obligations
80. Actions et participations
81. Créances sur des non résidents
82. Engagements envers des non résidents

1. Changement méthodologique.

Notes

- La moyenne du total des actifs/passifs (poste 29) est basée sur treize données de fin de mois.

- L'Ensemble des banques comprend les Banques commerciales et les Caisses d'épargne.

Changement méthodologique :

- Dû aux changements méthodologiques, pour l'année 1991, les ajustements en valeur (1,1 milliard de KrN en 1990) sont inclus sous la rubrique "Frais d'exploitation" (poste 6 ou poste 43 ou poste 56) et non sous la rubrique "Provisions (nettes)" (poste 8 ou poste 45 ou poste 58).

NORWAY

Commercial banks

Million Norwegian kroner

NORVEGE

Banques commerciales

Millions de couronnes norvégiennes

	1983	1984	1985	1986	1987	1988	1989	1990	1991	1992	
INCOME STATEMENT											**COMPTE DE RESULTATS**
1. Interest income	16421	20130	23179	30974	42243	45572	43709	43631	40234	38821	1. Produits financiers
2. Interest expenses	11162	14301	16945	23289	33352	36088	33093	33431	30930	28587	2. Frais financiers
3. Net interest income	5259	5829	6234	7685	8891	9484	10616	10200	9304	10234	3. Produits financiers nets
4. Non-interest income (net)	1917	2859	3551	4400	2443	4739	5229	3570	2188	3850	4. Produits non financiers (nets)
5. Gross income	7176	8688	9785	12085	11334	14223	15845	13770	11492	14084	5. Résultat brut
6. Operating expenses (1)	4843	5789	6676	7857	9358	9681	9522	10151	11742	8659	6. Frais d'exploitation (1)
7. Net income	2333	2899	3109	4228	1976	4542	6323	3619	-250	5425	7. Résultat net
8. Provisions (net) (1)	996	1391	1684	2500	2734	5712	5710	7593	16780	9842	8. Provisions (nettes) (1)
9. Profit before tax	1337	1508	1425	1728	-758	-1170	613	-3974	-17030	-4417	9. Bénéfices avant impôt
10. Income tax	231	264	298	328	151	78	287	61	8	77	10. Impôt
11. Profit after tax	1106	1244	1127	1400	-909	-1248	326	-4035	-17038	-4494	11. Bénéfices après impôt
12. Distributed profit	423	541	651	501	239	157	699	15	13	105	12. Bénéfices distribués
13. Retained profit	683	703	476	899	-1148	-1405	-373	-4050	-17051	-4599	13. Bénéfices mis en réserve
Memoranda											*Pour mémoire*
14. Staff costs	*2642*	*2954*	*3250*	*3925*	*4441*	*4833*	*4723*	*4928*	*4751*	*4348*	14. Frais de personnel
15. Provisions on loans	*616*	*745*	*736*	*794*	*2688*	*5673*	*5308*	*7051*	*16663*	*7800*	15. Provisions sur prêts
16. Provisions on securities	*..*	*..*	*..*	*..*	*..*	*..*	*..*	*..*	*..*	*..*	16. Provisions sur titres
BALANCE SHEET											**BILAN**
Assets											**Actif**
17. Cash & balance with Central bank	1621	893	1001	1136	1756	1512	1404	1283	1797	2535	17. Caisse & solde auprès de la Banque centrale
18. Interbank deposits	10377	13933	14832	27382	23939	17293	13416	17261	23493	36086	18. Dépôts interbancaires
19. Loans	91693	119184	152128	203608	237502	245541	272208	281433	258981	273155	19. Prêts
20. Securities	40546	50149	50296	52925	76414	54137	50082	48439	33969	40519	20. Valeurs mobilières
21. Other assets	3628	8022	5832	10226	20062	22231	23933	22850	19944	19628	21. Autres actifs
Liabilities											**Passif**
22. Capital & reserves	7046	9070	11271	14046	13906	13493	15202	13153	7122	8166	22. Capital et réserves
23. Borrowing from Central bank	1601	366	793	41936	41261	39518	27636	32814	29881	28544	23. Emprunts auprès de la Banque centrale
24. Interbank deposits	26315	36166	44224	52510	72292	58967	60811	62804	51388	39492	24. Dépôts interbancaires
25. Non-bank deposits	100792	125275	137290	135619	165776	169189	186288	193183	190008	218413	25. Dépôts non bancaires
26. Bonds	3263	6894	7910	27949	31955	38615	43067	44105	38446	57307	26. Obligations
27. Other liabilities	8848	14410	22601	23217	34483	20932	28038	25207	21339	20000	27. Autres engagements
Balance sheet total											**Total du bilan**
28. End-year total	147865	192181	224089	295277	359673	340713	361042	371266	338184	371923	28. En fin d'exercice
29. Average total	146175	176888	220953	270976	320318	361442	361350	387647	373090	349682	29. Moyen
Memoranda											*Pour mémoire*
30. Short-term securities	*2732*	*14690*	*17382*	*14086*	*26421*	*5546*	*6941*	*10318*	*5327*	*3807*	30. Titres à court terme
31. Bonds	*34452*	*30740*	*26420*	*30045*	*42132*	*40352*	*34291*	*28024*	*21172*	*29839*	31. Obligations
32. Shares and participations	*3362*	*4719*	*6493*	*8794*	*7861*	*8238*	*8850*	*10095*	*7470*	*6872*	32. Actions et participations
33. Claims on non-residents	*16789*	*24847*	*22673*	*41215*	*25853*	*20660*	*26830*	*30023*	*27120*	*39798*	33. Créances sur des non résidents
34. Liabilities to non-residents	*30032*	*45012*	*58367*	*85603*	*110579*	*106520*	*114870*	*112266*	*82903*	*66734*	34. Engagements envers des non résidents
SUPPLEMENTARY INFORMATION											**RENSEIGNEMENTS COMPLEMENTAIRES**
35. Number of institutions	22	21	27	29	28	29	28	22	21	21	35. Nombre d'institutions
36. Number of branches	640	670	673	702	740	713	602	602	540	488	36. Nombre de succursales
37. Number of employees (x 1000)	15.8	16.2	17.1	17.9	19.0	18.7	17.0	16.6	14.5	13.3	37. Nombre de salariés (x 1000)

NORWAY

Commercial banks

Per cent — *Pourcentage*

	1983	1984	1985	1986	1987	1988	1989	1990	1991	1992		
INCOME STATEMENT ANALYSIS												**ANALYSE DU COMPTE DE RESULTATS**
% of average balance sheet total												**% du total moyen du bilan**
38. Interest income	11.23	11.38	10.49	11.43	13.19	12.61	12.10	11.26	10.78	11.10	38.	Produits financiers
39. Interest expenses	7.64	8.08	7.67	8.59	10.41	9.98	9.16	8.62	8.29	8.18	39.	Frais financiers
40. Net interest income	3.60	3.30	2.82	2.84	2.78	2.62	2.94	2.63	2.49	2.93	40.	Produits financiers nets
41. Non-interest income (net)	1.31	1.62	1.61	1.62	0.76	1.31	1.45	0.92	0.59	1.10	41.	Produits non financiers (nets)
42. Gross income	4.91	4.91	4.43	4.46	3.54	3.94	4.38	3.55	3.08	4.03	42.	Résultat brut
43. Operating expenses (1)	3.31	3.27	3.02	2.90	2.92	2.68	2.64	2.62	3.15	2.48	43.	Frais d'exploitation (1)
44. Net income	1.60	1.64	1.41	1.56	0.62	1.26	1.75	0.93	-0.07	1.55	44.	Résultat net
45. Provisions (net) (1)	0.68	0.79	0.76	0.92	0.85	1.58	1.58	1.96	4.50	2.81	45.	Provisions (nettes) (1)
46. Profit before tax	0.91	0.85	0.64	0.64	-0.24	-0.32	0.17	-1.03	-4.56	-1.26	46.	Bénéfices avant impôt
47. Income tax	0.16	0.15	0.13	0.12	0.05	0.02	0.08	0.02	0.00	0.02	47.	Impôt
48. Profit after tax	0.76	0.70	0.51	0.52	-0.28	-0.35	0.09	-1.04	-4.57	-1.29	48.	Bénéfices après impôt
49. Distributed profit	0.29	0.31	0.29	0.18	0.07	0.04	0.19	0.00	0.00	0.03	49.	Bénéfices distribués
50. Retained profit	0.47	0.40	0.22	0.33	-0.36	-0.39	-0.10	-1.04	-4.57	-1.32	50.	Bénéfices mis en réserve
51. Staff costs	1.81	1.67	1.47	1.45	1.39	1.34	1.31	1.27	1.27	1.24	51.	Frais de personnel
52. Provisions on loans	0.42	0.42	0.33	0.29	0.84	1.57	1.47	1.82	4.47	2.23	52.	Provisions sur prêts
53. Provisions on securities	:	:	:	:	:	:	:	:	:	:	53.	Provisions sur titres
% of gross income												**% du total du résultat brut**
54. Net interest income	73.29	67.09	63.71	63.59	78.45	66.68	67.00	74.07	80.96	72.66	54.	Produits financiers nets
55. Non-interest income (net)	26.71	32.91	36.29	36.41	21.55	33.32	33.00	25.93	19.04	27.34	55.	Produits non financiers (nets)
56. Operating expenses (1)	67.49	66.63	68.23	65.01	82.57	68.07	60.09	73.72	102.18	61.48	56.	Frais d'exploitation (1)
57. Net income	32.51	33.37	31.77	34.99	17.43	31.93	39.91	26.28	-2.18	38.52	57.	Résultat net
58. Provisions (net) (1)	13.88	16.01	17.21	20.69	24.12	40.16	36.04	55.14	146.01	69.88	58.	Provisions (nettes) (1)
59. Profit before tax	18.63	17.36	14.56	14.30	-6.69	-8.23	3.87	-28.86	-148.19	-31.36	59.	Bénéfices avant impôt
60. Income tax	3.22	3.04	3.05	2.71	1.33	0.55	1.81	0.44	0.07	0.55	60.	Impôt
61. Profit after tax	15.41	14.32	11.52	11.58	-8.02	-8.77	2.06	-29.30	-148.26	-31.91	61.	Bénéfices après impôt
62. Staff costs	36.82	34.00	33.21	32.48	39.18	33.98	29.81	35.79	41.34	30.87	62.	Frais de personnel
% of net income												**% du total du résultat net**
63. Provisions (net)	42.69	47.98	54.17	59.13	138.36	125.76	90.31	209.81	:	181.42	63.	Provisions (nettes)
64. Profit before tax	57.31	52.02	45.83	40.87	-38.36	-25.76	9.69	-109.81	:	-81.42	64.	Bénéfices avant impôt
65. Income tax	9.90	9.11	9.59	7.76	7.64	1.72	4.54	1.69	:	1.42	65.	Impôt
66. Profit after tax	47.41	42.91	36.25	33.11	-46.00	-27.48	5.16	-111.49	:	-82.84	66.	Bénéfices après impôt

Commercial banks

Per cent

BALANCE SHEET ANALYSIS

% of year-end balance sheet total

	1983	1984	1985	1986	1987	1988	1989	1990	1991	1992
Assets										
67. Cash & balance with Central bank	1.10	0.46	0.45	0.38	0.49	0.44	0.39	0.35	0.53	0.68
68. Interbank deposits	7.02	7.25	6.62	9.27	6.66	5.08	3.72	4.65	6.95	9.70
69. Loans	62.01	62.02	67.89	68.95	66.03	72.07	75.40	75.80	76.58	73.44
70. Securities	27.42	26.09	22.44	17.92	21.25	15.89	13.87	13.05	10.04	10.89
71. Other assets	2.45	4.17	2.60	3.46	5.58	6.52	6.63	6.15	5.90	5.28
Liabilities										
72. Capital & reserves	4.77	4.72	5.03	4.76	3.87	3.96	4.21	3.54	2.11	2.20
73. Borrowing from Central bank	1.08	0.19	0.35	14.20	11.47	11.60	7.65	8.84	8.84	7.67
74. Interbank deposits	17.80	18.82	19.74	17.78	20.10	17.31	16.84	16.92	15.20	10.62
75. Non-bank deposits	68.16	65.19	61.27	45.93	46.09	49.66	51.60	52.03	56.18	58.73
76. Bonds	2.21	3.59	3.53	9.47	8.88	11.33	11.93	11.88	11.37	15.41
77. Other liabilities	5.98	7.50	10.09	7.86	9.59	6.14	7.77	6.79	6.31	5.38
Memoranda										
78. Short-term securities	*1.85*	*7.64*	*7.76*	*4.77*	*7.35*	*1.63*	*1.92*	*2.78*	*1.58*	*1.02*
79. Bonds	*23.30*	*16.00*	*11.79*	*10.18*	*11.71*	*11.84*	*9.50*	*7.55*	*6.26*	*8.02*
80. Shares and participations	*2.27*	*2.46*	*2.90*	*2.98*	*2.19*	*2.42*	*2.45*	*2.72*	*2.21*	*1.85*
81. Claims on non-residents	*11.35*	*12.93*	*10.12*	*13.96*	*7.19*	*6.06*	*7.43*	*8.09*	*8.02*	*10.70*
82. Liabilities to non-residents	*20.31*	*23.42*	*26.05*	*28.99*	*30.74*	*31.26*	*31.82*	*30.24*	*24.51*	*17.94*

1. Change in methodology.

Notes

- Average balance sheet totals (item 29) are based on thirteen end-month data.

Change in methodology:

- Due to methodological changes, in 1991, value adjustments are included under "Operating expenses" (item 6 or item 43 or item 56) and not under "Provisions (net)" (item 8 or item 45 or item 58).

Banques commerciales

Pourcentage

ANALYSE DU BILAN

% du total du bilan en fin d'exercice

Actif
67. Caisse & solde auprès de la Banque centrale
68. Dépôts interbancaires
69. Prêts
70. Valeurs mobilières
71. Autres actifs

Passif
72. Capital et réserves
73. Emprunts auprès de la Banque centrale
74. Dépôts interbancaires
75. Dépôts non bancaires
76. Obligations
77. Autres engagements

Pour mémoire
78. Titres à court terme
79. Obligations
80. Actions et participations
81. Créances sur des non résidents
82. Engagements envers des non résidents

1. Changement méthodologique.

Notes

- La moyenne du total des actifs/passifs (poste 29) est basée sur treize données de fin de mois.

Changement méthodologique :

- Dû aux changements méthodologiques, pour l'année 1991, les ajustements en valeur sont inclus sous la rubrique "Frais d'exploitation" (poste 6 ou poste 43 ou poste 56) et non sous la rubrique "Provisions (nettes)" (poste 8 ou poste 45 ou poste 58).

NORWAY

Savings banks

NORVEGE

Caisses d'épargne

Million Norwegian kroner / *Millions de couronnes norvégiennes*

	1983	1984	1985	1986	1987	1988	1989	1990	1991	1992	
INCOME STATEMENT											**COMPTE DE RESULTATS**
1. Interest income	11851	13836	17693	24296	31298	34693	32713	31391	29836	28849	1. Produits financiers
2. Interest expenses	7251	8759	12031	17201	22495	25544	22193	21376	19958	18350	2. Frais financiers
3. Net interest income	4600	5077	5662	7095	8803	9149	10520	10015	9878	10499	3. Produits financiers nets
4. Non-interest income (net)	482	622	1006	1405	1297	1581	2226	1585	1416	1705	4. Produits non financiers (nets)
5. Gross income	5082	5699	6668	8500	10100	10730	12746	11600	11294	12204	5. Résultat brut
6. Operating expenses (1)	3524	4070	5044	6069	6964	7757	7728	7782	8309	7200	6. Frais d'exploitation (1)
7. Net income	1558	1629	1624	2431	3136	2973	5018	3818	2985	5004	7. Résultat net
8. Provisions (net) (1)	736	860	1061	1549	1710	3170	4181	4062	4852	1865	8. Provisions (nettes) (1)
9. Profit before tax	822	769	563	882	1426	-197	837	-244	-1867	3139	9. Bénéfices avant impôt
10. Income tax	168	146	105	140	233	201	283	212	192	327	10. Impôt
11. Profit after tax	654	623	458	742	1193	-398	554	-456	-2059	2812	11. Bénéfices après impôt
12. Distributed profit	-	-	-	-	-	10	76	21	11	17	12. Bénéfices distribués
13. Retained profit	654	623	458	742	1193	-408	478	-477	-2070	2795	13. Bénéfices mis en réserve
Memoranda											*Pour mémoire*
14. Staff costs	*1881*	*2081*	*2537*	*2943*	*3229*	*3603*	*3539*	*3629*	*3665*	*3520*	14. Frais de personnel
15. Provisions on loans	*497*	*587*	*696*	*926*	*1744*	*3095*	*5173*	*3868*	*4708*	*3692*	15. Provisions sur prêts
16. Provisions on securities	*..*	*..*	*..*	*..*	*..*	*..*	*..*	*..*	*..*	*..*	16. Provisions sur titres
BALANCE SHEET											**BILAN**
Assets											**Actif**
17. Cash & balance with Central bank	1430	1195	1528	1757	2124	1624	1679	1853	1837	2355	17. Caisse & solde auprès de la Banque centrale
18. Interbank deposits	5140	4324	6885	13458	11794	6074	4383	3492	4977	5572	18. Dépôts interbancaires
19. Loans	64889	80505	111073	146547	168079	181965	187424	193320	192579	195420	19. Prêts
20. Securities	28775	33779	36567	30374	41095	42716	40963	35991	31834	26974	20. Valeurs mobilières
21. Other assets	1015	891	2219	2881	7906	9936	9214	8723	8669	8466	21. Autres actifs
Liabilities											**Passif**
22. Capital & reserves	6351	7092	8179	9122	9555	9338	11002	10615	9663	13343	22. Capital et réserves
23. Borrowing from Central bank	1500	796	2189	25740	32466	36736	30926	23066	14611	10632	23. Emprunts auprès de la Banque centrale
24. Interbank deposits	4208	6565	14751	17279	25412	21179	16406	13633	16684	11177	24. Dépôts interbancaires
25. Non-bank deposits	85661	102075	124774	132487	146689	156978	167897	177698	184342	189000	25. Dépôts non bancaires
26. Bonds	193	227	2237	4361	2614	5123	4971	6496	5413	7507	26. Obligations
27. Other liabilities	3336	3939	6142	6028	14263	12967	12461	11870	9183	7128	27. Autres engagements
Balance sheet total											**Total du bilan**
28. End-year total	101249	120694	158272	195017	230999	242320	243665	243379	239896	238787	28. En fin d'exercice
29. Average total	101588	117136	143262	187379	221112	252462	250833	251542	248570	241573	29. Moyen
Memoranda											*Pour mémoire*
30. Short-term securities	*1960*	*7690*	*11553*	*6384*	*6845*	*4808*	*2872*	*2810*	*3222*	*1613*	30. Titres à court terme
31. Bonds	*26082*	*25040*	*23349*	*21610*	*31573*	*35507*	*35479*	*30238*	*26073*	*22521*	31. Obligations
32. Shares and participations	*733*	*1049*	*1665*	*2380*	*2678*	*2402*	*2612*	*2942*	*2539*	*2841*	32. Actions et participations
33. Claims on non-residents	*2592*	*2746*	*5170*	*7834*	*5939*	*5475*	*4371*	*4060*	*3718*	*3358*	33. Créances sur des non résidents
34. Liabilities to non-residents	*3349*	*5634*	*12104*	*12517*	*21491*	*24751*	*19323*	*17049*	*13240*	*8701*	34. Engagements envers des non résidents
SUPPLEMENTARY INFORMATION											**RENSEIGNEMENTS COMPLEMENTAIRES**
35. Number of institutions	253	227	198	192	173	158	151	142	135	134	35. Nombre d'institutions
36. Number of branches	1300	1300	1328	1228	1426	1319	1194	1194	1121	1105	36. Nombre de succursales
37. Number of employees (x 1000)	12.2	12.8	12.8	14.7	15.6	15.7	14.9	14.6	13.3	13.4	37. Nombre de salariés (x 1000)

NORWAY

Savings banks

NORVEGE

Caisses d'épargne

Per cent — *Pourcentage*

INCOME STATEMENT ANALYSIS — ANALYSE DU COMPTE DE RESULTATS

		1983	1984	1985	1986	1987	1988	1989	1990	1991	1992		
% of average balance sheet total													**% du total moyen du bilan**
38. Interest income		11.67	11.81	12.35	12.97	14.15	13.74	13.04	12.48	12.00	11.94	38.	Produits financiers
39. Interest expenses		7.14	7.48	8.40	9.18	10.17	10.12	8.85	8.50	8.03	7.60	39.	Frais financiers
40. Net interest income		4.53	4.33	3.95	3.79	3.98	3.62	4.19	3.98	3.97	4.35	40.	Produits financiers nets
41. Non-interest income (net)		0.47	0.53	0.70	0.75	0.59	0.63	0.89	0.63	0.57	0.71	41.	Produits non financiers (nets)
42. Gross income		5.00	4.87	4.65	4.54	4.57	4.25	5.08	4.61	4.54	5.05	42.	Résultat brut
43. Operating expenses (1)		3.47	3.47	3.52	3.24	3.15	3.07	3.08	3.09	3.34	2.98	43.	Frais d'exploitation (1)
44. Net income		1.53	1.39	1.13	1.30	1.42	1.18	2.00	1.52	1.20	2.07	44.	Résultat net
45. Provisions (net) (1)		0.72	0.73	0.74	0.83	0.77	1.26	1.67	1.61	1.95	0.77	45.	Provisions (nettes) (1)
46. Profit before tax		0.81	0.66	0.39	0.47	0.64	-0.08	0.33	-0.10	-0.75	1.30	46.	Bénéfices avant impôt
47. Income tax		0.17	0.12	0.07	0.07	0.11	0.08	0.11	0.08	0.08	0.14	47.	Impôt
48. Profit after tax		0.64	0.53	0.32	0.40	0.54	-0.16	0.22	-0.18	-0.83	1.16	48.	Bénéfices après impôt
49. Distributed profit		-	-	-	-	-	0.00	0.03	0.01	0.00	0.01	49.	Bénéfices distribués
50. Retained profit		0.64	0.53	0.32	0.40	0.54	-0.16	0.19	-0.19	-0.83	1.16	50.	Bénéfices mis en réserve
51. Staff costs		1.85	1.78	1.77	1.57	1.46	1.43	1.41	1.44	1.47	1.46	51.	Frais de personnel
52. Provisions on loans		0.49	0.50	0.49	0.49	0.79	1.23	2.06	1.54	1.89	1.61	52.	Provisions sur prêts
53. Provisions on securities		..	..	..	..	..	..	..	..	..	..	53.	Provisions sur titres
% of gross income													**% du total du résultat brut**
54. Net interest income		90.52	89.09	84.91	83.47	87.16	85.27	82.54	86.34	87.46	86.03	54.	Produits financiers nets
55. Non-interest income (net)		9.48	10.91	15.09	16.53	12.84	14.73	17.46	13.66	12.54	13.97	55.	Produits non financiers (nets)
56. Operating expenses (1)		69.34	71.42	75.64	71.40	68.95	72.29	60.63	67.09	73.57	59.00	56.	Frais d'exploitation (1)
57. Net income		30.66	28.58	24.36	28.60	31.05	27.71	39.37	32.91	26.43	41.00	57.	Résultat net
58. Provisions (net) (1)		14.48	15.09	15.91	18.22	16.93	29.54	32.80	35.02	42.96	15.28	58.	Provisions (nettes) (1)
59. Profit before tax		16.17	13.49	8.44	10.38	14.12	-1.84	6.57	-2.10	-16.53	25.72	59.	Bénéfices avant impôt
60. Income tax		3.31	2.56	1.57	1.65	2.31	1.87	2.22	1.83	1.70	2.68	60.	Impôt
61. Profit after tax		12.87	10.93	6.87	8.73	11.81	-3.71	4.35	-3.93	-18.23	23.04	61.	Bénéfices après impôt
62. Staff costs		37.01	36.52	38.05	34.62	31.97	33.58	27.77	31.28	32.45	28.84	62.	Frais de personnel
% of net income													**% du total du résultat net**
63. Provisions (net)		47.24	52.79	65.33	63.72	54.53	106.63	83.32	106.39	162.55	37.27	63.	Provisions (nettes)
64. Profit before tax		52.76	47.21	34.67	36.28	45.47	-6.63	16.68	-6.39	-62.55	62.73	64.	Bénéfices avant impôt
65. Income tax		10.78	8.96	6.47	5.76	7.43	6.76	5.64	5.55	6.43	6.53	65.	Impôt
66. Profit after tax		41.98	38.24	28.20	30.52	38.04	-13.39	11.04	-11.94	-68.98	56.20	66.	Bénéfices après impôt

120

NORWAY

Savings banks

Per cent / *Pourcentage*

BALANCE SHEET ANALYSIS / ANALYSE DU BILAN

% of year-end balance sheet total / % du total du bilan en fin d'exercice

		1983	1984	1985	1986	1987	1988	1989	1990	1991	1992		
Assets													**Actif**
67.	Cash & balance with Central bank	1.41	0.99	0.97	0.90	0.92	0.67	0.69	0.76	0.77	0.99	67.	Caisse & solde auprès de la Banque centrale
68.	Interbank deposits	5.08	3.58	4.35	6.90	5.11	2.51	1.80	1.43	2.07	2.33	68.	Dépôts interbancaires
69.	Loans	64.09	66.70	70.18	75.15	72.76	75.09	76.92	79.43	80.28	81.84	69.	Prêts
70.	Securities	28.42	27.99	23.10	15.58	17.79	17.63	16.81	14.79	13.27	11.30	70.	Valeurs mobilières
71.	Other assets	1.00	0.74	1.40	1.48	3.42	4.10	3.78	3.58	3.61	3.55	71.	Autres actifs
Liabilities													**Passif**
72.	Capital & reserves	6.27	5.88	5.17	4.68	4.14	3.85	4.52	4.36	4.03	5.59	72.	Capital et réserves
73.	Borrowing from Central bank	1.48	0.66	1.38	13.20	14.05	15.16	12.69	9.48	6.09	4.45	73.	Emprunts auprès de la Banque centrale
74.	Interbank deposits	4.16	5.44	9.32	8.86	11.00	8.74	6.73	5.60	6.95	4.68	74.	Dépôts interbancaires
75.	Non-bank deposits	84.60	84.57	78.84	67.94	63.50	64.78	68.90	73.01	76.84	79.15	75.	Dépôts non bancaires
76.	Bonds	0.19	0.19	1.41	2.24	1.13	2.11	2.04	2.67	2.26	3.14	76.	Obligations
77.	Other liabilities	3.29	3.26	3.88	3.09	6.17	5.35	5.11	4.88	3.83	2.99	77.	Autres engagements
Memoranda													***Pour mémoire***
78.	*Short-term securities*	*1.94*	*6.37*	*7.30*	*3.27*	*2.96*	*1.98*	*1.18*	*1.15*	*1.34*	*0.68*	78.	*Titres à court terme*
79.	*Bonds*	*25.76*	*20.75*	*14.75*	*11.08*	*13.67*	*14.65*	*14.56*	*12.42*	*10.87*	*9.43*	79.	*Obligations*
80.	*Shares and participations*	*0.72*	*0.87*	*1.05*	*1.22*	*1.16*	*0.99*	*1.07*	*1.21*	*1.06*	*1.19*	80.	*Actions et participations*
81.	*Claims on non-residents*	*2.56*	*2.28*	*3.27*	*4.02*	*2.57*	*2.26*	*1.79*	*1.67*	*1.55*	*1.41*	81.	*Créances sur des non résidents*
82.	*Liabilities to non-residents*	*3.31*	*4.67*	*7.65*	*6.42*	*9.30*	*10.21*	*7.93*	*7.01*	*5.52*	*3.64*	82.	*Engagements envers des non résidents*

1. Change in methodology.

Notes

• Average balance sheet totals (item 29) are based on thirteen end-month data.

Change in methodology:

• Due to methodological changes, in 1991, value adjustments are included under "Operating expenses" (item 6 or item 43 or item 56) and not under "Provisions (net)" (item 8 or item 45 or item 58).

1. Changement méthodologique.

Notes

• La moyenne du total des actifs/passifs (poste 29) est basée sur treize données de fin de mois.

Changement méthodologique :

• Dû aux changements méthodologiques, pour l'année 1991, les ajustements en valeur sont inclus sous la rubrique "Frais d'exploitation" (poste 6 ou poste 43 ou poste 56) et non sous la rubrique "Provisions (nettes)" (poste 8 ou poste 45 ou poste 58).

PORTUGAL

All banks

Million escudos

		1983	1984	1985	1986	1987	1988	1989	1990 (1)	1991	1992
INCOME STATEMENT											
1.	Interest income	511086	737647	939400	880775	848092	944041	1171919	1526170	1853028	2166626
2.	Interest expenses	452165	663248	821707	718557	614871	649072	780109	980136	1197538	1511030
3.	Net interest income	58921	74399	117693	162218	233221	294969	391810	546034	655490	655596
4.	Non-interest income (net)	45375	48327	37271	36132	52303	64212	76182	126968	149699	214372
5.	Gross income	104296	122726	154964	198350	285524	359181	467992	673002	805189	869968
6.	Operating expenses	68077	85495	107744	132113	154510	183213	219080	280859	367504	460874
7.	Net income	36219	37231	47220	66237	131014	175968	248912	392143	437685	409094
8.	Provisions (net)	22667	23623	30831	49399	92362	115176	151446	231747	236298	252619
9.	Profit before tax	13552	13608	16389	16838	38652	60792	97466	160396	201387	156475
10.	Income tax	1103	1227	1622	1668	1846	4053	23304	38814	55937	40965
11.	Profit after tax	12449	12381	14767	15170	36806	56739	74162	121582	145450	115510
12.	Distributed profit	..	..	..	..	..	..	..	..	..	..
13.	Retained profit	..	..	..	..	..	..	..	..	..	..
	Memoranda										
14.	*Staff costs*	*49982*	*61249*	*76547*	*92062*	*106888*	*121684*	*141475*	*172837*	*216184*	*262319*
15.	*Provisions on loans*	*..*	*..*	*..*	*..*	*..*	*..*	*..*	*220452*	*217457*	*285555*
16.	*Provisions on securities*	*..*	*..*	*..*	*..*	*..*	*..*	*..*	*11493*	*19207*	*31868*
BALANCE SHEET											
	Assets										
17.	Cash & balance with Central bank	305567	306287	311083	284202	396356	465639	1319298	1424899	1807694	2006147
18.	Interbank deposits	131568	400402	798040	1072002	1192065	1263484	1242249	2267469	1981227	2880951
19.	Loans	2180816	2642474	2923807	3257965	3384853	3631461	3851876	4692485	5786290	6785826
20.	Securities	209588	197661	432504	573087	972915	1407330	1545134	2124880	3795675	4285416
21.	Other assets	709622	914242	987459	1132528	1432713	1971423	2342169	1257323	1249574	1335801
	Liabilities										
22.	Capital & reserves	201099	247872	305897	421556	609487	836160	1063216	1532464	1982141	2451728
23.	Borrowing from Central bank	43411	33110	57127	77083	60445	21686	30932	45412	196482	28493
24.	Interbank deposits	77728	60928	86839	106330	245149	333275	505209	1034466	1337458	1968283
25.	Non-bank deposits	2617830	3366521	4203635	4952503	5586231	6465273	7539688	8018707	9686631	11642527
26.	Bonds	22717	37779	43152	42025	69277	91676	92159	134255	169405	217846
27.	Other liabilities	574376	714856	756243	720287	808313	991267	1069522	1001752	1248343	985264
	Balance sheet total										
28.	End-year total	3537161	4461066	5452893	6319784	7378902	8739337	10300726	11767056	14620460	17294141
29.	Average total	3192550	3999114	4956980	5886339	6849343	8059120	9520032	NA	13193758	15957301
	Memoranda										
30.	*Short-term securities*	*179707*	*166259*	*45711*	*156355*	*293109*	*302597*	*522655*	*708908*	*1375478*	*1022243*
31.	*Bonds*	*32210*	*34361*	*345710*	*371191*	*572003*	*845926*	*816299*	*1096215*	*1898583*	*2511114*
32.	*Shares and participations*	*-*		*43628*	*46503*	*109391*	*131635*	*184629*	*280616*	*425311*	*570823*
33.	*Claims on non-residents*	*224292*	*312512*	*357334*	*339334*	*403409*	*611988*	*698218*	*734085*	*933953*	*1412845*
34.	*Liabilities to non-residents*	*221417*	*298942*	*257699*	*221513*	*229801*	*301338*	*466196*	*637619*	*935810*	*1224676*
SUPPLEMENTARY INFORMATION											
35.	Number of institutions	17	18	24	27	27	27	29	33	35	35
36.	Number of branches	1426	1469	1494	1510	1531	1607	1741	1991	2505	2852
37.	Number of employees (x 1000)	58.4	58.7	59.1	59.2	59.0	58.4	58.1	59.2	61.1	60.8

PORTUGAL

Ensemble des banques

Millions d'escudos

COMPTE DE RESULTATS
1. Produits financiers
2. Frais financiers
3. Produits financiers nets
4. Produits non financiers (nets)
5. Résultat brut
6. Frais d'exploitation
7. Résultat net
8. Provisions (nettes)
9. Bénéfices avant impôt
10. Impôt
11. Bénéfices après impôt
12. Bénéfices distribués
13. Bénéfices mis en réserve

Pour mémoire
14. *Frais de personnel*
15. *Provisions sur prêts*
16. *Provisions sur titres*

BILAN

Actif
17. Caisse & solde auprès de la Banque centrale
18. Dépôts interbancaires
19. Prêts
20. Valeurs mobilières
21. Autres actifs

Passif
22. Capital et réserves
23. Emprunts auprès de la Banque centrale
24. Dépôts interbancaires
25. Dépôts non bancaires
26. Obligations
27. Autres engagements

Total du bilan
28. En fin d'exercice
29. Moyen

Pour mémoire
30. *Titres à court terme*
31. *Obligations*
32. *Actions et participations*
33. *Créances sur des non résidents*
34. *Engagements envers des non résidents*

RENSEIGNEMENTS COMPLEMENTAIRES
35. Nombre d'institutions
36. Nombre de succursales
37. Nombre de salariés (x 1000)

All banks

Per cent

INCOME STATEMENT ANALYSIS

Ensemble des banques

Pourcentage

ANALYSE DU COMPTE DE RESULTATS

		1983	1984	1985	1986	1987	1988	1989	1990 (1)	1991	1992		
% of average balance sheet total													**% du total moyen du bilan**
38.	Interest income	16.01	18.45	18.95	14.96	12.38	11.71	12.31	NA	14.04	13.58	38.	Produits financiers
39.	Interest expenses	14.16	16.58	16.58	12.21	8.98	8.05	8.19	NA	9.08	9.47	39.	Frais financiers
40.	Net interest income	1.85	1.86	2.37	2.76	3.41	3.66	4.12	NA	4.97	4.11	40.	Produits financiers nets
41.	Non-interest income (net)	1.42	1.21	0.75	0.61	0.76	0.80	0.80	NA	1.13	1.34	41.	Produits non financiers (nets)
42.	Gross income	3.27	3.07	3.13	3.37	4.17	4.46	4.92	NA	6.10	5.45	42.	Résultat brut
43.	Operating expenses	2.13	2.14	2.17	2.24	2.26	2.27	2.30	NA	2.79	2.89	43.	Frais d'exploitation
44.	Net income	1.13	0.93	0.95	1.13	1.91	2.18	2.61	NA	3.32	2.56	44.	Résultat net
45.	Provisions (net)	0.71	0.59	0.62	0.84	1.35	1.43	1.59	NA	1.79	1.58	45.	Provisions (nettes)
46.	Profit before tax	0.42	0.34	0.33	0.29	0.56	0.75	1.02	NA	1.53	0.98	46.	Bénéfices avant impôt
47.	Income tax	0.03	0.03	0.03	0.03	0.03	0.05	0.24	NA	0.42	0.26	47.	Impôt
48.	Profit after tax	0.39	0.31	0.30	0.26	0.54	0.70	0.78	NA	1.10	0.72	48.	Bénéfices après impôt
49.	Distributed profit	..	..	..	..	..	..	..	..	..	..	49.	Bénéfices distribués
50.	Retained profit	..	..	..	..	..	..	..	..	..	..	50.	Bénéfices mis en réserve
51.	Staff costs	1.57	1.53	1.54	1.56	1.56	1.51	1.49	NA	1.64	1.64	51.	Frais de personnel
52.	Provisions on loans	..	..	..	..	..	..	..	NA	1.65	1.79	52.	Provisions sur prêts
53.	Provisions on securities	..	..	..	..	..	..	..	NA	0.15	0.20	53.	Provisions sur titres
% of gross income													**% du total du résultat brut**
54.	Net interest income	56.49	60.62	75.95	81.78	81.68	82.12	83.72	81.13	81.41	75.36	54.	Produits financiers nets
55.	Non-interest income (net)	43.51	39.38	24.05	18.22	18.32	17.88	16.28	18.87	18.59	24.64	55.	Produits non financiers (nets)
56.	Operating expenses	65.27	69.66	69.53	66.61	54.11	51.01	46.81	41.73	45.64	52.98	56.	Frais d'exploitation
57.	Net income	34.73	30.34	30.47	33.39	45.89	48.99	53.19	58.27	54.36	47.02	57.	Résultat net
58.	Provisions (net)	21.73	19.25	19.90	24.90	32.35	32.07	32.36	34.43	29.35	29.04	58.	Provisions (nettes)
59.	Profit before tax	12.99	11.09	10.58	8.49	13.54	16.93	20.83	23.83	25.01	17.99	59.	Bénéfices avant impôt
60.	Income tax	1.06	1.00	1.05	0.84	0.65	1.13	4.98	5.77	6.95	4.71	60.	Impôt
61.	Profit after tax	11.94	10.09	9.53	7.65	12.89	15.80	15.85	18.07	18.06	13.28	61.	Bénéfices après impôt
62.	Staff costs	47.92	49.91	49.40	46.41	37.44	33.88	30.23	25.68	26.85	30.15	62.	Frais de personnel
% of net income													**% du total du résultat net**
63.	Provisions (net)	62.58	63.45	65.29	74.58	70.50	65.45	60.84	59.10	53.99	61.75	63.	Provisions (nettes)
64.	Profit before tax	37.42	36.55	34.71	25.42	29.50	34.55	39.16	40.90	46.01	38.25	64.	Bénéfices avant impôt
65.	Income tax	3.05	3.30	3.43	2.52	1.41	2.30	9.36	9.90	12.78	10.01	65.	Impôt
66.	Profit after tax	34.37	33.25	31.27	22.90	28.09	32.24	29.79	31.00	33.23	28.24	66.	Bénéfices après impôt

PORTUGAL / PORTUGAL

All banks / **Ensemble des banques**

Per cent / *Pourcentage*

BALANCE SHEET ANALYSIS / ANALYSE DU BILAN

% of year-end balance sheet total / **% du total du bilan en fin d'exercice**

		1983	1984	1985	1986	1987	1988	1989	1990 (1)	1991	1992		
Assets													**Actif**
67.	Cash & balance with Central bank	8.64	6.87	5.70	4.50	5.37	5.33	12.81	12.11	12.36	11.60	67.	Caisse & solde auprès de la Banque centrale
68.	Interbank deposits	3.72	8.98	14.64	16.96	16.16	14.46	12.06	19.27	13.55	16.66	68.	Dépôts interbancaires
69.	Loans	61.65	59.23	53.62	51.55	45.87	41.55	37.39	39.88	39.58	39.24	69.	Prêts
70.	Securities	5.93	4.43	7.93	9.07	13.19	16.10	15.00	18.06	25.96	24.78	70.	Valeurs mobilières
71.	Other assets	20.06	20.49	18.11	17.92	19.42	22.56	22.74	10.69	8.55	7.72	71.	Autres actifs
Liabilities													**Passif**
72.	Capital & reserves	5.69	5.56	5.61	6.67	8.26	9.57	10.32	13.02	13.56	14.18	72.	Capital et réserves
73.	Borrowing from Central bank	1.23	0.74	1.05	1.22	0.82	0.25	0.30	0.39	1.34	0.16	73.	Emprunts auprès de la Banque centrale
74.	Interbank deposits	2.20	1.37	1.59	1.68	3.32	3.81	4.90	8.79	9.15	11.38	74.	Dépôts interbancaires
75.	Non-bank deposits	74.01	75.46	77.09	78.37	75.71	73.98	73.20	68.15	66.25	67.32	75.	Dépôts non bancaires
76.	Bonds	0.64	0.85	0.79	0.66	0.94	1.05	0.89	1.14	1.16	1.26	76.	Obligations
77.	Other liabilities	16.24	16.02	13.87	11.40	10.95	11.34	10.38	8.51	8.54	5.70	77.	Autres engagements
Memoranda													***Pour mémoire***
78.	*Short-term securities*		*-*	*0.84*	*2.47*	*3.97*	*3.46*	*5.07*	*6.02*	*9.41*	*5.91*	*78.*	*Titres à court terme*
79.	*Bonds*	*5.08*	*3.73*	*6.34*	*5.87*	*7.75*	*9.68*	*7.92*	*9.32*	*12.99*	*14.52*	*79.*	*Obligations*
80.	*Shares and participations*	*0.91*	*0.77*	*0.80*	*0.74*	*1.48*	*1.51*	*1.79*	*2.38*	*2.91*	*3.30*	*80.*	*Actions et participations*
81.	*Claims on non-residents*	*6.34*	*7.01*	*6.55*	*5.37*	*5.47*	*7.00*	*6.78*	*6.24*	*6.39*	*8.17*	*81.*	*Créances sur des non résidents*
82.	*Liabilities to non-residents*	*6.26*	*6.70*	*4.73*	*3.51*	*3.11*	*3.45*	*4.53*	*5.42*	*6.40*	*7.08*	*82.*	*Engagements envers des non résidents*

1. Break in series due to changes in methodology.

1. Rupture dans les séries consécutive aux changements méthodologiques.

Change in methodology:

- Until 1989, time deposits with the Central bank are included under "Interbank deposits" (item 18).

- As from 1990, data are based on the new accounting framework for the Portugese banking sector, introduced in January 1990.

Changement méthodologique :

- Jusqu'en 1989, les dépôts à terme auprès de la Banque centrale sont inclus sous "Dépôts interbancaires" (poste 18).

- A partir de 1990, les données sont établies à l'aide du nouveau cadre comptable pour le secteur bancaire portugais introduit en janvier 1990.

SPAIN

All banks

Billion pesetas

ESPAGNE

Ensemble des banques

Milliards de pesetas

	1983	1984	1985	1986	1987	1988	1989	1990	1991	1992		
INCOME STATEMENT (1)												**COMPTE DE RESULTATS (1)**
1. Interest income	3232	3775	4022	4172	4755	5075	6221	7589	8497	8909	1.	Produits financiers
2. Interest expenses	2020	2398	2522	2472	2816	2912	3822	4956	5567	5932	2.	Frais financiers
3. Net interest income	1212	1377	1500	1700	1939	2163	2399	2633	2930	2977	3.	Produits financiers nets
4. Non-interest income (net)	201	225	272	312	410	493	483	566	670	786	4.	Produits non financiers (nets)
5. Gross income	1413	1602	1772	2012	2349	2656	2882	3199	3600	3763	5.	Résultat brut
6. Operating expenses	910	1025	1144	1360	1456	1705	1756	1950	2108	2269	6.	Frais d'exploitation
7. Net income	503	577	628	652	893	951	1126	1249	1492	1494	7.	Résultat net
8. Provisions (net)	316	328	311	288	387	358	310	369	481	598	8.	Provisions (nettes)
9. Profit before tax	187	249	317	364	506	593	816	880	1011	896	9.	Bénéfices avant impôt
10. Income tax	43	49	69	85	120	158	231	239	249	219	10.	Impôt
11. Profit after tax	144	200	248	279	386	435	585	641	762	677	11.	Bénéfices après impôt
12. Distributed profit	82	84	94	102	135	188	243	262	317	315	12.	Bénéfices distribués
13. Retained profit	62	116	154	177	251	247	342	379	445	362	13.	Bénéfices mis en réserve
Memoranda												*Pour mémoire*
14. Staff costs	*605*	*677*	*756*	*939*	*979*	*1171*	*1144*	*1216*	*1278*	*1377*	14.	*Frais de personnel*
15. Provisions on loans	*260*	*226*	*186*	*137*	*181*	*206*	*156*	*195*	*377*	*523*	15.	*Provisions sur prêts*
16. Provisions on securities	*28*	*18*	*27*	*9*	*39*	*24*	*21*	*67*	*52*	*92*	16.	*Provisions sur titres*
BALANCE SHEET												**BILAN**
Assets												**Actif**
17. Cash & balance with Central bank	3582	3622	3668	3787	5033	5141	5930	5034	5788	4984	17.	Caisse & solde auprès de la Banque centrale
18. Interbank deposits	2953	3958	5146	5406	5750	6773	8301	9721	11744	14307	18.	Dépôts interbancaires
19. Loans	15401	15546	16828	18251	20650	23800	28055	31457	37340	40786	19.	Prêts
20. Securities	3807	7247	8667	10900	11718	13030	14145	15464	14273	15113	20.	Valeurs mobilières
21. Other assets	4456	5726	5891	5679	5920	6198	7050	8457	9721	11716	21.	Autres actifs
Liabilities												**Passif**
22. Capital & reserves	2446	2808	3164	3497	4132	4907	5572	6451	8231	8428	22.	Capital et réserves
23. Borrowing from Central bank	744	1057	980	1426	1384	957	2112	1590	1572	4282	23.	Emprunts auprès de la Banque centrale
24. Interbank deposits	3388	4252	5496	5584	5562	6250	6804	7563	9863	11574	24.	Dépôts interbancaires
25. Non-bank deposits	21074	24361	26262	28671	32748	37307	42709	48124	52773	57083	25.	Dépôts non bancaires
26. Bonds	802	1060	1310	1710	1463	1368	1093	1003	1208	1274	26.	Obligations
27. Other liabilities	1745	2562	2987	3134	3783	4153	5189	5402	5220	4267	27.	Autres engagements
Balance sheet total												**Total du bilan**
28. End-year total	30199	36100	40199	44021	49071	54942	63480	70133	78866	86907	28.	En fin d'exercice
29. Average total	28000	33150	38150	42110	46546	52007	59211	66807	74500	82887	29.	Moyen
Memoranda												*Pour mémoire*
30. Short-term securities	*172*	*2705*	*3831*	*4484*	*5412*	*6204*	*7237*	*8142*	*6064*	*6456*	30.	*Titres à court terme*
31. Bonds	*2904*	*3789*	*4052*	*5523*	*5291*	*5371*	*5180*	*5373*	*5477*	*5743*	31.	*Obligations*
32. Shares and participations	*731*	*754*	*784*	*893*	*1015*	*1456*	*1728*	*1949*	*2732*	*2915*	32.	*Actions et participations*
33. Claims on non-residents	*2495*	*3039*	*3089*	*3152*	*2804*	*2800*	*3019*	*3792*	*4511*	*7857*	33.	*Créances sur des non résidents*
34. Liabilities to non-residents	*3043*	*3678*	*3228*	*3372*	*3629*	*4246*	*4876*	*6447*	*7373*	*9342*	34.	*Engagements envers des non résidents*
SUPPLEMENTARY INFORMATION												**RENSEIGNEMENTS COMPLEMENTAIRES**
35. Number of institutions	376	369	364	355	346	334	333	327	323	319	35.	Nombre d'institutions
36. Number of branches	31053	31615	32462	32616	33049	33542	34519	35084	35811	35314	36.	Nombre de succursales
37. Number of employees (x 1000)	248.5	244.7	243.5	240.7	240.0	242.4	248.3	251.6	256.0	253.1	37.	Nombre de salariés (x 1000)

SPAIN

All banks

ESPAGNE

Ensemble des banques

Per cent / *Pourcentage*

INCOME STATEMENT ANALYSIS / ANALYSE DU COMPTE DE RESULTATS

		1983	1984	1985	1986	1987	1988	1989	1990	1991	1992		
% of average balance sheet total													**% du total moyen du bilan**
38.	Interest income	11.54	11.39	10.54	9.91	10.22	9.76	10.51	11.36	11.41	10.75	38.	Produits financiers
39.	Interest expenses	7.21	7.23	6.61	5.87	6.05	5.60	6.45	7.42	7.47	7.16	39.	Frais financiers
40.	Net interest income	4.33	4.15	3.93	4.04	4.17	4.16	4.05	3.94	3.93	3.59	40.	Produits financiers nets
41.	Non-interest income (net)	0.72	0.68	0.71	0.74	0.88	0.95	0.82	0.85	0.90	0.95	41.	Produits non financiers (nets)
42.	Gross income	5.05	4.83	4.64	4.78	5.05	5.11	4.87	4.79	4.83	4.54	42.	Résultat brut
43.	Operating expenses	3.25	3.09	3.00	3.23	3.13	3.28	2.97	2.92	2.83	2.74	43.	Frais d'exploitation
44.	Net income	1.80	1.74	1.65	1.55	1.92	1.83	1.90	1.87	2.00	1.80	44.	Résultat net
45.	Provisions (net)	1.13	0.99	0.82	0.68	0.83	0.69	0.52	0.55	0.65	0.72	45.	Provisions (nettes)
46.	Profit before tax	0.67	0.75	0.83	0.86	1.09	1.14	1.38	1.32	1.36	1.08	46.	Bénéfices avant impôt
47.	Income tax	0.15	0.15	0.18	0.20	0.26	0.30	0.39	0.36	0.33	0.26	47.	Impôt
48.	Profit after tax	0.51	0.60	0.65	0.66	0.83	0.84	0.99	0.96	1.02	0.82	48.	Bénéfices après impôt
49.	Distributed profit	0.29	0.25	0.25	0.24	0.29	0.36	0.41	0.39	0.43	0.38	49.	Bénéfices distribués
50.	Retained profit	0.22	0.35	0.40	0.42	0.54	0.47	0.58	0.57	0.60	0.44	50.	Bénéfices mis en réserve
51.	Staff costs	2.16	2.04	1.98	2.23	2.10	2.25	1.93	1.82	1.72	1.66	51.	Frais de personnel
52.	Provisions on loans	0.93	0.68	0.49	0.33	0.39	0.40	0.26	0.29	0.51	0.63	52.	Provisions sur prêts
53.	Provisions on securities	0.10	0.05	0.07	0.02	0.08	0.05	0.04	0.10	0.07	0.11	53.	Provisions sur titres
% of gross income													**% du total du résultat brut**
54.	Net interest income	85.77	85.96	84.65	84.49	82.55	81.44	83.24	82.31	81.39	79.11	54.	Produits financiers nets
55.	Non-interest income (net)	14.23	14.04	15.35	15.51	17.45	18.56	16.76	17.69	18.61	20.89	55.	Produits non financiers (nets)
56.	Operating expenses	64.40	63.98	64.56	67.59	61.98	64.19	60.93	60.96	58.56	60.30	56.	Frais d'exploitation
57.	Net income	35.60	36.02	35.44	32.41	38.02	35.81	39.07	39.04	41.44	39.70	57.	Résultat net
58.	Provisions (net)	22.36	20.47	17.55	14.31	16.48	13.48	10.76	11.53	13.36	15.89	58.	Provisions (nettes)
59.	Profit before tax	13.23	15.54	17.89	18.09	21.54	22.33	28.31	27.51	28.08	23.81	59.	Bénéfices avant impôt
60.	Income tax	3.04	3.06	3.89	4.22	5.11	5.95	8.02	7.47	6.92	5.82	60.	Impôt
61.	Profit after tax	10.19	12.48	14.00	13.87	16.43	16.38	20.30	20.04	21.17	17.99	61.	Bénéfices après impôt
62.	Staff costs	42.82	42.26	42.66	46.67	41.68	44.09	39.69	38.01	35.50	36.59	62.	Frais de personnel
% of net income													**% du total du résultat net**
63.	Provisions (net)	62.82	56.85	49.52	44.17	43.34	37.64	27.53	29.54	32.24	40.03	63.	Provisions (nettes)
64.	Profit before tax	37.18	43.15	50.48	55.83	56.66	62.36	72.47	70.46	67.76	59.97	64.	Bénéfices avant impôt
65.	Income tax	8.55	8.49	10.99	13.04	13.44	16.61	20.52	19.14	16.69	14.66	65.	Impôt
66.	Profit after tax	28.63	34.66	39.49	42.79	43.23	45.74	51.95	51.32	51.07	45.31	66.	Bénéfices après impôt

SPAIN

All banks

ESPAGNE

Ensemble des banques

Per cent

BALANCE SHEET ANALYSIS

Pourcentage

ANALYSE DU BILAN

% of year-end balance sheet total

% du total du bilan en fin d'exercice

	1983	1984	1985	1986	1987	1988	1989	1990	1991	1992	
Assets											**Actif**
67. Cash & balance with Central bank	11.86	10.03	9.12	8.60	10.26	9.36	9.34	7.18	7.34	5.73	67. Caisse & solde auprès de la Banque centrale
68. Interbank deposits	9.78	10.96	12.80	12.28	11.72	12.33	13.08	13.86	14.89	16.46	68. Dépôts interbancaires
69. Loans	51.00	43.06	41.86	41.46	42.08	43.32	44.20	44.85	47.35	46.93	69. Prêts
70. Securities	12.61	20.07	21.56	24.76	23.88	23.72	22.28	22.05	18.10	17.39	70. Valeurs mobilières
71. Other assets	14.76	15.86	14.65	12.90	12.06	11.28	11.11	12.06	12.33	13.48	71. Autres actifs
Liabilities											**Passif**
72. Capital & reserves	8.10	7.78	7.87	7.94	8.42	8.93	8.78	9.20	10.44	9.70	72. Capital et réserves
73. Borrowing from Central bank	2.46	2.93	2.44	3.24	2.82	1.74	3.33	2.27	1.99	4.93	73. Emprunts auprès de la Banque centrale
74. Interbank deposits	11.22	11.78	13.67	12.68	11.33	11.38	10.72	10.78	12.51	13.32	74. Dépôts interbancaires
75. Non-bank deposits	69.78	67.48	65.33	65.13	66.74	67.90	67.28	68.62	66.91	65.68	75. Dépôts non bancaires
76. Bonds	2.66	2.94	3.26	3.88	2.98	2.49	1.72	1.43	1.53	1.47	76. Obligations
77. Other liabilities	5.78	7.10	7.43	7.12	7.71	7.56	8.17	7.70	6.62	4.91	77. Autres engagements
Memoranda											***Pour mémoire***
78. Short-term securities	*0.57*	*7.49*	*9.53*	*10.19*	*11.03*	*11.29*	*11.40*	*11.61*	*7.69*	*7.43*	*78. Titres à court terme*
79. Bonds	*9.62*	*10.50*	*10.08*	*12.55*	*10.78*	*9.78*	*8.16*	*7.66*	*6.94*	*6.61*	*79. Obligations*
80. Shares and participations	*2.42*	*2.09*	*1.95*	*2.03*	*2.07*	*2.65*	*2.72*	*2.78*	*3.46*	*3.35*	*80. Actions et participations*
81. Claims on non-residents	*8.26*	*8.42*	*7.68*	*7.16*	*5.71*	*5.10*	*4.76*	*5.41*	*5.72*	*9.04*	*81. Créances sur des non résidents*
82. Liabilities to non-residents	*10.08*	*10.19*	*8.03*	*7.66*	*7.40*	*7.73*	*7.68*	*9.19*	*9.35*	*10.75*	*82. Engagements envers des non résidents*

1. Change in methodology.

1. Changement méthodologique.

Notes

Notes

* All banks include Commercial banks, Savings banks and Co-operative banks.

* L'Ensemble des banques comprend les Banques commerciales, les Caisses d'épargne et les Banques mutualistes.

Change in methodology:

Changement méthodologique :

* Historical data for Income statement were revised to reflect the modification of certain accounting principles which came into force 1 January 1992.

* Les données historiques pour le "Compte de résultats" ont été révisées afin de prendre en compte les modifications de certains principes comptables entrés en vigueur le 1er janvier 1992.

- Proceeds and costs relating to hedging operations are included in "Interest income/expenses (items 1 and 2) rather than "Non-interest income (net)" (item 4).

- Les produits et les coûts relatifs aux opérations de couverture à terme sont inclus dans "Produits/frais financiers" (postes 1 et 2) plutôt que dans "Produits non financiers (nets)" (poste 4).

- Cost imputed to internal pension funds, hitherto included in "Staff costs" (item 14), are now included as "Interest expenses" (item 2).

- Le coût imputé aux fonds de pensions internes, jusqu'ici inclut dans "Frais de personnel" (poste 14) est maintenant à la rubrique "Frais financiers" (poste 2).

- The country-risk allowance has been added to that for bad debts in "Provisions on loans" (item 15).

- L'indemnité risque-pays a été ajoutée à celle pour dettes douteuses à la rubrique "Provisions sur prêts" (poste 15).

* As from 1992, "Income tax" (item 10) includes tax on domestic activities of resident entities rather than total tax.

* A partir de 1992, la rubrique "Impôt" (poste 10) inclut l'impôt sur les activités domestiques des entités résidentes plutôt que l'impôt total.

SPAIN

Commercial banks

Billion pesetas

ESPAGNE

Banques commerciales

Milliards de pesetas

	1983	1984	1985	1986	1987	1988	1989	1990	1991	1992	
INCOME STATEMENT (1)											**COMPTE DE RESULTATS (1)**
1. Interest income	2267	2616	2710	2752	3157	3308	4036	4819	5520	5638	1. Produits financiers
2. Interest expenses	1501	1757	1787	1717	2004	1977	2566	3224	3690	3886	2. Frais financiers
3. Net interest income	766	859	923	1035	1153	1331	1470	1595	1830	1752	3. Produits financiers nets
4. Non-interest income (net)	182	180	207	226	314	373	362	433	535	574	4. Produits non financiers (nets)
5. Gross income	948	1039	1130	1261	1467	1704	1832	2028	2365	2326	5. Résultat brut
6. Operating expenses	601	660	727	830	906	1005	1049	1182	1326	1408	6. Frais d'exploitation
7. Net income	347	379	403	431	561	699	783	846	1039	918	7. Résultat net
8. Provisions (net)	222	243	217	205	262	252	208	223	317	342	8. Provisions (nettes)
9. Profit before tax	125	136	186	226	299	447	575	623	722	576	9. Bénéfices avant impôt
10. Income tax	34	38	48	61	83	134	179	189	185	145	10. Impôt
11. Profit after tax	91	98	138	165	216	313	396	434	537	431	11. Bénéfices après impôt
12. Distributed profit	53	52	61	68	91	141	186	207	262	255	12. Bénéfices distribués
13. Retained profit	38	46	77	97	125	172	210	227	275	176	13. Bénéfices mis en réserve
Memoranda											*Pour mémoire*
14. Staff costs	*403*	*441*	*486*	*577*	*627*	*688*	*689*	*750*	*813*	*867*	*14. Frais de personnel*
15. Provisions on loans	*182*	*205*	*152*	*152*	*176*	*219*	*138*	*127*	*257*	*335*	*15. Provisions sur prêts*
16. Provisions on securities	*19*	*14*	*22*	*4*	*26*	*24*	*17*	*47*	*41*	*46*	*16. Provisions sur titres*
BALANCE SHEET											**BILAN**
Assets											**Actif**
17. Cash & balance with Central bank	2152	2180	1938	1811	2791	2751	2979	2516	3105	2513	17. Caisse & solde auprès de la Banque centrale
18. Interbank deposits	2029	2843	3418	3481	4000	4585	5504	6384	7636	8678	18. Dépôts interbancaires
19. Loans	11193	11116	11943	12566	13722	15359	17773	19723	23922	25006	19. Prêts
20. Securities	2019	4212	5094	6623	6809	7020	7697	8508	8385	8873	20. Valeurs mobilières
21. Other assets	3415	4464	4538	4166	4220	4343	4791	5508	6640	8466	21. Autres actifs
Liabilities											**Passif**
22. Capital & reserves	1716	1935	2142	2342	2732	3318	3728	4231	5719	5639	22. Capital et réserves
23. Borrowing from Central bank	731	1030	919	1303	1257	919	1553	1296	1243	2593	23. Emprunts auprès de la Banque centrale
24. Interbank deposits	2714	3435	4791	4941	4986	5512	5978	6241	8554	9881	24. Dépôts interbancaires
25. Non-bank deposits	13735	15768	16077	16976	19184	20994	23637	27100	30198	32140	25. Dépôts non bancaires
26. Bonds	570	636	712	896	753	689	591	586	720	707	26. Obligations
27. Other liabilities	1343	2011	2290	2190	2631	2627	3255	3186	3254	2575	27. Autres engagements
Balance sheet total											**Total du bilan**
28. End-year total	20809	24815	26930	28648	31542	34059	38743	42639	49688	53535	28. En fin d'exercice
29. Average total	19433	22812	25873	27789	30095	32801	36401	40691	46164	51612	29. Moyen
Memoranda											*Pour mémoire*
30. Short-term securities	*80*	*1521*	*2330*	*3184*	*3486*	*3733*	*4016*	*4445*	*3221*	*3396*	*30. Titres à court terme*
31. Bonds	*1317*	*2058*	*2115*	*2743*	*2542*	*2175*	*2395*	*2628*	*2979*	*3214*	*31. Obligations*
32. Shares and participations	*622*	*633*	*650*	*696*	*782*	*1112*	*1285*	*1436*	*2185*	*2263*	*32. Actions et participations*
33. Claims on non-residents	*2461*	*2968*	*3020*	*3030*	*2676*	*2665*	*2821*	*3375*	*3983*	*6777*	*33. Créances sur des non résidents*
34. Liabilities to non-residents	*2864*	*3451*	*2976*	*3099*	*3312*	*3841*	*4420*	*5739*	*6603*	*8523*	*34. Engagements envers des non résidents*
SUPPLEMENTARY INFORMATION											**RENSEIGNEMENTS COMPLEMENTAIRES**
35. Number of institutions	140	139	139	138	138	138	145	154	160	164	35. Nombre d'institutions
36. Number of branches	16022	16215	16568	16468	16454	16549	16819	16836	18925	18180	36. Nombre de succursales
37. Number of employees (x 1000)	170.5	164.3	161.6	157.8	155.3	154.7	155.7	157.0	162.0	159.3	37. Nombre de salariés (x 1000)

SPAIN

Commercial banks

Banques commerciales

Per cent

Pourcentage

INCOME STATEMENT ANALYSIS

ANALYSE DU COMPTE DE RESULTATS

	1983	1984	1985	1986	1987	1988	1989	1990	1991	1992		
% of average balance sheet total												**% du total moyen du bilan**
38. Interest income	11.67	11.47	10.47	9.90	10.49	10.09	11.09	11.84	11.96	10.92	38.	Produits financiers
39. Interest expenses	7.72	7.70	6.91	6.18	6.66	6.03	7.05	7.92	7.99	7.53	39.	Frais financiers
40. Net interest income	3.94	3.77	3.57	3.72	3.83	4.06	4.04	3.92	3.96	3.39	40.	Produits financiers nets
41. Non-interest income (net)	0.94	0.79	0.80	0.81	1.04	1.14	0.99	1.06	1.16	1.11	41.	Produits non financiers (nets)
42. Gross income	4.88	4.55	4.37	4.54	4.87	5.20	5.03	4.98	5.12	4.51	42.	Résultat brut
43. Operating expenses	3.09	2.89	2.81	2.99	3.01	3.06	2.88	2.90	2.87	2.73	43.	Frais d'exploitation
44. Net income	1.79	1.66	1.56	1.55	1.86	2.13	2.15	2.08	2.25	1.78	44.	Résultat net
45. Provisions (net)	1.14	1.07	0.84	0.74	0.87	0.77	0.57	0.55	0.69	0.66	45.	Provisions (nettes)
46. Profit before tax	0.64	0.60	0.72	0.81	0.99	1.36	1.58	1.53	1.56	1.12	46.	Bénéfices avant impôt
47. Income tax	0.17	0.17	0.19	0.22	0.28	0.41	0.49	0.46	0.40	0.28	47.	Impôt
48. Profit after tax	0.47	0.43	0.53	0.59	0.72	0.95	1.09	1.07	1.16	0.84	48.	Bénéfices après impôt
49. Distributed profit	0.27	0.23	0.24	0.24	0.30	0.43	0.51	0.51	0.57	0.49	49.	Bénéfices distribués
50. Retained profit	0.20	0.20	0.30	0.35	0.42	0.52	0.58	0.56	0.60	0.34	50.	Bénéfices mis en réserve
51. Staff costs	2.07	1.93	1.88	2.08	2.08	2.10	1.89	1.84	1.76	1.68	51.	Frais de personnel
52. Provisions on loans	0.94	0.90	0.59	0.55	0.58	0.67	0.38	0.31	0.56	0.65	52.	Provisions sur prêts
53. Provisions on securities	0.10	0.06	0.09	0.01	0.09	0.07	0.05	0.12	0.09	0.09	53.	Provisions sur titres
% of gross income												**% du total du résultat brut**
54. Net interest income	80.80	82.68	81.68	82.08	78.60	78.11	80.24	78.65	77.38	75.32	54.	Produits financiers nets
55. Non-interest income (net)	19.20	17.32	18.32	17.92	21.40	21.89	19.76	21.35	22.62	24.68	55.	Produits non financiers (nets)
56. Operating expenses	63.40	63.52	64.34	65.82	61.76	58.98	57.26	58.28	56.07	60.53	56.	Frais d'exploitation
57. Net income	36.60	36.48	35.66	34.18	38.24	41.02	42.74	41.72	43.93	39.47	57.	Résultat net
58. Provisions (net)	23.42	23.39	19.20	16.26	17.86	14.79	11.35	11.00	13.40	14.70	58.	Provisions (nettes)
59. Profit before tax	13.19	13.09	16.46	17.92	20.38	26.23	31.39	30.72	30.53	24.76	59.	Bénéfices avant impôt
60. Income tax	3.59	3.66	4.25	4.84	5.66	7.86	9.77	9.32	7.82	6.23	60.	Impôt
61. Profit after tax	9.60	9.43	12.21	13.08	14.72	18.37	21.62	21.40	22.71	18.53	61.	Bénéfices après impôt
62. Staff costs	42.51	42.44	43.01	45.76	42.74	40.38	37.61	36.98	34.38	37.27	62.	Frais de personnel
% of net income												**% du total du résultat net**
63. Provisions (net)	63.98	64.12	53.85	47.56	46.70	36.05	26.56	26.36	30.51	37.25	63.	Provisions (nettes)
64. Profit before tax	36.02	35.88	46.15	52.44	53.30	63.95	73.44	73.64	69.49	62.75	64.	Bénéfices avant impôt
65. Income tax	9.80	10.03	11.91	14.15	14.80	19.17	22.86	22.34	17.81	15.80	65.	Impôt
66. Profit after tax	26.22	25.86	34.24	38.28	38.50	44.78	50.57	51.30	51.68	46.95	66.	Bénéfices après impôt

SPAIN

Commercial banks

Per cent — *Pourcentage*

BALANCE SHEET ANALYSIS — **ANALYSE DU BILAN**

% of year-end balance sheet total — *% du total du bilan en fin d'exercice*

	1983	1984	1985	1986	1987	1988	1989	1990	1991	1992	
Assets											**Actif**
67. Cash & balance with Central bank	10.34	8.79	7.20	6.32	8.85	8.08	7.69	5.90	6.25	4.69	67. Caisse & solde auprès de la Banque centrale
68. Interbank deposits	9.75	11.46	12.69	12.15	12.68	13.46	14.21	14.97	15.37	16.21	68. Dépôts interbancaires
69. Loans	53.79	44.80	44.35	43.86	43.50	45.10	45.87	46.26	48.14	46.71	69. Prêts
70. Securities	9.70	16.97	18.92	23.12	21.59	20.61	19.87	19.95	16.88	16.57	70. Valeurs mobilières
71. Other assets	16.41	17.99	16.85	14.54	13.38	12.75	12.37	12.92	13.36	15.81	71. Autres actifs
Liabilities											**Passif**
72. Capital & reserves	8.25	7.80	7.95	8.18	8.66	9.74	9.62	9.92	11.51	10.53	72. Capital et réserves
73. Borrowing from Central bank	3.51	4.15	3.41	4.55	3.99	2.70	4.01	3.04	2.50	4.84	73. Emprunts auprès de la Banque centrale
74. Interbank deposits	13.04	13.84	17.79	17.25	15.81	16.18	15.43	14.64	17.22	18.46	74. Dépôts interbancaires
75. Non-bank deposits	66.01	63.54	59.70	59.26	60.82	61.64	61.01	63.56	60.78	60.04	75. Dépôts non bancaires
76. Bonds	2.74	2.56	2.64	3.13	2.39	2.02	1.53	1.37	1.45	1.32	76. Obligations
77. Other liabilities	6.45	8.10	8.50	7.64	8.34	7.71	8.40	7.47	6.55	4.81	77. Autres engagements
Memoranda											*Pour mémoire*
78. Short-term securities	0.38	6.13	8.65	11.11	11.05	10.96	10.37	10.42	6.48	6.34	78. Titres à court terme
79. Bonds	6.33	8.29	7.85	9.57	8.06	6.39	6.18	6.16	6.00	6.00	79. Obligations
80. Shares and participations	2.99	2.55	2.41	2.43	2.48	3.26	3.32	3.37	4.40	4.23	80. Actions et participations
81. Claims on non-residents	11.83	11.96	11.21	10.58	8.48	7.82	7.28	7.92	8.02	12.66	81. Créances sur des non résidents
82. Liabilities to non-residents	13.76	13.91	11.05	10.82	10.50	11.28	11.41	13.46	13.29	15.92	82. Engagements envers des non résidents

1. Change in methodology.

Change in methodology:

- Revision of the historical series (see notes under All banks).

- As from 1992, "Income tax" (item 10) includes tax on domestic activities of resident entities rather than total tax.

1. Changement méthodologique.

Changement méthodologique :

- Révision des séries historiques (voir notes sous Ensemble des banques).

- A partir de 1992, la rubrique "Impôt" (poste 10) inclut l'impôt sur les activités domestiques des entités résidentes plutôt que l'impôt total.

SPAIN

Savings banks

Billion pesetas

ESPAGNE

Caisses d'épargne

Milliards de pesetas

	1983	1984	1985	1986	1987	1988	1989	1990	1991	1992	
INCOME STATEMENT (1)											**COMPTE DE RESULTATS (1)**
1. Interest income	856	1046	1182	1278	1434	1600	1999	2549	2721	2991	1. Produits financiers
2. Interest expenses	452	576	661	678	726	846	1159	1610	1734	1891	2. Frais financiers
3. Net interest income	404	470	521	600	708	754	840	939	987	1100	3. Produits financiers nets
4. Non-interest income (net)	29	36	56	80	89	116	116	128	129	206	4. Produits non financiers (nets)
5. Gross income	433	506	577	680	797	870	956	1067	1116	1306	5. Résultat brut
6. Operating expenses	276	330	377	487	502	649	650	704	709	779	6. Frais d'exploitation
7. Net income	157	176	200	193	295	221	306	363	407	527	7. Résultat net
8. Provisions (net)	76	80	84	75	112	97	95	136	153	243	8. Provisions (nettes)
9. Profit before tax	81	96	116	118	183	124	211	227	254	284	9. Bénéfices avant impôt
10. Income tax	9	10	20	23	35	22	49	47	59	68	10. Impôt
11. Profit after tax	72	86	96	95	148	102	162	180	195	216	11. Bénéfices après impôt
12. Distributed profit	24	27	27	28	38	43	50	47	47	50	12. Bénéfices distribués
13. Retained profit	48	59	69	67	110	59	112	133	148	166	13. Bénéfices mis en réserve
Memoranda											*Pour mémoire*
14. Staff costs	180	214	245	335	322	451	421	427	421	462	14. Frais de personnel
15. Provisions on loans	60	57	54	28	54	57	35	58	123	175	15. Provisions sur prêts
16. Provisions on securities	8	5	5	5	12	-1	3	18	11	46	16. Provisions sur titres
BALANCE SHEET											**BILAN**
Assets											**Actif**
17. Cash & balance with Central bank	1323	1361	1595	1825	2043	2183	2698	2249	2418	2253	17. Caisse & solde auprès de la Banque centrale
18. Interbank deposits	640	840	1402	1592	1428	1800	2412	2827	3494	4923	18. Dépôts interbancaires
19. Loans	3752	3949	4347	5094	6247	7735	9482	10824	12319	14484	19. Prêts
20. Securities	1719	2935	3442	4073	4666	5751	6203	6732	5664	6036	20. Valeurs mobilières
21. Other assets	976	1160	1234	1391	1576	1738	2139	2812	2927	3090	21. Autres actifs
Liabilities											**Passif**
22. Capital & reserves	649	783	916	1026	1239	1408	1640	1987	2244	2493	22. Capital et réserves
23. Borrowing from Central bank	12	27	62	123	127	39	559	294	329	1688	23. Emprunts auprès de la Banque centrale
24. Interbank deposits	529	745	627	552	471	640	739	1210	1205	1567	24. Dépôts interbancaires
25. Non-bank deposits	6626	7756	9182	10619	12359	15004	17641	19409	20686	22845	25. Dépôts non bancaires
26. Bonds	233	422	590	794	693	670	501	417	487	566	26. Obligations
27. Other liabilities	360	512	642	860	1069	1447	1854	2126	1873	1626	27. Autres engagements
Balance sheet total											**Total du bilan**
28. End-year total	8409	10245	12019	13975	15959	19207	22934	25444	26823	30785	28. En fin d'exercice
29. Average total	7649	9327	11132	12997	14967	17583	21071	24189	26134	28804	29. Moyen
Memoranda											*Pour mémoire*
30. Short-term securities	88	1173	1479	1246	1813	2335	3081	3556	2703	2959	30. Titres à court terme
31. Bonds	1526	1646	1834	2640	2626	3080	2687	2675	2429	2443	31. Obligations
32. Shares and participations	105	116	129	188	226	336	435	501	532	633	32. Actions et participations
33. Claims on non-residents	34	69	68	122	128	134	196	415	527	1065	33. Créances sur des non résidents
34. Liabilities to non-residents	172	220	245	266	309	399	450	699	758	804	34. Engagements envers des non résidents
SUPPLEMENTARY INFORMATION											**RENSEIGNEMENTS COMPLEMENTAIRES**
35. Number of institutions	83	81	79	79	79	79	78	66	57	54	35. Nombre d'institutions
36. Number of branches	11809	12201	12610	13062	13482	14092	14927	15356	13861	14145	36. Nombre de succursales
37. Number of employees (x 1000)	67.1	69.4	71.0	72.7	74.5	78.0	83.0	84.6	83.4	82.8	37. Nombre de salariés (x 1000)

131

Savings banks

Caisses d'épargne

Per cent / *Pourcentage*

INCOME STATEMENT ANALYSIS / ANALYSE DU COMPTE DE RESULTATS

	1983	1984	1985	1986	1987	1988	1989	1990	1991	1992	
% of average balance sheet total											**% du total moyen du bilan**
38. Interest income	11.19	11.21	10.62	9.83	9.58	9.10	9.49	10.54	10.41	10.38	38. Produits financiers
39. Interest expenses	5.91	6.18	5.94	5.22	4.85	4.81	5.50	6.66	6.64	6.57	39. Frais financiers
40. Net interest income	5.28	5.04	4.68	4.62	4.73	4.29	3.99	3.88	3.78	3.82	40. Produits financiers nets
41. Non-interest income (net)	0.38	0.39	0.50	0.62	0.59	0.66	0.55	0.53	0.49	0.72	41. Produits non financiers (nets)
42. Gross income	5.66	5.43	5.18	5.23	5.33	4.95	4.54	4.41	4.27	4.53	42. Résultat brut
43. Operating expenses	3.61	3.54	3.39	3.75	3.35	3.69	3.08	2.91	2.71	2.70	43. Frais d'exploitation
44. Net income	2.05	1.89	1.80	1.48	1.97	1.26	1.45	1.50	1.56	1.83	44. Résultat net
45. Provisions (net)	0.99	0.86	0.75	0.58	0.75	0.55	0.45	0.56	0.59	0.84	45. Provisions (nettes)
46. Profit before tax	1.06	1.03	1.04	0.91	1.22	0.71	1.00	0.94	0.97	0.99	46. Bénéfices avant impôt
47. Income tax	0.12	0.11	0.18	0.18	0.23	0.13	0.23	0.19	0.23	0.24	47. Impôt
48. Profit after tax	0.94	0.92	0.86	0.73	0.99	0.58	0.77	0.74	0.75	0.75	48. Bénéfices après impôt
49. Distributed profit	0.31	0.29	0.24	0.22	0.25	0.24	0.24	0.19	0.18	0.17	49. Bénéfices distribués
50. Retained profit	0.63	0.63	0.62	0.52	0.73	0.34	0.53	0.55	0.57	0.58	50. Bénéfices mis en réserve
51. Staff costs	2.35	2.29	2.20	2.58	2.15	2.56	2.00	1.77	1.61	1.60	51. Frais de personnel
52. Provisions on loans	0.78	0.61	0.49	0.22	0.36	0.32	0.17	0.24	0.47	0.61	52. Provisions sur prêts
53. Provisions on securities	0.10	0.05	0.04	0.04	0.08	-0.01	0.01	0.07	0.04	0.16	53. Provisions sur titres
% of gross income											**% du total du résultat brut**
54. Net interest income	93.30	92.89	90.29	88.24	88.83	86.67	87.87	88.00	88.44	84.23	54. Produits financiers nets
55. Non-interest income (net)	6.70	7.11	9.71	11.76	11.17	13.33	12.13	12.00	11.56	15.77	55. Produits non financiers (nets)
56. Operating expenses	63.74	65.22	65.34	71.62	62.99	74.60	67.99	65.98	63.53	59.65	56. Frais d'exploitation
57. Net income	36.26	34.78	34.66	28.38	37.01	25.40	32.01	34.02	36.47	40.35	57. Résultat net
58. Provisions (net)	17.55	15.81	14.56	11.03	14.05	11.15	9.94	12.75	13.71	18.61	58. Provisions (nettes)
59. Profit before tax	18.71	18.97	20.10	17.35	22.96	14.25	22.07	21.27	22.76	21.75	59. Bénéfices avant impôt
60. Income tax	2.08	1.98	3.47	3.38	4.39	2.53	5.13	4.40	5.29	5.21	60. Impôt
61. Profit after tax	16.63	17.00	16.64	13.97	18.57	11.72	16.95	16.87	17.47	16.54	61. Bénéfices après impôt
62. Staff costs	41.57	42.29	42.46	49.26	40.40	51.84	44.04	40.02	37.72	35.38	62. Frais de personnel
% of net income											**% du total du résultat net**
63. Provisions (net)	48.41	45.45	42.00	38.86	37.97	43.89	31.05	37.47	37.59	46.11	63. Provisions (nettes)
64. Profit before tax	51.59	54.55	58.00	61.14	62.03	56.11	68.95	62.53	62.41	53.89	64. Bénéfices avant impôt
65. Income tax	5.73	5.68	10.00	11.92	11.86	9.95	16.01	12.95	14.50	12.90	65. Impôt
66. Profit after tax	45.86	48.86	48.00	49.22	50.17	46.15	52.94	49.59	47.91	40.99	66. Bénéfices après impôt

SPAIN

Savings banks

Per cent / *Pourcentage*

BALANCE SHEET ANALYSIS / ANALYSE DU BILAN

% of year-end balance sheet total / % du total du bilan en fin d'exercice

	1983	1984	1985	1986	1987	1988	1989	1990	1991	1992		
Assets												**Actif**
67. Cash & balance with Central bank	15.73	13.28	13.27	13.06	12.80	11.37	11.76	8.84	9.01	7.32	67.	Caisse & solde auprès de la Banque centrale
68. Interbank deposits	7.61	8.20	11.66	11.39	8.95	9.37	10.52	11.11	13.03	15.99	68.	Dépôts interbancaires
69. Loans	44.62	38.55	36.17	36.45	39.14	40.27	41.34	42.54	45.93	47.05	69.	Prêts
70. Securities	20.44	28.65	28.64	29.14	29.24	29.94	27.05	26.46	21.12	19.61	70.	Valeurs mobilières
71. Other assets	11.61	11.32	10.27	9.95	9.88	9.05	9.33	11.05	10.91	10.04	71.	Autres actifs
Liabilities												**Passif**
72. Capital & reserves	7.72	7.64	7.62	7.34	7.76	7.33	7.15	7.81	8.37	8.10	72.	Capital et réserves
73. Borrowing from Central bank	0.14	0.26	0.52	0.88	0.80	0.20	2.44	1.16	1.23	5.48	73.	Emprunts auprès de la Banque centrale
74. Interbank deposits	6.29	7.27	5.22	3.95	2.95	3.33	3.22	4.76	4.49	5.09	74.	Dépôts interbancaires
75. Non-bank deposits	78.80	75.71	76.40	75.99	77.44	78.12	76.92	76.28	77.12	74.21	75.	Dépôts non bancaires
76. Bonds	2.77	4.12	4.91	5.68	4.34	3.49	2.18	1.64	1.82	1.84	76.	Obligations
77. Other liabilities	4.28	5.00	5.34	6.15	6.70	7.53	8.08	8.36	6.98	5.28	77.	Autres engagements
Memoranda												***Pour mémoire***
78. Short-term securities	*1.05*	*11.45*	*12.31*	*8.92*	*11.36*	*12.16*	*13.43*	*13.98*	*10.08*	*9.61*	*78.*	*Titres à court terme*
79. Bonds	*18.15*	*16.07*	*15.26*	*18.89*	*16.45*	*16.04*	*11.72*	*10.51*	*9.06*	*7.94*	*79.*	*Obligations*
80. Shares and participations	*1.25*	*1.13*	*1.07*	*1.35*	*1.42*	*1.75*	*1.90*	*1.97*	*1.98*	*2.06*	*80.*	*Actions et participations*
81. Claims on non-residents	*0.40*	*0.67*	*0.57*	*0.87*	*0.80*	*0.70*	*0.85*	*1.63*	*1.96*	*3.46*	*81.*	*Créances sur des non résidents*
82. Liabilities to non-residents	*2.05*	*2.15*	*2.04*	*1.90*	*1.94*	*2.08*	*1.96*	*2.75*	*2.83*	*2.61*	*82.*	*Engagements envers des non résidents*

1. Change in methodology.

Change in methodology:

- Revision of the historical series (see notes under All banks).

- As from 1992, "Income tax" (item 10) includes tax on domestic activities of resident entities rather than total tax.

1. Changement méthodologique.

Changement méthodologique :

- Révision des séries historiques (voir notes sous Ensemble des banques).

- A partir de 1992, la rubrique "Impôt" (poste 10) inclut l'impôt sur les activités domestiques des entités résidentes plutôt que l'impôt total.

Co-operative banks — Banques mutualistes

Billion pesetas — *Milliards de pesetas*

#	Item (EN)	Item (FR)	1983	1984	1985	1986	1987	1988	1989	1990	1991	1992
	INCOME STATEMENT (1)	**COMPTE DE RESULTATS (1)**										
1.	Interest income	Produits financiers	109	113	130	142	164	167	186	221	256	281
2.	Interest expenses	Frais financiers	67	66	74	75	82	88	97	122	143	156
3.	Net interest income	Produits financiers nets	42	47	56	67	82	79	89	99	113	125
4.	Non-interest income (net)	Produits non financiers (nets)	-10	9	9	5	4	4	5	6	7	7
5.	Gross income	Résultat brut	32	56	65	72	86	83	94	105	120	132
6.	Operating expenses	Frais d'exploitation	33	36	40	42	48	51	57	65	74	82
7.	Net income	Résultat net	-1	20	25	30	38	32	37	40	46	50
8.	Provisions (net)	Provisions (nettes)	19	6	10	9	12	9	7	10	11	13
9.	Profit before tax	Bénéfices avant impôt	-20	14	15	21	26	23	30	30	35	37
10.	Income tax	Impôt	1	1	1	2	2	2	3	3	5	6
11.	Profit after tax	Bénéfices après impôt	-21	13	14	19	24	21	27	27	30	31
12.	Distributed profit	Bénéfices distribués	4	5	5	6	6	5	7	8	9	10
13.	Retained profit	Bénéfices mis en réserve	-25	8	9	13	18	16	20	19	21	21
	Memoranda	*Pour mémoire*										
14.	Staff costs	Frais de personnel	22	23	26	27	30	33	35	39	44	48
15.	Provisions on loans	Provisions sur prêts	18	6	10	9	12	8	6	8	9	14
16.	Provisions on securities	Provisions sur titres	-	-	-	-	-	-	-	2	1	1
	BALANCE SHEET	**BILAN**										
	Assets	**Actif**										
17.	Cash & balance with Central bank	Caisse & solde auprès de la Banque centrale	107	81	136	151	199	207	253	269	265	219
18.	Interbank deposits	Dépôts interbancaires	284	276	326	332	323	388	385	511	613	707
19.	Loans	Prêts	456	481	538	591	681	706	800	910	1100	1296
20.	Securities	Valeurs mobilières	69	100	130	203	243	259	246	224	225	205
21.	Other assets	Autres actifs	65	102	119	122	124	116	120	137	153	161
	Liabilities	**Passif**										
22.	Capital & reserves	Capital et réserves	81	89	107	128	160	181	204	234	269	296
23.	Borrowing from Central bank	Emprunts auprès de la Banque centrale	-	-	-	-	-	-	-	-	-	-
24.	Interbank deposits	Dépôts interbancaires	145	73	78	91	105	98	87	112	104	127
25.	Non-bank deposits	Dépôts non bancaires	713	837	1003	1077	1206	1310	1431	1615	1889	2098
26.	Bonds	Obligations	-	2	8	19	17	9	1	1	-	-
27.	Other liabilities	Autres engagements	42	39	54	84	83	78	80	89	93	66
	Balance sheet total	**Total du bilan**										
28.	End-year total	En fin d'exercice	981	1040	1250	1399	1571	1676	1804	2050	2355	2587
29.	Average total	Moyen	920	1011	1145	1325	1485	1624	1740	1927	2203	2471
	Memoranda	*Pour mémoire*										
30.	Short-term securities	Titres à court terme	5	11	22	54	113	135	140	141	141	101
31.	Bonds	Obligations	61	85	104	141	123	116	98	70	69	86
32.	Shares and participations	Actions et participations	4	5	5	8	7	8	8	13	15	18
33.	Claims on non-residents	Créances sur des non résidents	-	2	1	-	-	1	1	1	2	14
34.	Liabilities to non-residents	Engagements envers des non résidents	7	6	7	7	8	5	6	9	12	15
	SUPPLEMENTARY INFORMATION	**RENSEIGNEMENTS COMPLEMENTAIRES**										
35.	Number of institutions	Nombre d'institutions	153	149	146	138	129	117	110	107	106	101
36.	Number of branches	Nombre de succursales	3222	3199	3284	3086	3113	2901	2773	2892	3025	2989
37.	Number of employees (x 1000)	Nombre de salariés (x 1000)	10.9	10.9	10.8	10.2	10.2	9.7	9.6	10.0	10.6	11.0

INCOME STATEMENT ANALYSIS / ANALYSE DU COMPTE DE RESULTATS

	1983	1984	1985	1986	1987	1988	1989	1990	1991	1992	
% of average balance sheet total											**% du total moyen du bilan**
38. Interest income	11.85	11.18	11.35	10.72	11.04	10.29	10.69	11.47	11.62	11.37	38. Produits financiers
39. Interest expenses	7.29	6.53	6.46	5.66	5.52	5.42	5.57	6.33	6.49	6.31	39. Frais financiers
40. Net interest income	4.57	4.65	4.89	5.06	5.52	4.87	5.11	5.14	5.13	5.06	40. Produits financiers nets
41. Non-interest income (net)	-1.09	0.89	0.79	0.38	0.27	0.25	0.29	0.31	0.32	0.28	41. Produits non financiers (nets)
42. Gross income	3.48	5.54	5.68	5.44	5.79	5.11	5.40	5.45	5.45	5.34	42. Résultat brut
43. Operating expenses	3.59	3.56	3.49	3.17	3.23	3.14	3.28	3.37	3.36	3.32	43. Frais d'exploitation
44. Net income	-0.11	1.98	2.18	2.27	2.56	1.97	2.13	2.08	2.09	2.02	44. Résultat net
45. Provisions (net)	2.07	0.59	0.87	0.68	0.81	0.55	0.40	0.52	0.50	0.53	45. Provisions (nettes)
46. Profit before tax	-2.18	1.39	1.31	1.59	1.75	1.42	1.72	1.56	1.59	1.50	46. Bénéfices avant impôt
47. Income tax	0.11	0.10	0.09	0.15	0.13	0.12	0.17	0.16	0.23	0.24	47. Impôt
48. Profit after tax	-2.28	1.29	1.22	1.43	1.62	1.29	1.55	1.40	1.36	1.25	48. Bénéfices après impôt
49. Distributed profit	0.44	0.49	0.44	0.45	0.40	0.31	0.40	0.42	0.41	0.40	49. Bénéfices distribués
50. Retained profit	-2.72	0.79	0.79	0.98	1.21	0.99	1.15	0.99	0.95	0.85	50. Bénéfices mis en réserve
51. Staff costs	2.39	2.28	2.27	2.04	2.02	2.03	2.01	2.02	2.00	1.94	51. Frais de personnel
52. Provisions on loans	1.96	0.59	0.87	0.68	0.81	0.49	0.34	0.42	0.41	0.57	52. Provisions sur prêts
53. Provisions on securities	-	-	-	-	-	-	-	0.10	0.05	0.04	53. Provisions sur titres
% of gross income											**% du total du résultat brut**
54. Net interest income	131.25	83.93	86.15	93.06	95.35	95.18	94.68	94.29	94.17	94.70	54. Produits financiers nets
55. Non-interest income (net)	-31.25	16.07	13.85	6.94	4.65	4.82	5.32	5.71	5.83	5.30	55. Produits non financiers (nets)
56. Operating expenses	103.13	64.29	61.54	58.33	55.81	61.45	60.64	61.90	61.67	62.12	56. Frais d'exploitation
57. Net income	-3.13	35.71	38.46	41.67	44.19	38.55	39.36	38.10	38.33	37.88	57. Résultat net
58. Provisions (net)	59.38	10.71	15.38	12.50	13.95	10.84	7.45	9.52	9.17	9.85	58. Provisions (nettes)
59. Profit before tax	-62.50	25.00	23.08	29.17	30.23	27.71	31.91	28.57	29.17	28.03	59. Bénéfices avant impôt
60. Income tax	3.13	1.79	1.54	2.78	2.33	2.41	3.19	2.86	4.17	4.55	60. Impôt
61. Profit after tax	-65.63	23.21	21.54	26.39	27.91	25.30	28.72	25.71	25.00	23.48	61. Bénéfices après impôt
62. Staff costs	68.75	41.07	40.00	37.50	34.88	39.76	37.23	37.14	36.67	36.36	62. Frais de personnel
% of net income											**% du total du résultat net**
63. Provisions (net)	-1900.00	30.00	40.00	30.00	31.58	28.13	18.92	25.00	23.91	26.00	63. Provisions (nettes)
64. Profit before tax	2000.00	70.00	60.00	70.00	68.42	71.88	81.08	75.00	76.09	74.00	64. Bénéfices avant impôt
65. Income tax	-100.00	5.00	4.00	6.67	5.26	6.25	8.11	7.50	10.87	12.00	65. Impôt
66. Profit after tax	2100.00	65.00	56.00	63.33	63.16	65.63	72.97	67.50	65.22	62.00	66. Bénéfices après impôt

SPAIN

Co-operative banks

ESPAGNE

Banques mutualistes

Per cent — *Pourcentage*

BALANCE SHEET ANALYSIS — **ANALYSE DU BILAN**

% of year-end balance sheet total — **% du total du bilan en fin d'exercice**

	1983	1984	1985	1986	1987	1988	1989	1990	1991	1992		
Assets												**Actif**
67. Cash & balance with Central bank	10.91	7.79	10.88	10.79	12.67	12.35	14.02	13.12	11.25	8.47	67.	Caisse & solde auprès de la Banque centrale
68. Interbank deposits	28.95	26.54	26.08	23.73	20.56	23.15	21.34	24.93	26.03	27.33	68.	Dépôts interbancaires
69. Loans	46.48	46.25	43.04	42.24	43.35	42.12	44.35	44.39	46.71	50.10	69.	Prêts
70. Securities	7.03	9.62	10.40	14.51	15.47	15.45	13.64	10.93	9.55	7.92	70.	Valeurs mobilières
71. Other assets	6.63	9.81	9.52	8.72	7.89	6.92	6.65	6.68	6.50	6.22	71.	Autres actifs
Liabilities												**Passif**
72. Capital & reserves	8.26	8.56	8.56	9.15	10.18	10.80	11.31	11.41	11.42	11.44	72.	Capital et réserves
73. Borrowing from Central bank	-	-	-	-	-	-	-	-	-	-	73.	Emprunts auprès de la Banque centrale
74. Interbank deposits	14.78	7.02	6.24	6.50	6.68	5.85	4.82	5.46	4.42	4.91	74.	Dépôts interbancaires
75. Non-bank deposits	72.68	80.48	80.24	76.98	76.77	78.16	79.32	78.78	80.21	81.10	75.	Dépôts non bancaires
76. Bonds	-	0.19	0.64	1.36	1.08	0.54	0.06	0.05	-	-	76.	Obligations
77. Other liabilities	4.28	3.75	4.32	6.00	5.28	4.65	4.43	4.34	3.95	2.55	77.	Autres engagements
Memoranda												**Pour mémoire**
78. Short-term securities	0.51	1.06	1.76	3.86	7.19	8.05	7.76	6.88	5.99	3.90	78.	Titres à court terme
79. Bonds	6.22	8.17	8.32	10.08	7.83	6.92	5.43	3.41	2.93	3.32	79.	Obligations
80. Shares and participations	0.41	0.48	0.40	0.57	0.45	0.48	0.44	0.63	0.64	0.70	80.	Actions et participations
81. Claims on non-residents	-	0.19	0.08	-	-	0.06	0.06	0.05	0.08	0.54	81.	Créances sur des non résidents
82. Liabilities to non-residents	0.71	0.58	0.56	0.50	0.51	0.30	0.33	0.44	0.51	0.58	82.	Engagements envers des non résidents

1. Change in methodology.

1. Changement méthodologique.

Change in methodology:

- Revision of the historical series (see notes under All banks).

- As from 1992, "Income tax" (item 10) includes tax on domestic activities of resident entities rather than total tax.

Changement méthodologique :

- Révision des séries historiques (voir notes sous Ensemble des banques).

- A partir de 1992, la rubrique "Impôt" (poste 10) inclut l'impôt sur les activités domestiques des entités résidentes plutôt que l'impôt total.

136

SWEDEN

Commercial banks

Million Swedish kroner

INCOME STATEMENT / COMPTE DE RESULTATS

#	Item	1983	1984	1985	1986	1987	1988	1989	1990	1991	1992	Poste (français)
1.	Interest income	48064	53625	58761	53282	58230	70837	97962	130929	131201	122619	Produits financiers
2.	Interest expenses	37516	42381	47811	38170	41768	51467	76559	105873	104914	96190	Frais financiers
3.	Net interest income	10548	11244	10950	15112	16462	19370	21403	25056	26287	26429	Produits financiers nets
4.	Non-interest income (net)	4241	4877	5883	8233	6482	7825	8565	8899	8848	17704	Produits non financiers (nets)
5.	Gross income	14789	16121	16833	23345	22944	27195	29968	33955	35135	44133	Résultat brut
6.	Operating expenses	8345	10491	10413	12673	12760	15112	16736	26568	42353	64668	Frais d'exploitation
7.	Net income	6444	5630	6420	10672	10184	12083	13232	7387	-7218	-20535	Résultat net
8.	Provisions (net)	4423	3853	4526	4888	5380	7397	8582	4786	-42895	-23564	Provisions (nettes)
9.	Profit before tax	2021	1777	1894	5784	4804	4686	4650	2601	35677	3029	Bénéfices avant impôt
10.	Income tax	953	737	636	3797	1638	2507	833	647	10576	510	Impôt
11.	Profit after tax	1068	1040	1258	1987	3166	2179	3817	1954	25101	2519	Bénéfices après impôt
12.	Distributed profit	784	810	1080	1296	1567	1873	2082	2014	2014	1727	Bénéfices distribués
13.	Retained profit	284	230	178	691	1599	306	1735	-60	23087	792	Bénéfices mis en réserve

Memoranda / Pour mémoire

#	Item	1983	1984	1985	1986	1987	1988	1989	1990	1991	1992	Poste (français)
14.	Staff costs	3421	3924	4307	4869	5718	6254	7016	8308	9242	10442	Frais de personnel
15.	Provisions on loans	9307	1520	1566	4989	5368	7602	3319	5680	47814	..	Provisions sur prêts
16.	Provisions on securities	-5444	2202	3017	99	42	-	5482	1154	9236	..	Provisions sur titres

BALANCE SHEET / BILAN

Assets / Actif

#	Item	1983	1984	1985	1986	1987	1988	1989	1990	1991	1992	Poste (français)
17.	Cash & balance with Central bank	9422	12450	16407	20156	19514	21016	20754	29467	13756	20577	Caisse & solde auprès de la Banque centrale
18.	Interbank deposits	61014	66936	67617	100242	134207	179948	189095	237934	194122	112209	Dépôts interbancaires
19.	Loans	222938	250728	261746	300322	338922	450616	579838	676529	625661	670191	Prêts
20.	Securities	145004	148651	136173	114419	108167	106185	125842	147546	316226	272689	Valeurs mobilières
21.	Other assets	38406	48968	58367	59566	65384	77240	104792	173158	57982	77890	Autres actifs

Liabilities / Passif

#	Item	1983	1984	1985	1986	1987	1988	1989	1990	1991	1992	Poste (français)
22.	Capital & reserves	29099	31987	33606	38772	47169	56944	65273	71307	65386	52898	Capital et réserves
23.	Borrowing from Central bank	13066	623	6891	4233	3455	19033	19946	14517	31415	60279	Emprunts auprès de la Banque centrale
24.	Interbank deposits	151169	169005	158724	173803	235065	314540	399495	526730	408906	300599	Dépôts interbancaires
25.	Non-bank deposits	224963	250906	261975	294776	292546	325616	372914	440738	503993	535982	Dépôts non bancaires
26.	Bonds	27562	27673	24734	22546	23905	39335	56383	85724	76723	89829	Obligations
27.	Other liabilities	30925	47539	54380	60578	64054	79535	106310	125616	121325	113968	Autres engagements

Balance sheet total / Total du bilan

#	Item	1983	1984	1985	1986	1987	1988	1989	1990	1991	1992	Poste (français)
28.	End-year total	476784	527734	540311	594707	666193	835005	1020321	1264632	1207745	1153554	En fin d'exercice
29.	Average total	463799	508851	552021	578578	660427	794416	994864	1202580	1254792	1209533	Moyen

Memoranda / Pour mémoire

#	Item	1983	1984	1985	1986	1987	1988	1989	1990	1991	1992	Poste (français)
30.	Short-term securities	6368	7319	8931	6312	2122	2566	3705	9720	21402	136911	Titres à court terme
31.	Bonds	136040	136476	129920	105119	98359	92876	108179	112899	86868	77073	Obligations
32.	Shares and participations	3307	4065	5113	6276	8888	8386	13624	25071	35877	27575	Actions et participations
33.	Claims on non-residents	12321	15614	14560	14395	17019	35366	65010	104230	303815	360649	Créances sur des non résidents
34.	Liabilities to non-residents	7466	13080	17340	24233	33592	50483	68976	103509	646684	563031	Engagements envers des non résidents

SUPPLEMENTARY INFORMATION / RENSEIGNEMENTS COMPLEMENTAIRES

#	Item	1983	1984	1985	1986	1987	1988	1989	1990	1991	1992	Poste (français)
35.	Number of institutions	14	15	15	14	14	14	14	12	9	8	Nombre d'institutions
36.	Number of branches	1450	1442	1436	1424	1403	1394	1376	1345	1288	1872	Nombre de succursales
37.	Number of employees (x 1000)	21.4	22.3	22.7	23.5	25.0	25.4	25.4	25.0	25.1	28.4	Nombre de salariés (x 1000)

SWEDEN

Commercial banks

Per cent

INCOME STATEMENT ANALYSIS

		1983	1984	1985	1986	1987	1988	1989	1990	1991	1992
% of average balance sheet total											
38.	Interest income	10.36	10.54	10.64	9.21	8.82	8.92	9.85	10.89	10.46	10.14
39.	Interest expenses	8.09	8.33	8.66	6.60	6.32	6.48	7.70	8.80	8.36	7.95
40.	Net interest income	2.27	2.21	1.98	2.61	2.49	2.44	2.15	2.08	2.09	2.19
41.	Non-interest income (net)	0.91	0.96	1.07	1.42	0.98	0.99	0.86	0.74	0.71	1.46
42.	Gross income	3.19	3.17	3.05	4.03	3.47	3.42	3.01	2.82	2.80	3.65
43.	Operating expenses	1.80	2.06	1.89	2.19	1.93	1.90	1.68	2.21	3.38	5.35
44.	Net income	1.39	1.11	1.16	1.84	1.54	1.52	1.33	0.61	-0.58	-1.70
45.	Provisions (net)	0.95	0.76	0.82	0.84	0.81	0.93	0.86	0.40	-3.42	-1.95
46.	Profit before tax	0.44	0.35	0.34	1.00	0.73	0.59	0.47	0.22	2.84	0.25
47.	Income tax	0.21	0.14	0.12	0.66	0.25	0.32	0.08	0.05	0.84	0.04
48.	Profit after tax	0.23	0.20	0.23	0.34	0.48	0.27	0.38	0.16	2.00	0.21
49.	Distributed profit	0.17	0.16	0.20	0.22	0.24	0.24	0.21	0.17	0.16	0.14
50.	Retained profit	0.06	0.05	0.03	0.12	0.24	0.04	0.17	0.00	1.84	0.07
51.	Staff costs	0.74	0.77	0.78	0.84	0.87	0.79	0.71	0.69	0.74	0.86
52.	Provisions on loans	2.01	0.30	0.28	0.86	0.81	0.96	0.33	0.47	3.81	..
53.	Provisions on securities	-1.17	0.43	0.55	0.02	0.01	-	0.55	0.10	0.74	..
% of gross income											
54.	Net interest income	71.32	69.75	65.05	64.73	71.75	71.23	71.42	73.79	74.82	59.88
55.	Non-interest income (net)	28.68	30.25	34.95	35.27	28.25	28.77	28.58	26.21	25.18	40.12
56.	Operating expenses	56.43	65.08	61.86	54.29	55.61	55.57	55.85	78.24	120.54	146.53
57.	Net income	43.57	34.92	38.14	45.71	44.39	44.43	44.15	21.76	-20.54	-46.53
58.	Provisions (net)	29.91	23.90	26.89	20.94	23.45	27.20	28.64	14.10	-122.09	-53.39
59.	Profit before tax	13.67	11.02	11.25	24.78	20.94	17.23	15.52	7.66	101.54	6.86
60.	Income tax	6.44	4.57	3.78	16.26	7.14	9.22	2.78	1.91	30.10	1.16
61.	Profit after tax	7.22	6.45	7.47	8.51	13.80	8.01	12.74	5.75	71.44	5.71
62.	Staff costs	23.13	24.34	25.59	20.86	24.92	23.00	23.41	24.47	26.30	23.66
% of net income											
63.	Provisions (net)	68.64	68.44	70.50	45.80	52.83	61.22	64.86	64.79	..	..
64.	Profit before tax	31.36	31.56	29.50	54.20	47.17	38.78	35.14	35.21	..	..
65.	Income tax	14.79	13.09	9.91	35.58	16.08	20.75	6.30	8.76	..	..
66.	Profit after tax	16.57	18.47	19.60	18.62	31.09	18.03	28.85	26.45	..	..

SUEDE

Banques commerciales

Pourcentage

ANALYSE DU COMPTE DE RESULTATS

% du total moyen du bilan
38. Produits financiers
39. Frais financiers
40. Produits financiers nets
41. Produits non financiers (nets)
42. Résultat brut
43. Frais d'exploitation
44. Résultat net
45. Provisions (nettes)
46. Bénéfices avant impôt
47. Impôt
48. Bénéfices après impôt
49. Bénéfices distribués
50. Bénéfices mis en réserve
51. Frais de personnel
52. Provisions sur prêts
53. Provisions sur titres

% du total du résultat brut
54. Produits financiers nets
55. Produits non financiers (nets)
56. Frais d'exploitation
57. Résultat net
58. Provisions (nettes)
59. Bénéfices avant impôt
60. Impôt
61. Bénéfices après impôt
62. Frais de personnel

% du total du résultat net
63. Provisions (nettes)
64. Bénéfices avant impôt
65. Impôt
66. Bénéfices après impôt

SWEDEN

Commercial banks

SUEDE

Banques commerciales

Per cent / *Pourcentage*

BALANCE SHEET ANALYSIS / ANALYSE DU BILAN

% of year-end balance sheet total / % du total du bilan en fin d'exercice

	1983	1984	1985	1986	1987	1988	1989	1990	1991	1992		
Assets												**Actif**
67. Cash & balance with Central bank	1.98	2.36	3.04	3.39	2.93	2.52	2.03	2.33	1.14	1.78	67.	Caisse & solde auprès de la Banque centrale
68. Interbank deposits	12.80	12.68	12.51	16.86	20.15	21.55	18.53	18.81	16.07	9.73	68.	Dépôts interbancaires
69. Loans	46.76	47.51	48.44	50.50	50.87	53.97	56.83	53.50	51.80	58.10	69.	Prêts
70. Securities	30.41	28.17	25.20	19.24	16.24	12.72	12.33	11.67	26.18	23.64	70.	Valeurs mobilières
71. Other assets	8.06	9.28	10.80	10.02	9.81	9.25	10.27	13.69	4.80	6.75	71.	Autres actifs
Liabilities												**Passif**
72. Capital & reserves	6.10	6.06	6.22	6.52	7.08	6.82	6.40	5.64	5.41	4.59	72.	Capital et réserves
73. Borrowing from Central bank	2.74	0.12	1.28	0.71	0.52	2.28	1.95	1.15	2.60	5.23	73.	Emprunts auprès de la Banque centrale
74. Interbank deposits	31.71	32.02	29.38	29.22	35.28	37.67	39.15	41.65	33.86	26.06	74.	Dépôts interbancaires
75. Non-bank deposits	47.18	47.54	48.49	49.57	43.91	39.00	36.55	34.85	41.73	46.46	75.	Dépôts non bancaires
76. Bonds	5.78	5.24	4.58	3.79	3.59	4.71	5.53	6.78	6.35	7.79	76.	Obligations
77. Other liabilities	6.49	9.01	10.06	10.19	9.61	9.53	10.42	9.93	10.05	9.88	77.	Autres engagements
Memoranda												*Pour mémoire*
78. Short-term securities	*1.34*	*1.39*	*1.65*	*1.06*	*0.32*	*0.31*	*0.36*	*0.77*	*1.77*	*11.87*	*78.*	*Titres à court terme*
79. Bonds	*28.53*	*25.86*	*24.05*	*17.68*	*14.76*	*11.12*	*10.60*	*8.93*	*7.19*	*6.68*	*79.*	*Obligations*
80. Shares and participations	*0.69*	*0.77*	*0.95*	*1.06*	*1.33*	*1.00*	*1.34*	*1.98*	*2.97*	*2.39*	*80.*	*Actions et participations*
81. Claims on non-residents	*2.58*	*2.96*	*2.69*	*2.42*	*2.55*	*4.24*	*6.37*	*8.24*	*25.16*	*31.26*	*81.*	*Créances sur des non résidents*
82. Liabilities to non-residents	*1.57*	*2.48*	*3.21*	*4.07*	*5.04*	*6.05*	*6.76*	*8.18*	*53.54*	*48.81*	*82.*	*Engagements envers des non résidents*

Notes

- Average balance sheet totals (item 29) are based on thirteen end-month data.

Change in methodology:

- For the year 1991, the Föreningsbankernas Bank is included under Co-operative banks and not under Commercial banks.

- As from 1992, Co-operative banks, which merged into one single commercial bank, are included under Commercial banks.

Notes

- La moyenne du total des actifs/passifs (poste 29) est basée sur treize données de fin de mois.

Changement méthodologique :

- Pour l'année 1991, la Föreningsbankernas Bank est comprise dans les Banques mutualistes et non pas dans les Banques commerciales.

- Depuis 1992, les Banques mutualistes, ayant fusionnées en une seule banque commerciale, sont classées dans les données concernant les Banques commerciales.

SWEDEN

Foreign commercial banks

Million Swedish kroner

SUEDE

Banques commerciales étrangères

Millions de couronnes suédoises

	1986	1987	1988	1989	1990	1991	1992	
INCOME STATEMENT								**COMPTE DE RESULTATS**
1. Interest income	417	1592	1591	2708	2959	2440	2541	1. Produits financiers
2. Interest expenses	322	1463	1462	2562	2722	2273	2454	2. Frais financiers
3. Net interest income	95	129	129	146	237	167	87	3. Produits financiers nets
4. Non-interest income (net)	103	80	80	96	121	231	451	4. Produits non financiers (nets)
5. Gross income	198	209	209	242	358	398	538	5. Résultat brut
6. Operating expenses	213	232	231	319	464	867	1369	6. Frais d'exploitation
7. Net income	-15	-23	-22	-77	-106	-469	-831	7. Résultat net
8. Provisions (net)	28	-2	4	5	-38	-5	157	8. Provisions (nettes)
9. Profit before tax	-43	-21	-26	-82	-68	-464	-988	9. Bénéfices avant impôt
10. Income tax	-	1	1	-	-	1	42	10. Impôt
11. Profit after tax	-43	-22	-27	-82	-68	-465	-1030	11. Bénéfices après impôt
12. Distributed profit	-	-	4	-	-	5	8	12. Bénéfices distribués
13. Retained profit	-43	-22	-31	-82	-68	-470	-1038	13. Bénéfices mis en réserve
Memoranda								*Pour mémoire*
14. Staff costs	78	137	136	130	148	161	171	14. Frais de personnel
15. Provisions on loans (1)	4	7	8	3	6171	13	..	15. Provisions sur prêts (1)
16. Provisions on securities (1)	23	3	4	10	600	23	..	16. Provisions sur titres (1)
BALANCE SHEET (2)								**BILAN (2)**
Assets								**Actif**
17. Cash & balance with Central bank	210	64	57	116	209	50	2794	17. Caisse & solde auprès de la Banque centrale
18. Interbank deposits	8341	11850	8175	8963	6380	3959	6362	18. Dépôts interbancaires
19. Loans	5741	9426	15337	18091	15564	13108	15732	19. Prêts
20. Securities	3011	2180	1086	1744	580	3033	5111	20. Valeurs mobilières
21. Other assets	784	1973	2834	3633	2252	640	1991	21. Autres actifs
Liabilities								**Passif**
22. Capital & reserves	914	887	942	890	835	528	664	22. Capital et réserves
23. Borrowing from Central bank	1129	113	326	603	377	169	5	23. Emprunts auprès de la Banque centrale
24. Interbank deposits	14138	21389	23726	28240	20687	16778	26951	24. Dépôts interbancaires
25. Non-bank deposits	364	731	1383	1145	1517	2024	2916	25. Dépôts non bancaires
26. Bonds	599	565	361	582	599	443	493	26. Obligations
27. Other liabilities	943	1808	753	1086	970	850	960	27. Autres engagements
Balance sheet total								**Total du bilan**
28. End-year total	18087	25493	27491	32547	24986	20793	31989	28. En fin d'exercice
29. Average total	NA	22242	28052	28568	25507	23931	25834	29. Moyen
Memoranda								*Pour mémoire*
30. Short-term securities	902	198	230	141	202	1961	10260	30. Titres à court terme
31. Bonds	2362	1602	873	1515	140	90	100	31. Obligations
32. Shares and participations	3	4	17	132	117	12	4	32. Actions et participations
33. Claims on non-residents	130	991	1612	3582	2907	5769	6736	33. Créances sur des non résidents
34. Liabilities to non-residents	72	108	486	396	524	17898	27839	34. Engagements envers des non résidents
SUPPLEMENTARY INFORMATION								**RENSEIGNEMENTS COMPLEMENTAIRES**
35. Number of institutions	12	11	10	9	9	8	8	35. Nombre d'institutions
36. Number of branches	-	-	1	-	-	-	10	36. Nombre de succursales
37. Number of employees (x 1000)	0.3	0.3	0.4	0.3	0.3	0.3	0.3	37. Nombre de salariés (x 1000)

140

SWEDEN

Foreign commercial banks

SUEDE

Banques commerciales étrangères

Per cent / *Pourcentage*

INCOME STATEMENT ANALYSIS / ANALYSE DU COMPTE DE RESULTATS

		1986	1987	1988	1989	1990	1991	1992	
% of average balance sheet total									**% du total moyen du bilan**
38.	Interest income	NA	7.16	5.67	9.48	11.60	10.20	9.84	Produits financiers
39.	Interest expenses	NA	6.58	5.21	8.97	10.67	9.50	9.50	Frais financiers
40.	Net interest income	NA	0.58	0.46	0.51	0.93	0.70	0.34	Produits financiers nets
41.	Non-interest income (net)	NA	0.36	0.29	0.34	0.47	0.97	1.75	Produits non financiers (nets)
42.	Gross income	NA	0.94	0.75	0.85	1.40	1.66	2.08	Résultat brut
43.	Operating expenses	NA	1.04	0.82	1.12	1.82	3.62	5.30	Frais d'exploitation
44.	Net income	NA	-0.10	-0.08	-0.27	-0.42	-1.96	-3.22	Résultat net
45.	Provisions (net)	NA	-0.01	0.01	0.02	-0.15	-0.02	0.61	Provisions (nettes)
46.	Profit before tax	NA	-0.09	-0.09	-0.29	-0.27	-1.94	-3.82	Bénéfices avant impôt
47.	Income tax	-	0.00	0.00	-	-	0.00	0.16	Impôt
48.	Profit after tax	NA	-0.10	-0.10	-0.29	-0.27	-1.94	-3.99	Bénéfices après impôt
49.	Distributed profit	-	-	0.01	-		0.02	0.03	Bénéfices distribués
50.	Retained profit	NA	-0.10	-0.11	-0.29	-0.27	-1.96	-4.02	Bénéfices mis en réserve
51.	Staff costs	NA	0.62	0.48	0.46	0.58	0.67	0.66	Frais de personnel
52.	Provisions on loans (1)	NA	0.03	0.03	0.01	24.19	0.05	..	Provisions sur prêts (1)
53.	Provisions on securities (1)	NA	0.01	0.01	0.04	2.35	0.10	..	Provisions sur titres (1)
% of gross income									**% du total du résultat brut**
54.	Net interest income	47.98	61.72	61.72	60.33	66.20	41.96	16.17	Produits financiers nets
55.	Non-interest income (net)	52.02	38.28	38.28	39.67	33.80	58.04	83.83	Produits non financiers (nets)
56.	Operating expenses	107.58	111.00	110.53	131.82	129.61	217.84	254.46	Frais d'exploitation
57.	Net income	-7.58	-11.00	-10.53	-31.82	-29.61	-117.84	-154.46	Résultat net
58.	Provisions (net)	14.14	-0.96	1.91	2.07	-10.61	-1.26	29.18	Provisions (nettes)
59.	Profit before tax	-21.72	-10.05	-12.44	-33.88	-18.99	-116.58	-183.64	Bénéfices avant impôt
60.	Income tax	-	0.48	0.48	-	-	0.25	7.81	Impôt
61.	Profit after tax	-21.72	-10.53	-12.92	-33.88	-18.99	-116.83	-191.45	Bénéfices après impôt
62.	Staff costs	39.39	65.55	65.07	53.72	41.34	40.45	31.78	Frais de personnel
% of net income									**% du total du résultat net**
63.	Provisions (net)	..	..	..	..	..	..	..	Provisions (nettes)
64.	Profit before tax	..	..	..	..	..	..	..	Bénéfices avant impôt
65.	Income tax	..	..	..	..	..	..	..	Impôt
66.	Profit after tax	..	..	..	..	..	..	..	Bénéfices après impôt

SWEDEN

Foreign commercial banks

SUEDE

Banques commerciales étrangères

Per cent / *Pourcentage*	1986	1987	1988	1989	1990	1991	1992	
BALANCE SHEET ANALYSIS								**ANALYSE DU BILAN**
% of year-end balance sheet total								**% du total du bilan en fin d'exercice**
Assets								**Actif**
67. Cash & balance with Central bank	1.16	0.25	0.21	0.36	0.84	0.24	8.73	67. Caisse & solde auprès de la Banque centrale
68. Interbank deposits	46.12	46.48	29.74	27.54	25.53	19.04	19.89	68. Dépôts interbancaires
69. Loans	31.74	36.97	55.79	55.58	62.29	63.04	49.18	69. Prêts
70. Securities	16.65	8.55	3.95	5.36	2.32	14.59	15.98	70. Valeurs mobilières
71. Other assets	4.33	7.74	10.31	11.16	9.01	3.08	6.22	71. Autres actifs
Liabilities								**Passif**
72. Capital & reserves	5.05	3.48	3.43	2.73	3.34	2.54	2.08	72. Capital et réserves
73. Borrowing from Central bank	6.24	0.44	1.19	1.85	1.51	0.81	0.02	73. Emprunts auprès de la Banque centrale
74. Interbank deposits	78.17	83.90	86.30	86.77	82.79	80.69	84.25	74. Dépôts interbancaires
75. Non-bank deposits	2.01	2.87	5.03	3.52	6.07	9.73	9.12	75. Dépôts non bancaires
76. Bonds	3.31	2.22	1.31	1.79	2.40	2.13	1.54	76. Obligations
77. Other liabilities	5.21	7.09	2.74	3.34	3.88	4.09	3.00	77. Autres engagements
Memoranda								**Pour mémoire**
78. *Short-term securities*	*4.99*	*0.78*	*0.84*	*0.43*	*0.81*	*9.43*	*32.07*	78. *Titres à court terme*
79. *Bonds*	*13.06*	*6.28*	*3.18*	*4.65*	*0.56*	*0.43*	*0.31*	79. *Obligations*
80. *Shares and participations*	*0.02*	*0.02*	*0.06*	*0.41*	*0.47*	*0.06*	*0.01*	80. *Actions et participations*
81. *Claims on non-residents*	*0.72*	*3.89*	*5.86*	*11.01*	*11.63*	*27.74*	*21.06*	81. *Créances sur des non résidents*
82. *Liabilities to non-residents*	*0.40*	*0.42*	*1.77*	*1.22*	*2.10*	*86.08*	*87.03*	82. *Engagements envers des non résidents*

1. As from 1992, change in methodology.
2. As from 1987, change in methodology.

1. A partir de 1992, changement méthodologique.
2. A partir de 1987, changement méthodologique.

Notes

- Average balance sheet totals (item 29) are based on thirteen end-month data.

Notes

- La moyenne du total des actifs/passifs (poste 29) est basée sur treize données de fin de mois.

Change in methodology:

- Beginning 1992, "Provisions on loans" (item 15 or item 52) and "Provisions on securities" (item 16 or item 53) are no longer available due to new accounting methods.
- As from 1987, balance sheet data are based on banks' annual balance figures. "Capital & reserves" (item 22 or item 72) also include reserves.

Changement méthodologique :

- A partir de 1992, "Provisions sur prêts" (poste 15 ou poste 52) et "Provisions sur titres" (poste 16 ou poste 53) ne sont plus disponibles du fait de nouvelles techniques comptables.
- Les données du bilan de 1987 ont été recalculées à partir des soldes annuels des banques. Les "Capital et réserves" (poste 22 ou poste 72) incluent aussi les réserves.

142

SWEDEN
Savings banks

SUEDE
Caisses d'épargne

Million Swedish kroner / *Millions de couronnes suédoises*

		1983	1984	1985	1986	1987	1988	1989	1990	1991	1992		
INCOME STATEMENT													**COMPTE DE RESULTATS**
1.	Interest income	14370	15536	17888	17053	18109	20328	24461	32005	31956	49806	1.	Produits financiers
2.	Interest expenses	10010	10851	12508	10765	11356	12593	15744	20871	19994	37020	2.	Frais financiers
3.	Net interest income	4360	4685	5360	6288	6753	7735	8717	11134	11962	12786	3.	Produits financiers nets
4.	Non-interest income (net)	826	1026	1352	2137	1828	2189	2371	2695	6210	19752	4.	Produits non financiers (nets)
5.	Gross income	5186	5711	6712	8425	8581	9924	11088	13829	18172	32538	5.	Résultat brut
6.	Operating expenses	3312	4159	5027	5965	6705	7406	8531	11231	11919	28310	6.	Frais d'exploitation
7.	Net income	1874	1552	1685	2460	1876	2518	2557	2598	-1747	4228	7.	Résultat net
8.	Provisions (net)	1672	1349	1457	1334	985	1731	2118	2448	-13356	-6458	8.	Provisions (nettes)
9.	Profit before tax	202	203	228	1126	891	787	439	150	11609	10686	9.	Bénéfices avant impôt
10.	Income tax	124	108	121	727	487	544	130	161	3587	549	10.	Impôt
11.	Profit after tax	78	95	107	399	404	243	309	-11	8022	10137	11.	Bénéfices après impôt
12.	Distributed profit	..	..	1	-	-	-	-	-	-	-	12.	Bénéfices distribués
13.	Retained profit	..	..	106	399	404	243	309	-11	8022	10137	13.	Bénéfices mis en réserve
Memoranda													*Pour mémoire*
14.	Staff costs	1769	2026	2270	2440	2770	2088	3651	4237	4549	5203	14.	Frais de personnel
15.	Provisions on loans	3678	679	544	989	980	1748	1078	2035	14692	..	15.	Provisions sur prêts
16.	Provisions on securities	7	485	807	103	8	5	1073	644	2197	..	16.	Provisions sur titres
BALANCE SHEET (1)													**BILAN (1)**
Assets													**Actif**
17.	Cash & balance with Central bank	1083	1556	1764	2291	2766	2822	3225	4230	4592	16375	17.	Caisse & solde auprès de la Banque centrale
18.	Interbank deposits	12541	16388	13287	13839	15098	19708	20368	26163	17460	22127	18.	Dépôts interbancaires
19.	Loans	77709	79889	83765	99869	111560	140385	170524	203904	189497	214186	19.	Prêts
20.	Securities	31160	31310	34717	38488	38437	31320	31368	33334	52710	61489	20.	Valeurs mobilières
21.	Other assets	4791	4397	5024	5575	5916	6742	8727	9851	9640	18925	21.	Autres actifs
Liabilities													**Passif**
22.	Capital & reserves	8704	10138	10777	12575	13938	16179	17547	19242	16241	21519	22.	Capital et réserves
23.	Borrowing from Central bank	-	-	-	-	-	-	-	-	88	8623	23.	Emprunts auprès de la Banque centrale
24.	Interbank deposits	6294	5642	6663	13847	18771	30976	51737	73242	48353	48931	24.	Dépôts interbancaires
25.	Non-bank deposits	108500	113709	116956	127979	135113	145601	155530	170544	180318	197526	25.	Dépôts non bancaires
26.	Bonds	693	770	895	1190	1735	2946	3826	3544	1139	21055	26.	Obligations
27.	Other liabilities	3093	3280	3269	4471	4218	5274	5572	10909	27761	35448	27.	Autres engagements
Balance sheet total													**Total du bilan**
28.	End-year total	127284	133539	138558	160063	173776	200976	234212	277482	273898	333101	28.	En fin d'exercice
29.	Average total (2)	121246	130412	136049	149311	166920	187376	217594	255847	275690	386763	29.	Moyen (2)
Memoranda													*Pour mémoire*
30.	Short-term securities	-	380	1742	889	1369	666	1426	4340	6846	38517	30.	Titres à court terme
31.	Bonds	28783	30781	33771	37412	37005	29388	31027	31037	24321	24190	31.	Obligations
32.	Shares and participations	1122	1360	1648	1924	1686	1869	1823	1890	1519	10920	32.	Actions et participations
33.	Claims on non-residents	764	124	75	293	467	1026	3405	8186	9340	35000	33.	Créances sur des non résidents
34.	Liabilities to non-residents	..	49	46	85	52	850	70	442	11407	74580	34.	Engagements envers des non résidents
SUPPLEMENTARY INFORMATION													**RENSEIGNEMENTS COMPLEMENTAIRES**
35.	Number of institutions	155	149	139	119	116	110	109	104	101	91	35.	Nombre d'institutions
36.	Number of branches	1265	1261	1179	1249	1249	1190	1273	1124	1129	1028	36.	Nombre de succursales
37.	Number of employees (x 1000)	12.4	13.1	13.5	14.6	14.6	15.6	15.8	14.9	15.3	15.4	37.	Nombre de salariés (x 1000)

143

SWEDEN

Savings banks

SUEDE

Caisses d'épargne

Per cent / *Pourcentage*

INCOME STATEMENT ANALYSIS — **ANALYSE DU COMPTE DE RESULTATS**

		1983	1984	1985	1986	1987	1988	1989	1990	1991	1992		
	% of average balance sheet total												**% du total moyen du bilan**
38.	Interest income	11.85	11.91	13.13	11.42	10.85	10.85	11.24	12.51	11.59	12.88	38.	Produits financiers
39.	Interest expenses	8.26	8.32	9.19	7.21	6.80	6.72	7.24	8.16	7.25	9.57	39.	Frais financiers
40.	Net interest income	3.60	3.59	3.94	4.21	4.05	4.13	4.01	4.35	4.34	3.31	40.	Produits financiers nets
41.	Non-interest income (net)	0.68	0.79	0.99	1.43	1.10	1.17	1.09	1.05	2.25	5.11	41.	Produits non financiers (nets)
42.	Gross income	4.28	4.38	4.93	5.64	5.14	5.30	5.10	5.41	6.59	8.41	42.	Résultat brut
43.	Operating expenses	2.73	3.19	3.70	4.00	4.02	3.95	3.92	4.39	7.23	7.32	43.	Frais d'exploitation
44.	Net income	1.55	1.19	1.24	1.65	1.12	1.34	1.18	1.02	-0.63	1.09	44.	Résultat net
45.	Provisions (net)	1.38	1.03	1.07	0.89	0.59	0.92	0.97	0.96	-4.84	-1.67	45.	Provisions (nettes)
46.	Profit before tax	0.17	0.16	0.17	0.75	0.53	0.42	0.20	0.06	4.21	2.76	46.	Bénéfices avant impôt
47.	Income tax	0.10	0.08	0.09	0.49	0.29	0.29	0.06	0.06	1.30	0.14	47.	Impôt
48.	Profit after tax	0.06	0.07	0.08	0.27	0.24	0.13	0.14	0.00	2.91	2.62	48.	Bénéfices après impôt
49.	Distributed profit	..	..	0.00	-	-	-	-	-	-	-	49.	Bénéfices distribués
50.	Retained profit	..	..	0.08	0.27	0.24	0.13	0.14	0.00	2.91	2.62	50.	Bénéfices mis en réserve
51.	Staff costs	1.46	1.55	1.67	1.63	1.66	1.11	1.68	1.66	1.65	1.35	51.	Frais de personnel
52.	Provisions on loans	3.03	0.52	0.40	0.66	0.59	0.93	0.50	0.80	5.33	..	52.	Provisions sur prêts
53.	Provisions on securities	0.01	0.37	0.59	0.07	0.00	0.00	0.49	0.25	0.80	..	53.	Provisions sur titres
	% of gross income												**% du total du résultat brut**
54.	Net interest income	84.07	82.03	79.86	74.64	78.70	77.94	78.62	80.51	65.83	39.30	54.	Produits financiers nets
55.	Non-interest income (net)	15.93	17.97	20.14	25.36	21.30	22.06	21.38	19.49	34.17	60.70	55.	Produits non financiers (nets)
56.	Operating expenses	63.86	72.82	74.90	70.80	78.14	74.63	76.94	81.21	109.61	87.01	56.	Frais d'exploitation
57.	Net income	36.14	27.18	25.10	29.20	21.86	25.37	23.06	18.79	-9.61	12.99	57.	Résultat net
58.	Provisions (net)	32.24	23.62	21.71	15.83	11.48	17.44	19.10	17.70	-73.50	-19.85	58.	Provisions (nettes)
59.	Profit before tax	3.90	3.55	3.40	13.36	10.38	7.93	3.96	1.08	63.88	32.84	59.	Bénéfices avant impôt
60.	Income tax	2.39	1.89	1.80	8.63	5.68	5.48	1.17	1.16	19.74	1.69	60.	Impôt
61.	Profit after tax	1.50	1.66	1.59	4.74	4.71	2.45	2.79	-0.08	44.14	31.15	61.	Bénéfices après impôt
62.	Staff costs	34.11	35.48	33.82	28.96	32.28	21.04	32.93	30.64	25.03	15.99	62.	Frais de personnel
	% of net income												**% du total du résultat net**
63.	Provisions (net)	89.22	86.92	86.47	54.23	52.51	68.75	82.83	94.23	..	-152.74	63.	Provisions (nettes)
64.	Profit before tax	10.78	13.08	13.53	45.77	47.49	31.25	17.17	5.77	..	252.74	64.	Bénéfices avant impôt
65.	Income tax	6.62	6.96	7.18	29.55	25.96	21.60	5.08	6.20	..	12.98	65.	Impôt
66.	Profit after tax	4.16	6.12	6.35	16.22	21.54	9.65	12.08	-0.42	..	239.76	66.	Bénéfices après impôt

SWEDEN

Savings banks

Per cent

BALANCE SHEET ANALYSIS

% of year-end balance sheet total

	1983	1984	1985	1986	1987	1988	1989	1990	1991	1992
Assets										
67. Cash & balance with Central bank	0.85	1.17	1.27	1.43	1.59	1.40	1.38	1.52	1.68	4.92
68. Interbank deposits	9.85	12.27	9.59	8.65	8.69	9.81	8.70	9.43	6.37	6.64
69. Loans	61.05	59.82	60.45	62.39	64.20	69.85	72.81	73.48	69.19	64.30
70. Securities	24.48	23.45	25.06	24.05	22.12	15.58	13.39	12.01	19.24	18.46
71. Other assets	3.76	3.29	3.63	3.48	3.40	3.35	3.73	3.55	3.52	5.68
Liabilities										
72. Capital & reserves	6.84	7.59	7.78	7.86	8.02	8.05	7.49	6.93	5.93	6.46
73. Borrowing from Central bank	-	-	-	-	-	-	-	-	0.03	2.59
74. Interbank deposits	4.94	4.22	4.81	8.65	10.80	15.41	22.09	26.40	17.65	14.69
75. Non-bank deposits	85.24	85.15	84.41	79.96	77.75	72.45	66.41	61.46	65.83	59.30
76. Bonds	0.54	0.58	0.65	0.74	1.00	1.47	1.63	1.28	0.42	6.32
77. Other liabilities	2.43	2.46	2.36	2.79	2.43	2.62	2.38	3.93	10.14	10.64
**Memoranda**										
78. Short-term securities	-	_0.28_	_1.26_	_0.56_	_0.79_	_0.33_	_0.61_	_1.56_	_2.50_	_11.56_
79. Bonds	_22.61_	_23.05_	_24.37_	_23.37_	_21.29_	_14.62_	_13.25_	_11.19_	_8.88_	_7.26_
80. Shares and participations	_0.88_	_1.02_	_1.19_	_1.20_	_0.97_	_0.93_	_0.78_	_0.68_	_0.55_	_3.28_
81. Claims on non-residents	_0.60_	_0.09_	_0.05_	_0.18_	_0.27_	_0.51_	_1.45_	_2.95_	_3.41_	_10.51_
82. Liabilities to non-residents	_.._	_0.04_	_0.03_	_0.05_	_0.03_	_0.42_	_0.03_	_0.16_	_4.16_	_22.39_

1. Change in methodology.

Change in methodology:

- Balance sheet data for 1983 were recalculated on the basis of banks' annual balance figures, bringing them in line with the years thereafter. "Capital & reserves" (item 22 or item 72) were also revised to include reserves.

- Beginning 1992, average balance sheet totals (item 29) are based on thirteen end-month data.

SUEDE

Caisses d'épargne

Pourcentage

ANALYSE DU BILAN

% du total du bilan en fin d'exercice

Actif
67. Caisse & solde auprès de la Banque centrale
68. Dépôts interbancaires
69. Prêts
70. Valeurs mobilières
71. Autres actifs

Passif
72. Capital et réserves
73. Emprunts auprès de la Banque centrale
74. Dépôts interbancaires
75. Dépôts non bancaires
76. Obligations
77. Autres engagements

**Pour mémoire**
78. Titres à court terme
79. Obligations
80. Actions et participations
81. Créances sur des non résidents
82. Engagements envers des non résidents

1. Changement méthodologique.

Changement méthodologique :

- Les données du bilan de 1983 ont été recalculées à partir des soldes annuels des banques afin qu'elles correspondent à celles des années précédentes. Les "Capital et réserves" (poste 22 ou poste 72) ont également été révisés pour inclure les réserves.

- A partir de 1992, la moyenne du total des actifs/passifs (poste 29) est basée sur treize données de fin de mois.

SWEDEN / SUEDE

Co-operative banks / Banques mutualistes

Million Swedish kroner / Millions de couronnes suédoises

INCOME STATEMENT / COMPTE DE RESULTATS

		1983	1984	1985	1986	1987	1988	1989	1990	1991
1.	Interest income / Produits financiers	3369	3728	4433	4314	4556	5323	6340	8249	12157
2.	Interest expenses / Frais financiers	2330	2581	3086	2687	2751	3200	3857	4942	8427
3.	Net interest income / Produits financiers nets	1039	1147	1347	1627	1805	2123	2483	3307	3730
4.	Non-interest income (net) / Produits non financiers (nets)	153	181	287	328	332	391	472	602	1144
5.	Gross income / Résultat brut	1192	1328	1634	1955	2137	2514	2955	3909	4874
6.	Operating expenses / Frais d'exploitation	816	1003	1208	1390	1625	1838	2159	2981	5717
7.	Net income / Résultat net	376	325	426	565	512	676	796	928	-843
8.	Provisions (net) / Provisions (nettes)	340	288	328	443	360	497	616	711	-2856
9.	Profit before tax / Bénéfices avant impôt	36	37	98	122	152	179	180	217	2013
10.	Income tax / Impôt	22	25	42	54	79	101	59	67	552
11.	Profit after tax / Bénéfices après impôt	14	12	56	68	73	78	121	150	1461
12.	Distributed profit / Bénéfices distribués	-	-	-	-	-	-	-	-	-
13.	Retained profit / Bénéfices mis en réserve	14	12	56	68	73	78	121	150	1461
	Memoranda / Pour mémoire									
14.	Staff costs / Frais de personnel	435	502	582	664	776	799	888	1092	1377
15.	Provisions on loans / Provisions sur prêts	604	160	140	177	268	-	366	523	3130
16.	Provisions on securities / Provisions sur titres	-	87	146	200	3	388	91	47	818

BALANCE SHEET (1) / BILAN (1)

		1983	1984	1985	1986	1987	1988	1989	1990	1991
	Assets / Actif									
17.	Cash & balance with Central bank / Caisse & solde auprès de la Banque centrale	150	188	223	269	327	368	443	593	1453
18.	Interbank deposits / Dépôts interbancaires	3901	4380	4296	5654	1950	2572	1067	1515	5548
19.	Loans / Prêts	17955	18846	19773	20825	26397	32805	40411	47201	60019
20.	Securities / Valeurs mobilières	6432	7253	7851	9484	10772	10009	10874	10828	23689
21.	Other assets / Autres actifs	1013	1177	1594	1688	1918	1499	1960	2352	3093
	Liabilities / Passif									
22.	Capital & reserves / Capital et réserves	1643	1848	2064	2380	4778	3407	4174	5035	4627
23.	Borrowing from Central bank / Emprunts auprès de la Banque centrale	-	31	1	1	151	1533	3487	2540	982
24.	Interbank deposits / Dépôts interbancaires	54	-	-	-	-	-	-	-	20381
25.	Non-bank deposits / Dépôts non bancaires	26565	28666	30262	33897	36480	41028	45690	52980	58682
26.	Bonds / Obligations	96	84	104	152	264	273	332	365	2396
27.	Other liabilities / Autres engagements	1093	1215	1306	1490	-309	1012	1073	1568	6733
	Balance sheet total / Total du bilan									
28.	End-year total / En fin d'exercice	29451	31844	33737	37920	41364	47253	54756	62488	93803
29.	Average total / Moyen	28854	31097	33152	36266	40232	45259	51406	57278	67395
	Memoranda / Pour mémoire									
30.	Short-term securities / Titres à court terme	-	-	-	-	-	381	480	615	2217
31.	Bonds / Obligations	6507	7375	8069	9886	10064	10062	10948	10479	9047
32.	Shares and participations / Actions et participations	14	30	107	108	122	122	122	436	1458
33.	Claims on non-residents / Créances sur des non résidents	-	-	-	-	-	-	-	-	1964
34.	Liabilities to non-residents / Engagements envers des non résidents	-	-	-	-	-	-	-	6	9316

SUPPLEMENTARY INFORMATION / RENSEIGNEMENTS COMPLEMENTAIRES

		1983	1984	1985	1986	1987	1988	1989	1990	1991
35.	Number of institutions / Nombre d'institutions	12	12	12	12	12	12	12	12	12
36.	Number of branches / Nombre de succursales	383	380	377	377	376	288	653	645	630
37.	Number of employees (x 1000) / Nombre de salariés (x 1000)	3.1	3.3	3.5	3.7	3.9	12.5	4.0	4.3	4.7

SWEDEN

Co-operative banks

Per cent

INCOME STATEMENT ANALYSIS

	1983	1984	1985	1986	1987	1988	1989	1990	1991
% of average balance sheet total									
38. Interest income	11.68	11.99	13.37	11.90	11.32	11.76	12.33	14.40	18.04
39. Interest expenses	8.08	8.30	9.31	7.41	6.84	7.07	7.50	8.63	12.50
40. Net interest income	3.60	3.69	4.06	4.49	4.49	4.69	4.83	5.77	5.53
41. Non-interest income (net)	0.53	0.58	0.87	0.90	0.83	0.86	0.92	1.05	1.70
42. Gross income	4.13	4.27	4.93	5.39	5.31	5.55	5.75	6.82	7.23
43. Operating expenses	2.83	3.23	3.64	3.83	4.04	4.06	4.20	5.20	8.48
44. Net income	1.30	1.05	1.28	1.56	1.27	1.49	1.55	1.62	-1.25
45. Provisions (net)	1.18	0.93	0.99	1.22	0.89	1.10	1.20	1.24	-4.24
46. Profit before tax	0.12	0.12	0.30	0.34	0.38	0.40	0.35	0.38	2.99
47. Income tax	0.08	0.08	0.13	0.15	0.20	0.22	0.11	0.12	0.82
48. Profit after tax	0.05	0.04	0.17	0.19	0.18	0.17	0.24	0.26	2.17
49. Distributed profit	-	-	-	-	-	-	-	-	-
50. Retained profit	0.05	0.04	0.17	0.19	0.18	0.17	0.24	0.26	2.17
51. Staff costs	1.51	1.61	1.76	1.83	1.93	1.77	1.73	1.91	2.04
52. Provisions on loans	2.09	0.51	0.42	0.49	0.67	-	0.71	0.91	4.64
53. Provisions on securities	-	0.28	0.44	0.55	0.01	0.86	0.18	0.08	1.21
% of gross income									
54. Net interest income	87.16	86.37	82.44	83.22	84.46	84.45	84.03	84.60	76.53
55. Non-interest income (net)	12.84	13.63	17.56	16.78	15.54	15.55	15.97	15.40	23.47
56. Operating expenses	68.46	75.53	73.93	71.10	76.04	73.11	73.06	76.26	117.30
57. Net income	31.54	24.47	26.07	28.90	23.96	26.89	26.94	23.74	-17.30
58. Provisions (net)	28.52	21.69	20.07	22.66	16.85	19.77	20.85	18.19	-58.60
59. Profit before tax	3.02	2.79	6.00	6.24	7.11	7.12	6.09	5.55	41.30
60. Income tax	1.85	1.88	2.57	2.76	3.70	4.02	2.00	1.71	11.33
61. Profit after tax	1.17	0.90	3.43	3.48	3.42	3.10	4.09	3.84	29.98
62. Staff costs	36.49	37.80	35.62	33.96	36.31	31.78	30.05	27.94	28.25
% of net income									
63. Provisions (net)	90.43	88.62	77.00	78.41	70.31	73.52	77.39	76.62	..
64. Profit before tax	9.57	11.38	23.00	21.59	29.69	26.48	22.61	23.38	..
65. Income tax	5.85	7.69	9.86	9.56	15.43	14.94	7.41	7.22	..
66. Profit after tax	3.72	3.69	13.15	12.04	14.26	11.54	15.20	16.16	..

SUEDE

Banques mutualistes

Pourcentage

ANALYSE DU COMPTE DE RESULTATS

% du total moyen du bilan
38. Produits financiers
39. Frais financiers
40. Produits financiers nets
41. Produits non financiers (nets)
42. Résultat brut
43. Frais d'exploitation
44. Résultat net
45. Provisions (nettes)
46. Bénéfices avant impôt
47. Impôt
48. Bénéfices après impôt
49. Bénéfices distribués
50. Bénéfices mis en réserve
51. Frais de personnel
52. Provisions sur prêts
53. Provisions sur titres

% du total du résultat brut
54. Produits financiers nets
55. Produits non financiers (nets)
56. Frais d'exploitation
57. Résultat net
58. Provisions (nettes)
59. Bénéfices avant impôt
60. Impôt
61. Bénéfices après impôt
62. Frais de personnel

% du total du résultat net
63. Provisions (nettes)
64. Bénéfices avant impôt
65. Impôt
66. Bénéfices après impôt

SWEDEN

Co-operative banks

Per cent

BALANCE SHEET ANALYSIS

% of year-end balance sheet total

	1983	1984	1985	1986	1987	1988	1989	1990	1991
Assets									
67. Cash & balance with Central bank	0.51	0.59	0.66	0.71	0.79	0.78	0.81	0.95	1.55
68. Interbank deposits	13.25	13.75	12.73	14.91	4.71	5.44	1.95	2.42	5.91
69. Loans	60.97	59.18	58.61	54.92	63.82	69.42	73.80	75.54	63.98
70. Securities	21.84	22.78	23.27	25.01	26.04	21.18	19.86	17.33	25.25
71. Other assets	3.44	3.70	4.72	4.45	4.64	3.17	3.58	3.76	3.30
Liabilities									
72. Capital & reserves	5.58	5.80	6.12	6.28	11.55	7.21	7.62	8.06	4.93
73. Borrowing from Central bank	-	-	-	-	-	-	-	-	1.05
74. Interbank deposits	0.18	0.10	0.00	0.00	0.37	3.24	6.37	4.06	21.73
75. Non-bank deposits	90.20	90.02	89.70	89.39	88.19	86.83	83.44	84.78	62.56
76. Bonds	0.33	0.26	0.31	0.40	0.64	0.58	0.61	0.58	2.55
77. Other liabilities	3.71	3.82	3.87	3.93	-0.75	2.14	1.96	2.51	7.18
Memoranda									
78. Short-term securities	*-*	*-*	*-*	*-*	*-*	*0.81*	*0.88*	*0.98*	*2.36*
79. Bonds	*22.09*	*23.16*	*23.92*	*26.07*	*24.33*	*21.29*	*19.99*	*16.77*	*9.64*
80. Shares and participations	*0.05*	*0.09*	*0.32*	*0.28*	*0.29*	*0.26*	*0.22*	*0.70*	*1.55*
81. Claims on non-residents	*-*	*-*	*-*	*-*	*-*	*-*	*-*	*-*	*2.09*
82. Liabilities to non-residents	*-*	*-*	*-*	*-*	*-*	*-*	*-*	*0.01*	*9.93*

1. Change in methodology.

Notes

- Average balance sheet totals (item 29) are based on thirteen end-month data.

Change in methodology:

- Balance sheet data for 1983-1987 were recalculated on the basis of banks' annual balance figures, bringing them in line with the years thereafter. "Capital & reserves" (item 22 or item 72) were also revised to include reserves.

- For the year 1991, the Föreningsbankernas Bank is included under Co-operative banks and not under Commercial banks.

- As from 1992, Co-operative banks, which merged into one single commercial bank, are included under Commercial banks.

SUEDE

Banques mutualistes

Pourcentage

ANALYSE DU BILAN

% du total du bilan en fin d'exercice

Actif
67. Caisse & solde auprès de la Banque centrale
68. Dépôts interbancaires
69. Prêts
70. Valeurs mobilières
71. Autres actifs

Passif
72. Capital et réserves
73. Emprunts auprès de la Banque centrale
74. Dépôts interbancaires
75. Dépôts non bancaires
76. Obligations
77. Autres engagements

Pour mémoire
78. Titres à court terme
79. Obligations
80. Actions et participations
81. Créances sur des non résidents
82. Engagements envers des non résidents

1. Changement méthodologique.

Notes

- La moyenne du total des actifs/passifs (poste 29) est basée sur treize données de fin de mois.

Changement méthodologique :

- Les données des bilans de 1983 à 1987 ont été recalculées à partir des soldes annuels des banques afin qu'elles correspondent à celles des années précédentes. Les "Capital et réserves" (poste 22 ou poste 72) ont également été révisés pour inclure les réserves.

- Pour l'année 1991, la Föreningsbankernas Bank est comprise dans les Banques mutualistes et non pas dans les Banques commerciales.

- Depuis 1992, les Banques mutualistes, ayant fusionnées en une seule banque commerciale, sont classées dans les données concernant les Banques commerciales.

SWITZERLAND / SUISSE

All banks / Ensemble des banques

Million Swiss francs / Millions de francs suisses

INCOME STATEMENT / COMPTE DE RESULTATS

#		1983	1984	1985	1986	1987	1988	1989	1990	1991	1992
1.	Interest income / Produits financiers	34077	39799	40021	39293	41233	45836	59594	70944	75442	74255
2.	Interest expenses / Frais financiers	25998	30800	30025	28705	30474	33563	46326	57257	58970	56246
3.	Net interest income / Produits financiers nets	8079	8999	9996	10588	10759	12273	13268	13687	16472	18009
4.	Non-interest income (net) / Produits non financiers (nets)	7020	7563	9000	10318	11462	10929	13737	13174	16992	17961
5.	Gross income / Résultat brut	15099	16562	18996	20906	22221	23202	27005	26861	33464	35970
6.	Operating expenses / Frais d'exploitation	8321	9067	10084	11302	12370	13386	14934	15939	17349	18408
7.	Net income / Résultat net	6778	7495	8912	9604	9851	9816	12071	10922	16115	17562
8.	Provisions (net) / Provisions (nettes)	2828	3101	3732	3972	4236	4134	5104	5561	10127	11386
9.	Profit before tax / Bénéfices avant impôt	3950	4394	5180	5632	5615	5682	6967	5561	5988	6176
10.	Income tax / Impôt	1184	1251	1474	1528	1531	1476	1535	1313	1382	1403
11.	Profit after tax / Bénéfices après impôt	2766	3143	3706	4104	4084	4206	5432	4048	4606	4773
12.	Distributed profit / Bénéfices distribués	1671	1922	2141	2370	2488	2523	3460	2715	2805	2829
13.	Retained profit / Bénéfices mis en réserve	1095	1221	1565	1734	1596	1683	1972	1333	1801	1944

Memoranda / Pour mémoire

#		1983	1984	1985	1986	1987	1988	1989	1990	1991	1992
14.	Staff costs / Frais de personnel	5671	6111	6738	7481	8189	8868	9828	10451	11419	11947
15.	Provisions on loans / Provisions sur prêts	..	..	..	..	..	..	..	..	..	..
16.	Provisions on securities / Provisions sur titres	..	..	..	..	..	..	..	..	..	..

BALANCE SHEET / BILAN

Assets / Actif

#		1983	1984	1985	1986	1987	1988	1989	1990	1991	1992
17.	Cash & balance with Central bank / Caisse & solde auprès de la Banque centrale	19920	22054	23832	25140	26375	12360	12332	11876	11715	11818
18.	Interbank deposits / Dépôts interbancaires	146786	166820	180879	207814	213523	226068	197365	196615	187439	196342
19.	Loans / Prêts	336230	373366	402795	431989	473369	540796	621374	670261	711407	726741
20.	Securities / Valeurs mobilières	70033	74190	82079	91261	93583	88245	97684	105054	110906	121896
21.	Other assets / Autres actifs	53069	52676	48555	48878	49634	48342	49591	48973	51855	55417

Liabilities / Passif

#		1983	1984	1985	1986	1987	1988	1989	1990	1991	1992
22.	Capital & reserves / Capital et réserves	36619	40094	45107	50349	54177	57993	63371	66743	68676	71439
23.	Borrowing from Central bank / Emprunts auprès de la Banque centrale	5124	8504	7008	10093	7605	4220	1585	1805	1239	1433
24.	Interbank deposits / Dépôts interbancaires	113393	115603	136182	160227	171115	179214	194091	208519	205741	209940
25.	Non-bank deposits / Dépôts non bancaires	342041	380761	387477	406571	432697	467158	494038	510663	534720	557064
26.	Bonds / Obligations	96026	104480	117260	130347	140314	151053	164228	181508	191779	194451
27.	Other liabilities / Autres engagements	32836	39664	45106	47495	50576	56175	61036	63546	71168	77887

Balance sheet total / Total du bilan

#		1983	1984	1985	1986	1987	1988	1989	1990	1991	1992
28.	End-year total / En fin d'exercice	626037	689106	738140	805082	856484	915812	978346	1032779	1073321	1112213
29.	Average total / Moyen	603053	657572	713623	771611	830783	886148	947079	1005563	1053050	1092767

Memoranda / Pour mémoire

#		1983	1984	1985	1986	1987	1988	1989	1990	1991	1992
30.	Short-term securities / Titres à court terme	25002	28896	31093	30730	29463	21328	25776	33898	29411	34438
31.	Bonds / Obligations	37744	37628	42389	49316	52547	53313	55961	56826	64916	68459
32.	Shares and participations / Actions et participations	7288	7666	8597	11215	11573	13604	15947	14331	16579	18999
33.	Claims on non-residents / Créances sur des non résidents	229375	264303	279251	305547	317222	337446	339306	354848	372834	392649
34.	Liabilities to non-residents / Engagements envers des non résidents	195477	212128	215294	234092	233768	255951	270950	293525	314501	325954

SUPPLEMENTARY INFORMATION / RENSEIGNEMENTS COMPLEMENTAIRES

#		1983	1984	1985	1986	1987	1988	1989	1990	1991	1992
35.	Number of institutions / Nombre d'institutions	431	439	441	448	452	454	455	457	445	435
36.	Number of branches / Nombre de succursales	5005	5179	5293	3948	4005	4082	4130	4191	4190	4111
37.	Number of employees (x 1000) / Nombre de salariés (x 1000)	91.8	93.7	98.1	105.4	112.5	115.1	119.3	121.4	120.9	118.5

SWITZERLAND

All banks

Per cent

INCOME STATEMENT ANALYSIS

SUISSE

Ensemble des banques

Pourcentage

ANALYSE DU COMPTE DE RESULTATS

	1983	1984	1985	1986	1987	1988	1989	1990	1991	1992		
% of average balance sheet total												**% du total moyen du bilan**
38. Interest income	5.65	6.05	5.61	5.09	4.96	5.17	6.29	7.06	7.16	6.80	38.	Produits financiers
39. Interest expenses	4.31	4.68	4.21	3.72	3.67	3.79	4.89	5.69	5.60	5.15	39.	Frais financiers
40. Net interest income	1.34	1.37	1.40	1.37	1.30	1.38	1.40	1.36	1.56	1.65	40.	Produits financiers nets
41. Non-interest income (net)	1.16	1.15	1.26	1.34	1.38	1.23	1.45	1.31	1.61	1.64	41.	Produits non financiers (nets)
42. Gross income	2.50	2.52	2.66	2.71	2.67	2.62	2.85	2.67	3.18	3.29	42.	Résultat brut
43. Operating expenses	1.38	1.38	1.41	1.46	1.49	1.51	1.58	1.59	1.65	1.68	43.	Frais d'exploitation
44. Net income	1.12	1.14	1.25	1.24	1.19	1.11	1.27	1.09	1.53	1.61	44.	Résultat net
45. Provisions (net)	0.47	0.47	0.52	0.51	0.51	0.47	0.54	0.55	0.96	1.04	45.	Provisions (nettes)
46. Profit before tax	0.66	0.67	0.73	0.73	0.68	0.64	0.74	0.53	0.57	0.57	46.	Bénéfices avant impôt
47. Income tax	0.20	0.19	0.21	0.20	0.18	0.17	0.16	0.13	0.13	0.13	47.	Impôt
48. Profit after tax	0.46	0.48	0.52	0.53	0.49	0.47	0.57	0.40	0.44	0.44	48.	Bénéfices après impôt
49. Distributed profit	0.28	0.29	0.30	0.31	0.30	0.28	0.37	0.27	0.27	0.26	49.	Bénéfices distribués
50. Retained profit	0.18	0.19	0.22	0.22	0.19	0.19	0.21	0.13	0.17	0.18	50.	Bénéfices mis en réserve
51. Staff costs	0.94	0.93	0.94	0.97	0.99	1.00	1.04	1.04	1.08	1.09	51.	Frais de personnel
52. Provisions on loans	:	:	:	:	:	:	:	:	:	:	52.	Provisions sur prêts
53. Provisions on securities	:	:	:	:	:	:	:	:	:	:	53.	Provisions sur titres
% of gross income												**% du total du résultat brut**
54. Net interest income	53.51	54.34	52.62	50.65	48.42	52.90	49.13	50.95	49.22	50.07	54.	Produits financiers nets
55. Non-interest income (net)	46.49	45.66	47.38	49.35	51.58	47.10	50.87	49.05	50.78	49.93	55.	Produits non financiers (nets)
56. Operating expenses	55.11	54.75	53.08	54.06	55.67	57.69	55.30	59.34	51.84	51.18	56.	Frais d'exploitation
57. Net income	44.89	45.25	46.92	45.94	44.33	42.31	44.70	40.66	48.16	48.82	57.	Résultat net
58. Provisions (net)	18.73	18.72	19.65	19.00	19.06	17.82	18.90	20.70	30.26	31.65	58.	Provisions (nettes)
59. Profit before tax	26.16	26.53	27.27	26.94	25.27	24.49	25.80	19.96	17.89	17.17	59.	Bénéfices avant impôt
60. Income tax	7.84	7.55	7.76	7.31	6.89	6.36	5.68	4.89	4.13	3.90	60.	Impôt
61. Profit after tax	18.32	18.98	19.51	19.63	18.38	18.13	20.11	15.07	13.76	13.27	61.	Bénéfices après impôt
62. Staff costs	37.56	36.90	35.47	35.78	36.85	38.22	36.39	38.91	34.12	33.21	62.	Frais de personnel
% of net income												**% du total du résultat net**
63. Provisions (net)	41.72	41.37	41.88	41.36	43.00	42.11	42.28	50.92	62.84	64.83	63.	Provisions (nettes)
64. Profit before tax	58.28	58.63	58.12	58.64	57.00	57.89	57.72	49.08	37.16	35.17	64.	Bénéfices avant impôt
65. Income tax	17.47	16.69	16.54	15.91	15.54	15.04	12.72	12.02	8.58	7.99	65.	Impôt
66. Profit after tax	40.81	41.93	41.58	42.73	41.46	42.85	45.00	37.06	28.58	27.18	66.	Bénéfices après impôt

SWITZERLAND

All banks

Per cent

BALANCE SHEET ANALYSIS

% of year-end balance sheet total

SUISSE

Ensemble des banques

Pourcentage

ANALYSE DU BILAN

% du total du bilan en fin d'exercice

		1983	1984	1985	1986	1987	1988	1989	1990	1991	1992	
Assets												**Actif**
67.	Cash & balance with Central bank	3.18	3.20	3.23	3.12	3.08	1.35	1.26	1.15	1.09	1.06	Caisse & solde auprès de la Banque centrale
68.	Interbank deposits	23.45	24.21	24.50	25.81	24.93	24.68	20.17	19.04	17.46	17.65	Dépôts interbancaires
69.	Loans	53.71	54.18	54.57	53.66	55.27	59.05	63.51	64.90	66.28	65.34	Prêts
70.	Securities	11.19	10.77	11.12	11.34	10.93	9.64	9.98	10.17	10.33	10.96	Valeurs mobilières
71.	Other assets	8.48	7.64	6.58	6.07	5.80	5.28	5.07	4.74	4.83	4.98	Autres actifs
Liabilities												**Passif**
72.	Capital & reserves	5.85	5.82	6.11	6.25	6.33	6.33	6.48	6.46	6.40	6.42	Capital et réserves
73.	Borrowing from Central bank	0.82	1.23	0.95	1.25	0.89	0.46	0.16	0.17	0.12	0.13	Emprunts auprès de la Banque centrale
74.	Interbank deposits	18.11	16.78	18.45	19.90	19.98	19.57	19.84	20.19	19.17	18.88	Dépôts interbancaires
75.	Non-bank deposits	54.64	55.25	52.49	50.50	50.52	51.01	50.50	49.45	49.82	50.09	Dépôts non bancaires
76.	Bonds	15.34	15.16	15.89	16.19	16.38	16.49	16.79	17.57	17.87	17.48	Obligations
77.	Other liabilities	5.25	5.76	6.11	5.90	5.91	6.13	6.24	6.15	6.63	7.00	Autres engagements
Memoranda												***Pour mémoire***
78.	*Short-term securities*	*3.99*	*4.19*	*4.21*	*3.82*	*3.44*	*2.33*	*2.63*	*3.28*	*2.74*	*3.10*	*Titres à court terme*
79.	*Bonds*	*6.03*	*5.46*	*5.74*	*6.13*	*6.14*	*5.82*	*5.72*	*5.50*	*6.05*	*6.16*	*Obligations*
80.	*Shares and participations*	*1.16*	*1.11*	*1.16*	*1.39*	*1.35*	*1.49*	*1.63*	*1.39*	*1.54*	*1.71*	*Actions et participations*
81.	*Claims on non-residents*	*36.64*	*38.35*	*37.83*	*37.95*	*37.04*	*36.85*	*34.68*	*34.36*	*34.74*	*35.30*	*Créances sur des non résidents*
82.	*Liabilities to non-residents*	*31.22*	*30.78*	*29.17*	*29.08*	*27.29*	*27.95*	*27.69*	*28.42*	*29.30*	*29.31*	*Engagements envers des non résidents*

Notes

- All banks include Large commercial banks, Cantonal banks, Regional and savings banks, Loan associations and agricultural co-operative banks and Other Swiss and foreign commercial banks.

Notes

- L'Ensemble des banques comprend les Grandes banques commerciales, les Banques cantonales, les Banques régionales et caisses d'épargne, les Caisses de crédit mutuel et les banques mutualistes agricoles, et les Autres banques suisses et étrangères.

151

SWITZERLAND

Large commercial banks

Million Swiss francs

SUISSE

Grandes banques commerciales

Millions de francs suisses

		1983	1984	1985	1986	1987	1988	1989	1990	1991	1992
INCOME STATEMENT	**COMPTE DE RESULTATS**										
1. Interest income	Produits financiers	18578	22496	21995	21157	22449	25335	33228	37805	39353	37330
2. Interest expenses	Frais financiers	14440	17800	16737	15530	16796	18894	26427	31374	31220	27990
3. Net interest income	Produits financiers nets	4138	4696	5258	5627	5653	6441	6801	6431	8133	9340
4. Non-interest income (net)	Produits non financiers (nets)	3806	4107	4885	5571	5965	5800	6879	6676	8544	9394
5. Gross income	Résultat brut	7944	8803	10143	11198	11618	12241	13680	13107	16677	18734
6. Operating expenses	Frais d'exploitation	4482	4848	5368	5984	6509	7030	7849	8086	9023	9765
7. Net income	Résultat net	3462	3955	4775	5214	5109	5211	5831	5021	7654	8969
8. Provisions (net)	Provisions (nettes)	1404	1612	1972	2153	2128	2177	2447	2280	4402	5650
9. Profit before tax	Bénéfices avant impôt	2058	2343	2803	3061	2981	3034	3384	2741	3252	3319
10. Income tax	Impôt	674	726	854	872	849	823	827	682	803	795
11. Profit after tax	Bénéfices après impôt	1384	1617	1949	2189	2132	2211	2557	2059	2449	2524
12. Distributed profit	Bénéfices distribués	923	1056	1257	1366	1423	1432	1623	1576	1585	1584
13. Retained profit	Bénéfices mis en réserve	461	561	692	823	709	779	934	483	864	940
Memoranda	***Pour mémoire***										
14. Staff costs	Frais de personnel	3076	3292	3611	3982	4340	4700	5242	5410	6060	6455
15. Provisions on loans	Provisions sur prêts	..	..	..	..	..	..	..	..	..	..
16. Provisions on securities	Provisions sur titres	..	..	..	..	..	..	..	..	..	..
BALANCE SHEET	**BILAN**										
Assets	**Actif**										
17. Cash & balance with Central bank	Caisse & solde auprès de la Banque centrale	11468	13002	13836	14588	14774	5523	5468	5189	5123	4889
18. Interbank deposits	Dépôts interbancaires	87419	101529	112359	132805	135700	142738	117329	110780	100290	103289
19. Loans	Prêts	146410	168729	182383	197894	219954	255872	302566	319625	344106	353135
20. Securities	Valeurs mobilières	43342	46349	51296	56863	55948	47052	52822	59255	64030	73671
21. Other assets	Autres actifs	40018	38620	34753	34675	34377	32313	31528	28678	29637	32297
Liabilities	**Passif**										
22. Capital & reserves	Capital et réserves	17890	19807	23290	26260	28051	29619	33143	33196	34148	35187
23. Borrowing from Central bank	Emprunts auprès de la Banque centrale	3851	6828	5043	7418	5408	3289	1203	1270	568	1107
24. Interbank deposits	Dépôts interbancaires	71362	71010	86610	105967	113804	112882	120732	125757	126306	127759
25. Non-bank deposits	Dépôts non bancaires	182657	209528	210121	220935	231597	247005	261719	271651	285212	303465
26. Bonds	Obligations	34878	38216	43374	48975	53041	57648	58710	58577	60272	59262
27. Other liabilities	Autres engagements	18019	22840	26189	27270	28852	33055	34206	33075	36682	40501
Balance sheet total	**Total du bilan**										
28. End-year total	En fin d'exercice	328657	368229	394627	436825	460752	483497	509713	523526	543187	567281
29. Average total	Moyen	317203	348443	381428	415726	448788	472125	496605	516620	533357	555234
Memoranda	***Pour mémoire***										
30. Short-term securities	Titres à court terme	20596	24873	27284	26777	25097	16756	19541	26556	21777	26889
31. Bonds	Obligations	17635	16135	17891	22105	22875	21059	22596	23619	30875	33756
32. Shares and participations	Actions et participations	5112	5341	6121	7981	7975	9237	10685	9080	11377	13026
33. Claims on non-residents	Créances sur des non résidents	163555	192836	205148	228827	237947	245803	242273	253852	267157	282046
34. Liabilities to non-residents	Engagements envers des non résidents	140943	156050	160604	180068	179045	193070	201479	220536	240443	248042
SUPPLEMENTARY INFORMATION	**RENSEIGNEMENTS COMPLEMENTAIRES**										
35. Number of institutions	Nombre d'institutions	5	5	5	5	5	5	5	4	4	4
36. Number of branches	Nombre de succursales	922	1007	1048	876	889	901	933	969	983	969
37. Number of employees (x 1000)	Nombre de salariés (x 1000)	50.3	50.5	52.7	56.6	59.9	60.8	62.9	62.4	62.5	61.9

SWITZERLAND

Large commercial banks

SUISSE

Grandes banques commerciales

Per cent / *Pourcentage*

INCOME STATEMENT ANALYSIS / ANALYSE DU COMPTE DE RESULTATS

		1983	1984	1985	1986	1987	1988	1989	1990	1991	1992		
% of average balance sheet total													**% du total moyen du bilan**
38.	Interest income	5.86	6.46	5.77	5.09	5.00	5.37	6.69	7.32	7.38	6.72	38.	Produits financiers
39.	Interest expenses	4.55	5.11	4.39	3.74	3.74	4.00	5.32	6.07	5.85	5.04	39.	Frais financiers
40.	Net interest income	1.30	1.35	1.38	1.35	1.26	1.36	1.37	1.24	1.52	1.68	40.	Produits financiers nets
41.	Non-interest income (net)	1.20	1.18	1.28	1.34	1.33	1.23	1.39	1.29	1.60	1.69	41.	Produits non financiers (nets)
42.	Gross income	2.50	2.53	2.66	2.69	2.59	2.59	2.75	2.54	3.13	3.37	42.	Résultat brut
43.	Operating expenses	1.41	1.39	1.41	1.44	1.45	1.49	1.58	1.57	1.69	1.76	43.	Frais d'exploitation
44.	Net income	1.09	1.14	1.25	1.25	1.14	1.10	1.17	0.97	1.44	1.62	44.	Résultat net
45.	Provisions (net)	0.44	0.46	0.52	0.52	0.47	0.46	0.49	0.44	0.83	1.02	45.	Provisions (nettes)
46.	Profit before tax	0.65	0.67	0.73	0.74	0.66	0.64	0.68	0.53	0.61	0.60	46.	Bénéfices avant impôt
47.	Income tax	0.21	0.21	0.22	0.21	0.19	0.17	0.17	0.13	0.15	0.14	47.	Impôt
48.	Profit after tax	0.44	0.46	0.51	0.53	0.48	0.47	0.51	0.40	0.46	0.45	48.	Bénéfices après impôt
49.	Distributed profit	0.29	0.30	0.33	0.33	0.32	0.30	0.33	0.31	0.30	0.29	49.	Bénéfices distribués
50.	Retained profit	0.15	0.16	0.18	0.20	0.16	0.16	0.19	0.09	0.16	0.17	50.	Bénéfices mis en réserve
51.	Staff costs	0.97	0.94	0.95	0.96	0.97	1.00	1.06	1.05	1.14	1.16	51.	Frais de personnel
52.	Provisions on loans	..	..	..	..	..	..	..	..	..	..	52.	Provisions sur prêts
53.	Provisions on securities	..	..	..	..	..	..	..	..	..	..	53.	Provisions sur titres
% of gross income													**% du total du résultat brut**
54.	Net interest income	52.09	53.35	51.84	50.25	48.66	52.62	49.71	49.07	48.77	49.86	54.	Produits financiers nets
55.	Non-interest income (net)	47.91	46.65	48.16	49.75	51.34	47.38	50.29	50.93	51.23	50.14	55.	Produits non financiers (nets)
56.	Operating expenses	56.42	55.07	52.92	53.44	56.03	57.43	57.38	61.69	54.10	52.12	56.	Frais d'exploitation
57.	Net income	43.58	44.93	47.08	46.56	43.97	42.57	42.62	38.31	45.90	47.88	57.	Résultat net
58.	Provisions (net)	17.67	18.31	19.44	19.23	18.32	17.78	17.89	17.40	26.40	30.16	58.	Provisions (nettes)
59.	Profit before tax	25.91	26.62	27.63	27.34	25.66	24.79	24.74	20.91	19.50	17.72	59.	Bénéfices avant impôt
60.	Income tax	8.48	8.25	8.42	7.79	7.31	6.72	6.05	5.20	4.82	4.24	60.	Impôt
61.	Profit after tax	17.42	18.37	19.22	19.55	18.35	18.06	18.69	15.71	14.68	13.47	61.	Bénéfices après impôt
62.	Staff costs	38.72	37.40	35.60	35.56	37.36	38.40	38.32	41.28	36.34	34.46	62.	Frais de personnel
% of net income													**% du total du résultat net**
63.	Provisions (net)	40.55	40.76	41.30	41.29	41.65	41.78	41.97	45.41	57.51	62.99	63.	Provisions (nettes)
64.	Profit before tax	59.45	59.24	58.70	58.71	58.35	58.22	58.03	54.59	42.49	37.01	64.	Bénéfices avant impôt
65.	Income tax	19.47	18.36	17.88	16.72	16.62	15.79	14.18	13.58	10.49	8.86	65.	Impôt
66.	Profit after tax	39.98	40.88	40.82	41.98	41.73	42.43	43.85	41.01	32.00	28.14	66.	Bénéfices après impôt

SWITZERLAND

Large commercial banks

Per cent

BALANCE SHEET ANALYSIS

% of year-end balance sheet total

		1983	1984	1985	1986	1987	1988	1989	1990	1991	1992
	Assets										
67.	Cash & balance with Central bank	3.49	3.53	3.51	3.34	3.21	1.14	1.07	0.99	0.94	0.86
68.	Interbank deposits	26.60	27.57	28.47	30.40	29.45	29.52	23.02	21.16	18.46	18.21
69.	Loans	44.55	45.82	46.22	45.30	47.74	52.92	59.36	61.05	63.35	62.25
70.	Securities	13.19	12.59	13.00	13.02	12.14	9.73	10.36	11.32	11.79	12.99
71.	Other assets	12.18	10.49	8.81	7.94	7.46	6.68	6.19	5.48	5.46	5.69
	Liabilities										
72.	Capital & reserves	5.44	5.38	5.90	6.01	6.09	6.13	6.50	6.34	6.29	6.20
73.	Borrowing from Central bank	1.17	1.85	1.28	1.70	1.17	0.68	0.24	0.24	0.10	0.20
74.	Interbank deposits	21.71	19.28	21.95	24.26	24.70	23.35	23.69	24.02	23.25	22.52
75.	Non-bank deposits	55.58	56.90	53.25	50.58	50.27	51.09	51.35	51.89	52.51	53.49
76.	Bonds	10.61	10.38	10.99	11.21	11.51	11.92	11.52	11.19	11.10	10.45
77.	Other liabilities	5.48	6.20	6.64	6.24	6.26	6.84	6.71	6.32	6.75	7.14
	Memoranda										
78.	*Short-term securities*	*6.27*	*6.75*	*6.91*	*6.13*	*5.45*	*3.47*	*3.83*	*5.07*	*4.01*	*4.74*
79.	*Bonds*	*5.37*	*4.38*	*4.53*	*5.06*	*4.96*	*4.36*	*4.43*	*4.51*	*5.68*	*5.95*
80.	*Shares and participations*	*1.56*	*1.45*	*1.55*	*1.83*	*1.73*	*1.91*	*2.10*	*1.73*	*2.09*	*2.30*
81.	*Claims on non-residents*	*49.76*	*52.37*	*51.99*	*52.38*	*51.64*	*50.84*	*47.53*	*48.49*	*49.18*	*49.72*
82.	*Liabilities to non-residents*	*42.88*	*42.38*	*40.70*	*41.22*	*38.86*	*39.93*	*39.53*	*42.13*	*44.27*	*43.72*

SUISSE

Grandes banques commerciales

Pourcentage

ANALYSE DU BILAN

% du total du bilan en fin d'exercice

Actif
67. Caisse & solde auprès de la Banque centrale
68. Dépôts interbancaires
69. Prêts
70. Valeurs mobilières
71. Autres actifs

Passif
72. Capital et réserves
73. Emprunts auprès de la Banque centrale
74. Dépôts interbancaires
75. Dépôts non bancaires
76. Obligations
77. Autres engagements

Pour mémoire
78. *Titres à court terme*
79. *Obligations*
80. *Actions et participations*
81. *Créances sur des non résidents*
82. *Engagements envers des non résidents*

SWITZERLAND

Other Swiss and foreign commercial banks

Million Swiss francs

SUISSE

Autres banques commerciales suisses et étrangères

Millions de francs suisses

	1983	1984	1985	1986	1987	1988	1989	1990	1991	1992	
INCOME STATEMENT											**COMPTE DE RESULTATS**
1. Interest income	6055	7247	7139	6542	6725	7791	11134	13187	13228	12771	1. Produits financiers
2. Interest expenses	4320	5290	4947	4318	4470	5126	8100	9963	9633	9054	2. Frais financiers
3. Net interest income	1735	1957	2192	2224	2255	2665	3034	3224	3595	3717	3. Produits financiers nets
4. Non-interest income (net)	2457	2635	3179	3693	4268	4007	5579	5061	6113	5892	4. Produits non financiers (nets)
5. Gross income	4192	4592	5371	5917	6523	6672	8613	8285	9708	9609	5. Résultat brut
6. Operating expenses	2095	2360	2694	3068	3456	3762	4281	4728	4991	5135	6. Frais d'exploitation
7. Net income	2097	2232	2677	2849	3067	2910	4332	3557	4717	4474	7. Résultat net
8. Provisions (net)	943	964	1155	1158	1355	1236	1794	2034	3003	2624	8. Provisions (nettes)
9. Profit before tax	1154	1268	1539	1691	1712	1674	2538	1523	1714	1850	9. Bénéfices avant impôt
10. Income tax	372	385	468	501	516	487	542	407	410	454	10. Impôt
11. Profit after tax	782	883	1071	1190	1196	1187	1996	1116	1304	1396	11. Bénéfices après impôt
12. Distributed profit	360	448	445	540	573	571	1270	554	654	673	12. Bénéfices distribués
13. Retained profit	422	435	626	650	623	616	726	562	650	723	13. Bénéfices mis en réserve
Memoranda											*Pour mémoire*
14. Staff costs	*1374*	*1532*	*1727*	*1979*	*2239*	*2444*	*2732*	*3028*	*3180*	*3246*	14. Frais de personnel
15. Provisions on loans	..	..	..	..	..	..	..	..	..	..	15. Provisions sur prêts
16. Provisions on securities	..	..	..	..	..	..	..	..	..	..	16. Provisions sur titres
BALANCE SHEET											**BILAN**
Assets											**Actif**
17. Cash & balance with Central bank	4769	5223	5890	6096	6762	3201	3377	3135	2880	3046	17. Caisse & solde auprès de la Banque centrale
18. Interbank deposits	34900	40320	42497	44419	44826	51339	50703	57381	58495	61590	18. Dépôts interbancaires
19. Loans	40055	43684	46251	47683	49673	59906	67353	74007	76536	77108	19. Prêts
20. Securities	11628	12001	13945	16729	18828	20728	24400	24266	25062	26448	20. Valeurs mobilières
21. Other assets	6261	6495	5788	6091	6693	6918	7795	8947	9262	8532	21. Autres actifs
Liabilities											**Passif**
22. Capital & reserves	9745	10775	11836	13275	14376	15964	17112	19455	19965	21026	22. Capital et réserves
23. Borrowing from Central bank	67	158	207	486	215	3	40	68	-	16	23. Emprunts auprès de la Banque centrale
24. Interbank deposits	33893	35722	39359	42786	43419	50315	54071	57935	56446	59279	24. Dépôts interbancaires
25. Non-bank deposits	42053	47400	47128	46924	49903	55965	59633	63942	67664	69333	25. Dépôts non bancaires
26. Bonds	5945	6712	7781	8745	9476	10050	11307	14730	14675	13158	26. Obligations
27. Other liabilities	5912	6956	8060	8802	9392	9795	11464	11607	13485	13911	27. Autres engagements
Balance sheet total											**Total du bilan**
28. End-year total	97614	107723	114371	121018	126782	142091	153628	167737	172235	176723	28. En fin d'exercice
29. Average total	92559	102668	111047	117694	123900	134437	147860	160683	169986	174479	29. Moyen
Memoranda											*Pour mémoire*
30. Short-term securities	*3180*	*2706*	*2559*	*2765*	*3245*	*3471*	*5328*	*6501*	*6875*	*6420*	30. Titres à court terme
31. Bonds	*7087*	*7829*	*9904*	*11953*	*13420*	*14587*	*15957*	*15068*	*15694*	*16689*	31. Obligations
32. Shares and participations	*1362*	*1466*	*1482*	*2011*	*2163*	*2670*	*3115*	*2698*	*2493*	*3339*	32. Actions et participations
33. Claims on non-residents	*59313*	*64626*	*66850*	*68618*	*70288*	*82017*	*87395*	*90756*	*95500*	*99193*	33. Créances sur des non résidents
34. Liabilities to non-residents	*49235*	*51707*	*50228*	*49455*	*49847*	*57374*	*63889*	*66742*	*67487*	*71069*	34. Engagements envers des non résidents
SUPPLEMENTARY INFORMATION											**RENSEIGNEMENTS COMPLEMENTAIRES**
35. Number of institutions	178	186	189	197	202	205	209	218	222	227	35. Nombre d'institutions
36. Number of branches	436	485	494	480	494	527	549	587	607	592	36. Nombre de succursales
37. Number of employees (x 1000)	18.0	19.1	20.2	22.4	25.0	25.9	27.0	28.9	28.1	26.8	37. Nombre de salariés (x 1000)

Other Swiss and foreign commercial banks

Autres banques commerciales suisses et étrangères

Per cent — *Pourcentage*

		1983	1984	1985	1986	1987	1988	1989	1990	1991	1992		
INCOME STATEMENT ANALYSIS													**ANALYSE DU COMPTE DE RESULTATS**
% of average balance sheet total													**% du total moyen du bilan**
38.	Interest income	6.54	7.06	6.43	5.56	5.43	5.80	7.53	8.21	7.78	7.32	38.	Produits financiers
39.	Interest expenses	4.67	5.15	4.45	3.67	3.61	3.81	5.48	6.20	5.67	5.19	39.	Frais financiers
40.	Net interest income	1.87	1.91	1.97	1.89	1.82	1.98	2.05	2.01	2.11	2.13	40.	Produits financiers nets
41.	Non-interest income (net)	2.65	2.57	2.86	3.14	3.44	2.98	3.77	3.15	3.60	3.38	41.	Produits non financiers (nets)
42.	Gross income	4.53	4.47	4.84	5.03	5.26	4.96	5.83	5.16	5.71	5.51	42.	Résultat brut
43.	Operating expenses	2.26	2.30	2.41	2.61	2.79	2.80	2.90	2.94	2.94	2.94	43.	Frais d'exploitation
44.	Net income	2.27	2.17	2.43	2.42	2.48	2.16	2.93	2.21	2.77	2.56	44.	Résultat net
45.	Provisions (net)	1.02	0.94	1.04	0.98	1.09	0.92	1.21	1.27	1.77	1.50	45.	Provisions (nettes)
46.	Profit before tax	1.25	1.24	1.39	1.44	1.38	1.25	1.72	0.95	1.01	1.06	46.	Bénéfices avant impôt
47.	Income tax	0.40	0.37	0.42	0.43	0.42	0.36	0.37	0.25	0.24	0.26	47.	Impôt
48.	Profit after tax	0.84	0.86	0.96	1.01	0.97	0.88	1.35	0.69	0.77	0.80	48.	Bénéfices après impôt
49.	Distributed profit	0.39	0.44	0.40	0.46	0.46	0.42	0.86	0.34	0.38	0.39	49.	Bénéfices distribués
50.	Retained profit	0.46	0.42	0.56	0.55	0.50	0.46	0.49	0.35	0.38	0.41	50.	Bénéfices mis en réserve
51.	Staff costs	1.48	1.49	1.56	1.68	1.81	1.82	1.85	1.88	1.87	1.86	51.	Frais de personnel
52.	Provisions on loans	..	..	..	..	..	..	..	..	..	..	52.	Provisions sur prêts
53.	Provisions on securities	..	..	..	..	..	..	..	..	..	..	53.	Provisions sur titres
% of gross income													**% du total du résultat brut**
54.	Net interest income	41.39	42.62	40.81	37.59	34.57	39.94	35.23	38.91	37.03	38.68	54.	Produits financiers nets
55.	Non-interest income (net)	58.61	57.38	59.19	62.41	65.43	60.06	64.77	61.09	62.97	61.32	55.	Produits non financiers (nets)
56.	Operating expenses	49.98	51.39	49.84	51.85	52.98	56.38	49.70	57.07	51.41	53.44	56.	Frais d'exploitation
57.	Net income	50.02	48.61	50.16	48.15	47.02	43.62	50.30	42.93	48.59	46.56	57.	Résultat net
58.	Provisions (net)	22.50	20.99	21.50	19.57	20.77	18.53	20.83	24.55	30.93	27.31	58.	Provisions (nettes)
59.	Profit before tax	27.53	27.61	28.65	28.58	26.25	25.09	29.47	18.38	17.66	19.25	59.	Bénéfices avant impôt
60.	Income tax	8.87	8.38	8.71	8.47	7.91	7.30	6.29	4.91	4.22	4.72	60.	Impôt
61.	Profit after tax	18.65	19.23	19.94	20.11	18.34	17.79	23.17	13.47	13.43	14.53	61.	Bénéfices après impôt
62.	Staff costs	32.78	33.36	32.15	33.45	34.32	36.63	31.72	36.55	32.76	33.78	62.	Frais de personnel
% of net income													**% du total du résultat net**
63.	Provisions (net)	44.97	43.19	42.87	40.65	44.18	42.47	41.41	57.18	63.66	58.65	63.	Provisions (nettes)
64.	Profit before tax	55.03	56.81	57.13	59.35	55.82	57.53	58.59	42.82	36.34	41.35	64.	Bénéfices avant impôt
65.	Income tax	17.74	17.25	17.37	17.59	16.82	16.74	12.51	11.44	8.69	10.15	65.	Impôt
66.	Profit after tax	37.29	39.56	39.76	41.77	39.00	40.79	46.08	31.37	27.64	31.20	66.	Bénéfices après impôt

SWITZERLAND

Other Swiss and foreign commercial banks

SUISSE

Autres banques commerciales suisses et étrangères

Per cent / *Pourcentage*

BALANCE SHEET ANALYSIS / **ANALYSE DU BILAN**

	1983	1984	1985	1986	1987	1988	1989	1990	1991	1992		
% of year-end balance sheet total												**% du total du bilan en fin d'exercice**
Assets												**Actif**
67. Cash & balance with Central bank	4.89	4.85	5.15	5.04	5.33	2.25	2.20	1.87	1.67	1.72	67.	Caisse & solde auprès de la Banque centrale
68. Interbank deposits	35.75	37.43	37.16	36.70	35.36	36.13	33.00	34.21	33.96	34.85	68.	Dépôts interbancaires
69. Loans	41.03	40.55	40.44	39.40	39.18	42.16	43.84	44.12	44.44	43.63	69.	Prêts
70. Securities	11.91	11.14	12.19	13.82	14.85	14.59	15.88	14.47	14.55	14.97	70.	Valeurs mobilières
71. Other assets	6.41	6.03	5.06	5.03	5.28	4.87	5.07	5.33	5.38	4.83	71.	Autres actifs
Liabilities												**Passif**
72. Capital & reserves	9.98	10.00	10.35	10.97	11.34	11.24	11.14	11.60	11.59	11.90	72.	Capital et réserves
73. Borrowing from Central bank	0.07	0.15	0.18	0.40	0.17	0.00	0.03	0.04	-	0.01	73.	Emprunts auprès de la Banque centrale
74. Interbank deposits	34.72	33.16	34.41	35.36	34.25	35.41	35.20	34.54	32.77	33.54	74.	Dépôts interbancaires
75. Non-bank deposits	43.08	44.00	41.21	38.77	39.36	39.39	38.82	38.12	39.29	39.23	75.	Dépôts non bancaires
76. Bonds	6.09	6.23	6.80	7.23	7.47	7.07	7.36	8.78	8.52	7.45	76.	Obligations
77. Other liabilities	6.06	6.46	7.05	7.27	7.41	6.89	7.46	6.92	7.83	7.87	77.	Autres engagements
Memoranda												*Pour mémoire*
78. Short-term securities	*3.26*	*2.51*	*2.24*	*2.28*	*2.56*	*2.44*	*3.47*	*3.88*	*3.99*	*3.63*	*78.*	*Titres à court terme*
79. Bonds	*7.26*	*7.27*	*8.66*	*9.88*	*10.59*	*10.27*	*10.39*	*8.98*	*9.11*	*9.44*	*79.*	*Obligations*
80. Shares and participations	*1.40*	*1.36*	*1.30*	*1.66*	*1.71*	*1.88*	*2.03*	*1.61*	*1.45*	*1.89*	*80.*	*Actions et participations*
81. Claims on non-residents	*60.76*	*59.99*	*58.45*	*56.70*	*55.44*	*57.72*	*56.89*	*54.11*	*55.45*	*56.13*	*81.*	*Créances sur des non résidents*
82. Liabilities to non-residents	*50.44*	*48.00*	*43.92*	*40.87*	*39.32*	*40.38*	*41.59*	*39.79*	*39.18*	*40.21*	*82.*	*Engagements envers des non résidents*

SWITZERLAND

Other Swiss commercial banks

SUISSE

Autres banques commerciales suisses

Million Swiss francs / Millions de francs suisses

	1983	1984	1985	1986	1987	1988	1989	1990	1991	1992	
INCOME STATEMENT											**COMPTE DE RESULTATS**
1. Interest income	1595	1863	2022	2254	2343	2557	3527	5547	5908	5737	1. Produits financiers
2. Interest expenses	948	1142	1199	1337	1406	1454	2214	3945	4055	3817	2. Frais financiers
3. Net interest income	647	721	823	917	937	1103	1313	1602	1853	1920	3. Produits financiers nets
4. Non-interest income (net)	892	1057	1336	1677	1914	1667	2063	2328	2293	2655	4. Produits non financiers (nets)
5. Gross income	1539	1778	2159	2594	2851	2770	3376	3930	4146	4575	5. Résultat brut
6. Operating expenses	860	997	1192	1402	1555	1587	1860	2219	2329	2400	6. Frais d'exploitation
7. Net income	679	781	967	1192	1296	1183	1516	1711	1817	2175	7. Résultat net
8. Provisions (net)	268	317	407	474	537	467	683	957	983	1216	8. Provisions (nettes)
9. Profit before tax	411	464	560	718	759	716	833	754	834	959	9. Bénéfices avant impôt
10. Income tax	148	159	191	252	269	249	252	206	190	235	10. Impôt
11. Profit after tax	263	305	369	466	490	467	581	548	644	724	11. Bénéfices après impôt
12. Distributed profit	127	146	173	213	229	231	270	290	369	390	12. Bénéfices distribués
13. Retained profit	136	159	196	253	261	236	311	258	275	334	13. Bénéfices mis en réserve
Memoranda											*Pour mémoire*
14. Staff costs	554	638	756	889	979	1000	1162	1407	1469	1510	14. Frais de personnel
15. Provisions on loans	..	..	..	..	..	..	..	..	..	..	15. Provisions sur prêts
16. Provisions on securities	..	..	..	..	..	..	..	..	..	..	16. Provisions sur titres
BALANCE SHEET											**BILAN**
Assets											**Actif**
17. Cash & balance with Central bank	1838	1995	2348	2591	2959	1351	1261	1296	1128	1083	17. Caisse & solde auprès de la Banque centrale
18. Interbank deposits	6845	7867	8558	12144	13064	12107	12697	20466	21116	22526	18. Dépôts interbancaires
19. Loans	15563	18247	20506	22518	24130	28666	32209	39791	42316	42436	19. Prêts
20. Securities	2813	3206	3826	4657	5002	5663	6629	11232	10817	12212	20. Valeurs mobilières
21. Other assets	2552	2594	2292	2549	2737	2777	3076	4518	4585	4343	21. Autres actifs
Liabilities											**Passif**
22. Capital & reserves	3003	3436	3913	4665	5285	5469	6070	8125	7893	8485	22. Capital et réserves
23. Borrowing from Central bank	6	69	78	118	113	-	40	68	-	16	23. Emprunts auprès de la Banque centrale
24. Interbank deposits	4749	5876	6846	8829	8844	10180	11126	16780	16001	17198	24. Dépôts interbancaires
25. Non-bank deposits	16316	18148	19231	22139	24172	24975	26768	36031	38948	40147	25. Dépôts non bancaires
26. Bonds	3553	3918	4557	5280	5709	6244	7654	11218	11433	10476	26. Obligations
27. Other liabilities	1984	2462	2905	3428	3766	3695	4215	5082	5688	6278	27. Autres engagements
Balance sheet total											**Total du bilan**
28. End-year total	29611	33909	37530	44459	47891	50564	55872	77304	79963	82600	28. En fin d'exercice
29. Average total	28275	31760	35720	40994	46175	49228	53218	66588	78634	81281	29. Moyen
Memoranda											*Pour mémoire*
30. Short-term securities	524	573	665	724	940	1254	1711	4667	4596	4315	30. Titres à court terme
31. Bonds	1882	1978	2487	2985	3086	3297	3403	5288	4955	5858	31. Obligations
32. Shares and participations	408	655	674	948	977	1111	1514	1277	1267	2039	32. Actions et participations
33. Claims on non-residents	9224	10874	11879	14957	15425	17047	19024	30140	32653	34826	33. Créances sur des non résidents
34. Liabilities to non-residents	8453	9188	9164	11834	12210	12759	14484	21644	25164	26160	34. Engagements envers des non résidents
SUPPLEMENTARY INFORMATION											**RENSEIGNEMENTS COMPLEMENTAIRES**
35. Number of institutions	82	82	85	88	91	89	91	92	92	93	35. Nombre d'institutions
36. Number of branches	242	264	277	266	273	287	301	327	333	317	36. Nombre de succursales
37. Number of employees (x 1000)	7.3	8.0	8.8	10.1	11.2	11.2	11.8	13.9	13.6	12.9	37. Nombre de salariés (x 1000)

SWITZERLAND

Other Swiss commercial banks

SUISSE

Autres banques commerciales suisses

	1983	1984	1985	1986	1987	1988	1989	1990	1991	1992		
Per cent												*Pourcentage*
INCOME STATEMENT ANALYSIS												**ANALYSE DU COMPTE DE RESULTATS**
% of average balance sheet total												**% du total moyen du bilan**
38. Interest income	5.64	5.87	5.66	5.50	5.07	5.19	6.63	8.33	7.51	7.06	38.	Produits financiers
39. Interest expenses	3.35	3.60	3.36	3.26	3.04	2.95	4.16	5.92	5.16	4.70	39.	Frais financiers
40. Net interest income	2.29	2.27	2.30	2.24	2.03	2.24	2.47	2.41	2.36	2.36	40.	Produits financiers nets
41. Non-interest income (net)	3.15	3.33	3.74	4.09	4.15	3.39	3.88	3.50	2.92	3.27	41.	Produits non financiers (nets)
42. Gross income	5.44	5.60	6.04	6.33	6.17	5.63	6.34	5.90	5.27	5.63	42.	Résultat brut
43. Operating expenses	3.04	3.14	3.34	3.42	3.37	3.22	3.50	3.33	2.96	2.95	43.	Frais d'exploitation
44. Net income	2.40	2.46	2.71	2.91	2.81	2.40	2.85	2.57	2.31	2.68	44.	Résultat net
45. Provisions (net)	0.95	1.00	1.14	1.16	1.16	0.95	1.28	1.44	1.25	1.50	45.	Provisions (nettes)
46. Profit before tax	1.45	1.46	1.57	1.75	1.64	1.45	1.57	1.13	1.06	1.18	46.	Bénéfices avant impôt
47. Income tax	0.52	0.50	0.53	0.61	0.58	0.51	0.47	0.31	0.24	0.29	47.	Impôt
48. Profit after tax	0.93	0.96	1.03	1.14	1.06	0.95	1.09	0.82	0.82	0.89	48.	Bénéfices après impôt
49. Distributed profit	0.45	0.46	0.48	0.52	0.50	0.47	0.51	0.44	0.47	0.48	49.	Bénéfices distribués
50. Retained profit	0.48	0.50	0.55	0.62	0.57	0.48	0.58	0.39	0.35	0.41	50.	Bénéfices mis en réserve
51. Staff costs	1.96	2.01	2.12	2.17	2.12	2.03	2.18	2.11	1.87	1.86	51.	Frais de personnel
52. Provisions on loans	:	:	:	:	:	:	:	:	:	:	52.	Provisions sur prêts
53. Provisions on securities	:	:	:	:	:	:	:	:	:	:	53.	Provisions sur titres
% of gross income												**% du total du résultat brut**
54. Net interest income	42.04	40.55	38.12	35.35	32.87	39.82	38.89	40.76	44.69	41.97	54.	Produits financiers nets
55. Non-interest income (net)	57.96	59.45	61.88	64.65	67.13	60.18	61.11	59.24	55.31	58.03	55.	Produits non financiers (nets)
56. Operating expenses	55.88	56.07	55.21	54.05	54.54	57.29	55.09	56.46	56.17	52.46	56.	Frais d'exploitation
57. Net income	44.12	43.93	44.79	45.95	45.46	42.71	44.91	43.54	43.83	47.54	57.	Résultat net
58. Provisions (net)	17.41	17.83	18.85	18.27	18.84	16.86	20.23	24.35	23.71	26.58	58.	Provisions (nettes)
59. Profit before tax	26.71	26.10	25.94	27.68	26.62	25.85	24.67	19.19	20.12	20.96	59.	Bénéfices avant impôt
60. Income tax	9.62	8.94	8.85	9.71	9.44	8.99	7.46	5.24	4.58	5.14	60.	Impôt
61. Profit after tax	17.09	17.15	17.09	17.96	17.19	16.86	17.21	13.94	15.53	15.83	61.	Bénéfices après impôt
62. Staff costs	36.00	35.88	35.02	34.27	34.34	36.10	34.42	35.80	35.43	33.01	62.	Frais de personnel
% of net income												**% du total du résultat net**
63. Provisions (net)	39.47	40.59	42.09	39.77	41.44	39.48	45.05	55.93	54.10	55.91	63.	Provisions (nettes)
64. Profit before tax	60.53	59.41	57.91	60.23	58.56	60.52	54.95	44.07	45.90	44.09	64.	Bénéfices avant impôt
65. Income tax	21.80	20.36	19.75	21.14	20.76	21.05	16.62	12.04	10.46	10.80	65.	Impôt
66. Profit after tax	38.73	39.05	38.16	39.09	37.81	39.48	38.32	32.03	35.44	33.29	66.	Bénéfices après impôt

SWITZERLAND

Other Swiss commercial banks

SUISSE

Autres banques commerciales suisses

Per cent

Pourcentage

BALANCE SHEET ANALYSIS

ANALYSE DU BILAN

% of year-end balance sheet total

% du total du bilan en fin d'exercice

	1983	1984	1985	1986	1987	1988	1989	1990	1991	1992		
Assets												**Actif**
67. Cash & balance with Central bank	6.21	5.88	6.26	5.83	6.18	2.67	2.26	1.68	1.41	1.31	67.	Caisse & solde auprès de la Banque centrale
68. Interbank deposits	23.12	23.20	22.80	27.32	27.28	23.94	22.73	26.47	26.41	27.27	68.	Dépôts interbancaires
69. Loans	52.56	53.81	54.64	50.65	50.39	56.69	57.65	51.47	52.92	51.38	69.	Prêts
70. Securities	9.50	9.45	10.19	10.47	10.44	11.20	11.86	14.53	13.53	14.78	70.	Valeurs mobilières
71. Other assets	8.62	7.65	6.11	5.73	5.72	5.49	5.51	5.84	5.73	5.26	71.	Autres actifs
Liabilities												**Passif**
72. Capital & reserves	10.14	10.13	10.43	10.49	11.04	10.82	10.86	10.51	9.87	10.27	72.	Capital et réserves
73. Borrowing from Central bank	0.02	0.20	0.21	0.27	0.24	-	0.07	0.09	-	0.02	73.	Emprunts auprès de la Banque centrale
74. Interbank deposits	16.04	17.33	18.24	19.86	18.47	20.13	19.91	21.71	20.01	20.82	74.	Dépôts interbancaires
75. Non-bank deposits	55.10	53.52	51.24	49.80	50.47	49.39	47.91	46.61	48.71	48.60	75.	Dépôts non bancaires
76. Bonds	12.00	11.55	12.14	11.88	11.92	12.35	13.70	14.51	14.30	12.68	76.	Obligations
77. Other liabilities	6.70	7.26	7.74	7.71	7.86	7.31	7.54	6.57	7.11	7.60	77.	Autres engagements
Memoranda												***Pour mémoire***
78. Short-term securities	*1.77*	*1.69*	*1.77*	*1.63*	*1.96*	*2.48*	*3.06*	*6.04*	*5.75*	*5.22*	*78.*	*Titres à court terme*
79. Bonds	*6.36*	*5.83*	*6.63*	*6.71*	*6.44*	*6.52*	*6.09*	*6.84*	*6.20*	*7.09*	*79.*	*Obligations*
80. Shares and participations	*1.38*	*1.93*	*1.80*	*2.13*	*2.04*	*2.20*	*2.71*	*1.65*	*1.58*	*2.47*	*80.*	*Actions et participations*
81. Claims on non-residents	*31.15*	*32.07*	*31.65*	*33.64*	*32.21*	*33.71*	*34.05*	*38.99*	*40.84*	*42.16*	*81.*	*Créances sur des non résidents*
82. Liabilities to non-residents	*28.55*	*27.10*	*24.42*	*26.62*	*25.50*	*25.23*	*25.92*	*28.00*	*31.47*	*31.67*	*82.*	*Engagements envers des non résidents*

Notes

- Other Swiss commercial banks are a sub-group of Other Swiss and foreign commercial banks.

Notes

- Les Autres banques commerciales suisses sont un sous-groupe des Autres banques commerciales suisses et étrangères.

SWITZERLAND

Foreign commercial banks

Million Swiss francs

SUISSE

Banques commerciales étrangères

Millions de francs suisses

	1983	1984	1985	1986	1987	1988	1989	1990	1991	1992	
INCOME STATEMENT											**COMPTE DE RESULTATS**
1. Interest income	4460	5384	5117	4288	4382	5235	7607	7640	7320	7034	1. Produits financiers
2. Interest expenses	3373	4148	3748	2981	3064	3672	5886	6017	5578	5237	2. Frais financiers
3. Net interest income	1087	1236	1369	1307	1318	1563	1721	1623	1742	1797	3. Produits financiers nets
4. Non-interest income (net)	1565	1578	1843	2016	2354	2340	3516	2734	3820	3237	4. Produits non financiers (nets)
5. Gross income	2652	2814	3212	3323	3672	3903	5237	4357	5562	5034	5. Résultat brut
6. Operating expenses	1236	1363	1485	1666	1901	2175	2421	2509	2682	2734	6. Frais d'exploitation
7. Net income	1416	1451	1727	1657	1771	1728	2816	1848	2662	2300	7. Résultat net
8. Provisions (net)	675	647	748	684	818	769	1112	1077	2021	1408	8. Provisions (nettes)
9. Profit before tax	741	804	979	973	953	959	1704	771	879	892	9. Bénéfices avant impôt
10. Income tax	224	226	277	249	247	238	290	201	220	219	10. Impôt
11. Profit after tax	517	578	702	724	706	721	1414	570	659	673	11. Bénéfices après impôt
12. Distributed profit	233	303	272	327	344	340	1000	264	285	283	12. Bénéfices distribués
13. Retained profit	284	275	430	397	362	381	414	306	374	390	13. Bénéfices mis en réserve
Memoranda											*Pour mémoire*
14. Staff costs	820	894	971	1090	1260	1444	1569	1621	1712	1736	14. Frais de personnel
15. Provisions on loans	..	..	..	..	..	..	..	..	..	..	15. Provisions sur prêts
16. Provisions on securities	..	..	..	..	..	..	..	..	..	..	16. Provisions sur titres
BALANCE SHEET											**BILAN**
Assets											**Actif**
17. Cash & balance with Central bank	2932	3228	3542	3505	3805	1850	2116	1839	1753	1963	17. Caisse & solde auprès de la Banque centrale
18. Interbank deposits	28055	32453	33939	32275	31762	39232	38006	36915	37379	39064	18. Dépôts interbancaires
19. Loans	24492	25437	25745	25165	25543	31239	35144	34215	34220	34672	19. Prêts
20. Securities	8815	8795	10119	12072	13826	15065	17771	13034	14244	14236	20. Valeurs mobilières
21. Other assets	3709	3901	3496	3542	3956	4141	4719	4429	4677	4189	21. Autres actifs
Liabilities											**Passif**
22. Capital & reserves	6742	7339	7923	8610	9091	10494	11042	11329	12072	12541	22. Capital et réserves
23. Borrowing from Central bank	-	89	129	368	102	3	-	-	-	-	23. Emprunts auprès de la Banque centrale
24. Interbank deposits	29205	29846	32513	33957	34575	40134	42946	41156	40444	42081	24. Dépôts interbancaires
25. Non-bank deposits	25736	29252	27897	24785	25731	30990	32865	27910	28716	29186	25. Dépôts non bancaires
26. Bonds	2392	2794	3224	3465	3767	3806	3653	3512	3243	2682	26. Obligations
27. Other liabilities	3927	4494	5155	5374	5626	6099	7249	6525	7797	7633	27. Autres engagements
Balance sheet total											**Total du bilan**
28. End-year total	68003	73814	76841	76559	78891	91527	97756	90433	92272	94124	28. En fin d'exercice
29. Average total	64283	70908	75328	76700	77725	85209	94642	94095	91353	93198	29. Moyen
Memoranda											*Pour mémoire*
30. Short-term securities	2656	2133	1894	2041	2305	2217	3617	1834	2280	2105	30. Titres à court terme
31. Bonds	5205	5851	7417	8968	10334	11289	12554	9780	10739	10831	31. Obligations
32. Shares and participations	954	811	808	1063	1186	1559	1601	1421	1226	1300	32. Actions et participations
33. Claims on non-residents	50088	53752	54971	53661	54863	64970	68371	60616	62847	64367	33. Créances sur des non résidents
34. Liabilities to non-residents	40782	42519	41064	37621	37637	44614	49405	45098	42323	44909	34. Engagements envers des non résidents
SUPPLEMENTARY INFORMATION											**RENSEIGNEMENTS COMPLEMENTAIRES**
35. Number of institutions	96	104	104	109	111	116	118	126	130	134	35. Nombre d'institutions
36. Number of branches	194	221	217	214	221	240	248	260	274	275	36. Nombre de succursales
37. Number of employees (x 1000)	10.6	11.1	11.5	12.3	13.9	14.7	15.2	15.0	14.5	13.9	37. Nombre de salariés (x 1000)

161

Foreign commercial banks

Per cent — *Pourcentage*

INCOME STATEMENT ANALYSIS — ANALYSE DU COMPTE DE RESULTATS

	1983	1984	1985	1986	1987	1988	1989	1990	1991	1992	
% of average balance sheet total											**% du total moyen du bilan**
38. Interest income	6.94	7.59	6.79	5.59	5.64	6.14	8.04	8.12	8.01	7.55	38. Produits financiers
39. Interest expenses	5.25	5.85	4.98	3.89	3.94	4.31	6.22	6.39	6.11	5.62	39. Frais financiers
40. Net interest income	1.69	1.74	1.82	1.70	1.70	1.83	1.82	1.72	1.91	1.93	40. Produits financiers nets
41. Non-interest income (net)	2.43	2.23	2.45	2.63	3.03	2.75	3.72	2.91	4.18	3.47	41. Produits non financiers (nets)
42. Gross income	4.13	3.97	4.26	4.33	4.72	4.58	5.53	4.63	6.09	5.40	42. Résultat brut
43. Operating expenses	1.92	1.92	1.97	2.17	2.45	2.55	2.56	2.67	2.91	2.93	43. Frais d'exploitation
44. Net income	2.20	2.05	2.29	2.16	2.28	2.03	2.98	1.96	3.17	2.47	44. Résultat net
45. Provisions (net)	1.05	0.91	0.99	0.89	1.05	0.90	1.17	1.14	2.21	1.51	45. Provisions (nettes)
46. Profit before tax	1.15	1.13	1.30	1.27	1.23	1.13	1.80	0.82	0.96	0.96	46. Bénéfices avant impôt
47. Income tax	0.35	0.32	0.37	0.32	0.32	0.28	0.31	0.21	0.24	0.23	47. Impôt
48. Profit after tax	0.80	0.82	0.93	0.94	0.91	0.85	1.49	0.61	0.72	0.72	48. Bénéfices après impôt
49. Distributed profit	0.36	0.43	0.36	0.43	0.44	0.40	1.06	0.28	0.31	0.30	49. Bénéfices distribués
50. Retained profit	0.44	0.39	0.57	0.52	0.47	0.45	0.44	0.33	0.41	0.42	50. Bénéfices mis en réserve
51. Staff costs	1.28	1.26	1.29	1.42	1.62	1.69	1.66	1.72	1.87	1.86	51. Frais de personnel
52. Provisions on loans	..	..	..	..	..	..	..	..	..	..	52. Provisions sur prêts
53. Provisions on securities	..	..	..	..	..	..	..	..	..	..	53. Provisions sur titres
% of gross income											**% du total du résultat brut**
54. Net interest income	40.99	43.92	42.62	39.33	35.89	40.05	32.86	37.25	31.32	35.70	54. Produits financiers nets
55. Non-interest income (net)	59.01	56.08	57.38	60.67	64.11	59.95	67.14	62.75	68.68	64.30	55. Produits non financiers (nets)
56. Operating expenses	46.61	48.44	46.23	50.14	51.77	55.73	46.23	57.59	47.86	54.31	56. Frais d'exploitation
57. Net income	53.39	51.56	53.77	49.86	48.23	44.27	53.77	42.41	52.14	45.69	57. Résultat net
58. Provisions (net)	25.45	22.99	23.29	20.58	22.28	19.70	21.23	24.72	36.34	27.97	58. Provisions (nettes)
59. Profit before tax	27.94	28.57	30.48	29.28	25.95	24.57	32.54	17.70	15.80	17.72	59. Bénéfices avant impôt
60. Income tax	8.45	8.03	8.62	7.49	6.73	6.10	5.54	4.61	3.96	4.35	60. Impôt
61. Profit after tax	19.49	20.54	21.86	21.79	19.23	18.47	27.00	13.08	11.85	13.37	61. Bénéfices après impôt
62. Staff costs	30.92	31.77	30.23	32.80	34.31	37.00	29.96	37.20	30.78	34.49	62. Frais de personnel
% of net income											**% du total du résultat net**
63. Provisions (net)	47.67	44.59	43.31	41.28	46.19	44.50	39.49	58.28	69.69	61.22	63. Provisions (nettes)
64. Profit before tax	52.33	55.41	56.69	58.72	53.81	55.50	60.51	41.72	30.31	38.78	64. Bénéfices avant impôt
65. Income tax	15.82	15.58	16.04	15.03	13.95	13.77	10.30	10.88	7.59	9.52	65. Impôt
66. Profit after tax	36.51	39.83	40.65	43.69	39.86	41.72	50.21	30.84	22.72	29.26	66. Bénéfices après impôt

SWITZERLAND

Foreign commercial banks

Per cent

BALANCE SHEET ANALYSIS

% of year-end balance sheet total

	1983	1984	1985	1986	1987	1988	1989	1990	1991	1992
Assets										
67. Cash & balance with Central bank	4.31	4.37	4.61	4.58	4.82	2.02	2.16	2.03	1.90	2.09
68. Interbank deposits	41.26	43.97	44.17	42.16	40.26	42.86	38.88	40.82	40.51	41.50
69. Loans	36.02	34.46	33.50	32.87	32.38	34.13	35.95	37.83	37.09	36.84
70. Securities	12.96	11.92	13.17	15.77	17.53	16.46	18.18	14.41	15.44	15.12
71. Other assets	5.45	5.28	4.55	4.63	5.01	4.52	4.83	4.90	5.07	4.45
Liabilities										
72. Capital & reserves	9.91	9.94	10.31	11.25	11.52	11.47	11.30	12.53	13.08	13.32
73. Borrowing from Central bank	-	0.12	0.17	0.48	0.13	0.00	-	-	-	-
74. Interbank deposits	42.95	40.43	42.31	44.35	43.83	43.85	43.93	45.51	43.83	44.71
75. Non-bank deposits	37.85	39.63	36.30	32.37	32.62	33.86	33.62	30.86	31.12	31.01
76. Bonds	3.52	3.79	4.20	4.53	4.77	4.16	3.74	3.88	3.51	2.85
77. Other liabilities	5.77	6.09	6.71	7.02	7.13	6.66	7.42	7.22	8.45	8.11
Memoranda										
78. Short-term securities	3.91	2.89	2.46	2.67	2.92	2.42	3.70	2.03	2.47	2.24
79. Bonds	7.65	7.93	9.65	11.71	13.10	12.33	12.84	10.81	11.64	11.51
80. Shares and participations	1.40	1.10	1.05	1.39	1.50	1.70	1.64	1.57	1.33	1.38
81. Claims on non-residents	73.66	72.82	71.54	70.09	69.54	70.98	69.94	67.03	68.11	68.39
82. Liabilities to non-residents	59.97	57.60	53.44	49.14	47.71	48.74	50.54	49.87	45.87	47.71

Notes

- Foreign commercial banks are a sub-group of Other Swiss and foreign commercial banks.

SUISSE

Banques commerciales étrangères

Pourcentage

ANALYSE DU BILAN

% du total du bilan en fin d'exercice

Actif
67. Caisse & solde auprès de la Banque centrale
68. Dépôts interbancaires
69. Prêts
70. Valeurs mobilières
71. Autres actifs

Passif
72. Capital et réserves
73. Emprunts auprès de la Banque centrale
74. Dépôts interbancaires
75. Dépôts non bancaires
76. Obligations
77. Autres engagements

Pour mémoire
78. Titres à court terme
79. Obligations
80. Actions et participations
81. Créances sur des non résidents
82. Engagements envers des non résidents

Notes

- Les Banques commerciales étrangères sont un sous-groupe des Autres banques commerciales suisses et étrangères.

SWITZERLAND

Cantonal banks

Million Swiss francs

SUISSE

Banques cantonales

Millions de francs suisses

	1983	1984	1985	1986	1987	1988	1989	1990	1991	1992	
INCOME STATEMENT											**COMPTE DE RESULTATS**
1. Interest income	5902	6297	6825	7216	7470	7834	9504	12441	14496	15597	1. Produits financiers
2. Interest expenses	4547	4850	5246	5519	5704	5879	7387	9950	11531	12456	2. Frais financiers
3. Net interest income	1355	1447	1579	1697	1766	1955	2117	2491	2965	3141	3. Produits financiers nets
4. Non-interest income (net)	517	544	625	707	794	740	845	937	1794	1999	4. Produits non financiers (nets)
5. Gross income	1872	1991	2204	2404	2560	2695	2962	3428	4759	5140	5. Résultat brut
6. Operating expenses	1113	1183	1297	1422	1523	1636	1771	2006	2173	2312	6. Frais d'exploitation
7. Net income	759	808	907	982	1037	1059	1191	1422	2586	2828	7. Résultat net
8. Provisions (net)	336	357	417	458	482	468	546	732	1980	2236	8. Provisions (nettes)
9. Profit before tax	423	451	490	524	555	591	645	690	606	592	9. Bénéfices avant impôt
10. Income tax	43	42	49	52	60	60	60	114	64	46	10. Impôt
11. Profit after tax	380	409	441	472	495	531	585	576	542	546	11. Bénéfices après impôt
12. Distributed profit	283	305	321	338	360	379	413	427	406	418	12. Bénéfices distribués
13. Retained profit	97	104	120	134	135	152	172	149	136	128	13. Bénéfices mis en réserve
Memoranda											*Pour mémoire*
14. Staff costs	808	846	921	994	1053	1124	1210	1320	1455	1516	14. Frais de personnel
15. Provisions on loans	..	..	..	..	..	..	..	..	..	..	15. Provisions sur prêts
16. Provisions on securities	..	..	..	..	..	..	..	..	..	..	16. Provisions sur titres
BALANCE SHEET											**BILAN**
Assets											**Actif**
17. Cash & balance with Central bank	2137	2249	2439	2688	2942	2146	2024	2080	2203	2311	17. Caisse & solde auprès de la Banque centrale
18. Interbank deposits	17918	18552	19155	22901	24626	23943	20976	19885	20112	22311	18. Dépôts interbancaires
19. Loans	92779	98702	106569	112661	122697	134904	152419	170371	182581	189022	19. Prêts
20. Securities	9568	10023	10774	11251	12011	13218	13513	14639	15121	15414	20. Valeurs mobilières
21. Other assets	4303	4811	5070	5069	5205	5490	6241	6904	8265	9773	21. Autres actifs
Liabilities											**Passif**
22. Capital & reserves	5480	5798	6094	6582	7214	7603	8078	8838	9182	9827	22. Capital et réserves
23. Borrowing from Central bank	930	1137	1303	1573	1396	691	199	338	213	246	23. Emprunts auprès de la Banque centrale
24. Interbank deposits	6314	6542	7160	7491	8854	9819	11736	15500	15821	16819	24. Dépôts interbancaires
25. Non-bank deposits	72744	76428	80065	85217	92911	100577	106657	109647	115245	117334	25. Dépôts non bancaires
26. Bonds	34986	37432	41656	45500	48334	51554	57677	66223	72846	77677	26. Obligations
27. Other liabilities	6252	7000	7729	8207	8772	9457	10831	13337	14978	16927	27. Autres engagements
Balance sheet total											**Total du bilan**
28. End-year total	126705	134337	144007	154570	167481	179701	195173	213879	228282	238830	28. En fin d'exercice
29. Average total	122860	130521	139172	149289	161025	173591	187437	204526	221081	233556	29. Moyen
Memoranda											*Pour mémoire*
30. Short-term securities	1004	1058	1002	974	941	932	712	660	588	992	30. Titres à court terme
31. Bonds	8123	8500	9240	9574	10215	11224	11396	12167	12653	12635	31. Obligations
32. Shares and participations	441	465	532	703	855	1062	1405	1812	1880	1786	32. Actions et participations
33. Claims on non-residents	5740	6020	6251	7051	7938	8632	8620	9208	9342	10673	33. Créances sur des non résidents
34. Liabilities to non-residents	4539	3588	3600	3684	3905	4475	4569	5283	5679	5854	34. Engagements envers des non résidents
SUPPLEMENTARY INFORMATION											**RENSEIGNEMENTS COMPLEMENTAIRES**
35. Number of institutions	29	29	29	29	29	29	29	29	28	28	35. Nombre d'institutions
36. Number of branches	1316	1330	1359	709	722	741	755	768	771	779	36. Nombre de succursales
37. Number of employees (x 1000)	14.4	14.7	15.3	16.1	16.9	17.3	18.0	18.8	19.5	19.3	37. Nombre de salariés (x 1000)

SWITZERLAND

Cantonal banks

Per cent

INCOME STATEMENT ANALYSIS

		1983	1984	1985	1986	1987	1988	1989	1990	1991	1992	
	% of average balance sheet total											**% du total moyen du bilan**
38.	Interest income	4.80	4.82	4.90	4.83	4.64	4.51	5.07	6.08	6.56	6.68	Produits financiers
39.	Interest expenses	3.70	3.72	3.77	3.70	3.54	3.39	3.94	4.86	5.22	5.33	Frais financiers
40.	Net interest income	1.10	1.11	1.13	1.14	1.10	1.13	1.13	1.22	1.34	1.34	Produits financiers nets
41.	Non-interest income (net)	0.42	0.42	0.45	0.47	0.49	0.43	0.45	0.46	0.81	0.86	Produits non financiers (nets)
42.	Gross income	1.52	1.53	1.58	1.61	1.59	1.55	1.58	1.68	2.15	2.20	Résultat brut
43.	Operating expenses	0.91	0.91	0.93	0.95	0.95	0.94	0.94	0.98	0.98	0.99	Frais d'exploitation
44.	Net income	0.62	0.62	0.65	0.66	0.64	0.61	0.64	0.70	1.17	1.21	Résultat net
45.	Provisions (net)	0.27	0.27	0.30	0.31	0.30	0.27	0.29	0.36	0.90	0.96	Provisions (nettes)
46.	Profit before tax	0.34	0.35	0.35	0.35	0.34	0.34	0.34	0.34	0.27	0.25	Bénéfices avant impôt
47.	Income tax	0.03	0.03	0.04	0.03	0.04	0.03	0.03	0.06	0.03	0.02	Impôt
48.	Profit after tax	0.31	0.31	0.32	0.32	0.31	0.31	0.31	0.28	0.25	0.23	Bénéfices après impôt
49.	Distributed profit	0.23	0.23	0.23	0.23	0.22	0.22	0.22	0.21	0.18	0.18	Bénéfices distribués
50.	Retained profit	0.08	0.08	0.09	0.09	0.08	0.09	0.09	0.07	0.06	0.05	Bénéfices mis en réserve
51.	Staff costs	0.66	0.65	0.66	0.67	0.65	0.65	0.65	0.65	0.66	0.65	Frais de personnel
52.	Provisions on loans	..	..	..	..	..	..	..	..	..	..	Provisions sur prêts
53.	Provisions on securities	..	..	..	..	..	..	..	..	..	..	Provisions sur titres
	% of gross income											**% du total du résultat brut**
54.	Net interest income	72.38	72.68	71.64	70.59	68.98	72.54	71.47	72.67	62.30	61.11	Produits financiers nets
55.	Non-interest income (net)	27.62	27.32	28.36	29.41	31.02	27.46	28.53	27.33	37.70	38.89	Produits non financiers (nets)
56.	Operating expenses	59.46	59.42	58.85	59.15	59.49	60.71	59.79	58.52	45.66	44.98	Frais d'exploitation
57.	Net income	40.54	40.58	41.15	40.85	40.51	39.29	40.21	41.48	54.34	55.02	Résultat net
58.	Provisions (net)	17.95	17.93	18.92	19.05	18.83	17.37	18.43	21.35	41.61	43.50	Provisions (nettes)
59.	Profit before tax	22.60	22.65	22.23	21.80	21.68	21.93	21.78	20.13	12.73	11.52	Bénéfices avant impôt
60.	Income tax	2.30	2.11	2.22	2.16	2.34	2.23	2.03	3.33	1.34	0.89	Impôt
61.	Profit after tax	20.30	20.54	20.01	19.63	19.34	19.70	19.75	16.80	11.39	10.62	Bénéfices après impôt
62.	Staff costs	43.16	42.49	41.79	41.35	41.13	41.71	40.85	38.51	30.57	29.49	Frais de personnel
	% of net income											**% du total du résultat net**
63.	Provisions (net)	44.27	44.18	45.98	46.64	46.48	44.19	45.84	51.48	76.57	79.07	Provisions (nettes)
64.	Profit before tax	55.73	55.82	54.02	53.36	53.52	55.81	54.16	48.52	23.43	20.93	Bénéfices avant impôt
65.	Income tax	5.67	5.20	5.40	5.30	5.79	5.67	5.04	8.02	2.47	1.63	Impôt
66.	Profit after tax	50.07	50.62	48.62	48.07	47.73	50.14	49.12	40.51	20.96	19.31	Bénéfices après impôt

SUISSE

Banques cantonales

Pourcentage

ANALYSE DU COMPTE DE RESULTATS

SWITZERLAND

Cantonal banks

SUISSE

Banques cantonales

Per cent — *Pourcentage*

BALANCE SHEET ANALYSIS — ANALYSE DU BILAN

% of year-end balance sheet total — **% du total du bilan en fin d'exercice**

	1983	1984	1985	1986	1987	1988	1989	1990	1991	1992		
Assets												**Actif**
67. Cash & balance with Central bank	1.69	1.67	1.69	1.74	1.76	1.19	1.04	0.97	0.97	0.97	67.	Caisse & solde auprès de la Banque centrale
68. Interbank deposits	14.14	13.81	13.30	14.82	14.70	13.32	10.75	9.30	8.81	9.34	68.	Dépôts interbancaires
69. Loans	73.22	73.47	74.00	72.89	73.26	75.07	78.09	79.66	79.98	79.14	69.	Prêts
70. Securities	7.55	7.46	7.48	7.28	7.17	7.36	6.92	6.84	6.62	6.45	70.	Valeurs mobilières
71. Other assets	3.40	3.58	3.52	3.28	3.11	3.06	3.20	3.23	3.62	4.09	71.	Autres actifs
Liabilities												**Passif**
72. Capital & reserves	4.33	4.32	4.23	4.26	4.31	4.23	4.14	4.13	4.02	4.11	72.	Capital et réserves
73. Borrowing from Central bank	0.73	0.85	0.90	1.02	0.83	0.38	0.10	0.16	0.09	0.10	73.	Emprunts auprès de la Banque centrale
74. Interbank deposits	4.98	4.87	4.97	4.85	5.29	5.46	6.01	7.25	6.93	7.04	74.	Dépôts interbancaires
75. Non-bank deposits	57.41	56.89	55.60	55.13	55.48	55.97	54.65	51.27	50.48	49.13	75.	Dépôts non bancaires
76. Bonds	27.61	27.86	28.93	29.44	28.86	28.69	29.55	30.96	31.91	32.52	76.	Obligations
77. Other liabilities	4.93	5.21	5.37	5.31	5.24	5.26	5.55	6.24	6.56	7.09	77.	Autres engagements
Memoranda												*Pour mémoire*
78. Short-term securities	*0.79*	*0.79*	*0.70*	*0.63*	*0.56*	*0.52*	*0.36*	*0.31*	*0.26*	*0.42*	*78.*	*Titres à court terme*
79. Bonds	*6.41*	*6.33*	*6.42*	*6.19*	*6.10*	*6.25*	*5.84*	*5.69*	*5.54*	*5.29*	*79.*	*Obligations*
80. Shares and participations	*0.35*	*0.35*	*0.37*	*0.45*	*0.51*	*0.59*	*0.72*	*0.85*	*0.82*	*0.75*	*80.*	*Actions et participations*
81. Claims on non-residents	*4.53*	*4.48*	*4.34*	*4.56*	*4.74*	*4.80*	*4.42*	*4.31*	*4.09*	*4.47*	*81.*	*Créances sur des non résidents*
82. Liabilities to non-residents	*3.58*	*2.67*	*2.50*	*2.38*	*2.33*	*2.49*	*2.34*	*2.47*	*2.49*	*2.45*	*82.*	*Engagements envers des non résidents*

SWITZERLAND

Regional and savings banks

Million Swiss francs

SUISSE

Banques régionales et caisses d'épargne

Millions de francs suisses

	1983	1984	1985	1986	1987	1988	1989	1990	1991	1992	
INCOME STATEMENT											**COMPTE DE RESULTATS**
1. Interest income	2737	2886	3102	3319	3460	3666	4306	5606	6085	6053	1. Produits financiers
2. Interest expenses	2050	2168	2334	2494	2603	2708	3276	4402	4707	4677	2. Frais financiers
3. Net interest income	687	718	768	825	857	958	1030	1204	1378	1376	3. Produits financiers nets
4. Non-interest income (net)	213	242	272	303	386	327	370	418	446	549	4. Produits non financiers (nets)
5. Gross income	900	960	1040	1128	1243	1285	1400	1622	1824	1925	5. Résultat brut
6. Operating expenses	517	548	596	662	700	755	803	859	873	871	6. Frais d'exploitation
7. Net income	383	412	444	466	543	530	597	763	951	1054	7. Résultat net
8. Provisions (net)	121	138	152	163	230	201	252	411	596	704	8. Provisions (nettes)
9. Profit before tax	262	274	292	303	313	329	345	352	355	350	9. Bénéfices avant impôt
10. Income tax	81	82	87	87	90	90	91	92	87	87	10. Impôt
11. Profit after tax	181	192	205	216	223	239	254	260	268	263	11. Bénéfices après impôt
12. Distributed profit	102	109	114	122	128	137	149	153	155	149	12. Bénéfices distribués
13. Retained profit	79	83	91	94	95	102	105	107	113	114	13. Bénéfices mis en réserve
Memoranda											*Pour mémoire*
14. *Staff costs*	*351*	*370*	*399*	*435*	*456*	*489*	*519*	*553*	*566*	*558*	14. *Frais de personnel*
15. *Provisions on loans*	*..*	*..*	*..*	*..*	*..*	*..*	*..*	*..*	*..*	*..*	15. *Provisions sur prêts*
16. *Provisions on securities*	*..*	*..*	*..*	*..*	*..*	*..*	*..*	*..*	*..*	*..*	16. *Provisions sur titres*
BALANCE SHEET											**BILAN**
Assets											**Actif**
17. Cash & balance with Central bank	1277	1306	1370	1452	1543	1143	1108	1112	1119	1142	17. Caisse & solde auprès de la Banque centrale
18. Interbank deposits	3734	3531	3896	4384	4625	4141	4382	4303	3841	4185	18. Dépôts interbancaires
19. Loans	43557	47279	50924	55236	60738	67342	73364	78230	77898	75047	19. Prêts
20. Securities	5368	5682	5921	6252	6628	7045	6725	6665	6464	6120	20. Valeurs mobilières
21. Other assets	1979	2156	2277	2297	2548	2743	3028	3284	3418	3447	21. Autres actifs
Liabilities											**Passif**
22. Capital & reserves	2888	3059	3192	3499	3767	4000	4193	4369	4456	4435	22. Capital et réserves
23. Borrowing from Central bank	275	381	455	616	586	236	143	111	439	50	23. Emprunts auprès de la Banque centrale
24. Interbank deposits	1494	1864	2350	2830	3622	4572	5376	6975	4868	3823	24. Dépôts interbancaires
25. Non-bank deposits	32411	34164	35909	38035	41198	44577	46076	45037	44756	43445	25. Dépôts non bancaires
26. Bonds	16644	18110	19903	22006	23963	25833	29091	32677	33547	33125	26. Obligations
27. Other liabilities	2202	2376	2579	2635	2946	3195	3727	4425	4675	5063	27. Autres engagements
Balance sheet total											**Total du bilan**
28. End-year total	55914	59954	64388	69621	76082	82414	88607	93595	92741	89941	28. En fin d'exercice
29. Average total	54048	57934	62171	67004	72851	79248	85511	91101	93168	91341	29. Moyen
Memoranda											*Pour mémoire*
30. *Short-term securities*	*222*	*254*	*241*	*203*	*167*	*152*	*172*	*152*	*142*	*109*	30. *Titres à court terme*
31. *Bonds*	*4887*	*5149*	*5333*	*5664*	*6016*	*6425*	*5994*	*5953*	*5676*	*5359*	31. *Obligations*
32. *Shares and participations*	*259*	*279*	*347*	*385*	*446*	*468*	*559*	*560*	*646*	*652*	32. *Actions et participations*
33. *Claims on non-residents*	*767*	*821*	*1002*	*1051*	*1049*	*994*	*1018*	*1032*	*834*	*738*	33. *Créances sur des non résidents*
34. *Liabilities to non-residents*	*760*	*783*	*862*	*885*	*971*	*1032*	*1013*	*963*	*892*	*990*	34. *Engagements envers des non résidents*
SUPPLEMENTARY INFORMATION											**RENSEIGNEMENTS COMPLEMENTAIRES**
35. Number of institutions	217	217	216	215	214	213	210	204	189	174	35. Nombre d'institutions
36. Number of branches	1086	1106	1111	640	658	672	664	654	637	602	36. Nombre de succursales
37. Number of employees (x 1000)	6.9	7.1	7.4	7.7	8.0	8.2	8.4	8.5	8.2	7.9	37. Nombre de salariés (x 1000)

SWITZERLAND

Regional and savings banks

SUISSE

Banques régionales et caisses d'épargne

Per cent — *Pourcentage*

INCOME STATEMENT ANALYSIS — ANALYSE DU COMPTE DE RESULTATS

		1983	1984	1985	1986	1987	1988	1989	1990	1991	1992		
% of average balance sheet total													**% du total moyen du bilan**
38.	Interest income	5.06	4.98	4.99	4.95	4.75	4.63	5.04	6.15	6.53	6.63	38.	Produits financiers
39.	Interest expenses	3.79	3.74	3.75	3.72	3.57	3.42	3.83	4.83	5.05	5.12	39.	Frais financiers
40.	Net interest income	1.27	1.24	1.24	1.23	1.18	1.21	1.20	1.32	1.48	1.51	40.	Produits financiers nets
41.	Non-interest income (net)	0.39	0.42	0.44	0.45	0.53	0.41	0.43	0.46	0.48	0.60	41.	Produits non financiers (nets)
42.	Gross income	1.67	1.66	1.67	1.68	1.71	1.62	1.64	1.78	1.96	2.11	42.	Résultat brut
43.	Operating expenses	0.96	0.95	0.96	0.99	0.96	0.95	0.94	0.94	0.94	0.95	43.	Frais d'exploitation
44.	Net income	0.71	0.71	0.71	0.70	0.75	0.67	0.70	0.84	1.02	1.15	44.	Résultat net
45.	Provisions (net)	0.22	0.24	0.24	0.24	0.32	0.25	0.29	0.45	0.64	0.77	45.	Provisions (nettes)
46.	Profit before tax	0.48	0.47	0.47	0.45	0.43	0.42	0.40	0.39	0.38	0.38	46.	Bénéfices avant impôt
47.	Income tax	0.15	0.14	0.14	0.13	0.12	0.11	0.11	0.10	0.09	0.10	47.	Impôt
48.	Profit after tax	0.33	0.33	0.33	0.32	0.31	0.30	0.30	0.29	0.29	0.29	48.	Bénéfices après impôt
49.	Distributed profit	0.19	0.19	0.18	0.18	0.18	0.17	0.17	0.17	0.17	0.16	49.	Bénéfices distribués
50.	Retained profit	0.15	0.14	0.15	0.14	0.13	0.13	0.12	0.12	0.12	0.12	50.	Bénéfices mis en réserve
51.	Staff costs	0.65	0.64	0.64	0.65	0.63	0.62	0.61	0.61	0.61	0.61	51.	Frais de personnel
52.	Provisions on loans	..	..	..	..	..	..	..	..	..	..	52.	Provisions sur prêts
53.	Provisions on securities	..	..	..	..	..	..	..	..	..	..	53.	Provisions sur titres
% of gross income													**% du total du résultat brut**
54.	Net interest income	76.33	74.79	73.85	73.14	68.95	74.55	73.57	74.23	75.55	71.48	54.	Produits financiers nets
55.	Non-interest income (net)	23.67	25.21	26.15	26.86	31.05	25.45	26.43	25.77	24.45	28.52	55.	Produits non financiers (nets)
56.	Operating expenses	57.44	57.08	57.31	58.69	56.32	58.75	57.36	52.96	47.86	45.25	56.	Frais d'exploitation
57.	Net income	42.56	42.92	42.69	41.31	43.68	41.25	42.64	47.04	52.14	54.75	57.	Résultat net
58.	Provisions (net)	13.44	14.38	14.62	14.45	18.50	15.64	18.00	25.34	32.68	36.57	58.	Provisions (nettes)
59.	Profit before tax	29.11	28.54	28.08	26.86	25.18	25.60	24.64	21.70	19.46	18.18	59.	Bénéfices avant impôt
60.	Income tax	9.00	8.54	8.37	7.71	7.24	7.00	6.50	5.67	4.77	4.52	60.	Impôt
61.	Profit after tax	20.11	20.00	19.71	19.15	17.94	18.60	18.14	16.03	14.69	13.66	61.	Bénéfices après impôt
62.	Staff costs	39.00	38.54	38.37	38.56	36.69	38.05	37.07	34.09	31.03	28.99	62.	Frais de personnel
% of net income													**% du total du résultat net**
63.	Provisions (net)	31.59	33.50	34.23	34.98	42.36	37.92	42.21	53.87	62.67	66.79	63.	Provisions (nettes)
64.	Profit before tax	68.41	66.50	65.77	65.02	57.64	62.08	57.79	46.13	37.33	33.21	64.	Bénéfices avant impôt
65.	Income tax	21.15	19.90	19.59	18.67	16.57	16.98	15.24	12.06	9.15	8.25	65.	Impôt
66.	Profit after tax	47.26	46.60	46.17	46.35	41.07	45.09	42.55	34.08	28.18	24.95	66.	Bénéfices après impôt

SWITZERLAND

Regional and savings banks

SUISSE

Banques régionales et caisses d'épargne

Per cent — *Pourcentage*

BALANCE SHEET ANALYSIS — ANALYSE DU BILAN

% of year-end balance sheet total — % du total du bilan en fin d'exercice

	1983	1984	1985	1986	1987	1988	1989	1990	1991	1992	
Assets											**Actif**
67. Cash & balance with Central bank	2.28	2.18	2.13	2.09	2.03	1.39	1.25	1.19	1.21	1.27	67. Caisse & solde auprès de la Banque centrale
68. Interbank deposits	6.68	5.89	6.05	6.30	6.08	5.02	4.95	4.60	4.14	4.65	68. Dépôts interbancaires
69. Loans	77.90	78.86	79.09	79.34	79.83	81.71	82.80	83.58	84.00	83.44	69. Prêts
70. Securities	9.60	9.48	9.20	8.98	8.71	8.55	7.59	7.12	6.97	6.80	70. Valeurs mobilières
71. Other assets	3.54	3.60	3.54	3.30	3.35	3.33	3.42	3.51	3.69	3.83	71. Autres actifs
Liabilities											**Passif**
72. Capital & reserves	5.17	5.10	4.96	5.03	4.95	4.85	4.73	4.67	4.80	4.93	72. Capital et réserves
73. Borrowing from Central bank	0.49	0.64	0.71	0.88	0.77	0.29	0.16	0.12	0.47	0.06	73. Emprunts auprès de la Banque centrale
74. Interbank deposits	2.67	3.11	3.65	4.06	4.76	5.55	6.07	7.45	5.25	4.25	74. Dépôts interbancaires
75. Non-bank deposits	57.97	56.98	55.77	54.63	54.15	54.09	52.00	48.12	48.26	48.30	75. Dépôts non bancaires
76. Bonds	29.77	30.21	30.91	31.61	31.50	31.35	32.83	34.91	36.17	36.83	76. Obligations
77. Other liabilities	3.94	3.96	4.01	3.78	3.87	3.88	4.21	4.73	5.04	5.63	77. Autres engagements
Memoranda											***Pour mémoire***
78. Short-term securities	*0.40*	*0.42*	*0.37*	*0.29*	*0.22*	*0.18*	*0.19*	*0.16*	*0.15*	*0.12*	*78. Titres à court terme*
79. Bonds	*8.74*	*8.59*	*8.28*	*8.14*	*7.91*	*7.80*	*6.76*	*6.36*	*6.12*	*5.96*	*79. Obligations*
80. Shares and participations	*0.46*	*0.47*	*0.54*	*0.55*	*0.59*	*0.57*	*0.63*	*0.60*	*0.70*	*0.72*	*80. Actions et participations*
81. Claims on non-residents	*1.37*	*1.37*	*1.56*	*1.51*	*1.38*	*1.21*	*1.15*	*1.10*	*0.90*	*0.82*	*81. Créances sur des non résidents*
82. Liabilities to non-residents	*1.36*	*1.31*	*1.34*	*1.27*	*1.28*	*1.25*	*1.14*	*1.03*	*0.96*	*1.10*	*82. Engagements envers des non résidents*

SWITZERLAND

Loan associations and agricultural co-operative banks

Million Swiss francs

SUISSE

Caisses de crédit mutuel et banques mutualistes agricoles

Millions de francs suisses

	1983	1984	1985	1986	1987	1988	1989	1990	1991	1992	
INCOME STATEMENT											**COMPTE DE RESULTATS**
1. Interest income	804	873	960	1059	1129	1209	1422	1906	2280	2504	1. Produits financiers
2. Interest expenses	640	692	761	844	901	955	1137	1567	1878	2070	2. Frais financiers
3. Net interest income	164	181	199	215	228	254	285	339	402	434	3. Produits financiers nets
4. Non-interest income (net)	28	34	39	44	49	55	63	81	96	128	4. Produits non financiers (nets)
5. Gross income	192	215	238	259	277	309	348	420	498	562	5. Résultat brut
6. Operating expenses	113	128	146	166	183	203	230	259	291	325	6. Frais d'exploitation
7. Net income	79	87	92	93	94	106	118	161	207	237	7. Résultat net
8. Provisions (net)	24	30	36	40	42	53	64	106	146	172	8. Provisions (nettes)
9. Profit before tax	55	57	56	53	52	53	54	55	61	65	9. Bénéfices avant impôt
10. Income tax	15	16	16	16	15	16	15	18	18	21	10. Impôt
11. Profit after tax	40	41	40	37	37	37	39	37	43	44	11. Bénéfices après impôt
12. Distributed profit	3	4	4	4	4	4	5	5	5	5	12. Bénéfices distribués
13. Retained profit	37	37	36	33	33	33	34	32	38	39	13. Bénéfices mis en réserve
Memoranda											*Pour mémoire*
14. Staff costs	62	70	80	91	101	111	125	139	158	173	14. Frais de personnel
15. Provisions on loans	..	..	..	..	..	..	..	..	..	..	15. Provisions sur prêts
16. Provisions on securities	..	..	..	..	..	..	..	..	..	..	16. Provisions sur titres
BALANCE SHEET											**BILAN**
Assets											**Actif**
17. Cash & balance with Central bank	270	274	297	316	353	347	355	360	389	431	17. Caisse & solde auprès de la Banque centrale
18. Interbank deposits	2814	2888	2972	3305	3747	3907	3975	4266	4700	4967	18. Dépôts interbancaires
19. Loans	13429	14972	16668	18515	20310	22773	25672	28028	30286	32429	19. Prêts
20. Securities	127	135	143	166	168	204	223	229	229	244	20. Valeurs mobilières
21. Other assets	508	594	667	746	809	878	999	1159	1273	1368	21. Autres actifs
Liabilities											**Passif**
22. Capital & reserves	616	655	695	733	770	807	845	885	926	964	22. Capital et réserves
23. Borrowing from Central bank	-	-	-	-	-	-	-	18	20	13	23. Emprunts auprès de la Banque centrale
24. Interbank deposits	331	465	703	1153	1414	1627	2176	2352	2301	2260	24. Dépôts interbancaires
25. Non-bank deposits	12177	13241	14254	15460	17089	19034	19953	20386	21844	23487	25. Dépôts non bancaires
26. Bonds	3573	4010	4546	5121	5501	5968	7443	9301	10439	11229	26. Obligations
27. Other liabilities	451	492	549	581	612	674	808	1101	1347	1485	27. Autres engagements
Balance sheet total											**Total du bilan**
28. End-year total	17148	18863	20747	23048	25387	28109	31225	34042	36876	39438	28. En fin d'exercice
29. Average total	16385	18006	19805	21898	24217	26748	29667	32634	35459	38157	29. Moyen
Memoranda											*Pour mémoire*
30. Short-term securities	..	5	7	11	12	18	24	28	29	28	30. Titres à court terme
31. Bonds	13	15	21	20	21	18	18	20	17	20	31. Obligations
32. Shares and participations	115	115	115	135	135	167	181	181	183	197	32. Actions et participations
33. Claims on non-residents	..	..	..	..	..	..	..	..	..	..	33. Créances sur des non résidents
34. Liabilities to non-residents	..	..	..	..	..	..	..	..	..	..	34. Engagements envers des non résidents
SUPPLEMENTARY INFORMATION											**RENSEIGNEMENTS COMPLEMENTAIRES**
35. Number of institutions	2	2	2	2	2	2	2	2	2	2	35. Nombre d'institutions
36. Number of branches	1245	1251	1281	1243	1242	1241	1229	1213	1192	1169	36. Nombre de succursales
37. Number of employees (x 1000)	2.2	2.3	2.4	2.6	2.7	2.8	3.0	2.7	2.6	2.6	37. Nombre de salariés (x 1000)

SWITZERLAND

SUISSE

Loan associations and agricultural co-operative banks

Caisses de crédit mutuel et banques mutualistes agricoles

	1983	1984	1985	1986	1987	1988	1989	1990	1991	1992		Pourcentage
Per cent												
INCOME STATEMENT ANALYSIS												**ANALYSE DU COMPTE DE RESULTATS**
% of average balance sheet total												**% du total moyen du bilan**
38. Interest income	4.91	4.85	4.85	4.84	4.66	4.52	4.79	5.84	6.43	6.56	38.	Produits financiers
39. Interest expenses	3.91	3.84	3.84	3.85	3.72	3.57	3.83	4.80	5.30	5.42	39.	Frais financiers
40. Net interest income	1.00	1.01	1.00	0.98	0.94	0.95	0.96	1.04	1.13	1.14	40.	Produits financiers nets
41. Non-interest income (net)	0.17	0.19	0.20	0.20	0.20	0.21	0.21	0.25	0.27	0.34	41.	Produits non financiers (nets)
42. Gross income	1.17	1.19	1.20	1.18	1.14	1.16	1.17	1.29	1.40	1.47	42.	Résultat brut
43. Operating expenses	0.69	0.71	0.74	0.76	0.76	0.76	0.78	0.79	0.82	0.85	43.	Frais d'exploitation
44. Net income	0.48	0.48	0.46	0.42	0.39	0.40	0.40	0.49	0.58	0.62	44.	Résultat net
45. Provisions (net)	0.15	0.17	0.18	0.18	0.17	0.20	0.22	0.32	0.41	0.45	45.	Provisions (nettes)
46. Profit before tax	0.34	0.32	0.28	0.24	0.21	0.20	0.18	0.17	0.17	0.17	46.	Bénéfices avant impôt
47. Income tax	0.09	0.09	0.08	0.07	0.06	0.06	0.05	0.06	0.05	0.06	47.	Impôt
48. Profit after tax	0.24	0.23	0.20	0.17	0.15	0.14	0.13	0.11	0.12	0.12	48.	Bénéfices après impôt
49. Distributed profit	0.02	0.02	0.02	0.02	0.02	0.01	0.02	0.02	0.01	0.01	49.	Bénéfices distribués
50. Retained profit	0.23	0.21	0.18	0.15	0.14	0.12	0.11	0.10	0.11	0.10	50.	Bénéfices mis en réserve
51. Staff costs	0.38	0.39	0.40	0.42	0.42	0.41	0.42	0.43	0.45	0.45	51.	Frais de personnel
52. Provisions on loans	..	..	..	..	..	..	..	..	..	..	52.	Provisions sur prêts
53. Provisions on securities	..	..	..	..	..	..	..	..	..	..	53.	Provisions sur titres
% of gross income												**% du total du résultat brut**
54. Net interest income	85.42	84.19	83.61	83.01	82.31	82.20	81.90	80.71	80.72	77.22	54.	Produits financiers nets
55. Non-interest income (net)	14.58	15.81	16.39	16.99	17.69	17.80	18.10	19.29	19.28	22.78	55.	Produits non financiers (nets)
56. Operating expenses	58.85	59.53	61.34	64.09	66.06	65.70	66.09	61.67	58.43	57.83	56.	Frais d'exploitation
57. Net income	41.15	40.47	38.66	35.91	33.94	34.30	33.91	38.33	41.57	42.17	57.	Résultat net
58. Provisions (net)	12.50	13.95	15.13	15.44	15.16	17.15	18.39	25.24	29.32	30.60	58.	Provisions (nettes)
59. Profit before tax	28.65	26.51	23.53	20.46	18.77	17.15	15.52	13.10	12.25	11.57	59.	Bénéfices avant impôt
60. Income tax	7.81	7.44	6.72	6.18	5.42	5.18	4.31	4.29	3.61	3.74	60.	Impôt
61. Profit after tax	20.83	19.07	16.81	14.29	13.36	11.97	11.21	8.81	8.63	7.83	61.	Bénéfices après impôt
62. Staff costs	32.29	32.56	33.61	35.14	36.46	35.92	35.92	33.10	31.73	30.78	62.	Frais de personnel
% of net income												**% du total du résultat net**
63. Provisions (net)	30.38	34.48	39.13	43.01	44.68	50.00	54.24	65.84	70.53	72.57	63.	Provisions (nettes)
64. Profit before tax	69.62	65.52	60.87	56.99	55.32	50.00	45.76	34.16	29.47	27.43	64.	Bénéfices avant impôt
65. Income tax	18.99	18.39	17.39	17.20	15.96	15.09	12.71	11.18	8.70	8.86	65.	Impôt
66. Profit after tax	50.63	47.13	43.48	39.78	39.36	34.91	33.05	22.98	20.77	18.57	66.	Bénéfices après impôt

SWITZERLAND

Loan associations and agricultural co-operative banks

SUISSE

Caisses de crédit mutuel et banques mutualistes agricoles

Per cent / *Pourcentage*

BALANCE SHEET ANALYSIS / **ANALYSE DU BILAN**

% of year-end balance sheet total / % du total du bilan en fin d'exercice

	1983	1984	1985	1986	1987	1988	1989	1990	1991	1992		
Assets											**Actif**	
67. Cash & balance with Central bank	1.57	1.45	1.43	1.37	1.39	1.23	1.14	1.06	1.05	1.09	67.	Caisse & solde auprès de la Banque centrale
68. Interbank deposits	16.41	15.31	14.32	14.34	14.76	13.90	12.73	12.53	12.75	12.59	68.	Dépôts interbancaires
69. Loans	78.31	79.37	80.34	80.33	80.00	81.02	82.22	82.33	82.13	82.23	69.	Prêts
70. Securities	0.74	0.72	0.69	0.72	0.66	0.73	0.71	0.67	0.62	0.62	70.	Valeurs mobilières
71. Other assets	2.96	3.15	3.21	3.24	3.19	3.12	3.20	3.40	3.45	3.47	71.	Autres actifs
Liabilities											**Passif**	
72. Capital & reserves	3.59	3.47	3.35	3.18	3.03	2.87	2.71	2.60	2.51	2.44	72.	Capital et réserves
73. Borrowing from Central bank	-	-	-	-	-	-	-	0.05	0.05	0.03	73.	Emprunts auprès de la Banque centrale
74. Interbank deposits	1.93	2.47	3.39	5.00	5.57	5.79	6.97	6.91	6.24	5.73	74.	Dépôts interbancaires
75. Non-bank deposits	71.01	70.20	68.70	67.08	67.31	67.71	63.90	59.88	59.24	59.55	75.	Dépôts non bancaires
76. Bonds	20.84	21.26	21.91	22.22	21.67	21.23	23.84	27.32	28.31	28.47	76.	Obligations
77. Other liabilities	2.63	2.61	2.65	2.52	2.41	2.40	2.59	3.23	3.65	3.77	77.	Autres engagements
Memoranda											*Pour mémoire*	
78. Short-term securities	..	0.03	0.03	0.05	0.05	0.06	0.08	0.08	0.08	0.07	78.	Titres à court terme
79. Bonds	0.08	0.08	0.10	0.09	0.08	0.06	0.06	0.06	0.05	0.05	79.	Obligations
80. Shares and participations	0.67	0.61	0.55	0.59	0.53	0.59	0.58	0.53	0.50	0.50	80.	Actions et participations
81. Claims on non-residents	..	..	..	..	..	..	..	..	..	..	81.	Créances sur des non résidents
82. Liabilities to non-residents	..	..	..	..	..	..	..	..	..	..	82.	Engagements envers des non résidents

TURKEY

Commercial banks

Billion Turkish liras

TURQUIE

Banques commerciales

Milliards de livres turques

INCOME STATEMENT / COMPTE DE RESULTATS

		1983	1984	1985	1986	1987	1988	1989	1990	1991	1992	
1.	Interest income	859	1567	2609	4317	6314	12165	20232	33243	63597	117540	Produits financiers
2.	Interest expenses	727	1325	2386	3437	4482	9177	17250	23803	42282	78163	Frais financiers
3.	Net interest income	132	242	223	880	1832	2988	2982	9440	21315	39377	Produits financiers nets
4.	Non-interest income (net)	115	180	229	185	417	1098	2854	1963	-1956	-2471	Produits non financiers (nets)
5.	Gross income	247	422	452	1065	2249	4086	5836	11403	19359	36906	Résultat brut
6.	Operating expenses	180	243	346	534	855	1658	3014	5943	10896	20146	Frais d'exploitation
7.	Net income	67	179	106	531	1394	2428	2822	5460	8463	16760	Résultat net
8.	Provisions (net)	16	36	39	128	498	841	947	1341	2430	2073	Provisions (nettes)
9.	Profit before tax	51	143	67	403	896	1587	1875	4119	6033	14687	Bénéfices avant impôt
10.	Income tax	9	25	24	50	81	185	406	637	804	2134	Impôt
11.	Profit after tax	42	118	43	353	815	1402	1469	3482	5229	12553	Bénéfices après impôt
12.	Distributed profit	17	43	54	163	321	695	762	1788	2399	3848	Bénéfices distribués
13.	Retained profit	25	75	-11	190	494	707	707	1694	2830	8705	Bénéfices mis en réserve

Memoranda / Pour mémoire

		1983	1984	1985	1986	1987	1988	1989	1990	1991	1992	
14.	Staff costs	144	202	286	433	684	1313	2420	4820	8353	15507	Frais de personnel
15.	Provisions on loans	-	-	-	119	438	654	671	861	1772	1438	Provisions sur prêts
16.	Provisions on securities	-	-	-	-	-	-	-	7	142	40	Provisions sur titres

BALANCE SHEET / BILAN

Assets / Actif

		1983	1984	1985	1986	1987	1988	1989	1990	1991	1992	
17.	Cash & balance with Central bank	492	736	1317	2143	3984	5331	7340	10349	16911	29766	Caisse & solde auprès de la Banque centrale
18.	Interbank deposits	501	1154	1615	2415	3375	8037	9733	14701	32039	85047	Dépôts interbancaires
19.	Loans	2630	3479	6080	10378	16989	24496	38904	68887	111813	206434	Prêts
20.	Securities	195	663	1458	2279	4180	6987	12476	17111	34283	60357	Valeurs mobilières
21.	Other assets	2051	2998	4395	6042	9702	16701	28229	41544	74912	128810	Autres actifs

Liabilities / Passif

		1983	1984	1985	1986	1987	1988	1989	1990	1991	1992	
22.	Capital & reserves	288	454	677	726	1407	2793	4517	6999	13635	23960	Capital et réserves
23.	Borrowing from Central bank	524	284	450	657	2033	2538	3088	3129	4013	8003	Emprunts auprès de la Banque centrale
24.	Interbank deposits	103	232	244	1375	1984	3222	4262	6837	8259	20435	Dépôts interbancaires
25.	Non-bank deposits	3336	5256	8627	14452	22128	35111	58141	88726	160595	285234	Dépôts non bancaires
26.	Bonds	12	9	7	7	7	54	389	413	704	6187	Obligations
27.	Other liabilities	1606	2794	4859	6040	10671	17834	26285	46488	82752	166595	Autres engagements

Balance sheet total / Total du bilan

		1983	1984	1985	1986	1987	1988	1989	1990	1991	1992	
28.	End-year total	5868	9029	14865	23257	38230	61552	96682	152592	269958	510414	En fin d'exercice
29.	Average total	4985	7449	11947	19061	30744	49891	79117	124637	211275	390186	Moyen

Memoranda / Pour mémoire

		1983	1984	1985	1986	1987	1988	1989	1990	1991	1992	
30.	Short-term securities	..	..	..	..	..	..	..	..	..	..	Titres à court terme
31.	Bonds	185	482	1073	1627	2611	3961	9417	12579	19296	41965	Obligations
32.	Shares and participations	117	161	257	355	706	1305	2666	4081	6370	11096	Actions et participations
33.	Claims on non-residents	51	160	26	1635	2351	6848	9208	13931	36108	81980	Créances sur des non résidents
34.	Liabilities to non-residents	45	177	36	1015	2192	3578	5040	12821	22428	55466	Engagements envers des non résidents

SUPPLEMENTARY INFORMATION / RENSEIGNEMENTS COMPLEMENTAIRES

		1983	1984	1985	1986	1987	1988	1989	1990	1991	1992	
35.	Number of institutions	44	44	48	50	51	53	53	56	56	58	Nombre d'institutions
36.	Number of branches	6272	6193	6259	6338	6407	6517	6579	6543	6463	6188	Nombre de succursales
37.	Number of employees (x 1000)	131.0	133.4	136.3	141.8	147.3	149.4	151.1	152.0	150.8	144.6	Nombre de salariés (x 1000)

TURKEY

Commercial banks

TURQUIE

Banques commerciales

Per cent — *Pourcentage*

INCOME STATEMENT ANALYSIS — ANALYSE DU COMPTE DE RESULTATS

		1983	1984	1985	1986	1987	1988	1989	1990	1991	1992		
	% of average balance sheet total												**% du total moyen du bilan**
38.	Interest income	17.23	21.04	21.84	22.65	20.54	24.38	25.57	26.67	30.10	30.12	38.	Produits financiers
39.	Interest expenses	14.58	17.79	19.97	18.03	14.58	18.39	21.80	19.10	20.01	20.03	39.	Frais financiers
40.	Net interest income	2.65	3.25	1.87	4.62	5.96	5.99	3.77	7.57	10.09	10.09	40.	Produits financiers nets
41.	Non-interest income (net)	2.31	2.42	1.92	0.97	1.36	2.20	3.61	1.57	-0.93	-0.63	41.	Produits non financiers (nets)
42.	Gross income	4.95	5.67	3.78	5.59	7.32	8.19	7.38	9.15	9.16	9.46	42.	Résultat brut
43.	Operating expenses	3.61	3.26	2.90	2.80	2.78	3.32	3.81	4.77	5.16	5.16	43.	Frais d'exploitation
44.	Net income	1.34	2.40	0.89	2.79	4.53	4.87	3.57	4.38	4.01	4.30	44.	Résultat net
45.	Provisions (net)	0.32	0.48	0.33	0.67	1.62	1.69	1.20	1.08	1.15	0.53	45.	Provisions (nettes)
46.	Profit before tax	1.02	1.92	0.56	2.11	2.91	3.18	2.37	3.30	2.86	3.76	46.	Bénéfices avant impôt
47.	Income tax	0.18	0.34	0.20	0.26	0.26	0.37	0.51	0.51	0.38	0.55	47.	Impôt
48.	Profit after tax	0.84	1.58	0.36	1.85	2.65	2.81	1.86	2.79	2.47	3.22	48.	Bénéfices après impôt
49.	Distributed profit	0.34	0.58	0.45	0.86	1.04	1.39	0.96	1.43	1.14	0.99	49.	Bénéfices distribués
50.	Retained profit	0.50	1.01	-0.09	1.00	1.61	1.42	0.89	1.36	1.34	2.23	50.	Bénéfices mis en réserve
51.	Staff costs	2.89	2.71	2.39	2.27	2.22	2.63	3.06	3.87	3.95	3.97	51.	Frais de personnel
52.	Provisions on loans	-	-	-	0.62	1.42	1.31	0.85	0.69	0.84	0.37	52.	Provisions sur prêts
53.	Provisions on securities	-	-	-	-	-	-	-	0.01	0.07	0.01	53.	Provisions sur titres
	% of gross income												**% du total du résultat brut**
54.	Net interest income	53.44	57.35	49.34	82.63	81.46	73.13	51.10	82.79	110.10	106.70	54.	Produits financiers nets
55.	Non-interest income (net)	46.56	42.65	50.66	17.37	18.54	26.87	48.90	17.21	-10.10	-6.70	55.	Produits non financiers (nets)
56.	Operating expenses	72.87	57.58	76.55	50.14	38.02	40.58	51.64	52.12	56.28	54.59	56.	Frais d'exploitation
57.	Net income	27.13	42.42	23.45	49.86	61.98	59.42	48.36	47.88	43.72	45.41	57.	Résultat net
58.	Provisions (net)	6.48	8.53	8.63	12.02	22.14	20.58	16.23	11.76	12.55	5.62	58.	Provisions (nettes)
59.	Profit before tax	20.65	33.89	14.82	37.84	39.84	38.84	32.13	36.12	31.16	39.80	59.	Bénéfices avant impôt
60.	Income tax	3.64	5.92	5.31	4.69	3.60	4.53	6.96	5.59	4.15	5.78	60.	Impôt
61.	Profit after tax	17.00	27.96	9.51	33.15	36.24	34.31	25.17	30.54	27.01	34.01	61.	Bénéfices après impôt
62.	Staff costs	58.30	47.87	63.27	40.66	30.41	32.13	41.47	42.27	43.15	42.02	62.	Frais de personnel
	% of net income												**% du total du résultat net**
63.	Provisions (net)	23.88	20.11	36.79	24.11	35.72	34.64	33.56	24.56	28.71	12.37	63.	Provisions (nettes)
64.	Profit before tax	76.12	79.89	63.21	75.89	64.28	65.36	66.44	75.44	71.29	87.63	64.	Bénéfices avant impôt
65.	Income tax	13.43	13.97	22.64	9.42	5.81	7.62	14.39	11.67	9.50	12.73	65.	Impôt
66.	Profit after tax	62.69	65.92	40.57	66.48	58.46	57.74	52.06	63.77	61.79	74.90	66.	Bénéfices après impôt

TURKEY

Commercial banks

TURQUIE

Banques commerciales

Per cent — *Pourcentage*

BALANCE SHEET ANALYSIS — **ANALYSE DU BILAN**

% of year-end balance sheet total — **% du total du bilan en fin d'exercice**

	1983	1984	1985	1986	1987	1988	1989	1990	1991	1992
Assets										
67. Cash & balance with Central bank	8.38	8.15	8.86	9.21	10.42	8.66	7.59	6.78	6.26	5.83
68. Interbank deposits	8.54	12.78	10.86	10.38	8.83	13.06	10.07	9.63	11.87	16.66
69. Loans	44.82	38.53	40.90	44.62	44.44	39.80	40.24	45.14	41.42	40.44
70. Securities	3.32	7.34	9.81	9.80	10.93	11.35	12.90	11.21	12.70	11.83
71. Other assets	34.95	33.20	29.57	25.98	25.38	27.13	29.20	27.23	27.75	25.24
Liabilities										
72. Capital & reserves	4.91	5.03	4.55	3.12	3.68	4.54	4.67	4.59	5.05	4.69
73. Borrowing from Central bank	8.93	3.15	3.03	2.82	5.32	4.12	3.19	2.05	1.49	1.57
74. Interbank deposits	1.76	2.57	1.64	5.91	5.19	5.23	4.41	4.48	3.06	4.00
75. Non-bank deposits	56.85	58.21	58.04	62.14	57.88	57.04	60.14	58.15	59.49	55.88
76. Bonds	0.20	0.10	0.05	0.03	0.02	0.09	0.40	0.27	0.26	1.21
77. Other liabilities	27.37	30.94	32.69	25.97	27.91	28.97	27.19	30.47	30.65	32.64
Memoranda										
78. Short-term securities	*3.15*	*5.34*	*7.22*	*7.00*	*6.83*	*6.44*	*9.74*	*8.24*	*7.15*	*8.22*
79. Bonds	*1.99*	*1.78*	*1.73*	*1.53*	*1.85*	*2.12*	*2.76*	*2.67*	*2.36*	*2.17*
80. Shares and participations	..	..	..	..	..	..	..	..	..	..
81. Claims on non-residents	*0.87*	*1.77*	*0.17*	*7.03*	*6.15*	*11.13*	*9.52*	*9.13*	*13.38*	*16.06*
82. Liabilities to non-residents	*0.77*	*1.96*	*0.24*	*4.36*	*5.73*	*5.81*	*5.21*	*8.40*	*8.31*	*10.87*

Actif
67. Caisse & solde auprès de la Banque centrale
68. Dépôts interbancaires
69. Prêts
70. Valeurs mobilières
71. Autres actifs

Passif
72. Capital et réserves
73. Emprunts auprès de la Banque centrale
74. Dépôts interbancaires
75. Dépôts non bancaires
76. Obligations
77. Autres engagements

Pour mémoire
78. Titres à court terme
79. Obligations
80. Actions et participations
81. Créances sur des non résidents
82. Engagements envers des non résidents

Change in methodology

- Iller Bankasi, although not being a full commercial bank, is included in the data until end-1988.

- Until 1986, "Interest income" (item 1) includes interest paid by the Central bank on required reserves for Turkish lira denominated deposits.

- "Operating expenses" (item 6) do not include rents for the period 1981-85.

- Data include, as from 1986, the foreign branches of domestic banks.

Changement méthodologique :

- Jusqu'en fin 1988, Iller Bankasi, bien que celle-ci ne soit pas à tous égards une banque commerciale, est incluse dans les données.

- Jusqu'en 1986 les "Produits financiers" (poste 1) couvrent la rémunération par la Banque centrale des réserves obligatoires assises sur les dépôts en livres turques.

- Les "Frais d'exploitation" (poste 6) ne comprennent pas les loyers pour la période 1981-85.

- A compter de 1986 les données incluent les filiales étrangères des banques domestiques.

UNITED KINGDOM
Commercial banks

ROYAUME-UNI
Banques commerciales

Million pounds sterling / *Millions de livres sterling*

		1984	1985	1986	1987	1988	1989	1990	1991	1992	
INCOME STATEMENT											**COMPTE DE RESULTATS**
1.	Interest income	31359	31941	31684	34363	39998	56101	63140	57737	52975	Produits financiers
2.	Interest expenses	22665	22544	21607	23124	27121	41736	48286	42199	36910	Frais financiers
3.	Net interest income	8694	9397	10077	11239	12877	14365	14854	15538	16065	Produits financiers nets
4.	Non-interest income (net)	4807	4951	5750	6710	7300	8772	9474	10645	11582	Produits non financiers (nets)
5.	Gross income	13501	14348	15827	17949	20177	23137	24328	26183	27647	Résultat brut
6.	Operating expenses	9025	9378	10319	11583	13159	14977	16021	17197	17717	Frais d'exploitation
7.	Net income	4476	4970	5508	6366	7018	8160	8307	8986	9930	Résultat net
8.	Provisions (net)	1956	1676	1733	5382	1228	7325	4766	6885	8134	Provisions (nettes)
9.	Profit before tax	2520	3294	3775	984	5790	835	3541	2101	1796	Bénéfices avant impôt
10.	Income tax	1356	1488	1345	763	2113	550	1630	872	1018	Impôt
11.	Profit after tax	1164	1806	2430	221	3677	285	1911	1229	778	Bénéfices après impôt
12.	Distributed profit	369	450	576	710	949	1201	1262	1273	1238	Bénéfices distribués
13.	Retained profit	795	1356	1854	-489	2728	-916	649	-44	-460	Bénéfices mis en réserve
	Memoranda										*Pour mémoire*
14.	Staff costs	5397	5612	6167	6749	7719	8658	9114	9519	9839	Frais de personnel
15.	Provisions on loans	..	..	..	..	..	..	..	..	..	Provisions sur prêts
16.	Provisions on securities	..	..	..	..	..	..	..	..	..	Provisions sur titres
BALANCE SHEET											**BILAN**
	Assets										**Actif**
17.	Cash & balance with Central bank	5984	5879	6091	5864	6107	7433	7249	7057	7594	Caisse & solde auprès de la Banque centrale
18.	Interbank deposits	66411	62873	70466	72308	77191	79191	80039	79774	89174	Dépôts interbancaires
19.	Loans	181924	179618	191201	219420	257865	306456	319817	322240	339391	Prêts
20.	Securities	17281	20347	23878	28987	27986	34189	38401	45448	63022	Valeurs mobilières
21.	Other assets	31016	33133	42994	43463	52112	65416	69913	77832	90086	Autres actifs
	Liabilities										**Passif**
22.	Capital & reserves	12099	13632	17506	19791	23833	24728	24614	24440	24639	Capital et réserves
23.	Borrowing from Central bank	–	–	–	–	–	–	–	–	–	Emprunts auprès de la Banque centrale
24.	Interbank deposits (1)	–	–	–	–	–	–	–	–	–	Dépôts interbancaires (1)
25.	Non-bank deposits	275619	269036	290594	326047	366372	429820	453145	465404	511398	Dépôts non bancaires
26.	Bonds	8364	10495	12677	11230	13941	16778	15077	16616	19356	Obligations
27.	Other liabilities	6534	8687	13853	12974	17115	21359	22583	25891	33873	Autres engagements
	Balance sheet total										**Total du bilan**
28.	End-year total	302616	301850	334630	370042	421261	492685	515419	532351	589266	En fin d'exercice
29.	Average total	286369	302233	318240	352336	395652	456973	504052	523885	560809	Moyen
	Memoranda										*Pour mémoire*
30.	Short-term securities	4237	5639	5993	8709	10718	15405	16403	17458	23829	Titres à court terme
31.	Bonds	..	..	..	..	..	..	..	..	..	Obligations
32.	Shares and participations	..	..	..	..	..	..	..	..	..	Actions et participations
33.	Claims on non-residents	..	..	..	..	..	..	..	..	..	Créances sur des non résidents
34.	Liabilities to non-residents	..	..	..	..	..	..	..	..	..	Engagements envers des non résidents
SUPPLEMENTARY INFORMATION											**RENSEIGNEMENTS COMPLÉMENTAIRES**
35.	Number of institutions	48	54	53	53	52	49	47	41	39	Nombre d'institutions
36.	Number of branches	13683	13615	13332	13813	13702	13467	12994	12306	11598	Nombre de succursales
37.	Number of employees (x 1000)	335.9	340.0	350.0	374.6	402.6	414.2	411.5	399.9	375.8	Nombre de salariés (x 1000)

UNITED KINGDOM

Commercial banks

ROYAUME-UNI

Banques commerciales

Per cent / *Pourcentage*

INCOME STATEMENT ANALYSIS / ANALYSE DU COMPTE DE RESULTATS

		1984	1985	1986	1987	1988	1989	1990	1991	1992		
	% of average balance sheet total										**% du total moyen du bilan**	
38.	Interest income	10.95	10.57	9.96	9.75	10.11	12.28	12.53	11.02	9.45	Produits financiers	38.
39.	Interest expenses	7.91	7.46	6.79	6.56	6.85	9.13	9.58	8.06	6.58	Frais financiers	39.
40.	Net interest income	3.04	3.11	3.17	3.19	3.25	3.14	2.95	2.97	2.86	Produits financiers nets	40.
41.	Non-interest income (net)	1.68	1.64	1.81	1.90	1.85	1.92	1.88	2.03	2.07	Produits non financiers (nets)	41.
42.	Gross income	4.71	4.75	4.97	5.09	5.10	5.06	4.83	5.00	4.93	Résultat brut	42.
43.	Operating expenses	3.15	3.10	3.24	3.29	3.33	3.28	3.18	3.28	3.16	Frais d'exploitation	43.
44.	Net income	1.56	1.64	1.73	1.81	1.77	1.79	1.65	1.72	1.77	Résultat net	44.
45.	Provisions (net)	0.68	0.55	0.54	1.53	0.31	1.60	0.95	1.31	1.45	Provisions (nettes)	45.
46.	Profit before tax	0.88	1.09	1.19	0.28	1.46	0.18	0.70	0.40	0.32	Bénéfices avant impôt	46.
47.	Income tax	0.47	0.49	0.42	0.22	0.53	0.12	0.32	0.17	0.18	Impôt	47.
48.	Profit after tax	0.41	0.60	0.76	0.06	0.93	0.06	0.38	0.23	0.14	Bénéfices après impôt	48.
49.	Distributed profit	0.13	0.15	0.18	0.20	0.24	0.26	0.25	0.24	0.22	Bénéfices distribués	49.
50.	Retained profit	0.28	0.45	0.58	-0.14	0.69	-0.20	0.13	-0.01	-0.08	Bénéfices mis en réserve	50.
51.	Staff costs	1.88	1.86	1.94	1.92	1.95	1.89	1.81	1.82	1.75	Frais de personnel	51.
52.	Provisions on loans	:	:	:	:	:	:	:	:	:	Provisions sur prêts	52.
53.	Provisions on securities	:	:	:	:	:	:	:	:	:	Provisions sur titres	53.
	% of gross income										**% du total du résultat brut**	
54.	Net interest income	64.40	65.49	63.67	62.62	63.82	62.09	61.06	59.34	58.11	Produits financiers nets	54.
55.	Non-interest income (net)	35.60	34.51	36.33	37.38	36.18	37.91	38.94	40.66	41.89	Produits non financiers (nets)	55.
56.	Operating expenses	66.85	65.36	65.20	64.53	65.22	64.73	65.85	65.68	64.08	Frais d'exploitation	56.
57.	Net income	33.15	34.64	34.80	35.47	34.78	35.27	34.15	34.32	35.92	Résultat net	57.
58.	Provisions (net)	14.49	11.68	10.95	29.98	6.09	31.66	19.59	26.30	29.42	Provisions (nettes)	58.
59.	Profit before tax	18.67	22.96	23.85	5.48	28.70	3.61	14.56	8.02	6.50	Bénéfices avant impôt	59.
60.	Income tax	10.04	10.37	8.50	4.25	10.47	2.38	6.70	3.33	3.68	Impôt	60.
61.	Profit after tax	8.62	12.59	15.35	1.23	18.22	1.23	7.86	4.69	2.81	Bénéfices après impôt	61.
62.	Staff costs	39.97	39.11	38.97	37.60	38.26	37.42	37.46	36.36	35.59	Frais de personnel	62.
	% of net income										**% du total du résultat net**	
63.	Provisions (net)	43.70	33.72	31.46	84.54	17.50	89.77	57.37	76.62	81.91	Provisions (nettes)	63.
64.	Profit before tax	56.30	66.28	68.54	15.46	82.50	10.23	42.63	23.38	18.09	Bénéfices avant impôt	64.
65.	Income tax	30.29	29.94	24.42	11.99	30.11	6.74	19.62	9.70	10.25	Impôt	65.
66.	Profit after tax	26.01	36.34	44.12	3.47	52.39	3.49	23.00	13.68	7.83	Bénéfices après impôt	66.

UNITED KINGDOM

Commercial banks

Per cent

BALANCE SHEET ANALYSIS

% of year-end balance sheet total

	1984	1985	1986	1987	1988	1989	1990	1991	1992
Assets									
67. Cash & balance with Central bank	1.98	1.95	1.82	1.58	1.45	1.51	1.41	1.33	1.29
68. Interbank deposits	21.95	20.83	21.06	19.54	18.32	16.07	15.53	14.99	15.13
69. Loans	60.12	59.51	57.14	59.30	61.21	62.20	62.05	60.53	57.60
70. Securities	5.71	6.74	7.14	7.83	6.64	6.94	7.45	8.54	10.70
71. Other assets	10.25	10.98	12.85	11.75	12.37	13.28	13.56	14.62	15.29
Liabilities									
72. Capital & reserves	4.00	4.52	5.23	5.35	5.66	5.02	4.78	4.59	4.18
73. Borrowing from Central bank	–	–	–	–	–	–	–	–	–
74. Interbank deposits (1)	..	..	..	..	..	..	..	..	..
75. Non-bank deposits	91.08	89.13	86.84	88.11	86.97	87.24	87.92	87.42	86.79
76. Bonds	2.76	3.48	3.79	3.03	3.31	3.41	2.93	3.12	3.28
77. Other liabilities	2.16	2.88	4.14	3.51	4.06	4.34	4.38	4.86	5.75
Memoranda									
78. Short-term securities	*1.40*	*1.87*	*1.79*	*2.35*	*2.54*	*3.13*	*3.18*	*3.28*	*4.04*
79. Bonds	..	..	..	..	..	..	..	..	..
80. Shares and participations	..	..	..	..	..	..	..	..	..
81. Claims on non-residents	..	..	..	..	..	..	..	..	..
82. Liabilities to non-residents	..	..	..	..	..	..	..	..	..

1. Included under "Non-bank deposits" (item 25 or item 75).

Notes

- Data on London clearing banks' groups (consolidated worldwide) for the years 1980-84 are included in "Bank Profitability, Statistical Supplement, Financial Statements of Banks 1982-86" (OECD, Paris, 1988). Series for this banking group have been discontinued.

Change in methodology:

- As from 1987 data include Abbey National Plc.

ROYAUME-UNI

Banques commerciales

Pourcentage

ANALYSE DU BILAN

% du total du bilan en fin d'exercice

Actif
67. Caisse & solde auprès de la Banque centrale
68. Dépôts interbancaires
69. Prêts
70. Valeurs mobilières
71. Autres actifs

Passif
72. Capital et réserves
73. Emprunts auprès de la Banque centrale
74. Dépôts interbancaires (1)
75. Dépôts non bancaires
76. Obligations
77. Autres engagements

Pour mémoire
78. Titres à court terme
79. Obligations
80. Actions et participations
81. Créances sur des non résidents
82. Engagements envers des non résidents

1. Inclus sous "Dépôts non bancaires" (poste 25 ou poste 75).

Notes

- Les chiffres relatifs aux "Grandes banques de Londres (consolidées à l'échelle mondiale)" pour les années 1980 à 1984 figurent dans "Rentabilité des banques, Supplément statistique, Comptes des banques 1982-86" (OCDE, Paris, 1988). Cette série de données a été interrompue.

Changement méthodologique :

- A compter de 1987 les données incluent Abbey National Plc.

UNITED STATES
Commercial banks

ETATS-UNIS
Banques commerciales

Million US dollars — *Millions de dollars des EU*

			1983	1984	1985	1986	1987	1988	1989	1990	1991	1992
INCOME STATEMENT		**COMPTE DE RESULTATS**										
1.	Interest income	Produits financiers	214182	249348	247047	236290	243740	270954	315724	318787	287356	253588
2.	Interest expenses	Frais financiers	143421	168470	156650	142024	144352	164254	204134	203932	166323	121045
3.	Net interest income	Produits financiers nets	70761	80878	90397	94266	99388	106700	111590	114855	121033	132543
4.	Non-interest income (net)	Produits non financiers (nets)	25563	26548	32701	39937	43003	45893	51968	55996	63133	69802
5.	Gross income	Résultat brut	96324	107426	123098	134203	142391	152593	163558	170851	184166	202345
6.	Operating expenses	Frais d'exploitation	66603	73487	81898	89628	96784	100810	107555	114994	124071	130115
7.	Net income	Résultat net	29721	33939	41200	44575	45607	51783	56003	55857	60095	72230
8.	Provisions (net)	Provisions (nettes)	10656	13753	17601	21929	37452	16998	30920	31734	34096	25807
9.	Profit before tax	Bénéfices avant impôt	19065	20186	23599	22646	8155	34785	25083	24123	25999	46423
10.	Income tax	Impôt	4098	4717	5588	5265	5387	9964	9611	7785	8218	14467
11.	Profit after tax	Bénéfices après impôt	14967	15469	18011	17381	2768	24821	15472	16338	17781	31956
12.	Distributed profit	Bénéfices distribués	7338	7606	8497	9183	10634	13190	14046	13842	14260	14125
13.	Retained profit	Bénéfices mis en réserve	7629	7863	9514	8198	-7866	11631	1426	2496	3521	17831
	Memoranda	*Pour mémoire*										
14.	Staff costs	Frais de personnel	33719	36706	39765	42617	44948	46316	48891	51442	52765	54438
15.	Provisions on loans	Provisions sur prêts	10649	13716	17535	21879	37376	16833	30811	31738	34066	25883
16.	Provisions on securities	Provisions sur titres	..	..	..	..	..	..	..	..	..	..
BALANCE SHEET		**BILAN**										
	Assets	**Actif**										
17.	Cash & balance with Central bank	Caisse & solde auprès de la Banque centrale	130632	129618	146601	168246	145135	158039	165772	167049	154177	153849
18.	Interbank deposits	Dépôts interbancaires	203959	151162	153425	165107	172428	160223	151887	121267	124216	120660
19.	Loans	Prêts	1391275	1596117	1734729	1857726	1901949	2004151	2141682	2187635	2133463	2122165
20.	Securities	Valeurs mobilières	439378	412298	477817	524840	550941	569013	598113	648749	753320	845548
21.	Other assets	Autres actifs	167769	209569	205941	208638	215392	224276	225818	243258	244011	239643
	Liabilities	**Passif**										
22.	Capital & reserves	Capital et réserves	140036	153506	168464	181097	179815	195704	203764	217501	230048	261713
23.	Borrowing from Central bank	Emprunts auprès de la Banque centrale										
24.	Interbank deposits	Dépôts interbancaires	183064	163926	163460	163398	165018	144602	144132	122878	136260	124263
25.	Non-bank deposits	Dépôts non bancaires	1652230	1790797	1944314	2106379	2158471	2274436	2390972	2508565	2533050	2554088
26.	Bonds	Obligations	9798	13100	17528	19668	20203	20042	22083	25897	26763	35408
27.	Other liabilities	Autres engagements	347885	377435	424747	454015	462338	480917	522321	493116	483067	506394
	Balance sheet total	**Total du bilan**										
28.	End-year total	En fin d'exercice	2333013	2498764	2718513	2924557	2985845	3115701	3283271	3367958	3409187	3481865
29.	Average total	Moyen	2261084	2415889	2608639	2821535	2955201	3050773	3199486	3325615	3388573	3445526
	Memoranda	*Pour mémoire*										
30.	Short-term securities	Titres à court terme	..	..	..	..	..	..	..	..	..	..
31.	Bonds	Obligations	..	..	..	..	..	..	..	..	..	..
32.	Shares and participations	Actions et participations	..	..	..	..	..	..	..	..	..	..
33.	Claims on non-residents	Créances sur des non résidents	..	..	..	..	..	..	..	..	..	..
34.	Liabilities to non-residents	Engagements envers des non résidents	..	..	..	..	..	..	..	..	..	..
SUPPLEMENTARY INFORMATION		**RENSEIGNEMENTS COMPLEMENTAIRES**										
35.	Number of institutions	Nombre d'institutions	14454	14460	14357	14130	13669	13094	12689	12319	11877	11417
36.	Number of branches	Nombre de succursales	NA	NA	NA	NA	NA	NA	NA	NA	NA	NA
37.	Number of employees (x 1000)	Nombre de salariés (x 1000)	NA	NA	NA	NA	NA	NA	NA	NA	NA	NA

UNITED STATES

Commercial banks

Per cent

INCOME STATEMENT ANALYSIS

ETATS-UNIS

Banques commerciales

Pourcentage

ANALYSE DU COMPTE DE RESULTATS

		1983	1984	1985	1986	1987	1988	1989	1990	1991	1992		
	% of average balance sheet total												**% du total moyen du bilan**
38.	Interest income	9.47	10.32	9.47	8.37	8.25	8.88	9.87	9.59	8.48	7.36	38.	Produits financiers
39.	Interest expenses	6.34	6.97	6.01	5.03	4.88	5.38	6.38	6.13	4.91	3.51	39.	Frais financiers
40.	Net interest income	3.13	3.35	3.47	3.34	3.36	3.50	3.49	3.45	3.57	3.85	40.	Produits financiers nets
41.	Non-interest income (net)	1.13	1.10	1.25	1.42	1.46	1.50	1.62	1.68	1.86	2.03	41.	Produits non financiers (nets)
42.	Gross income	4.26	4.45	4.72	4.76	4.82	5.00	5.11	5.14	5.43	5.87	42.	Résultat brut
43.	Operating expenses	2.95	3.04	3.14	3.18	3.28	3.30	3.36	3.46	3.66	3.78	43.	Frais d'exploitation
44.	Net income	1.31	1.40	1.58	1.58	1.54	1.70	1.75	1.68	1.77	2.10	44.	Résultat net
45.	Provisions (net)	0.47	0.57	0.67	0.78	1.27	0.56	0.97	0.95	1.01	0.75	45.	Provisions (nettes)
46.	Profit before tax	0.84	0.84	0.90	0.80	0.28	1.14	0.78	0.73	0.77	1.35	46.	Bénéfices avant impôt
47.	Income tax	0.18	0.20	0.21	0.19	0.18	0.33	0.30	0.23	0.24	0.42	47.	Impôt
48.	Profit after tax	0.66	0.64	0.69	0.62	0.09	0.81	0.48	0.49	0.52	0.93	48.	Bénéfices après impôt
49.	Distributed profit	0.32	0.31	0.33	0.33	0.36	0.43	0.44	0.42	0.42	0.41	49.	Bénéfices distribués
50.	Retained profit	0.34	0.33	0.36	0.29	-0.27	0.38	0.04	0.08	0.10	0.52	50.	Bénéfices mis en réserve
51.	Staff costs	1.49	1.52	1.52	1.51	1.52	1.52	1.53	1.55	1.56	1.58	51.	Frais de personnel
52.	Provisions on loans	0.47	0.57	0.67	0.78	1.26	0.55	0.96	0.95	1.01	0.75	52.	Provisions sur prêts
53.	Provisions on securities	:	:	:	:	:	:	:	:	:	:	53.	Provisions sur titres
	% of gross income												**% du total du résultat brut**
54.	Net interest income	73.46	75.29	73.43	70.24	69.80	69.92	68.23	67.23	65.72	65.50	54.	Produits financiers nets
55.	Non-interest income (net)	26.54	24.71	26.57	29.76	30.20	30.08	31.77	32.77	34.28	34.50	55.	Produits non financiers (nets)
56.	Operating expenses	69.14	68.41	66.53	66.79	67.97	66.06	65.76	67.31	67.37	64.30	56.	Frais d'exploitation
57.	Net income	30.86	31.59	33.47	33.21	32.03	33.94	34.24	32.69	32.63	35.70	57.	Résultat net
58.	Provisions (net)	11.06	12.80	14.30	16.34	26.30	11.14	18.90	18.57	18.51	12.75	58.	Provisions (nettes)
59.	Profit before tax	19.79	18.79	19.17	16.87	5.73	22.80	15.34	14.12	14.12	22.94	59.	Bénéfices avant impôt
60.	Income tax	4.25	4.39	4.54	3.92	3.78	6.53	5.88	4.56	4.46	7.15	60.	Impôt
61.	Profit after tax	15.54	14.40	14.63	12.95	1.94	16.27	9.46	9.56	9.65	15.79	61.	Bénéfices après impôt
62.	Staff costs	35.01	34.17	32.30	31.76	31.57	30.35	29.89	30.11	28.65	26.90	62.	Frais de personnel
	% of net income												**% du total du résultat net**
63.	Provisions (net)	35.85	40.52	42.72	49.20	82.12	32.83	55.21	56.81	56.74	35.73	63.	Provisions (nettes)
64.	Profit before tax	64.15	59.48	57.28	50.80	17.88	67.17	44.79	43.19	43.26	64.27	64.	Bénéfices avant impôt
65.	Income tax	13.79	13.90	13.56	11.81	11.81	19.24	17.16	13.94	13.68	20.03	65.	Impôt
66.	Profit after tax	50.36	45.58	43.72	38.99	6.07	47.93	27.63	29.25	29.59	44.24	66.	Bénéfices après impôt

UNITED STATES

Commercial banks

ETATS-UNIS

Banques commerciales

Per cent / *Pourcentage*

BALANCE SHEET ANALYSIS / **ANALYSE DU BILAN**

% of year-end balance sheet total / % du total du bilan en fin d'exercice

	1983	1984	1985	1986	1987	1988	1989	1990	1991	1992	
Assets											**Actif**
67. Cash & balance with Central bank	5.60	5.19	5.39	5.75	4.86	5.07	5.05	4.96	4.52	4.42	67. Caisse & solde auprès de la Banque centrale
68. Interbank deposits	8.74	6.05	5.64	5.65	5.77	5.14	4.63	3.60	3.64	3.47	68. Dépôts interbancaires
69. Loans	59.63	63.88	63.81	63.52	63.70	64.32	65.23	64.95	62.58	60.95	69. Prêts
70. Securities	18.83	16.50	17.58	17.95	18.45	18.26	18.22	19.26	22.10	24.28	70. Valeurs mobilières
71. Other assets	7.19	8.39	7.58	7.13	7.21	7.20	6.88	7.22	7.16	6.88	71. Autres actifs
Liabilities											**Passif**
72. Capital & reserves	6.00	6.14	6.20	6.19	6.02	6.28	6.21	6.46	6.75	7.52	72. Capital et réserves
73. Borrowing from Central bank	..	..	..	..	..	..	..	..	..	..	73. Emprunts auprès de la Banque centrale
74. Interbank deposits	7.85	6.56	6.01	5.59	5.53	4.64	4.39	3.65	4.00	3.57	74. Dépôts interbancaires
75. Non-bank deposits	70.82	71.67	71.52	72.02	72.29	73.00	72.82	74.48	74.30	73.35	75. Dépôts non bancaires
76. Bonds	0.42	0.52	0.64	0.67	0.68	0.64	0.67	0.77	0.79	1.02	76. Obligations
77. Other liabilities	14.91	15.10	15.62	15.52	15.48	15.44	15.91	14.64	14.17	14.54	77. Autres engagements
Memoranda											*Pour mémoire*
78. Short-term securities	..	..	..	..	..	..	..	..	..	..	78. Titres à court terme
79. Bonds	..	..	..	..	..	..	..	..	..	..	79. Obligations
80. Shares and participations	..	..	..	..	..	..	..	..	..	..	80. Actions et participations
81. Claims on non-residents	..	..	..	..	..	..	..	..	..	..	81. Créances sur des non résidents
82. Liabilities to non-residents	..	..	..	..	..	..	..	..	..	..	82. Engagements envers des non résidents

Notes

- The term Commercial banks corresponds to the term Insured commercial banks used in United States publications.

Notes

- Le terme Banques commerciales correspond à la rubrique Banques commerciales assurées des publications américaines.

181

UNITED STATES

Large commercial banks

Million US dollars

ETATS-UNIS

Grandes banques commerciales

Millions de dollars des EU

		1983	1984	1985	1986	1987	1988	1989	1990	1991	1992	
INCOME STATEMENT												**COMPTE DE RESULTATS**
1.	Interest income	130099	156427	156651	151729	163337	188200	224285	226559	199781	177464	1. Produits financiers
2.	Interest expenses	92578	110687	103389	94174	100856	118630	151652	151151	119088	87805	2. Frais financiers
3.	Net interest income	37521	45740	53262	57555	62481	69570	72633	75408	80693	89659	3. Produits financiers nets
4.	Non-interest income (net)	18449	18869	23852	29817	33839	37049	42296	46157	51724	57603	4. Produits non financiers (nets)
5.	Gross income	55970	64609	77114	87372	96320	106619	114929	121565	132417	147262	5. Résultat brut
6.	Operating expenses	38908	44460	51185	57892	65094	69338	75349	81976	89130	94558	6. Frais d'exploitation
7.	Net income	17062	20149	25929	29480	31226	37281	39580	39589	43287	52704	7. Résultat net
8.	Provisions (net)	6806	9055	10888	13784	31117	11742	25871	25994	28085	21136	8. Provisions (nettes)
9.	Profit before tax	10256	11094	15041	15696	109	25539	13709	13595	15202	31568	9. Bénéfices avant impôt
10.	Income tax	2614	2993	3838	3784	3067	7220	6249	4669	4894	9862	10. Impôt
11.	Profit after tax	7642	8101	11203	11912	-2958	18319	7460	8926	10308	21706	11. Bénéfices après impôt
12.	Distributed profit	4013	3994	4593	5387	6734	8830	9172	8851	9481	9196	12. Bénéfices distribués
13.	Retained profit	3629	4107	6610	6525	-9692	9489	-1712	75	827	12510	13. Bénéfices mis en réserve
Memoranda													*Pour mémoire*
14.	Staff costs	*20089*	*22460*	*25111*	*27867*	*30288*	*31790*	*33868*	*36182*	*37105*	*38480*	14. Frais de personnel
15.	Provisions on loans	*6799*	*9019*	*10824*	*13736*	*31041*	*11587*	*25769*	*25998*	*28055*	*21212*	15. Provisions sur prêts
16.	Provisions on securities	..	..	..	..	..	..	..	..	..	..	16. Provisions sur titres
BALANCE SHEET												**BILAN**
Assets												**Actif**
17.	Cash & balance with Central bank	97653	106301	122800	141487	122822	134678	142180	144020	131182	131017	17. Caisse & solde auprès de la Banque centrale
18.	Interbank deposits	145829	125671	128446	137490	147859	137214	131386	102223	106348	104539	18. Dépôts interbancaires
19.	Loans	898966	1043432	1154006	1255740	1304663	1405018	1513367	1554404	1516176	1518075	19. Prêts
20.	Securities	185860	177599	237792	283584	305231	321587	352720	383338	458325	533297	20. Valeurs mobilières
21.	Other assets	129654	130037	127943	125595	138083	150078	154726	173680	175460	175370	21. Autres actifs
Liabilities												**Passif**
22.	Capital & reserves	72509	82895	94767	107057	104631	119991	124617	135155	145947	173897	22. Capital et réserves
23.	Borrowing from Central bank	..	..	..	..	..	..	..	..	..	..	23. Emprunts auprès de la Banque centrale
24.	Interbank deposits	175239	155072	155001	155444	158033	137956	137503	116972	130174	118619	24. Dépôts interbancaires
25.	Non-bank deposits	901880	1004695	1128235	1254682	1322324	1438049	1537914	1636025	1647214	1672172	25. Dépôts non bancaires
26.	Bonds	6888	10439	15203	17357	17825	18279	19851	24472	25551	34470	26. Obligations
27.	Other liabilities	301446	329939	377781	409351	415845	434299	474493	445041	438607	463138	27. Autres engagements
Balance sheet total												**Total du bilan**
28.	End-year total	1457962	1583040	1770987	1943896	2018658	2148574	2294379	2357665	2387492	2462297	28. En fin d'exercice
29.	Average total	1414964	1520501	1677014	1857442	1981277	2083616	2221477	2326022	2372579	2424895	29. Moyen
Memoranda													*Pour mémoire*
30.	Short-term securities	..	..	..	..	..	..	..	..	..	..	30. Titres à court terme
31.	Bonds	..	..	..	..	..	..	..	..	..	..	31. Obligations
32.	Shares and participations	..	..	..	..	..	..	..	..	..	..	32. Actions et participations
33.	Claims on non-residents	..	..	..	..	..	..	..	..	..	..	33. Créances sur des non résidents
34.	Liabilities to non-residents	..	..	..	..	..	..	..	..	..	..	34. Engagements envers des non résidents
SUPPLEMENTARY INFORMATION												**RENSEIGNEMENTS COMPLEMENTAIRES**
35.	Number of institutions	253	274	311	335	348	360	373	370	364	375	35. Nombre d'institutions
36.	Number of branches	NA	NA	NA	NA	NA	NA	NA	NA	NA	NA	36. Nombre de succursales
37.	Number of employees (x 1000)	NA	NA	NA	NA	NA	NA	NA	NA	NA	NA	37. Nombre de salariés (x 1000)

UNITED STATES

Large commercial banks

Per cent — *Pourcentage*

INCOME STATEMENT ANALYSIS — ANALYSE DU COMPTE DE RESULTATS

		1983	1984	1985	1986	1987	1988	1989	1990	1991	1992		
	% of average balance sheet total												**% du total moyen du bilan**
38.	Interest income	9.19	10.29	9.34	8.17	8.24	9.03	10.10	9.74	8.42	7.32	38.	Produits financiers
39.	Interest expenses	6.54	7.28	6.17	5.07	5.09	5.69	6.83	6.50	5.02	3.62	39.	Frais financiers
40.	Net interest income	2.65	3.01	3.18	3.10	3.15	3.34	3.27	3.24	3.40	3.70	40.	Produits financiers nets
41.	Non-interest income (net)	1.30	1.24	1.42	1.61	1.71	1.78	1.90	1.98	2.18	2.38	41.	Produits non financiers (nets)
42.	Gross income	3.96	4.25	4.60	4.70	4.86	5.12	5.17	5.23	5.58	6.07	42.	Résultat brut
43.	Operating expenses	2.75	2.92	3.05	3.12	3.29	3.33	3.39	3.52	3.76	3.90	43.	Frais d'exploitation
44.	Net income	1.21	1.33	1.55	1.59	1.58	1.79	1.78	1.70	1.82	2.17	44.	Résultat net
45.	Provisions (net)	0.48	0.60	0.65	0.74	1.57	0.56	1.16	1.12	1.18	0.87	45.	Provisions (nettes)
46.	Profit before tax	0.72	0.73	0.90	0.85	0.01	1.23	0.62	0.58	0.64	1.30	46.	Bénéfices avant impôt
47.	Income tax	0.18	0.20	0.23	0.20	0.15	0.35	0.28	0.20	0.21	0.41	47.	Impôt
48.	Profit after tax	0.54	0.53	0.67	0.64	-0.15	0.88	0.34	0.38	0.43	0.90	48.	Bénéfices après impôt
49.	Distributed profit	0.28	0.26	0.27	0.29	0.34	0.42	0.41	0.38	0.40	0.38	49.	Bénéfices distribués
50.	Retained profit	0.26	0.27	0.39	0.35	-0.49	0.46	-0.08	0.00	0.03	0.52	50.	Bénéfices mis en réserve
51.	Staff costs	1.42	1.48	1.50	1.50	1.53	1.53	1.52	1.56	1.56	1.59	51.	Frais de personnel
52.	Provisions on loans	0.48	0.59	0.65	0.74	1.57	0.56	1.16	1.12	1.18	0.87	52.	Provisions sur prêts
53.	Provisions on securities	:	:	:	:	:	:	:	:	:	:	53.	Provisions sur titres
	% of gross income												**% du total du résultat brut**
54.	Net interest income	67.04	70.80	69.07	65.87	64.87	65.25	63.20	62.03	60.94	60.88	54.	Produits financiers nets
55.	Non-interest income (net)	32.96	29.20	30.93	34.13	35.13	34.75	36.80	37.97	39.06	39.12	55.	Produits non financiers (nets)
56.	Operating expenses	69.52	68.81	66.38	66.26	67.58	65.03	65.56	67.43	67.31	64.21	56.	Frais d'exploitation
57.	Net income	30.48	31.19	33.62	33.74	32.42	34.97	34.44	32.57	32.69	35.79	57.	Résultat net
58.	Provisions (net)	12.16	14.02	14.12	15.78	32.31	11.01	22.51	21.38	21.21	14.35	58.	Provisions (nettes)
59.	Profit before tax	18.32	17.17	19.50	17.96	0.11	23.95	11.93	11.18	11.48	21.44	59.	Bénéfices avant impôt
60.	Income tax	4.67	4.63	4.98	4.33	3.18	6.77	5.44	3.84	3.70	6.70	60.	Impôt
61.	Profit after tax	13.65	12.54	14.53	13.63	-3.07	17.18	6.49	7.34	7.78	14.74	61.	Bénéfices après impôt
62.	Staff costs	35.89	34.76	32.56	31.89	31.45	29.82	29.47	29.76	28.02	26.13	62.	Frais de personnel
	% of net income												**% du total du résultat net**
63.	Provisions (net)	39.89	44.94	41.99	46.76	99.65	31.50	65.36	65.66	64.88	40.10	63.	Provisions (nettes)
64.	Profit before tax	60.11	55.06	58.01	53.24	0.35	68.50	34.64	34.34	35.12	59.90	64.	Bénéfices avant impôt
65.	Income tax	15.32	14.85	14.80	12.84	9.82	19.37	15.79	11.79	11.31	18.71	65.	Impôt
66.	Profit after tax	44.79	40.21	43.21	40.41	-9.47	49.14	18.85	22.55	23.81	41.18	66.	Bénéfices après impôt

UNITED STATES

Large commercial banks

Per cent — *Pourcentage*

BALANCE SHEET ANALYSIS — ANALYSE DU BILAN

% of year-end balance sheet total — % du total du bilan en fin d'exercice

	1983	1984	1985	1986	1987	1988	1989	1990	1991	1992		
Assets												**Actif**
67. Cash & balance with Central bank	6.70	6.71	6.93	7.28	6.08	6.27	6.20	6.11	5.49	5.32	67.	Caisse & solde auprès de la Banque centrale
68. Interbank deposits	10.00	7.94	7.25	7.07	7.32	6.39	5.73	4.34	4.45	4.25	68.	Dépôts interbancaires
69. Loans	61.66	65.91	65.16	64.60	64.63	65.39	65.96	65.93	63.50	61.65	69.	Prêts
70. Securities	12.75	11.22	13.43	14.59	15.12	14.97	15.37	16.26	19.20	21.66	70.	Valeurs mobilières
71. Other assets	8.89	8.21	7.22	6.46	6.84	6.99	6.74	7.37	7.35	7.12	71.	Autres actifs
Liabilities												**Passif**
72. Capital & reserves	4.97	5.24	5.35	5.51	5.18	5.58	5.43	5.73	6.11	7.06	72.	Capital et réserves
73. Borrowing from Central bank	..	..	..	..	..	..	..	..	..	..	73.	Emprunts auprès de la Banque centrale
74. Interbank deposits	12.02	9.80	8.75	8.00	7.83	6.42	5.99	4.96	5.45	4.82	74.	Dépôts interbancaires
75. Non-bank deposits	61.86	63.47	63.71	64.54	65.51	66.93	67.03	69.39	68.99	67.91	75.	Dépôts non bancaires
76. Bonds	0.47	0.66	0.86	0.89	0.88	0.85	0.87	1.04	1.07	1.40	76.	Obligations
77. Other liabilities	20.68	20.84	21.33	21.06	20.60	20.21	20.68	18.88	18.37	18.81	77.	Autres engagements
Memoranda												***Pour mémoire***
78. Short-term securities	..	..	..	..	..	..	..	..	..	..	78.	Titres à court terme
79. Bonds	..	..	..	..	..	..	..	..	..	..	79.	Obligations
80. Shares and participations	..	..	..	..	..	..	..	..	..	..	80.	Actions et participations
81. Claims on non-residents	..	..	..	..	..	..	..	..	..	..	81.	Créances sur des non résidents
82. Liabilities to non-residents	..	..	..	..	..	..	..	..	..	..	82.	Engagements envers des non résidents

Notes

- The term Large commercial banks corresponds to the term Large insured commercial banks used in United States publications.
- Large commercial banks are a sub-group of Commercial banks and include institutions with total assets of US$ 1000 million or more.

Notes

- Le terme Grandes banques commerciales correspond à la rubrique Grandes banques commerciales assurées des publications américaines.
- Les Grandes banques commerciales, qui sont un sous-groupe des Banques commerciales, sont les banques dont le total du bilan atteint ou dépasse $US 1000 million.

UNITED STATES
Mutual savings banks

ETATS-UNIS
Caisses d'épargne mutuelles

Million US dollars — *Millions de dollars des EU*

#	Item (EN) / (FR)	1983	1984	1985	1986	1987	1988	1989	1990	1991	1992
	INCOME STATEMENT / **COMPTE DE RESULTATS**										
1.	Interest income / Produits financiers	14586	12619	14220	15910	18005	20056	22085	21014	17365	14645
2.	Interest expenses / Frais financiers	13399	11129	11118	11007	12118	14018	16168	15265	11699	7899
3.	Net interest income / Produits financiers nets	1187	1490	3102	4903	5887	6038	5917	5749	5666	6746
4.	Non-interest income (net) / Produits non financiers (nets)	1458	1025	1374	1545	1280	1288	1450	1200	1435	1577
5.	Gross income / Résultat brut	2645	2515	4476	6448	7167	7326	7367	6949	7101	8323
6.	Operating expenses / Frais d'exploitation	2522	2172	2630	3432	4195	4768	5222	5574	5235	5041
7.	Net income / Résultat net	123	343	1846	3016	2972	2558	2145	1375	1866	3282
8.	Provisions (net) / Provisions (nettes)	51	68	180	265	361	624	1925	2787	2019	1037
9.	Profit before tax / Bénéfices avant impôt	72	275	1666	2751	2611	1934	220	-1412	-153	2245
10.	Income tax / Impôt	120	134	457	1025	1054	903	450	189	417	891
11.	Profit after tax / Bénéfices après impôt	-48	141	1209	1726	1557	1031	-230	-1601	-570	1354
12.	Distributed profit / Bénéfices distribués	NA	NA	NA	50	211	339	494	-353	302	405
13.	Retained profit (1) / Bénéfices mis en réserve (1)	NA	NA	NA	1676	1346	692	-724	-1954	-872	949
	Memoranda / *Pour mémoire*										
14.	*Staff costs* / *Frais de personnel*	*1145*	*1001*	*1231*	*1539*	*1885*	*2081*	*2171*	*2193*	*1973*	*2005*
15.	*Provisions on loans* / *Provisions sur prêts*	*51*	*68*	*180*	*265*	*361*	*624*	*1925*	*2787*	*2019*	*1037*
16.	*Provisions on securities* / *Provisions sur titres*	..	..	..	..	..	..	..	..	..	..
	BALANCE SHEET / **BILAN**										
	Assets / **Actif**										
17.	Cash & balance with Central bank / Caisse & solde auprès de la Banque centrale	5634	4089	4665	6666	6334	7537	5939	5418	5273	4544
18.	Interbank deposits / Dépôts interbancaires	..	..	..	..	..	..	..	..	..	..
19.	Loans / Prêts	103564	84966	101041	116017	140616	161359	166242	154429	137791	120657
20.	Securities / Valeurs mobilières	53515	40403	42469	47310	53488	50048	48967	46982	48013	52784
21.	Other assets / Autres actifs	8069	6043	7588	8019	10157	11518	12455	14349	12887	13395
	Liabilities / **Passif**										
22.	Capital & reserves / Capital et réserves	8244	7004	9378	13871	16339	17489	17200	15275	14484	15278
23.	Borrowing from Central bank / Emprunts auprès de la Banque centrale	..	..	..	..	..	..	..	..	..	..
24.	Interbank deposits / Dépôts interbancaires	..	..	..	..	..	..	..	..	..	..
25.	Non-bank deposits / Dépôts non bancaires	153785	121559	137317	148251	168329	182795	188592	182191	172930	162132
26.	Bonds / Obligations	593	476	647	844	906	927	668	627	420	235
27.	Other liabilities / Autres engagements	8160	6462	8421	15046	25021	29251	27143	23086	16130	13734
	Balance sheet total / **Total du bilan**										
28.	End-year total / En fin d'exercice	170782	135501	155763	178012	210595	230462	233603	221179	203964	191379
29.	Average total / Moyen	163055	153142	145632	166888	194304	220529	232033	227391	212572	197672
	Memoranda / *Pour mémoire*										
30.	*Short-term securities* / *Titres à court terme*	*5104*	*5403*	*7004*	..	..	..	..	..	..	..
31.	*Bonds* / *Obligations*	..	..	..	..	..	..	..	..	..	..
32.	*Shares and participations* / *Actions et participations*	..	..	..	..	..	..	..	..	..	..
33.	*Claims on non-residents* / *Créances sur des non résidents*	..	..	..	..	..	..	..	..	..	..
34.	*Liabilities to non-residents* / *Engagements envers des non résidents*	..	..	..	..	..	..	..	..	..	..
	SUPPLEMENTARY INFORMATION / **RENSEIGNEMENTS COMPLEMENTAIRES**										
35.	Number of institutions / Nombre d'institutions	294	267	343	359	371	375	374	356	337	330
36.	Number of branches / Nombre de succursales	NA	NA	NA	NA	NA	NA	NA	NA	NA	NA
37.	Number of employees (x 1000) / Nombre de salariés (x 1000)	NA	NA	NA	NA	NA	NA	NA	NA	NA	NA

UNITED STATES

Mutual savings banks

Per cent / *Pourcentage*

INCOME STATEMENT ANALYSIS / ANALYSE DU COMPTE DE RESULTATS

		1983	1984	1985	1986	1987	1988	1989	1990	1991	1992		
	% of average balance sheet total												**% du total moyen du bilan**
38.	Interest income	8.95	8.24	9.76	9.53	9.27	9.09	9.52	9.24	8.17	7.41	38.	Produits financiers
39.	Interest expenses	8.22	7.27	7.63	6.60	6.24	6.36	6.97	6.71	5.50	4.00	39.	Frais financiers
40.	Net interest income	0.73	0.97	2.13	2.94	3.03	2.74	2.55	2.53	2.67	3.41	40.	Produits financiers nets
41.	Non-interest income (net)	0.89	0.67	0.94	0.93	0.66	0.58	0.62	0.53	0.68	0.80	41.	Produits non financiers (nets)
42.	Gross income	1.62	1.64	3.07	3.86	3.69	3.32	3.17	3.06	3.34	4.21	42.	Résultat brut
43.	Operating expenses	1.55	1.42	1.81	2.06	2.16	2.16	2.25	2.45	2.46	2.55	43.	Frais d'exploitation
44.	Net income	0.08	0.22	1.27	1.81	1.53	1.16	0.92	0.60	0.88	1.66	44.	Résultat net
45.	Provisions (net)	0.03	0.04	0.12	0.16	0.19	0.28	0.83	1.23	0.95	0.52	45.	Provisions (nettes)
46.	Profit before tax	0.04	0.18	1.14	1.65	1.34	0.88	0.09	-0.62	-0.07	1.14	46.	Bénéfices avant impôt
47.	Income tax	0.07	0.09	0.31	0.61	0.54	0.41	0.19	0.08	0.20	0.45	47.	Impôt
48.	Profit after tax	-0.03	0.09	0.83	1.03	0.80	0.47	-0.10	-0.70	-0.27	0.68	48.	Bénéfices après impôt
49.	Distributed profit	NA	NA	NA	0.03	0.11	0.15	0.21	0.16	0.14	0.20	49.	Bénéfices distribués
50.	Retained profit (1)	NA	NA	NA	1.00	0.69	0.31	-0.31	-0.86	-0.41	0.48	50.	Bénéfices mis en réserve (1)
51.	Staff costs	0.70	0.65	0.85	0.92	0.97	0.94	0.94	0.96	0.93	1.01	51.	Frais de personnel
52.	Provisions on loans	0.03	0.04	0.12	0.16	0.19	0.28	0.83	1.23	0.95	0.52	52.	Provisions sur prêts
53.	Provisions on securities	:	:	:	:	:	:	:	:	:	:	53.	Provisions sur titres
	% of gross income												**% du total du résultat brut**
54.	Net interest income	44.88	59.24	69.30	76.04	82.14	82.42	80.32	82.73	79.79	81.05	54.	Produits financiers nets
55.	Non-interest income (net)	55.12	40.76	30.70	23.96	17.86	17.58	19.68	17.27	20.21	18.95	55.	Produits non financiers (nets)
56.	Operating expenses	95.35	86.36	58.76	53.23	58.53	65.08	70.88	80.21	73.72	60.57	56.	Frais d'exploitation
57.	Net income	4.65	13.64	41.24	46.77	41.47	34.92	29.12	19.79	26.28	39.43	57.	Résultat net
58.	Provisions (net)	1.93	2.70	4.02	4.11	5.04	8.52	26.13	40.11	28.43	12.46	58.	Provisions (nettes)
59.	Profit before tax	2.72	10.93	37.22	42.66	36.43	26.40	2.99	-20.32	-2.15	26.97	59.	Bénéfices avant impôt
60.	Income tax	4.54	5.33	10.21	15.90	14.71	12.33	6.11	2.72	5.87	10.71	60.	Impôt
61.	Profit after tax	-1.81	5.61	27.01	26.77	21.72	14.07	-3.12	-23.04	-8.03	16.27	61.	Bénéfices après impôt
62.	Staff costs	43.29	39.80	27.50	23.87	26.30	28.41	29.47	31.56	27.78	24.09	62.	Frais de personnel
	% of net income												**% du total du résultat net**
63.	Provisions (net)	41.46	19.83	9.75	8.79	12.15	24.39	89.74	202.69	108.20	31.60	63.	Provisions (nettes)
64.	Profit before tax	58.54	80.17	90.25	91.21	87.85	75.61	10.26	-102.69	-8.20	68.40	64.	Bénéfices avant impôt
65.	Income tax	97.56	39.07	24.76	33.99	35.46	35.30	20.98	13.75	22.35	27.15	65.	Impôt
66.	Profit after tax	-39.02	41.11	65.49	57.23	52.39	40.30	-10.72	-116.44	-30.55	41.26	66.	Bénéfices après impôt

UNITED STATES
Mutual savings banks

ETATS-UNIS
Caisses d'épargne mutuelles

Per cent

Pourcentage

BALANCE SHEET ANALYSIS

ANALYSE DU BILAN

% of year-end balance sheet total

% du total du bilan en fin d'exercice

	1983	1984	1985	1986	1987	1988	1989	1990	1991	1992		
Assets												**Actif**
67. Cash & balance with Central bank	3.30	3.02	2.99	3.74	3.01	3.27	2.54	2.45	2.59	2.37	67.	Caisse & solde auprès de la Banque centrale
68. Interbank deposits	..	..	..	..	..	..	..	..	..	..	68.	Dépôts interbancaires
69. Loans	60.64	62.71	64.87	65.17	66.77	70.02	71.16	69.82	67.56	63.05	69.	Prêts
70. Securities	31.34	29.82	27.27	26.58	25.40	21.72	20.96	21.24	23.54	27.58	70.	Valeurs mobilières
71. Other assets	4.72	4.46	4.87	4.50	4.82	5.00	5.33	6.49	6.32	7.00	71.	Autres actifs
Liabilities												**Passif**
72. Capital & reserves	4.83	5.17	6.02	7.79	7.76	7.59	7.36	6.91	7.10	7.98	72.	Capital et réserves
73. Borrowing from Central bank	..	..	..	..	..	..	..	..	..	..	73.	Emprunts auprès de la Banque centrale
74. Interbank deposits	..	..	..	..	..	..	..	..	..	..	74.	Dépôts interbancaires
75. Non-bank deposits	90.05	89.71	88.16	83.28	79.93	79.32	80.73	82.37	84.78	84.72	75.	Dépôts non bancaires
76. Bonds	0.35	0.35	0.42	0.47	0.43	0.40	0.29	0.28	0.21	0.12	76.	Obligations
77. Other liabilities	4.78	4.77	5.41	8.45	11.88	12.69	11.62	10.44	7.91	7.18	77.	Autres engagements
Memoranda												*Pour mémoire*
78. Short-term securities	*2.99*	*3.99*	*4.50*	..	..	..	..	..	..	..	*78.*	*Titres à court terme*
79. Bonds	..	..	..	..	..	..	..	..	..	..	*79.*	*Obligations*
80. Shares and participations	..	..	..	..	..	..	..	..	..	..	*80.*	*Actions et participations*
81. Claims on non-residents	..	..	..	..	..	..	..	..	..	..	*81.*	*Créances sur des non résidents*
82. Liabilities to non-residents	..	..	..	..	..	..	..	..	..	..	*82.*	*Engagements envers des non résidents*

1. Exclusive of dividend payouts.

1. A l'exclusion des dividendes payés.

MAIN SALES OUTLETS OF OECD PUBLICATIONS
PRINCIPAUX POINTS DE VENTE DES PUBLICATIONS DE L'OCDE

ARGENTINA – ARGENTINE
Carlos Hirsch S.R.L.
Galería Güemes, Florida 165, 4° Piso
1333 Buenos Aires   Tel. (1) 331.1787 y 331.2391
                                         Telefax: (1) 331.1787

AUSTRALIA – AUSTRALIE
D.A. Information Services
648 Whitehorse Road, P.O.B 163
Mitcham, Victoria 3132   Tel. (03) 873.4411
                                            Telefax: (03) 873.5679

AUSTRIA – AUTRICHE
Gerold & Co.
Graben 31
Wien I   Tel. (0222) 533.50.14

BELGIUM – BELGIQUE
Jean De Lannoy
Avenue du Roi 202
B-1060 Bruxelles   Tel. (02) 538.51.69/538.08.41
                                    Telefax: (02) 538.08.41

CANADA
Renouf Publishing Company Ltd.
1294 Algoma Road
Ottawa, ON K1B 3W8   Tel. (613) 741.4333
                                            Telefax: (613) 741.5439
Stores:
61 Sparks Street
Ottawa, ON K1P 5R1   Tel. (613) 238.8985
211 Yonge Street
Toronto, ON M5B 1M4   Tel. (416) 363.3171
                                            Telefax: (416)363.59.63

Les Éditions La Liberté Inc.
3020 Chemin Sainte-Foy
Sainte-Foy, PQ G1X 3V6   Tel. (418) 658.3763
                                                Telefax: (418) 658.3763

Federal Publications Inc.
165 University Avenue, Suite 701
Toronto, ON M5H 3B8   Tel. (416) 860.1611
                                            Telefax: (416) 860.1608

Les Publications Fédérales
1185 Université
Montréal, QC H3B 3A7   Tel. (514) 954.1633
                                            Telefax : (514) 954.1635

CHINA – CHINE
China National Publications Import
Export Corporation (CNPIEC)
16 Gongti E. Road, Chaoyang District
P.O. Box 88 or 50
Beijing 100704 PR   Tel. (01) 506.6688
                                      Telefax: (01) 506.3101

DENMARK – DANEMARK
Munksgaard Book and Subscription Service
35, Nørre Søgade, P.O. Box 2148
DK-1016 København K   Tel. (33) 12.85.70
                                              Telefax: (33) 12.93.87

FINLAND – FINLANDE
Akateeminen Kirjakauppa
Keskuskatu 1, P.O. Box 128
00100 Helsinki

Subscription Services/Agence d'abonnements :
P.O. Box 23
00371 Helsinki   Tel. (358 0) 12141
                                      Telefax: (358 0) 121.4450

FRANCE
OECD/OCDE
Mail Orders/Commandes par correspondance:
2, rue André-Pascal
75775 Paris Cedex 16   Tel. (33-1) 45.24.82.00
                                            Telefax: (33-1) 49.10.42.76
                                            Telex: 640048 OCDE

OECD Bookshop/Librairie de l'OCDE :
33, rue Octave-Feuillet
75016 Paris   Tel. (33-1) 45.24.81.67
                                      (33-1) 45.24.81.81

Documentation Française
29, quai Voltaire
75007 Paris   Tel. 40.15.70.00

Gibert Jeune (Droit-Économie)
6, place Saint-Michel
75006 Paris   Tel. 43.25.91.19

Librairie du Commerce International
10, avenue d'Iéna
75016 Paris   Tel. 40.73.34.60

Librairie Dunod
Université Paris-Dauphine
Place du Maréchal de Lattre de Tassigny
75016 Paris   Tel. (1) 44.05.40.13

Librairie Lavoisier
11, rue Lavoisier
75008 Paris   Tel. 42.65.39.95

Librairie L.G.D.J. - Montchrestien
20, rue Soufflot
75005 Paris   Tel. 46.33.89.85

Librairie des Sciences Politiques
30, rue Saint-Guillaume
75007 Paris   Tel. 45.48.36.02

P.U.F.
49, boulevard Saint-Michel
75005 Paris   Tel. 43.25.83.40

Librairie de l'Université
12a, rue Nazareth
13100 Aix-en-Provence   Tel. (16) 42.26.18.08

Documentation Française
165, rue Garibaldi
69003 Lyon   Tel. (16) 78.63.32.23

Librairie Decitre
29, place Bellecour
69002 Lyon   Tel. (16) 72.40.54.54

GERMANY – ALLEMAGNE
OECD Publications and Information Centre
August-Bebel-Allee 6
D-53175 Bonn 2   Tel. (0228) 959.120
                              Telefax: (0228) 959.12.17

GREECE – GRÈCE
Librairie Kauffmann
Mavrokordatou 9
106 78 Athens   Tel. (01) 32.55.321
                                      Telefax: (01) 36.33.967

HONG-KONG
Swindon Book Co. Ltd.
13–15 Lock Road
Kowloon, Hong Kong   Tel. 366.80.31
                                            Telefax: 739.49.75

HUNGARY – HONGRIE
Euro Info Service
POB 1271
1464 Budapest   Tel. (1) 111.62.16
                                      Telefax : (1) 111.60.61

ICELAND – ISLANDE
Mál Mog Menning
Laugavegi 18, Pósthólf 392
121 Reykjavik   Tel. 162.35.23

INDIA – INDE
Oxford Book and Stationery Co.
Scindia House
New Delhi 110001   Tel.(11) 331.5896/5308
                                      Telefax: (11) 332.5993
17 Park Street
Calcutta 700016   Tel. 240832

INDONESIA – INDONÉSIE
Pdii-Lipi
P.O. Box 269/JKSMG/88
Jakarta 12790   Tel. 583467
                                      Telex: 62 875

IRELAND – IRLANDE
TDC Publishers – Library Suppliers
12 North Frederick Street
Dublin 1   Tel. (01) 874.48.35
                                      Telefax: (01) 874.84.16

ISRAEL
Electronic Publications only
Publications électroniques seulement
Praedicta
5 Shatna Street
P.O. Box 34030
Jerusalem 91340   Tel. (2) 52.84.90/1/2
                                      Telefax: (2) 52.84.93

ITALY – ITALIE
Libreria Commissionaria Sansoni
Via Duca di Calabria 1/1
50125 Firenze   Tel. (055) 64.54.15
                                      Telefax: (055) 64.12.57
Via Bartolini 29
20155 Milano   Tel. (02) 36.50.83

Editrice e Libreria Herder
Piazza Montecitorio 120
00186 Roma   Tel. 679.46.28
                                      Telefax: 678.47.51

Libreria Hoepli
Via Hoepli 5
20121 Milano   Tel. (02) 86.54.46
                                      Telefax: (02) 805.28.86

Libreria Scientifica
Dott. Lucio de Biasio 'Aeiou'
Via Coronelli, 6
20146 Milano   Tel. (02) 48.95.45.52
                                      Telefax: (02) 48.95.45.48

JAPAN – JAPON
OECD Publications and Information Centre
Landic Akasaka Building
2-3-4 Akasaka, Minato-ku
Tokyo 107   Tel. (81.3) 3586.2016
                                      Telefax: (81.3) 3584.7929

KOREA – CORÉE
Kyobo Book Centre Co. Ltd.
P.O. Box 1658, Kwang Hwa Moon
Seoul   Tel. 730.78.91
                                      Telefax: 735.00.30

MALAYSIA – MALAISIE
Co-operative Bookshop Ltd.
University of Malaya
P.O. Box 1127, Jalan Pantai Baru
59700 Kuala Lumpur
Malaysia   Tel. 756.5000/756.5425
                                      Telefax: 757.3661

MEXICO – MEXIQUE
Revistas y Periodicos Internacionales S.A. de C.V.
Florencia 57 - 1004
Mexico, D.F. 06600   Tel. 207.81.00
                                      Telefax : 208.39.79

NETHERLANDS – PAYS-BAS
SDU Uitgeverij Plantijnstraat
Externe Fondsen
Postbus 20014
2500 EA's-Gravenhage   Tel. (070) 37.89.880
Voor bestellingen: Telefax: (070) 34.75.778

OECD PUBLICATIONS, 2 rue André-Pascal, 75775 PARIS CEDEX 16
PRINTED IN FRANCE
(21 94 03 3) ISBN 92-64-04114-1 - No. 47220 1994